Queer Print in Europe

Queer Print in Europe

Edited by
Glyn Davis and Laura Guy

BLOOMSBURY VISUAL ARTS
LONDON • NEW YORK • OXFORD • NEW DELHI • SYDNEY

BLOOMSBURY VISUAL ARTS
Bloomsbury Publishing Plc
50 Bedford Square, London, WC1B 3DP, UK
1385 Broadway, New York, NY 10018, USA
29 Earlsfort Terrace, Dublin 2, Ireland

BLOOMSBURY, BLOOMSBURY VISUAL ARTS and the Diana logo are trademarks of Bloomsbury Publishing Plc

First published in Great Britain 2022

Cover design: Louise Dugdale
Cover images: *FUORI!*, Issue 13, 1974. Fondazione Sandro Penna / FUORI!
G.L.A.L. magazine (Grup en Lluita per l'Alliberament de la Lesbiana), Issue 3, 1981.

A catalogue record for this book is available from the British Library.

Library of Congress Cataloging-in-Publication Data

Names: Davis, Glyn, editor. | Guy, Laura, editor.
Title: Queer print in Europe / edited by Glyn Davis and Laura Guy.
Description: London ; New York : Bloomsbury Visual Arts, 2022. | Includes
bibliographical references and index.
Identifiers: LCCN 2022005849 (print) | LCCN 2022005850 (ebook) | ISBN
9781350273498 (paperback) | ISBN 9781350158665 (hardback) | ISBN
9781350158672 (epub) | ISBN 9781350158689 (pdf)
Subjects: LCSH: Gay press publications--Europe. | Gay press--Europe. |
Prints, European--Themes, motives. | Homosexuality and the arts--Europe.
Classification: LCC HQ76.95.E85 Q44 2022 (print) | LCC HQ76.95.E85
(ebook) | DDC 306.76/6094--dc23/eng/20220217
LC record available at https://lccn.loc.gov/2022005849
LC ebook record available at https://lccn.loc.gov/2022005850

ISBN: HB: 978–1–3501–5866–5
PB: 978–1–3502–7349–8
ePDF: 978–1–3501–5868–9
eBook: 978–1–3501–5867–2

Design, editorial, layout and colour production by Tom Cabot/Ketchup
Printed and bound in India

To find out more about our authors and books visit **www.bloomsbury.com** and sign up for our newsletters.

Contents

Introduction: Queer Print in Europe
Glyn Davis and Laura Guy   1

PART 1: THE POLITICS OF COMMUNITY BUILDING

1 Silent Voices: The 'Arabs' and Gay Liberation in France
   Antoine Idier   17

2 'Happiness was in the pages of this monthly': The Birth of the Lesbian Press
   in France and the Fabric of a Space of One's Own (1976–90)
   Ilana Eloit   39

3 Seeking Acceptance or Revolution? An Overview of the First Italian
   LGBTQ Magazines (1971–79)
   Dario Pasquini   55

4 Change Always Has to Build: In Conversation with Gail Lewis
   Taylor Le Melle   81

PART 2: MATERIALS AND MAKING

5 The Sexual Revolt in Spain in the 1970s Through Its Publications:
   Ideas, Fears and Aesthetics
   Alberto Berzosa and Gracia Trujillo   99

6 Sexual Difference and Queer Subjectivity in Slovak
   LGBTQ Print Periodicals
   Viera Lorencova   116

7 Revolt Press, Pornography and the Development of Gay Markets
   in Sweden
   Thomas Cubbin   140

8 *Mietje*: In Conversation with Gert Hekma and Mattias Duyves
   Benny Nemer   159

PART 3: GENERATIONAL INTERACTIONS

9   This Too is Polish Culture: In Conversation With Karol Radziszewski
    Aleksandra Gajowy   177

10 Queer Memory in (Re)constituting the Trans Lesbian 1970s in the UK
    Nat Raha   197

11 Uses of the Past: Sexuality, Self-image and Group Identity in
    German Lesbian Magazines in the 1970s
    Janin Afken   218

12 Lavender Menace Revisited: In Conversation With Sigrid Nielsen,
    Bob Orr and James Ley
    Fiona Anderson   237

Index   259

Introduction: Queer Print in Europe

GLYN DAVIS AND LAURA GUY

etween 1971 and 1974, over twenty issues of *Lunch*, a magazine 'for the new homosexual man and woman', were published. *Lunch* was assembled by members of the magazine committee of the Campaign for Homosexual Equality (CHE), a gay rights organisation with a significant number of chapters spread geographically across England and Wales. The magazine was of higher quality than other CHE publications – such as its typed-and-copied *Bulletin*, produced during the same years – with clean typesetting, heavy paper stock, and some smartly-designed covers. *Lunch* included articles and commentary on CHE activities, on lesbian and gay politics, and on issues adjudged to be of cultural interest to its readers. The cover of issue 19 (April 1973), for instance, featured an image of a knight on horseback, sword raised aloft, with both animal and rider clad in chain mail armour; the words 'To Morecambe!' appear in gothic script above the knight's head, a reference to an upcoming CHE conference. The illustration seems to suggest the event should be understood as a battleground, or at least a site for playful jousting. Articles in the issue included an interrogation of the notion of a 'gay life-style', and a piece on Dutch novelist Gerard Reve. Like many print publications, *Lunch* did not last long, but its issues serve collectively as a rich and fascinating record of a particular moment in British queer history, albeit a record refracted through the particular politics of the CHE. And like other print publications, *Lunch* raises both possibilities and problems for historians of queer culture.

Encounters with *Lunch* are shaped by material conditions circumscribed by strategies of preservation and access. Copies of the magazine are held in various collections, both personal and public, and each context organises the ways that we come into contact with the materials of queer history. Collections of the magazine are not always complete; they are largely concentrated in a main urban centre, London. As is often the case with queer print ephemera produced before the advent of the internet, *Lunch* 'disappeared' from public view when queer cultures moved online, left behind with countless other undigitized materials. At the time of writing this introduction, archivists at the Bishopsgate Institute have begun the process of digitising the full set of *Lunch* held in their own collection. As Cait McKinney has recently argued in *Information Activism* (2020), the digitisation of queer culture's paper archives does not necessarily address inequalities that organise preservation strategies or access.[1] Yet undertaken by an institution like Bishopsgate, which is underpinned by principles of community ownership, digitisation

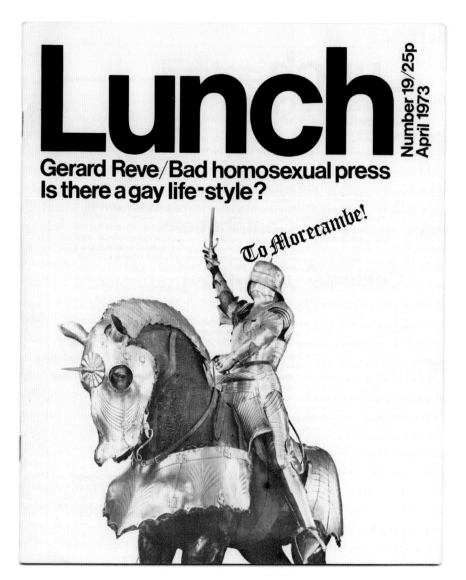

Cover of *Lunch*, Issue 19, April 1973. Courtesy of Bishopsgate Institute.

will surely help to make the magazine more available to queer readers. Behind these considerations of preservation and access lie pertinent questions about how we might conceptualise queer print. Rather than fetishize the ephemeral qualities of print, or celebrate another discovery of a 'lost' artefact of the recent queer past, how might print inform ways of thinking about queer history in the present? It is to this line of inquiry that many of this book's contributors are attuned.

Lunch is just one example of the enormous mass of LGBTQ+ printed materials that have circulated – usually locally or nationally, sometimes more widely – across Europe since the advent of a widespread gay rights movement in the 1960s. Yet it serves as emblematic in many ways: little known beyond those who accessed it at the time; swiftly defunct, revealing its ephemerality; created by and for members of a particular activist community; simultaneously local (if not parochial) and tantalisingly internationalist in its intentions; threaded through with political tensions as well as the historiographic issues outlined above (though, as many of the contributors to this collection show, the two are not easily separable). *Queer Print in Europe* is the first book to examine in detail the history and politics of European queer print cultures. Our conception of print culture is an expansive one, foregrounding newsletters, zines, magazines, journals and books, and also including flyers, manifestos, posters and pamphlets. Printed materials and print publishing have been central to histories of queer struggle – as they have with many other cultures of dissent, agitation and activism – and have proliferated exponentially since the 1970s, with the growth of an international above-ground network of queer activists, readers, writers, and artists. McKinney emphasises that queer feminist communities employed print media in ways that networked information systems long before the advent of the internet.[2] Even since the rise of online networking and archiving, the circulation of books, magazines and zines remains central to the kinship ties and political affiliations of international queer community.

Tackling the extraordinary volume of European queer print culture is, of course, impossible. There is simply too much to include: where to begin with the overflowing boxes of scrappy but seductive ephemera held in legitimate archives, never mind the individual collections of materials hoarded in personal storage that need to be accessed through one-to-one connections? At the same time, so much is already lost: disposed of by previous owners because judged as ephemeral, or not deigned worthy of entering the holdings of a formal archive. The selection of material included in this volume is merely the tiny, glistening tip of a big queer iceberg – one whose underwater mass is difficult to fully discern. In these introductory pages, we want to outline the choices that we have made, and the ways in which the essays and conversations included in this collection help us to open up broader questions about queer history and historiography, about national, international and postnational formations of queerness, and about the imbrications of activist communities and material cultures.

Queer Print in Europe does not present *a* history of LGBTQ+ print cultures: its content is not organised chronologically, and its editors and contributors do not subscribe to, or advocate for, the narrative of increasing rights achievements, acceptance and tolerance that some politicians and activists espouse. We would argue that the nature of print asks that we tell less schematic histories of queer 'liberation', and challenge understandings of evolving political gains. Circulating through diverse readerships at the time of publication, and finding new readers out of time, print publishing challenges the spatial and temporal lines that often fix queer struggle to particular geographies or events. The most casual encounters with archival queer print materials will reveal a polyphony of voices and perspectives, many of which became side-lined or subdued, shunted to the margins by the spread of mainstream assimilationist LGBTQ+ rights politics; those perspectives can retain a vital charge, ripe for rediscovery and reawakening as queer struggle against homophobic and transphobic erasure and violence persists.

This book began life as a conference held in February 2017 at the Centre for Contemporary Arts (CCA) in Glasgow, entitled 'Between the Sheets: Radical Print Cultures Before the Queer Bookshop', the first major event of a three-year pan-European queer history project, 'Cruising the Seventies: Unearthing Pre-HIV/AIDS Queer Sexual Cultures.'[3] *Queer Print in Europe* is one of the main material outputs of that project, our own contribution to LGBTQ+ print culture.[4] Traces of the original event manifest in these pages – most notably in the contributions by Fiona Anderson, co-organiser with Laura Guy of 'Between the Sheets', and Nat Raha – but the bulk of its content has been assembled subsequently. The event surfaced key topics of interrogation, methodological approaches, and political positions that threaded themselves through the rest of the 'Cruising the Seventies' project and which are core to this collection of essays: a belief in the value of scrutinising historical instances of queer material culture and examining their interaction with lived activist experience; a recognition of the necessity of intergenerational conversation as a force of pedagogical and dynamic exchange; and an investment in creative approaches to queer historiography, in which innovative methods could foment and activate insight. Indeed, the contributors to this volume adopt a variety of methodological approaches to their topics of enquiry, revealing the extent to which any sustained examination of queer print cultures and histories requires an intellectual malleability, a willingness to adopt a prismatic approach that throws light on varied facets of the objects under interrogation.

One of the barriers to assembling a comprehensive catalogue of queer European history and its associated print cultures (even if such an undertaking was desirable) is the differing national manifestations of activist activity, which have been shaped by specific circumstances. Of course, the constitution of national or transnational contexts is always in flux and even within countries, there are major divisions and distinctions between regions or zones to take into account (East versus West Germany, for instance).

The circulation of print culture often eschews any such borders, however, or at least works across them. This book offers up queer print culture as a way to think through queer Europe in the 1970s and after, insisting that the lines drawn by state and regional boundaries be remapped through the more contingent and ephemeral associations represented by queer political movements – and the movements of queer political actants. Just as our conceptualisation of print culture is expansive, so is our understanding of Europe – an entity that has shifted and redefined itself repeatedly since the formation of the EEC in 1957, and which continues to do so. There is no one way of conceptualising Europe – what it might be and mean – and this collection does not draw hard geographical borders. Likewise, we recognize Sara Ahmed's critique of theories that characterize migrancy as inherently transgressive, acknowledging the patterns of alienation, discrimination and violence that can accompany experiences of movement both into and within Europe, including the experiences of LGBTQ+ migrants.[5] We are most interested in what the material history the book explores can reveal: how do queer print publications help us to imagine Europe, and also to challenge the force and implication of national boundaries or borders? How has queer print culture worked at various points to imagine a queer Europe, and what forms did that take? In what ways does the history of queer print culture from the 1970s onwards offer critical perspectives on Europe and its colonies? We believe that queer print can allow us to engage with the challenge of Europe as an entity, as well as the notion of 'other Europes', at a historical juncture where this feels politically vital. Europe has not been a unanimously welcoming context for queers; indeed, the essays and conversations contained within this collection repeatedly return to, and trouble at, the tensions between Europe and queerness.

This book purposefully pivots away from North America to focus on Europe. Timelines of LGBTQ+ politics and queer culture are often organised around a North American perspective. Whilst the riots at New York's Stonewall Inn in 1969 and the Stateside activism addressing the crises surrounding HIV/AIDS from the 1980s onwards evidently had significant global repercussions, other dates and events were of particular significance in specific locations: the passing of the 1967 Sexual Offences Act in England and Wales; the death of Franco in 1975 in Spain, which marked the end of a lengthy period of dictatorial repression; the 1985 Operation Hyacinth police activities in Poland; the 1989 fall of the Berlin Wall and dismantling of the Soviet Bloc. Across Europe, queer cultures have emerged into visibility unevenly, in ways that challenge not only geographic parameters but also temporal ones. Terminology has been adopted and adapted in distinct ways – as editors we have honoured our authors' measured and sensitive use of various permutations of the LGBTQ+ acronym in their contributions, whilst noticing the extent to which 'queer' retains widespread value and currency as an expansive category and referent. There are contributions to this book that focus on particular local and national queer print cultures (of Spain, Italy, and Slovakia, for instance).

Others emphasise the challenges of thinking and working across and between countries, the movement of print materials echoing the journeys and interpersonal connections of LGBTQ+ people. Though this book began with a project exploring the 'queer seventies', the periods addressed here are more varied, accounting for distinct chronologies shaped by divergent social, cultural and political factors.

Perhaps because this book began as part of the 'Cruising the Seventies' project, and a workshop dedicated to queer print in that decade, many of the essays published here focus on a range of activities that took place before the onset of the AIDS crisis. The ongoing crisis has reshaped political and queer community relations across Europe and the globe. It has also transformed the terms on which we might approach histories before the HIV/AIDS crisis. Some of the essays in this book touch upon these changes. In his discussion of the activities of Revolt Press, Tom Cubbin addresses the gradual erosion of sexual liberation in Sweden in the 1980s, a consequence of legislation surrounding HIV/AIDS, such as the closure of bathhouses, that intersected with increased regulation of sex and pornography. Interviewed by Alexsandra Gajowy for this collection, the artist Karol Radziszewski describes the increasing visibility of homosexuality within public discourse in Poland as a consequence of the crises surrounding HIV/AIDS, and how this framed Operation Hyacinth, the first widespread attempt by the state-run Polish police force to target homosexuals. Concluding his conversation with Gert Hekma and Mattias Duyves, Benny Nemer comments on how HIV/AIDS frames his own understanding of grassroots queer political activity in the 1970s. This is something that is challenged through his interaction with Hekma and Duyves, revealing the complexities of historical return that permeate many of the contributions to this publication.

Intergenerational conversation – indeed, conversational exchange in general – was of vital importance to the 'Cruising the Seventies' project, and is central to this collection. Essays and conversations are mixed in the book's three sections. We see conversation as commensurate with print culture, each forging alliances through personal connections, inviting individuals to become members of larger groups, and allowing the silenced to find their voices. Conversation does not always flow easily: the wider circulation of queer print materials across Europe has sometimes been restricted by linguistic barriers. The ability to read and translate between various languages has been a vital component of the flow of information, activist tactics, and poetic interventions. Queer practices, cultural materials and personal connections are often heavily coded, operating within linguistic realms of idiolect and vernacular. These informal languages have largely developed outside of more formalised, institutional infrastructures. As a result, their assimilation into academic discourse is complicated, sometimes contradictory and at other times not possible. Here we might note again that queer studies and queer theory has been dominated by certain institutional contexts in the US.[6] Its insights do not always sit comfortably with LGBTQ+ experience outside of these centres. Queer perspectives have entered fields of scholarship in Europe in ways that are varied, complex and significant. Yet academic settings are not always commensurate with, and are in some instances hostile to, queer work. Likewise, although the European Union facilitates and resources exchange between its member states, as editors based in the UK, we are acutely aware of the contingent economic and political relations that underpin these exchanges. Operating more autonomously than we tend to as researchers, the histories and materials addressed in *Queer Print in Europe* reveal extraordinary efforts to build queer ties between countries, in defiance of linguistic limits and institutional omissions; they also highlight the palpable echoes and resonances between specific localised struggles and the queer activist responses to them.

Conversations are ephemeral, their pleasures located in part in their immediacy, urgency, and impermanence. The same can be argued of much print culture: it is designed to be discarded. As Bruce LaBruce has said of fanzines, they:

> aren't supposed to be catalogued and historicized and analysed to death, for Christsake. They're supposed to be disposable. That's the whole point. Throw your fanzines away right now. Go ahead. Xeroxed material doesn't last forever anyway, you know. It fades.[7]

Although little attention has been paid until recently to the role of print ephemera in queer social movements, a broader concern with the subject – or attitude – of ephemerality is written through accounts of queer life. Since it surfaced within the academy in the late 1980s, queer studies and associated fields have often attended to ephemeral traces, foregrounding the informal or undocumented quality of materials that make up the stuff of queer history. José Esteban Muñoz drew connections between queerness and the ephemeral:

> Instead of being clearly available as visible evidence, queerness has instead existed as innuendo, gossip, fleeting moments, and performances that are meant to be interacted with by those within its epistemological sphere – while evaporating at the touch of those who would eliminate queer possibility.[8]

Ephemera, he noted, 'does not rest on epistemological foundations but is instead interested in following traces, glimmers, residues, and specks of things'; further, it 'is a mode of proofing and producing arguments often worked by minoritarian culture and criticism makers.'[9] As an example of this in practice, Gavin Butt's valuable scholarship on gossip within the queer New York art worlds of the 1950s and 1960s asks readers to consider the reasons why recourse to ephemeral forms is necessary for those engaged in writing accounts of queer art practice and queer history more generally.[10]

This is to acknowledge that there are blatant tensions built into *Queer Print in Europe* that centre on ephemerality and the archive. As a book devoted to the history of material cultural practices, it pays sustained attention to objects that, on the whole, were designed to be transient. The contributors explore matters of aesthetics, and their essays are accompanied by high-quality reproductions of the print materials under discussion. Many of the print materials discussed in these pages, from the Spanish newsletter *Aghois* to the Polish zine *Filo*, adopted DIY aesthetics; others, however, such as *Lunch* or the Dutch publication *Mietje*, had a much higher level of finish. Our intention is not to create a canon of these materials, or to enshrine the examples chosen as somehow exemplary; these are merely fragments, ice crystals, at once beautiful but in many instances designed to melt away. Most queer print materials are not adequately archived or even comprehensively collected in personal attics or basements (or under-the-bed storage boxes); their ephemerality is ontological, and any account of their making and circulation should attempt to prevent the cohesion of a permanent and final history.

In this regard, the thinking behind this collection has been guided by two particular texts: Lisa Gitelman's *Paper Knowledge: Toward a Media History of Documents* and Kate Eichhorn's *Adjusted Margin: Xerography, Art and Activism in the Late Twentieth Century*. Gitelman tangles with documents as 'epistemic objects', 'evidential structures in the long human history of clues.'[11] Documents, she writes, 'are integral to the ways people think as well as to the social order that they inhabit'.[12] Gitelman wrestles with the notion of 'print culture' as overly expansive: as she asks, 'how widely, how unanimously, and how continuously can the meanings of printedness be shared, and what exactly are their structuring roles?'[13] Despite her scepticism, however, we have found it useful to think across multiple manifestations of print culture in this collection, with the queerness of the creators, distributors and consumers of these materials providing valuable threads between forms. Eichhorn, in contrast, engages with print culture in relation to feminist and queer political movements, considering the effects on language occasioned through the use of the Xerox machine, a messy but standardizing process, and in turn reflecting on the opportunities print produces for disturbing such mechanisms of standardisation.[14] Central to Eichhorn's argument is the conviction that the copy machine had a profound impact on the activities of activists and corresponding knowledge production in the late twentieth century. Not only did widespread access to Xeroxing allow for the production and circulation of materials that 'might otherwise have been subject to censorship'[15] but the aesthetics of these machines have become central to a political imaginary, 'synonymous with a certain politics or ethos, if not a particular mode of production'.[16] In thinking through and tarrying with the diversity of queer print cultures produced across Europe since the 1970s, our contributors have attempted to wrestle the tensions between form and content, and with tools of production as both limits and enablers.

This book builds upon existing scholarship relating to queer print in Europe and is in dialogue with ongoing work in this area. *LGBTQs, Media and Culture in Europe* (2016), edited by Alexander Dhoest, Lukasz Szulc and Bart Eeckhout, is an important contribution to the field of queer media studies in Europe and includes essays on national contexts not addressed in this book, such as Ana Maria Brandão, Tânia Cristina Machado and Joana Afonso's chapter on the lesbian press in Portugal.[17] Joachim C. Häberlen, Mark Keck-Szajbel and Kate Mahoney's edited collection *The Politics of Authenticity* (2018) examines the history of post-1968 counter-cultures and features contributions by Maria Bühner, whose work on lesbian activism in the German Democratic Republic includes examination of a variety of print periodicals, and Antoine Idier – whose writing also appears in this collection – on the writer Guy Hocquenghem and the Radical Left in France.[18] In the UK, Leila Kassir and Richard Espley's 2021 collection *Queer Between the Covers: Histories of Queer Publishing and Publishing Queer Voices* takes a long view on radical queer publishing from the nineteenth-century to the present day and includes Graham McKerrow's important account of state censorship in the context of one queer bookshop, Gay's the Word in London.[19] A forthcoming volume edited by Sarah Crook and Charlie Jeffries, dedicated to the subject of feminist and queer activism in Britain and the United States in the long 1980s, promises to extend histories of queer print in Britain through contributions by Flora Dunster – on the 'Lesbians Talk…' series published by Scarlet Press in the 1990s – and Taous R. Dahmani – on the journal *Polareyes* created by and for Black women in photography.[20]

The tracing and articulation of histories of queer print in Europe is not being done by academics alone. For example, a recent roundtable between Naomie Pieter, Wigbertson Julian Isenia, Anne Krul, Tieneke Sumter, Andre Reeder, Marlon Reina and Ajamu, dedicated to the subject of archiving queer of colour politics in the Netherlands and published online on the occasion of the exhibition Sonsbeek 20–24, foregrounded the work of artists in collecting and interpreting materials of queer culture and counteracting occlusions, especially around the LGBTQI activism of Black and other people of colour.[21] This roundtable also gestured to the important role that the protagonists of queer activism play in historicizing: many of the discussants provided accounts of their own role in recent histories of queer print, for example through groups that were active in the 1980s and 1990s such as SUHO (Surinamese Homosexuals), Flamboyant and Strange Fruit. In a conversation between artist Evan Ifekoya and cultural activist Nazmia Jamal that took place at the 2017 'Between the Sheets' conference, the kernel source event of this edited collection, productive aesthetic and political connections between queer POC DIY publishing strategies and archival artistic practices were articulated. Activist groups and networks have also made significant contributions to historicizing queer print cultures: for instance the International Lesbian Information Service (ILIS), which was in operation in Europe from 1980 to 1998, disseminated information about lesbian print publications via regular conferences and newsletters, and exemplifies the transnational possibilities that McKinney postulates in her book.

The essays and interviews collected together in the pages of *Queer Print in Europe* are divided into three sections, each highlighting a key thematic concern. These groupings purposefully invite reflection on the complex links between seemingly distinct histories, materials, and arguments. At the same time, conceptual and affective resonances ripple across the book as a whole; topics of connection bleed between the contributions to the collection like the ink on poorly Xeroxed zines. The first section, 'The Politics of Community Building', examines the ways in which the production, content, and circulation of queer print materials can foster social, affective and erotic connections between individuals – or reveal the divisions between factions. Spaces of dispute and dissent as much as they are of consensus and kinship, print materials afford opportunities for the sometimes contradictory and fragmented nature of political community to find expression. Antoine Idier, in his opening contribution, addresses the politically problematic ways in which some 'gay liberation' print publications produced in France in the early 1970s treated race. Focusing on two specific publications associated with the activist group FHAR (Front homosexuel d'action révolutionnaire), Idier unpacks the diversity of opinions aired in each, focusing in particular on the attitudes expressed in their pages towards sexual encounters with North African men (grouped under the epithet 'Arabs'). The racism of some of these writings, grounded in France's colonial relation with parts of Africa and broader xenophobic assumptions and stereotypes, intersects in complex ways with understandings of gay liberation being articulated and debated at the time. Queer print publications may foster community, but they may also purposefully exclude. As Idier notes, it is vital to interrogate the intentional and unconscious omissions from any group formation, including that group's representations of itself and debates between its members that appear in its print culture.

Ilana Eloit's essay (previously published in French, made available in English here for the first time) explores the origins of the lesbian press in France in the late 1970s and early 1980s. Eloit highlights that lesbianism was 'a question, a lack to be filled, a ritually invoked and repeatedly pointed out absence' in feminist publications. The formation of the lesbian press thus had, as one of its principal functions, the creation of opportunities for social connections. Magazines such as *Lesbia* and *Lettres à Sappho* generated ties between individuals, but also offered the space to debate community politics. Community differences of opinion were also on display in the pages of various Italian queer print publications of the 1970s, as Dario Pasquini reveals in his essay. *FUORI!*, the publication of the eponymous group, often included radical perspectives on queer culture and politics; in contrast, *Homo* and *con NOI* expressed more assimilationist positions. Approaches to sex and desire, as well as to the forms that political revolution could take, were aired by contributors, their debate revealing tensions between particular conceptions of queer identity and activism that had echoes and resonance far beyond Italy. In Taylor Le Melle's interview with Gail Lewis, which rounds out the book's first section, the latter notes how instances of print culture that emerge from within Black political activist movements in Britain in the 1970s and '80s record the impulses and concerns of that moment, serving as traces of ongoing vital change that are picked up, worked on, and evolved across the decades. Although those print traces may seem ephemeral, they can also bring generations into conversation with each other: the younger queer researcher and activist enters into a productive dialogue with an older figure from the community, centred on shared and divergent experiences through which 'a third space or a new space which shows us that change always has to build' might emerge, one which 'is always a vision to the future'.

The second section of *Queer Print in Europe*, 'Materials and Making', specifically draws attention to the pragmatics of queer print production: the sourcing of content, the establishment (however makeshift or fleeting) of spaces for design and fabrication, the creation or extant availability of distribution networks, the reasoning behind certain aesthetic choices. Alberto Berzosa and Gracia Trujillo, in their discussion of a number of queer print publications in Spain in the 1970s, identify the ways in which related queer political messages were disseminated across manifestos, political posters hastily pasted up in public spaces, and magazines. They situate these cultural manifestations of dissident opinion in relation to the independent activist media of the anti-Franco political resistance: 'political commitment', they argue, 'had a clear aesthetic implication, since the means of production … were precarious and the conditions of exception and illegality required urgent and non-systematic forms of work.' Viera Lorencova's essay explores the emergence and expansion of Slovakia's queer print culture from the 1990s to the present day. The publications discussed have adopted varied aesthetics, which Lorencova examines in detail: the zine-like DIY format of *L-Listy* and *Séparé* are compared with the 'sleek aesthetic' of *Q Archiv*. The essay concludes with a discussion of *QYS* magazine, which is mainly distributed online but retains a printed analogue version. Despite its aesthetic and digital distribution methods differing to some of the earlier examples Lorencova discusses, its production is driven by a similar perceived need, described by one of its editors as his belief 'that Slovak LGBTI community deserves to have [a magazine]'.

Thomas Cubbin, in his essay on Sweden's Revolt Press, reveals the impact that situating the publisher's headquarters in a non-urban location had on the content of the pornography that the company generated. Cubbin highlights the international dimension of queer pornographic production: the borrowing of photo shoots between companies, the national censorship limits imposed on distributing certain kinds of material, the international identification of niche markets that needed nurturing but that also could be capitalised on. Benny Nemer's conversation with Gert Hekma and Mattias Duyves explores the making of *Mietje*, a colourful, sexy, political and poetic zine created by the Rooie Flikkers (Red Faggots) group of communist queers in the Netherlands. The interaction between the trio reveals not only how the publication's finances came together, but the ways in which a group of young queers laboured together – in amongst their socialising – to create a high-quality, aesthetically bold object.

In the third and final section of the book, 'Generational Interactions', contributors explore the complex ways in which traces of queer print materials persist across time, how artists have engaged with those traces (or their absence), and the relationship of particular queer publications to real or imagined historical LGBTQ+ cultures. Queer print culture is written through or overlaid with complex temporalities, indebted to phantasmatic pasts or futures, reworking facets from the archive for a contemporary and future readership. In the conversation between art historian Aleksandra Gajowy and artist Karol Radziszewski that opens this section, the latter discusses the ways in which archival trawls for elements of occluded queer history across Central and Eastern Europe (CEE) have informed his practice. Radziszewski reveals the queer print publications he has unearthed from Poland and elsewhere, discusses his collabourative working relationship with Ryszard Kisiel (creator of the Polish queer zine *Filo* in the 1980s), and outlines the working practices on his own publication, *DIK Fagazine*. *DIK* gathers together, often in themed issues, queer print materials such as photographs and zines; as a collectible art object, the magazine transmutes disposable ephemera into culturally valuable residue. Nat Raha's contribution draws attention to the significant gaps in recent queer historical accounts of the 1970s: the lack of detail about trans lesbian activists and agency, and the subsequent forgetting of intersectional connections between various groups, movements and struggles that this can entail. Reflecting on a conversation between Raha and Roz Kaveney that took place at the 'Between the Sheets' conference, and exploring London Gay Liberation Front's TS/TV Group, Raha presents 'a liberationist vision of trans life that explicitly emerges from a feminist revolution and from lesbian separatism.'

Janin Afken discusses two lesbian magazines of the 1970s from West Germany, *UkZ* and *Lesbenpresse*. She identifies how the former was indebted to Weimar culture and earlier models of lesbian identity and socialisation, and the ways in which the latter engaged with a combination of mythic female archetype, 1960s counterculture, and matriarchal visions of the future. Despite appearing in the same year, *UkZ* and *Lesbenpresse* had distinct temporal registers, each collapsing into their form and content traces of other times. Finally, Fiona Anderson's conversation with Sigrid Nielsen, Bob Orr and James Ley focuses on Nielsen and Orr's collabourative work running LGBTQ+ bookstores in Edinburgh – Lavender Menace, West and Wilde – and Ley's authoring of a play about the former, *Love Song to Lavender Menace*. Nielsen and Orr relate the history of their involvements in selling books, magazines and other print culture, the politics of running a queer bookshop, and the colla;bouration involved in working with Ley on his script. Queer bookshops remain vital if fragile enterprises wherever they appear; Ley's play pays tribute, but also reveals the continued currency of the political and community connections that take place through such spaces.

The array of material served up in *Queer Print in Europe* can only be a taster. The sampling of material that we have selected for this collection only gestures towards the extraordinary richness of the queer print materials and their associated cultures that have flourished across Europe, however evanescently, over the last six decades. It is our hope that the essays and conversations here will provoke further research on artists and makers, activist groups and their material publications, production and distribution companies, bookstores and their owners. *Lunch* is just one delicious morsel: fruity, zesty, even nourishing. But as we hope this collection of words and images reveals, there is a banquet waiting to be feasted upon.

ACKNOWLEDGEMENTS

The production of *Queer Print in Europe* was financially supported by HERA and the European Commission, as part of the 'Cruising the Seventies: Unearthing Pre-HIV/AIDS Queer Sexual Cultures' project. Additional financial assistance was provided by the Research and Knowledge Exchange committee of Edinburgh College of Art, University of Edinburgh.

The editors would like to extend our thanks to all those who contributed to 'Between the Sheets: Radical Print Cultures Before the Queer Book Shop' at the Centre for Contemporary Art, Glasgow, 23–24 February 2017, where many of the ideas for this book began to take shape: Fiona Anderson, Jonathan Bay, Mark Clintberg, Evan Ifekoya, Nazmia Jamal, Roz Kaveney, James Ley, Benny Nemer, Sigrid Nielsen, Bob Orr and Nat Raha.

NOTES

1   Cait McKinney, *Information Activism: A Queer History of Lesbian Media Technologies*, Durham, NC: Duke University Press, 2020.

2   Ibid.

3   'Cruising the Seventies' ran from July 2016 to November 2019. It was funded by HERA and the European Commission. For further information on the project, see https://www.crusev.ed.ac.uk.

4   The other main 'Cruising the Seventies' publications include: Alberto Berzosa and Gracia Trujillo (eds), *Fiestas, memorias y archivos: Politica sexual disidente y resistencias cotidianas en Espana en los anos setenta*, Madrid: Brumeria, 2019; Janin Afken and Benedikt Wolf (eds), *Sexual Culture in Germany in the 1970s: A Golden Age for Queers?*, London: Palgrave Macmillan, 2020; Tomasz Basiuk and Jedrzej Burszta (eds), *Queers in State Socialism: Cruising 1970s Poland*, London: Routledge, 2020; Tomasz Basiuk and Agnieszka Koscianska (eds), *Sexual Citizenship, Archives, Oral History: Central Europe in a Comparative Perspective*, Warsaw: University of Warsaw Press, 2021; Alberto Berzosa, Lucas Platero, Juan Antonio Suárez and Gracia Trujillo (eds), *Reimaginar la disidencia sexual en la Espana de los 70s: redes, vidas, archivos*, Barcelona: Bellaterra, 2020; Fiona Anderson, Glyn Davis and Nat Raha (eds), 'Imagining Queer Europe Then and Now', *Third Text*, No. 168, 2021.

5   Sara Ahmed, 'Home and Away: Narratives of migration and estrangement', in *International Journal of Cultural Studies*, Vol. 2, Issue 3, 1999, 329–347.

6   Matt Brim, *Poor Queer Theory: Confronting Elitism in the University*, Durham, NC: Duke University Press, 2020.

7   Bruce LaBruce, 'The Wild, Wild World of Fanzines: Notes from a Reluctant Pornographer', in Paul Burston and Colin Richardson (eds), *A Queer Romance: Lesbians, Gay Men and Popular Culture*, London: Routledge, 1995, 193.

8   José Esteban Muñoz, 'Ephemera as Evidence: Introductory Notes to Queer Acts', *Women and Performance: A Journal of Feminist Theory*, Vol. 8 Issue 2, 1996, 6.

9   Ibid., 10.

10 Gavin Butt, *Between You and Me: Queer Disclosures in the New York Art World, 1948–1963*, 2nd edn, Durham, NC: Duke University Press, 2006.

11 Lisa Gitelman, *Paper Knowledge: Toward a Media History of Documents*, Durham, NC: Duke University Press, 2014, 1.

12 Ibid., 5.

13 Ibid., 9.

14 Kate Eichhorn, *Adjusted Margin: Xerography, Art and Activism in the Late Twentieth Century*, Cambridge, MA: MIT Press, 2016.

15 Ibid., 7.

16 Ibid., 145.

17 Alexander Dhoest, Lukasz Szulc and Bart Eeckhout (eds), *LGBTQs, Media and Culture in Europe*, London: Routledge, 2016.

18 Joachim C. Häberlin, Mark Keck-Szajbel and Kate Mahoney (eds), *The Politics of Authenticity: Countercultures and Radical Movements across the Iron Curtain, 1968–1989*, New York: Berghahn Books, 2018.

19 Leila Kassir and Richard Espley (eds), *Queer Between the Covers: Histories of Queer Publishing and Publishing Queer Voices*, London: University of London Press, 2021.

20 See also Jess Baines's research on radical print collectives in Britain. Jess Baines 'Experiments in democratic participation: feminist printshop collectives'. *Cultural Policy, Criticism & Management Research* (6), 2012, pp. 29–51 and Jess Baines, Suzy Mackie, Anne Robinson and Pru Stevenson, *See Red Women's Workshop: Feminist Posters 1974–1990*, Four Corners, London, 2016.

21 Naomie Pieter, Wigbertson Julian Isenia et al., 'Archiving Queer of Colour Politics in the Netherlands', no date. Available online at: https://www.sonsbeek20-24.org/en/editorial-room/glaring-world-through-rear-view/archiving-queer-colour-politics-netherlands/ [Accessed on 23 June 2021].

Part 1

THE POLITICS OF
COMMUNITY BUILDING

1 Silent Voices: The 'Arabs' and Gay Liberation in France

ANTOINE IDIER

(Translated by Daniella Shreir)

n the subject of literature in the fledgling United States, Toni Morrison writes in *Playing in the Dark*:

> For a people who made much of their 'newness' – their potential, freedom, and innocence – it is striking how dour, how troubled, how frightened and haunted our early and founding literature truly is.[1]

At the risk of slightly twisting the original meaning, it's tempting to use this quotation from Morrison to consider the writings of French 'gay liberation' movements at the beginning of the 1970s and their treatment of race. Through their formulation of a strong political directive on homosexuality these movements undoubtedly constituted a radically new event. By breaking with the *homophilic* movements of the '50s and '60s (namely the Arcadie movement in France),[2] they instead offered an unprecedented politicisation of homosexuality and homosexual subjectivity and challenged the terms through which a left-wing politics had usually been tackled, instead defending the existence of oppression and struggles that were specifically sexual, in addition to and not instead of economic domination and class struggle.

Driven by this powerful newness, these movements were equally haunted by race and the intersection of racial and sexual questions. To pick up Morrison's words again, this 'presence informs in compelling and inescapable ways the texture' of certain gay liberation writings:

It is a dark and abiding presence, there for the literary imagination as both a visible and an invisible mediating force [...] the shadow hovers in implication, in sign, in line of demarcation.[3]

Racialised subjects – most often from the Maghreb, where France had colonies until the 1960s – are ubiquitous in a range of writings by gay activists produced at the beginning of the 1970s. Yet, only present under the epithet 'Arabs', they remain silent, dealt with but not given a voice. There is indeed an 'absent voice' (Didier Eribon's concept, taken from Pierre Bourdieu), a reminder that it's imperative to interrogate 'the question of a subjugated person's right to speak, of access to speech for those who don't speak or aren't heard. Who is speaking? Who is able to speak? And who doesn't speak when others do?' We must at the same time interrogate the structure and the social mechanisms that produce this absence: 'These absent voices reveal, through their very absence, the profound truth of this system: its violence and its brutality.'[4]

The FHAR (Front homosexuel d'action révolutionnaire) emerged at the beginning of 1971 in Paris. It was founded by militant feminists, some of whom had participated in the MLF (Mouvement de Libération des Femmes), whose creation had come a few months before. These women were joined by 'leftist' activists – that is to say activists who challenged the Communist Party line and who had been very involved in May '68, as well as in groups considered to be Trotskyist or Maoist.[5] The FHAR's activities were varied: on the 10th of March 1971, for example, the group interrupted the broadcast of a radio show dedicated to the subject of homosexuality; they participated in traditional left-wing protests (such as the May Day march); they organised weekly general assemblies (held at Paris's École des Beaux-Arts) and were responsible for the creation of several publications. Notable among these was the 12th issue of the journal *Tout!*, an organ for the *mao-spontex* (a neologism for Mao-spontaneity) group Vive la revolution, published on the 23rd of April 1971, which included several pages dedicated to sexuality and homosexuality. There was also the 12th issue of the journal *Recherches* (whose founder was the philosopher-psychoanalyst Félix Guattari), published in March 1973, whose title was 'Trois milliards de pervers: Grande encyclopédie des homosexualités' ('Three Billion Perverts: The Big Encyclopedia of Homosexualities').[6] These two publications caused a scandal. In the case of *Tout!*, the assertion of homosexuality outraged a number of leftist activists, some of whom refused to sell the issue. The *Recherches* special issue, meanwhile, was seized by the police and Guattari was sentenced in 1974 for an 'affront to public decency.'

Despite their associations with the FHAR movement, neither publication presented a single, unequivocal viewpoint: the texts are far-ranging, written by different, often anonymous, authors, sometimes openly in conversation or opposition with each other. These journals therefore constitute a heterogeneous assemblage of viewpoints.

Front cover of *Tout!*,
Issue 12, 23 April 1971.

It's also necessary to note that the FHAR didn't constitute an organised or hierarchised group, but rather an informal movement – what activist Guy Hocquenghem, who played a central role in the selection of texts and the production of the *Tout!* and *Recherches* issues, called a 'nebula of feelings and actions'[7] – that played a central role in the selection of texts and the production of the *Tout!* and *Recherches* issues. Moreover,

Tout!, Issue 12,
23 April 1971, page 6.

although the very fact of 'speaking up' was considered a political act in and of itself, one of the specific aims behind the production of these two issues was the publication of diverse voices and perspectives.

Amongst the diversity of viewpoints, both publications paid special attention to expressions of sexuality involving 'Arabs'. This term covers North African immigrants

Tout!, Issue 12,
23 April 1971, page 7.

living in France, principally in Paris (to the extent that the FHAR's texts were predominantly written by militants living in the capital region), as well as, in some cases, North Africans met during these men's travels to the region. The category is problematic from the outset, inscribed as part of a history of ethnic divisions. Berbers and Kabyle people were, for example, sometimes included and sometimes excluded. Thus one text specifies

Front cover of
Recherches, Issue 12,
March 1973.

that 'Arabs' are 'most often Berbers, more or less Arabicised and Islamised.'[8] On the other hand, another text seems to put 'Arabs' and 'Berbers' in opposition, drawing up an original ethno-sexual typology: 'I don't like Tunisians because they are all Arabised. Algerians and Moroccans are different. I've learned the difference between Arabs and Berbers through fucking. And I prefer Berbers, even when they're Arabised.'[9] These texts are testament to an initial paradox: while they are produced by an anti-racist, anti-colonial project, and thought of as belonging to a progressive movement which takes racism, immigration and the material conditions of the lives of individuals involved into account, these writings generate a set of patterns that are racist, colonial and orientalist in their own way. This 'orientalism' is conveyed in the sense that Edward Said gave to the term, that is to say the setting up of the 'Orient' as opposed to the 'Occident' and the formation of 'Orientals' as Othered subjects, irremediably different to westerners and united in that difference (despite their own social, geographic, cultural and political disparities), especially in a sexual context.[10] We can also find the schema described by Frantz Fanon in *Black Skin, White Masks*, according to which the comprehension of the 'racial situation' necessitates attaching 'considerable importance [...] to sexual phenomena'. Racism based on 'the fear of the sexual potency of the Negro' can also be found here, applied to 'Arabs' rather than 'Negros' and given the inverse value (there's no 'fear' but celebration).[11]

A second paradox is the following: the racist character of these texts doesn't totally escape their authors or editors. Instead, this racism is knowingly included in the FHAR's publications as testament to a certain conception of 'gay liberation.'

THE LOGIC OF 'US'

One of the most important issues in the creation of a political movement, but also in the critical analysis of this creation, concerns the *nous*: the 'us.' Who is this 'us' as the group defines it? The establishment of a political movement, with its claim to represent a social class or group, necessitates the interrogation of the definition of the group that is formed. But who this group leaves to one side – whether this is intentional, in identifying a group as opposite to 'us', or unintentional, through unconscious omission – also requires examination.[12]

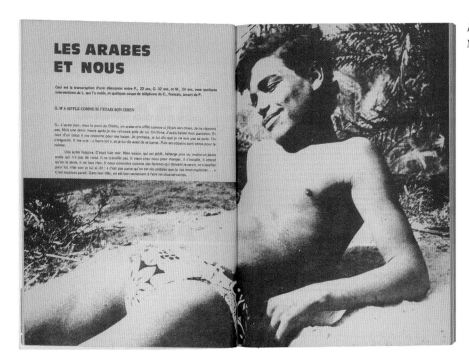

Recherches, Issue 12,
March 1973, pp.12–13.

The twelfth issue of *Recherches* was divided into several thematically-organised chapters, the first of which was entitled 'Arabes et pédés' ('Arabs and Faggots'). As the content of the chapter very quickly makes evident, the intention here wasn't to think through the intersection of these two identities – the fact that some individuals are 'Arabs' *and* 'faggots', but rather to consider them as two distinct social groups: the 'Arabs' on one side and the 'faggots' on the other. Specifically, the chapter opens with a long roundtable discussion between three gay activists (identified only by their initials) entitled 'Les Arabes et nous' ('The Arabs and us'). If 'Arabs' can't be 'faggots', there must also be a singular 'Arab' sexuality, distinct from that of the 'Europeans', separate from the relationship between the categories of 'homosexuality' and 'heterosexuality', but embedded in the relationship between social norms and prohibitions ('Arab' sexuality is said to be more 'free' or less guilt-ridden) or in the forms it takes ('Arab' sexuality is also said, for example, to be devoid of 'sentimentality').[13] Moreover, the interview supposes that 'faggots' aren't 'Arab' but French, European and white. These latter identities aren't discussed by the authors of the texts, no more so than an interrogation of the perceptions of the world and the social arrangements that they entail, or the views that those in possession of these identities espouse in interactions with non-white people.

On the contrary, the repeated use of this 'us', in opposition to 'them', only reinforces the establishment of 'Arabs' as divergent subjects, by charting a *demarcation*, to use Morrison's word, without ever reflecting on their social identity. Where the gay activists are

Recherches, Issue 12,
March 1973, pp.14–15.

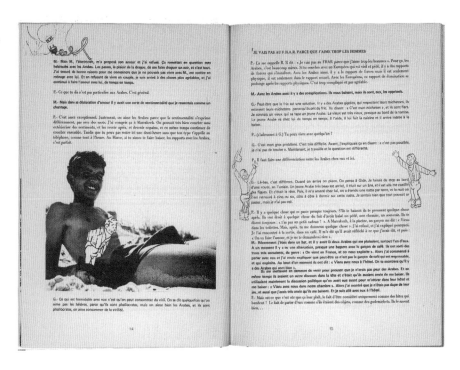

Recherches, Issue 12,
March 1973, pp.32–3.

Recherches, Issue 12, March 1973, pp.64–5.

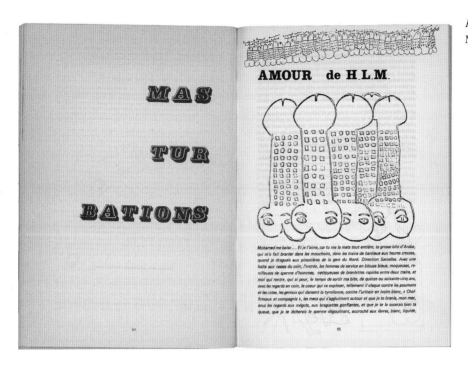

identifiable by their initials and ages, and sometimes even a few biographical details, the 'Arabs' have no name, no trajectory, no elements through which they might be identified beyond a small summary of the circumstances of the sexual encounter (often fleeting; predominantly in cruising spots). They seem only to exist in and through their sexual interactions with Europeans. For the 14 pages the discussion occupies, there are therefore only references to 'an Arab', 'a young Arab', 'Arabs', 'five Arab guys', 'sex with Arabs', a 'young Moroccan gigolo', etc. One of the participants recognises this: 'One Arab can easily be replaced by another. They form a sort of collection.'[14]

The only features affixed to 'Arabs' are general, falling within a broad typology, within a group whose members are not individualised, but interchangeable. It is claimed accordingly that there is a marked difference in approach to sexual power:

If you sleep with a European faggot who is manly, a power struggle sets in. With the Arabs too, there is a power struggle, but it is only physical, it is only part of the sexual relationship. With Europeans, this power relation continues beyond the physical side of the relationship.

Similarly, the roundtable contributors claim a difference in approach to sentimentality: 'It's sometimes said that sentiment doesn't exist among Arabs. But sentimentality is expressed differently. Not through words. Not through our usual code.'[15] A 'complex, tedious psychology' is associated with Europeans, so much so that one of the activists explains: 'When I sleep with a European, I'm bored shitless.'[16] In the course of the discussion, a range of qualifiers is used to describe the Arabs: they're strong, clean, lazy, liars, thieves, virile; their penises are beautiful, they want to be served, they play the dominant role in the sexual relation and hold contempt for the 'fags' they're sleeping with. Furthermore, although the interview is testament to a porosity of racialised categories, this idea is rejected by the gay activists. At one point, one of them describes 'Arab guys' who are, according to them, 'very Europeanised'; another activist says he stopped having a relationship with an Algerian student because he was too 'Europeanised'. One activist states: 'I really don't want […] them to become European in their relationship to sexuality.'[17]

It must be noted that this interview, like the issue of *Recherches* from which it is taken, includes qualifications and reservations in relationship to these opinions, but these are minor. One of the participants asks: 'But are we sure they like being seen as erect penises? The fact we talk about them like objects, like dildos?' A bit further on, he adds: 'It's a bit shitty to talk about them like objects…' One of the others also states: 'I wonder if we're not being a bit racist at the moment' (however, he opposes this racism with his assessment of the misogyny and homophobia of 'Arabs'). One of the men relates something that a 'mixed-race Antillean' told him: 'These men [European gays] love having sex with me in the parks of Paris. But in the clubs they don't want to dance with me.'[18]

It must also be noted that when sexual relations with 'Arabs' are discussed, this discussion above all centres on what it provides for the European activists. This connects to a more general feature of colonialism and orientalism as highlighted by Said: the Other (the oriental) is what allows the speaker to find their own truth, and less their counterpart's.

In 'The Arabs and us' it's mostly a question of the distinctive pleasure, of the *jouissance* that the interview participants take. 'I take enjoyment from the idea that I'm giving myself over. He's fucking me but he doesn't have the intellectual distance I have. We remain intellectuals who are playing at giving themselves over to savageness, to the beast', 'I was drunk and I had that same mental pleasure. That of being the whore who is sacrificed', 'You feel negated, slaughtered, by this Arab who's fucking you up the ass. And it's amazing.'[19] But it's much more than that and this is made abundantly clear in another account featured in the journal (in which the author relates his sexual relations with 'Arabs' as well as his discovery of his own racism and the links he forged with separatists): 'These little Algerian proles are a lot like me. […] This universe makes clear to me my own hatreds. […] I understand that I'm becoming Algerian, that Arab Algeria is me.' The author then adds: 'I'm neither just French nor a pure and simple faggot.' The transformation the European undergoes as a result of his sexual relations with non-Europeans, as well as the link established between desire for the other and a hatred for his own homeland ('I threw up the North'), are features that can be found more generally in literature relating to colonialism.[20]

As Todd Shepard has established, racism is not unique to gay activists: the structures that these contributions to *Recherches* expose were largely shared with and deeply engrained in French society in the '60s and '70s, on the left as well as the right.[21] The racism under examination here is publicised and refracted through the mechanisms built into the FHAR and into gay activism. However, it remains a major blind spot: while the deconstruction of sexual and social norms is asserted and practiced by the FHAR, sometimes in a fairly sophisticated way, this willing deconstruction gets tripped up by the racial question. In this respect, the question of 'us' acts all the more as an indicator of this thoughtlessness than its problematisation – that is to say that the interrogation of the creation of a social group defined by its sexuality and the social conditions surrounding this sexuality is what played a major role in the foundation of these gay movements.

In April 1971, for example, Hocquenghem authored a text called 'An address to those who are like us', calling for the 'destruction of "sexual and fascist normality"'. He reported on the group's internal contradictions, notably between men and women, all the while purporting that he was not making 'any distinction between us.'[22] This address was the counterpart to another address, 'To those who think they're "normal"', which clearly established an antagonistic counter group which dominated the 'us' of the former. This address developed a conflict between 'us' and 'you': 'Your society [...] has treated us like a social evil', 'You're individually responsible for the vile mutilation you've made us undergo by rebuking our desire', etc.[23] The creation of this 'us' is even more vital because it had previously been suppressed: in spring of 1968 the short-lived CAPR – Comité d'action pédérastique révolutionnaire (Committee of Revolutionary Pederastic Action) – was formed in an occupied Sorbonne University but their posters were quickly torn down by left-wing activists.

What's more, the contours of this 'us' were subject to discussions that aimed to know how exactly it was constituted, and notably to know to what extent the creation of this group could supersede other divides, such as the class divide. In another text, Hocquenghem returns to the beginnings of the FHAR and the decision to distribute leaflets in 'gay clubs.' This expression in itself carries social and political baggage: gays who frequented night clubs and were members of clubs were thought to belong to the bourgeois or middle class (the latter of whom would be complicit with the bourgeoisie through being aspirational), and were considered to be apolitical.[24] In April 1971, however, Hocquenghem clarified: 'When you start to discover that you're a community, it seems infinitely important that even those guys that I used to hate – those office-working-club-goers who are also fags – were with me.'[25] I will return to this point later: the social definition of gay activism has been the subject of lively debate; here, the question of the tension between sexuality and class has been posed. Similarly, the relationship between men and women, between gays and lesbians, created such tensions that, for example, a faction of lesbian activists left the FHAR from summer 1971 onwards to found an autonomous group,

Les Gouines Rouges (Red Dykes). However, the fact remains that the 'us' was supposed to go beyond divides of gender and class, but this was not accompanied by a similar interrogation of racial divides.

AN ANTI-RACIST POLITICS

One of the singularities of this collection of writing on 'Arabs' lies in the fact that it can be read from various angles, according to different layers. Alongside the texts cited above, there are also texts that recognise their racism (all of which reach a consensus that the former should be published) and manifest an anti-racist politics, and it is worth discussing them further. However, even though the contours of the 'us' are interrogated in these contributions in terms of race, the exclusion of racialised subjects from this 'us' still persists.

It's necessary to remember that the remarks of these gay activists are part of a particularly racist period and context. For activists, the assertion of a sexuality that linked French people to 'Arabs' was transgressive in the context of a society that strongly condemned interracial sexual relations. A good example of this condemnation and a wider account of racial-sexual prohibitions can be found in Claire Etcherelli's *Élise ou la vraie vie*, which received the prestigious Prix Femina in 1967. The novel tells the love story of Élise, a white worker, and Arezki, an Algerian worker, who meet in Paris during the Algerian war. Élise discovers the impropriety of this relationship in 'the gaze of others, the expression of the waiter who took our order', and expresses her shame at going out with a *crouillat*, a *raton*, a *bicot* (slang words for 'Arabs'). She describes herself as being 'satisfied that no one saw us together.'[26]

A fraction of gay activists was motivated to fight such prohibitions, which led notably to them overturning taboos and celebrating socially condemned relationships, without however questioning the terms of this condemnation and celebration. Several of the FHAR's texts thus maintain solidarity between homosexuals and 'Arabs.' One of the main interlocutors of the 'Les Arabes et nous' discussion talks about 'the coming together of two sexual afflictions. Two afflictions that connect to each other.'[27] Another text mentions 'the strong solidarity between oppressed groups that I feel with Arabs.'[28] However, as we have seen, this is a solidarity that is expressed as being between two groups that are thought of as distinct and only as distinct. In the issue of *Recherches*, the discussion 'Les Arabes et nous' is enhanced by an appendix text. The introduction explains that, following the first discussion, 'it seemed opportune to many of us who read it that we undertake a similar project with the participation of Arab guys.'[29] This discussion, held 'in an Arab café', and occupying only three pages, is fairly tedious and is quickly cut short by a man who interrupts the conversation. The contributions are not very substantial and the questions are still directed by the gay activists according to their preoccupations.

Inside this issue of *Recherches* a few dissonant and marginal voices go against the grain of the issue's dominant tone. *Three Billion Perverts* includes four anonymously-written pages entitled 'Les Arabes et les "blancs"' ('Arabs and "whites"'). This title is rich in meaning, with *blancs* standing both for the contributions which weren't accepted into the issue[30] (the text's author complains of the atmosphere in which the creation of this issue was conducted), the thoughtlessness of the ideological orientation of the coordinators, but also the individuals of the white race, as opposed to the 'imaginary Arabs' that populate the issue. On this occasion, the anonymous author describes 'a special issue on Arabs without any Arabs.'[31]

Moreover, the FHAR's publications are accompanied by several warnings pertaining to their racist character. This awareness did not prevent them from being published but, on the contrary, actually sparked interest (a mix of 'racism and "revolutionary" spirit', according to one of the texts in *Trois milliards de pervers*).[32] In the 12th issue of *Tout!* a young man describes his first gay experience involving anal penetration: violent and painful, it left him wounded. His sexual partner is described in this way: 'He had an ugly Arab face and his perfume wasn't exactly rose-scented.' The text was published with the following comment:

> The text below struck some of our non-gay comrades as racist. [...] It's true that French homosexuals, in their own way, espouse a certain form of racism: how might you imagine that a young white boy of 15, even if he's a faggot, can escape a racist atmosphere?

This warning is accompanied by the definition of a gay, anti-racist politics. The activists assert:

> Let us point out that in France it is our Arab friends who fuck us and never the other way around. How can we not see in this a consensual form of revenge on us, the colonising West? Do you think that we can have the same relationship with the Arabs as everyone else or as the average Frenchman when we commit the act that bourgeois morality sees as the most shameful with them? Yes, we feel the type of strong solidarity felt between oppressed groups with the Arabs.[33]

These few lines are important in so far as they condense the elements that enrich these texts on 'Arabs'. There is certainly an awareness about racism and a 'solidarity between oppressed peoples.'[34] There is also the reassertion of two different groups, even when the 'Arabs' are considered 'friends.' Equally, there's a politicisation of what the FHAR had previously termed 'sexual roles', meaning the distinction between 'top' and 'bottom' positions during penetration: here the writers of these lines seem to draw conclusions from the fact that it's the 'Arabs' who 'fuck' them, even if, on other occasions, activists railed against the idea of the active/passive dichotomy of roles, and against the hierarchies these roles implied. Finally, there's the assertion of a specific relationship that gay men reportedly have with 'Arabs', due to the reprobate sexuality they share. This is a unique way of thinking about the intersection of dominations, as if social repression against homosexuality, if not outweighing racism, does at least reconfigure racial relations. Herein lies the paradox of these texts: the power relations aren't removed – colonialism and its history are summoned – but racialised relations are seemingly dismantled by the fact of sexuality.

DISTINGUISHING ONESELF

As Toni Morrison wrote, the establishment of the Other is also the establishment of the self, the taking up of a position on one's own self-definition. Thus, 'The urgency of distinguishing between those who belong to the human race and those who are decidedly non-human is so powerful the spotlight turns away and shines not on the object of degradation but on its creator.'[35] The use by Morrison of the word 'distinguishing', is similar to a key term in Pierre Bourdieu's sociology, *la distinction* (distinction).[36] Distinguishing oneself, for an individual, is the taking up of a position (cultural, political, etc.) that allows one both to assert that one belongs to a social group and to distinguish oneself from another (or several other) social groups. In a more general way, this distinction is present in colonial literature (I'm thinking, for example, of texts by Michel Leiris and Pierre Herbart). The colonial experience – travelling into colonies – allowed the individual to assert their hatred for France or European civilisation, and to state their contempt for their compatriots. In the context of the gay liberation of the '70s in France, the racial question supports this process of distinction.

On one hand, this distinction is made regarding left-wing activists and is a form of competition regarding the definition of revolutionary behaviour. In *Tout!* gay activists assert: 'We're sure that the racism of [non-gay] activists, whose only relationship with Arabs is through rhetoric, is more alienating than our own.'[37] This statement demonstrates how the racial question must be understood in the light of the fight the gay activists led to assert their membership within the Left. Gay activists faced great difficulties in establishing homosexual struggle as a significant fight inside the radical left, and they suffered violent homophobia from other activists. A hierarchy of fights and divides also relegated sexual questions far behind class struggle. It is for that reason that some of the texts and actions of the FHAR could be seen as being directed against the radical left in itself. 'It seems that there's no relationship possible between homosexuality and the revolutionary struggle', writes Christian Maurel in *Tout!* 'At least that's what lots of leftists think, who don't hesitate to exclude fags and lesbians from the revolution.'[38]

This is why, in the context of tensions within the left, gay activists endowed desire and sexuality with a specific strength: it was thought that these things might allow for a singular social comprehension by which gay activists could better understand racism than other left-wing activists. While colonialism – particularly in the form of the Algerian war, but also the war in Vietnam – was the background that constituted the political education of activists of the '60s and '70s ('leftist' movements were often set up to challenge the positions of the Parti communiste francais on Algeria), the journal *Tout!* recalls Jean Genet's statement: 'Homosexuality was what made me realise that Algerians were no different from other men.' This statement outraged the Lutte Ouvrière – a Trotskyist group according to whom the FHAR embodied 'petty-bourgeois individualism' – but the FHAR responded noting that the 'sexual relation allows for the deepening of this realisation to an instinctual level.'[39] For his part, in his book *Le Désir homosexuel* (*Homosexual Desire*), Hocquenghem talked about 'an intervention based not on a kind of solidarity of principle but on a desiring relation.'[40] What must be understood from these quotations is that, engaged in a battle to (re)define what the politics of the left was, gay activists took up the racial question to distinguish themselves from other left-wing activists; to assert that they would naturally be more to the left of other activists, or at the least in a position to lead a specific and more effective politics.

An alternative type of distinction refers to what it is to be gay, with race supporting a definition of what a politicised homosexuality should be. We find an example of this in the long interview 'Three Billion Perverts', during the course of which one of the participants distinguishes between the practice of sodomy depending on whether it takes place with a 'European' or an 'Arab.' The former asks to use lubricant, while the second uses saliva, 'spit[ting] into his hand.' The man telling this anecdote indicates that lubricant 'is part of [a] gay culture' that the 'Arab' isn't imagined to be part of. Another participant adds that lubricant 'is the queens from Saint-Germain to Saint-Trop' with their little bags and the last remaining cream from the pharmacy, like the last disinfectant.'[41] This last statement is important: it unfavourably condenses that which gay activists wanted to establish themselves against. Saint-Germain stands for Saint-Germain-des-Prés which was, at the time, the centre of intellectual life in Paris but also the centre of a gay life (due to the presence of bars and clubs), considered to be bourgeois. Saint-Trop is Saint-Tropez, a fashionable seaside town in the Côte d'Azur. Dismissing lubricant as something that's part of the life of 'queens from Saint-Germain to Saint-Tropez', is a way of self-distinguishing, in the most Bourdieusian sense of the term, from a homosexuality that is considered bourgeois; by the same token, it's also a way of associating sexual relations with an 'Arab' with a sexuality that isn't bourgeois, that is in opposition to the bourgeoisie and instead indicative of a transgressive gay culture.

We find this opposition in some of Hocquenghem's later writing, despite what he wrote in 1971 about the necessity of creating a 'community' with 'clubgo[ing]' gays.[42] In 1976, for example, taking Pasolini's death as a starting point, he denounced 'groups of "respectable" homosexuals' as well as 'a great move [...] towards neutralising and making homosexuality respectable.' He then contrasts several types of gay:

The traditional queen, likable or wicked, the lover of young thugs, the specialist of street urinals, all these exotic types inherited from the nineteenth century, give way to the reassuring modern young homosexual (aged 25 to 40) with moustache and briefcase, without complexes or affectations, cold and polite, in an advertising job or sales position at a large department store, opposed to outlandishness, respectful of power, and a lover of enlightened liberalism and culture. Gone are the sordid and the grandiose, the amusing and the evil. Sado-masochism itself is no longer anything more than a vestiary fashion for the proper queen.[43]

Beyond a historical argument (which is, moreover, debatable), what seems to be important here is the pitting of one 'type' of homosexuality against others. What appears from out of this quote is a homosexuality that is supposedly anti-establishment, defined by social practices and positions that aren't exclusively sexual. In the same text, which is very rich in social distinction in its rejection of the middle classes, Hocquenghem regrets the fact that 'everyone will fuck in his own social class, the dynamic junior executives will breathe with rapture the smell of their partners' aftershave.'[44]

It's within this structure that race can be inserted: as a desire towards a marginalised individual in a racist society, sexual desire for an Arab might therefore carry with it a subversive charge, and would define the bearer of this desire as a subversive subject. As a result, the gay liberation movement remains more inflected by psychoanalysis than it might like to think, despite the anti-psychoanalytical critique brought to bear by the FHAR and raised in the *Recherches* issue (which, in its introduction, contrasts psychoanalytical knowledge with knowledge produced by the activists themselves). Indeed, something very 'object-related' persists: the definition of subversive desire respects the Freudian hypothesis according to which perversion is characterised by the object towards which the desire is borne. With the possibility that this could be someone of the same sex, a subversive force in and of itself is attributed to homosexual desire – but also the 'Arab' or the foreigner (or, elsewhere in Hocquenghem, 'the thug'). The simple fact of being drawn to immigrants, to marginalised people, in a racist society, would render this desire transgressive – which however still says nothing about the political position of the bearer of this desire who contributes, once again, to the essentialisation of the other as different.

CRITIQUE OF GAY LIBERATION

An important part of the *Recherches* issue on 'Arabs' is a text spanning four pages, published anonymously but which, according to several sources, can be attributed to Gilles Deleuze. Titled 'Sex-pol en acte' (Sexual politics in action), it immediately follows the 'Arabs and us' discussion, which it proposes to analyse. At the time Deleuze was fairly close to members of the FHAR: as a result of his links with Félix Guattari, naturally, and the response to their 1972 book *L'anti-Œdipe*, which gay activists (notably Hocquenghem) had seized upon to think through gay liberation, but also because of his teaching at the Université de Vincennes, an institution that welcomed a great many left-wing thinkers as well as activists. In 1973, Michel Cressole, a member of the FHAR, authored a small book about him (which Hocquenghem participated in writing) which ends with a lively correspondence, a testament to many disagreements.[45] In 1974, Deleuze also prefaced Hocquenghem's *L'Après-mai des faunes*.[46]

Deleuze's text in *Recherches* allows for an understanding as to why gay activists might be able to publish racist texts, while being aware of this racism: the very production of these texts belonged to the way in which Deleuze conceptualised gay liberation. The philosopher recalls in broad strokes the thesis of *L'anti-Œdipe*: society is filled with relationships based on desire – 'libidinal investments' – and not only economic connections (as Marxism would claim). These libidinal investments are in the realm of the unconscious. Hence a dual political task: unveiling unconscious investments and analysing them politically. As Deleuze explains:

> If we stop at political *consciousness*, it is, generally speaking, fairly easy to designate what is revolutionary and what is fascist [...] But the introduction of desire, libido and the unconscious into the political field complicates things: because fascist *and* revolutionary, racist *and* anti-racist libidinal investments intermingle or are scattered in the same person and in new conditions which at least allow for the beginning of an analysis of desire's *entanglements*, independent from any reference to notions like that of appearance, mystification or betrayal.[47]

As much as an analysis of desire, this text also shows Deleuze (and Guattari) thinking through political and social positions in terms of the unconscious (which, in the end, in spite of all that separates their work, isn't so far from the *habitus* of Pierre Bourdieu's sociological theory), as well as through the contradictions between the conscious and the unconscious present in an individual or individuals in the same social group. This is the precise problem posed by the text about 'Arabs' in *Three Billion Perverts*: a political position that *consciously* proclaims itself 'revolutionary' (in this case, anti-racist) which *unconsciously* turns out to be 'fascist' (in this case, racist).

As Deleuze continues, the task of revolutionary movements should therefore be to uncover these unconscious investments in order to work on them and transform them:

> Only a revolutionary-oriented group can accommodate desire employed in this way; only this kind of group can ensure little by little, progressively, the defusions capable of eliminating real reactionary elements and can flip desire over onto the side of revolution.[48]

33

Thus the importance of the publication of these texts on 'Arabs': despite their 'unconscious fascism', their 'racist themes' and the 'racist and fascist desire' they exhibit, they still constitute a stage of revolutionary work. 'As long as these investments of desire aren't uncovered, there will always be unconscious fascism on the side of the revolutionaries', Deleuze clarifies, describing it as necessary to bring to light, to uncover these unconsciously reactionary features:

> To rid oneself of them, it's not enough to, it's not a question of making love with Arabs [...]. You have to know with whom and with what machine, what device, what organisation of desire, you're making love if you're also doing politics.

In other words, it's about bringing unconscious elements over to the side of the conscious: 'You won't be able to get rid of racism in the course of a brief conversation. But you will at least have brought it to light.'[49]

In this text, Deleuze suggests a keen understanding of the way in which French gay activists conceived of gay liberation. One text in this issue of *Recherches* reflects this conceptualisation in particular: entitled 'Les Culs énergumènes' ('The Screwball Asses') and published anonymously, it was written by Christian Maurel but was wrongly attributed to Guy Hocquenghem upon its translation into English.[50] In this text Maurel, who expresses his disagreement with several theses espoused by some other activists (notably Hocquenghem and his *Le Désir homosexuel*) reflects on the texts about 'Arabs', notably the discussion 'Les Arabes et nous'. Although he mentions 'intense, almost nauseating, doubt', he also talks about a 'stupefying honesty.' In his view, the text is 'exemplary', its authors aren't 'liars', although the 'Arabs' form 'a collection of dildos, and we must not forget that a collector is always somehow a bourgeois.' He also writes, 'Those who live them and dare tell us about it at least do so fully'.[51] Maurel's vocabulary ('honesty', 'dare', 'liars' etc) underlines how fundamental the question of 'speaking truthfully' was to these gay activists – something that would justify, in their minds, the publication of these texts on 'Arabs'. We understand this all the better if we recall that it was precisely this project that Michel Foucault opposed in *La volonté de savoir* (*The Will to Knowledge*), reminding us how 'speaking truthfully' is a mechanism of power, and that the *aveu/mensonge* (avowal/lie) binary is embedded in a long history of controlling sexuality.[52]

As much as an understanding or a justification of the project carried out by the gay activists, Deleuze's text could also be read as a critique, or at least a reminder of the limits of the activists' approach, if they stop mid-way. As he reminds us in *Recherches*, the texts also evidence an 'ordinary, completely Oedipal sexuality',[53] which can be understood as a reminder of the fact that sexual practices are never free from all power or completely fall outside of social norms. This text demonstrates the position that Deleuze held towards the gay movement more generally: support accompanied by a critique of certain positions held by activists and notably what could today be considered a naivety or form of blindness. Several times, if only to remind us that one must superimpose the unconscious positions over the conscious positions, Deleuze underlined that it's not enough to claim to be revolutionary to be it. In his letter addressed to Michel Cressole (one of the 'Les Arabes et nous' participants), he clarifies this position:

> One has never fought against Oedipal secretions without fighting against oneself, without experimenting against oneself […] Having a non-oedipal love is no small matter. And you should know that it is not enough to be single, without children, queer, a member of a group, to avoid Oedipus, as there are group Oedipodes: Oedipal homosexuals, Oedipianised MLF members, etc. Take the model text 'The Arabs and us', which is even more Oedipal than my daughter.[54]

CONCLUSION

There are of course 'absent voices' in this reading of the FHAR's writings – that of racialised subjects in France in the 1970s. If on the one hand the writings of the 'gay liberation' teach us little about these voices – if it's the case that, as is in one of the few opinions presented in direct discourse in *Recherches*, the French want to 'fuck them' but not 'dance' with them in nightclubs[55] – they, on the other, tell us a lot about racist and sexist structures, about the entanglement between race and gay liberation. While the FHAR, from its conception, was animated by the project of 'giving a voice' to minority subjects, it is also the case that, through the production of one's own discourse about oneself, not every individual has access to this right to speak and instead remains, if it can be said, spoken *for* by others. An introductory note to the 12th issue of *Recherches* recalls all these ambiguities of 'gay liberation' productions: Guattari underscores that 'it's not good enough […] to "give voice" to the subjects concerned […], the conditions for a total exercise, or even breakthrough, of this articulation, must still be created.'[56] More generally, this essay's quick foray into one particular political and cultural moment recalls others: a longer history, since the beginning of the 19th century, of relationships between anti-colonialism, race and sexuality, in the sense that it seems to me that gay activists can be seen as part of older social structures, linking a hatred of Europe, a celebration (mostly sexual) of the 'Other' and a denunciation of colonialism; a history, too, that runs up to the present day, of speech by minority sexual and racial groups, and of social conditions that make this speaking possible.[57]

NOTES

1 Toni Morrison. 1992. *Playing in the Dark*. Cambridge, MA: Harvard University Press. 65.

2 See Julian Jackson. 2009. *Living in Arcadia: Homosexuality, Politics, and Morality in France from the Liberation to AIDS*. Chicago: The University of Chicago Press.

3 Morrison. *Playing in the Dark*. Op. cit. 78.

4 Didier Eribon. 2016. 'La voix absente.' In Eribon, *Principes d'une pensée critique*. Paris: Fayard. 130, 135. Translator's own translation.

5 On the wider context of 'gay liberation' in France, see Antoine Idier. 2017. *Les Vies de Guy Hocquenghem. Politique, sexualité, culture*. Paris: Fayard; Idier, 2020. 'A Genealogy of a Politics of Subjectivity : Guy Hocquenghem, Homosexuality, and the Radical Left in Post-1968 France.' In Joachim C. Häberlen, Mark Keck-Szajbel and Kate Mahoney. Eds. *The Politics of Authenticity: Countercultures and Radical Movements across the Iron Curtain, 1968–1989*. New York/Oxford: Berghahn. 89–109.

6 These weren't the only publications to come from the FHAR: the journal *Le Fléau social* appeared in 1972 (the title is a reference to a piece of French legislation from 1960 which considered homosexuality as a 'fléau social', a 'social ill') as well as the journal *L'Antinorm*. It should be noted that, thanks to a collective interest in the movements of the 1970s, several publications have been reissued in recent years. The *Recherches* issue 'Trois milliards de pervers', for instance, was republished in 2015 (La Bussière: Acratie). Previously, a partially digitised version was available on the internet. *Le Rapport contre la normalité,* the FHAR manifesto-book published in 1971, was also reissued in 2013 (Montpellier: GayKitschCamp). This is not unique to France: several translations of texts by Guy Hocquenghem have recently emerged, for example, in German (*Das homosexuelle Begehren*. 2019. Hamburg: Nautilus) and in English (*The Amphitheater of the Dead*. 2018. New York: Guillotine).

7 Guy Hocquenghem. 1974. *L'Après-mai des faunes*. Paris: Grasset. 159.

8 *Recherches*. No. 12. March 1973. 33.

9 Ibid. 38.

10 Edward W. Said. 1978. *Orientalism*. New York: Pantheon Books.

11 Frantz Fanon. 1986. Translated by Charles Lam Markmann. *Black Skin, White Masks*. London: Pluto Press. 123, 126. The absence of 'Black' subjects, who barely appear, should be noted. It should also be considered that when one or two references to 'nègres' appear, these are opposed to 'Arabs': 'Les autres sont comme tous les nègres, un peu plus incertains que les Arabes pour les affaires de cul.' ('The others are, like all negroes, a little more uncertain than the Arabs about sexual matters.' *Recherches*. Op. cit. 41).

12 Pierre Bourdieu. 2001. *Langage et pouvoir symbolique*. Paris: Seuil.

13 For example, according to another text in the journal, while 'Europeans [...] quite often experience their homosexuality in a "pathological" way', conversely 'the Arab [...] experiences homosexual relations without problems, without guilt; he only asks that it not be too visible on the outside' (*Recherches*. Op. cit. 34).

14 Ibid. 11–13, 20.

15 Ibid. 15, 17. See also: 'I understood it when I went to Marrakech. We could very well sleep together without expressing feelings, and see each other afterwards, and become friends, and at the same time continue to sleep together. Whereas here you can't be alone for half an hour without your guy calling you on the phone.' Ibid. 14. According to another text in the publication, 'to ask an "Arab" for "love" is to ask for the impossible.' Ibid. 34.

16 Ibid. 21.

17 Ibid. 13, 20.

18 Ibid. 15–17.

19 Ibid. 18, 16.

20 Ibid. 57, 59.

21 Todd Shepard. 2018. *Sex, France, and Arab Men, 1962–1979*. Chicago: University of Chicago Press.

22 Hocquenghem. *L'Après-mai des faunes*. Op. cit. 147–148.

23 Ibid. 145.

24 These categories are not exempt from social contempt or distinction, especially as the majority of gay activists were young intellectuals, students, cultural producers, etc. Hocquenghem himself was born into a Parisian bourgeois family, to parents who had been to the prestigious École Normale and were teachers, and he himself studied at the École Normale de la rue d'Ulm.

25 Hocquenghem. *L'Après-mai des faunes*. Op. cit. 155.

26 Claire Etcherell. 1972. *Élise ou la vraie vie*. Paris: Gallimard, «Folio». 132, 134. Translator's own translation.

27 *Recherches*. Op. cit. 13.

28 *Rapport contre la normalité*. Op. cit. 104.

29 *Recherches. Op. cit.* 25.

30 Translator's note: In French, blanc means both 'white' and 'unused.'

31 *Recherches*, Op. cit. 206–7.

32 Ibid. 35.

33 *Rapport contre la normalité*. Op. cit. 102, 104.

34 This 'solidarity' can be found in the support given to the FHAR by the homosexual, anarchist and anti-colonialist writer Daniel Guérin: 'I am signing your manifesto. [...] All my life, I have practiced a very strong solidarity of oppressed peoples with the Arabs.' (*Tout !* No. 13. 17 May 1971.)

35 Toni Morrison. 2017. *The Origin of Others*. Cambridge, MA: Harvard University Press. 29.

36 Pierre Bourdieu. 1979. *La Distinction. Critique sociale du jugement*. Paris, Minuit. On the friendship and shared political and theoretical ties between Morrison and Bourdieu, see '"Voir comme on ne voit jamais": dialogue entre Pierre Bourdieu et Toni Morrison.' *Vacarme*. No. 6. Winter 1998. https://vacarme.org/article807.html

37 *Rapport contre la normalité*. Op. cit. 104.

38 Ibid. 50.

39 Ibid. 25, 28.

40 Guy Hocquenghem. 1993. *Homosexual Desire*, Durham, NC: Duke University Press. 141.

41 *Recherches*. Op. cit. 23.

42 Hocquenghem. *Après-mai des faunes*. Op. cit. 155.

43 Guy Hocquenghem. 2017. 'Tout le monde ne peut pas mourir dans son lit.' In Hocquenghem. *Un journal de rêve*. Paris: Verticales. 42–43.

44 Ibid. 44.

45 Michel Cressole. 1973. *Gilles Deleuze*. Paris: Éditions universitaires.

46 My own writing on the relationship between Deleuze and gay liberation can be found in *Les Vies de Guy Hocquenghem*. Op. cit.

47 *Recherches*. Op. cit. 28.

48 Ibid. 28–29.

49 Ibid. 29.

50 The publisher Semiotext(e) translated 'Les Culs énergumènes' into English, attributing it to Hocquenghem (*The Screwball Asses*. Los Angeles: Semiotext(e). 2010); the attribution to Christian Maurel was rectified in a recent German translation (*Für den Arsch*. Berlin: August Verlag. 2019). On this misattribution, see Idier, *Les Vies de Guy Hocquenghem*, Op. cit. 20–22. It seems important to me in the context of a book dedicated to queer print cultures of the 1970s, to underline the more general problems of power posed by this misattribution: beyond Hocquenghem himself these problems concern the way in which a certain number of writings (often initially published anonymously) have recently been rediscovered. In the context of a movement towards rediscovery, republication and translation of texts from the 1970s, it must be remembered that, on one hand, publishing consists of taking ownership of a certain capital and, on the other hand, committing a certain violence. On circulation,

translation and the power of recognition, see Pascale Casanova. 2004. *The World Republic of Letters.* Cambridge, MA: Harvard University Press.

51 Hocquenghem [Maurel]. *The Screwball Asses.* Op. cit. 9–14.

52 Michel Foucault. 1976. *La Volonté de savoir*. Paris: Gallimard. See Didier Eribon. 2004. *Insult and the Making of the Gay Self.* Durham, NC: Duke University Press, for his analysis of the genealogy of Foucault's book in the context of sexual and gay liberation in the 1970s.

53 *Recherches*. Op. cit. 30.

54 Michel Cressole, *Deleuze.* Op. cit. 116.

55 *Recherches*. Op. cit. 16.

56 Ibid. 2.

57 *Mithly* (2019), a multi-screen video work by Julian Volz, is an example of the link made between the gay liberation of the 1970s and contemporary gay and queer Arab movements. See: https://www.schirn.de/en/magazine/schirn_tipps/2020/open_confident_arab_and_queer/ I'm also thinking of the Instagram account 'Personnes racisées vs grindr' which collects and interrogates the racism of dating apps: https://www.instagram.com/pracisees_vs_grindr/.

2 'Happiness was in the pages of this magazine': The Birth of the French Lesbian Press and the Construction of a Space of One's Own (1976–90)

ILANA ELOIT

(Translated by Merl Storr)

I n 1980, following the publication of Monique Wittig's articles 'The straight mind' and 'One is not born a woman' in the journal *Questions féministes* (Feminist Questions) (1977–1980), a conflict that had been brewing for years between feminism and political lesbianism came to a head. The conflict involved a violent opposition between feminists and radical lesbians on the *Questions féministes* editorial board over the issue of the connection between heterosexuality and women's oppression.[1] It ended with the closure of the journal, which was replaced after a lengthy court case by the journal *Nouvelles Questions Féministes* (New Feminist Questions) (1981–) organised by some of the former editorial board members. This conflict, which extended far beyond the journal itself and penetrated every stratum of feminist activism, formed part of the wider emergence of a lesbian movement during the 1980s; but that decade opened, almost inevitably, with another major political question, namely mixed-gender alliances with gay men.

Masques (Masks) (1979–1985), a quarterly 'journal of homosexualities', was founded in 1979 by male and female activists from the *Ligue communiste révolutionnaire* (Revolutionary Communist League).[2] In April 1982, two founder members and six contributors – all of them women – walked out of the journal, condemning 'the systematic blindness and deafness that have constantly set the editors against our questions, concerns and critiques, and even against our very existence as lesbians'. Exasperated by the gradual depoliticisation of a journal 'where the requirement of consensus [...] rules', by 'the predominance of the masculine', and by 'repeated attacks on feminism' by certain members of the journal, the eight leavers wished henceforth to 'contribute to the consolidation of the autonomous Lesbian Movement'.[3]

The juxtaposition of these two examples is revealing of the profoundly political and social nature of the space of the feminist, homosexual and lesbian press in France at the turn of the 1980s. Indeed, this activist press was much more than a tool of information for a political community: it was the space where those communities were formed, and where the political questions that occupied them were articulated. In this sense, the press was the geographical place where these communities came to life, gained substance, gathered, split and re-formed. To write the history of the lesbian press during this period is thus inevitably to write the political and social history of the construction of these political identities, and to interrogate the role of the press in those constructions.

The history of the conflicts within the editorial boards of *Questions féministes* and *Masques* sheds equal light on another important factor: lesbians often experienced the feminist and mixed homosexual press as spaces of confrontation and development, where some of the theoretical contradictions that lesbian subjectivity posed for feminist or homosexual unity became manifest. Thus these two conflicts, which occurred just two years apart, heralded the major discursive shake-ups from which a lesbian political subjectivity emerged in France, falteringly and precariously, in these early years of the 1980s – a lesbian political subjectivity that would itself take shape through the growth of an autonomous and specifically lesbian press throughout the 1980s.

The lesbian press differed from the feminist press in that it was a space not only of politicisation, but also of escape from isolation and the homosexual closet. A survey conducted by the *Mouvement d'information et d'expression des lesbiennes* (MIEL,[4] Movement for Lesbian Information and Expression) in 1986 revealed that 93.7% of lesbians asked felt a 'need for lesbian information', thus demonstrating 'the need to have a relationship with the lesbian world, to know what is being organised, thought and created in that world, and to compare one's own experiences with those of other lesbians'.[5] The solitude that characterised homosexual life allows us to understand the press's crucial role in community-building: it constituted a link to the community, just as much as it acted as a sign of the community's existence – the latter being a particular necessity for lesbians, whose sexual sociality lacked the presence and public visibility of gay men's. Thus the lesbian press had two faces: because it was at once a tool for politicisation and a tool for connecting isolated subjectivities, it blended the political with the intimate, activist tracts with life stories, historical investigations with lonely hearts ads, grievances against women's groups with languid poetry, reports on activist meetings with announcements of lesbian festivals. The lesbian press constituted a polymorphous, hybrid and overflowing space that went beyond both the feminist press and the homosexual press in its political, intimate and poetic quest for a space of its own. This essay does not set out to provide an exhaustive inventory of the French lesbian press at the turn of the 1980s and throughout the decade.[6] Rather, it aims to ponder the social, political and cultural role of the lesbian press in the construction of a collective identity, by asking: what did the lesbian press do for lesbians in France?[7]

LESBIANS AND THE FEMINIST PRESS: A PEOPLE WHO ARE MISSING[8]

The term 'female homosexual' (*homosexuelle*) had occupied a significant place in *Le Torchon brûle* (The Tea Towel Is Burning) (1971–1973)[9], the first journal of the *Mouvement de libération de femmes* (MLF, Women's Liberation Movement), emphasising lesbians' strong presence at the heart of the women's movement. But lesbians were soon relegated to the sidelines in feminist publications, the numbers of which nevertheless grew exponentially throughout the 1970s. Far from being continually asserted, the presence of lesbians manifested itself in the feminist press during the second half of the 1970s as a question, a lack to be filled, a ritually invoked and repeatedly pointed out absence that haunted the space of the feminist press.

Whether they concerned abortion, contraception or childcare, the 'women-specific issues'[10] addressed by the feminist movement for the most part were actually those of heterosexual women.[11] In this context it is not difficult to understand the alienation some lesbians felt from the feminist press, which remained silent on lesbian-specific issues such as violence against lesbians, anti-lesbian discrimination at work, lesbian reproduction and motherhood, or coming out. While the politicisation or non-politicisation of homosexuality took different forms according to the intellectual currents within the MLF[12] (detailed discussion of which is beyond the scope of this article), it is clear that although homosexuality 'appeared to prevail in the everyday practices of the movement, in that it inspired activism and a new form of conviviality among women, it was quickly relegated to second place in the movement's collective concerns'.[13]

Thus, in the October 1979 issue of *Histoires d'Elles* (Stories of Women[14]) (1977–1980) – a monthly feminist journal created in 1977 with the aim of taking a 'women's look' at current affairs – one reader complained of the journal's sustained silence on lesbianism:

> I just want to bring up one topic: why such silence on homosexuality in Histoires d'Elles? Every month I hope to read about women whose joys and sorrows in life somewhat resemble my own, but nothing – complete silence. Unless this topic has nothing to do with either politics, everyday life or fantasy?? So no hard feelings, but a little sadness deep in my heart.[15]

Similarly, it was only under the pressure of external criticism that *Le Temps des Femmes* (Women's Times) (1978–1982), a journal produced by the class struggle strand of the MLF, broached the topic of lesbianism. Following the publication in 1981 of a special issue looking back over the previous decade of feminism, Suzette Triton published in *Masques* – a journal she had co-founded – a scathing opinion piece titled 'Women's Times are not lesbians' times',[16] in which she condemned the absence of any consideration of lesbian struggles.

Histoires d'Elles' and *Le Temps des Femmes'* respective responses to these two points of view are particularly illuminating. In reply to Suzette Triton's critique, the editors of *Le Temps des Femmes* stated that it was not possible to 'cover everything on a whistle-stop tour' and mentioned the imminent possibility of making the 'women omitted from this issue […] the sole focus of a future issue'.[17] As for the editors of *Histoires d'Elles*, they greeted the words of the reader who had criticised them for 'such silence on homosexuality' with the following reply: 'thank you for the message. Perhaps it is because what is something of a fantasy for every woman is an everyday reality for only a few'.

In a few terse sentences, these two responses bring together three modes of exteriorisation of the lesbian viewpoint: particularisation, derealisation (or fetishisation) and depoliticisation. The particularisation lay in the idea that because lesbianism concerned only a minority of women, it should be content with a reduced level of representation (or no representation at all) in the discursive field of feminism, or with separate representation in a special issue. The derealisation lay in the description of homosexuality as an imaginary elsewhere, a ghostly but ardently desired presence: 'a fantasy for every woman'. Lastly, the depoliticisation worked by reducing the power relations between heterosexuality and homosexuality in the women's movement, and in society in general, to a numerical relationship: 'reality for only a few'. Overall, the publication of these expressions of lesbian discontent and disquiet enabled the editors to short-circuit the issue: by publishing the texts, they protected themselves against accusations of censorship, and provided a space where the issue of lesbianism could be raised without affecting the general organisation or dominant order of discourse. In this sense, publishing and responding to criticism by defending oneself in one way or another was another means of closing down the debate and inoculating the dominant discourse against the corrosive power of minoritarian critique. Simultaneously inside and outside the movement, lesbians had to position themselves in relation to this political and discursive dilemma in the 1970s. Indeed, for Joan W. Scott, French feminists since Olympe de Gouges (the author of the *Declaration of the Rights of Woman and Citizen* in 1791) have been 'paradoxical citizens' insofar as they have highlighted the 'intractable contradictions'[18] of an 'exclusive democracy'[19] founded on the exclusion of women from the field of politics; that being the case, have not lesbians become 'paradoxical feminists' in turn by inhabiting a thoroughly 'paradoxical' position within feminism, one that reveals the omissions, displacements and exclusions at the heart of the political subject 'women'?

In 1978, a reader wrote to *Des femmes en mouvements* (Women in Movements) (1977–1979), a journal of the group *Psychanalyse et Politique* (Psychoanalysis and

Politics) from the MLF's differentialist strand: 'I am a lesbian – I use this term as a quick self-definition, but I'm not very attached to it – and I miss hearing from women like myself. It's impossible for me to open any publication on women without this desire for recognition…'.[20] At the end of the 1970s, lesbians set off in quest of this recognition that they could not find in the feminist press.

THE LESBIAN PRESS AND THE CREATION OF SOCIAL CONNECTIONS

By enabling the formation of a community of 'fellow-readers'[21] and thereby making visible 'in the mind of each […] the image of their communion',[22] as Benedict Anderson notes, journals in general enable identification with a collective subject. Drawing on Sartrean concepts, Didier Eribon argues that the mobilisation of homosexuals is the result of a shift: the 'passive' unity of a 'collective' that has been imposed on its members – who are strangers connected only through 'the mediation of their lived relation to the homophobic society' – transforms into a 'fused group' when those members, 'animated by a common project',[23] mutually recognise one another. Thus, although of course political questions were not absent from the first lesbian gatherings, it is clear that the search for social connections – the absence of which was traumatic in the personal accounts of so many lesbians – was one of the principal functions of the lesbian press at the turn of the 1980s.

There is evidence of this need to escape from isolation in the editorial statements of the first two French lesbian journals. The *Journal des lesbiennes féministes* (Journal of Feminist Lesbians) (1976–1977) was created in 1976 by the *Groupe des lesbiennes féministes* (Feminist Lesbians' Group),[24] one of the first lesbian groups; in the editorial, the editors asserted: 'we do not have a position on the "Women's movement"; we are all the Movement. But for us there is also the desire to make ourselves known as lesbians, and above all to know and recognise ourselves and each other among women'.[25] Similarly, the journal *Quand les femmes s'aiment* (When Women Love Each Other[26]) (1978–1980), launched in 1978 by the *Groupe de Lesbiennes du Centre des Femmes de Lyon* (Lyons Women's Centre Lesbian Group) and published alternately by the Lyons group and the *Groupe Lesbiennes de Paris* (Paris Lesbians Group), wanted to bring lesbians together:

Front cover of *Quand les femmes s'aiment*, Issue 1, April 1978. Artwork by Madé Tissé.

It was a great moment when we talked in the group about meeting people, organising things, about places where we could tell each other things, about a way of getting to know each other, lesbians from all over... We receive a fair bit of post: from lesbians in isolated areas who are prepared to travel miles to attend the group, from other groups asking for news about us, from women 'interested by our existence' who ask who we are. [...] We would like [the journal] to enable isolated lesbians to gather together [...], and for it to take active part in the debates and in the affirmation of a lesbian movement.[27]

The year 1982 saw the creation of *Lesbia* (1982–2012), a monthly lesbian journal that had national distribution and was entirely produced by volunteers. *Lesbia* marked a crucial stage in the history of lesbianism in France thanks to its longevity and the extent of its circulation, which grew from a print run of 500 for the first issues to 7,000 in 1987 and 10,000 in 1988.[28] Similarly, from issue 2 onwards, the magazine took on the objective of 'breaking down isolation and providing a link, a connection between all lesbians'.[29] Lastly, in the editorial for issue 2 of *Désormais* (Henceforth) (1979–1980), a journal that sought to bring women's homosexuality 'out of every ghetto', Nella Nobili wrote: 'On opening the pages of this journal, every reader must be able to say to herself "HENCEFORTH I am no longer alone"!'[30] In short, while a group can bring together a certain number of individuals within a *local* geographical area, only a journal is in a position to access the symbolic dimension of identity by establishing an imaginary space in which each member of the 'collective' is potentially able to recognise the other members in a reciprocal relationship.

In this quest for contact, a crucial role was played by *Lesbia*'s small ads, which allowed readers to initiate romantic, friendly or political encounters. In June 1986, a meeting was organised in Toulouse for *Lesbia* subscribers in south-western France to 'bring together isolated women [...] who are unaware of each other'.[31] An article was published about this meeting which allowed participants to speak for themselves: '*Before*, certainly, the letter sent out by *Lesbia* is an open door and a promise. In dark solitude, the sudden, unhoped-for possibility of meeting. One gets ready [...], as if for a departure, a new departure',[32] said one participant. Another reports: 'That Sunday 22 June for me will always be a day like no other, a day apart, in a different universe from my ordinary life [...] how happy I was!'[33] In a survey conducted by the journal to profile its readers, the editors noted that '[small ads] have now become fully a part of the lesbian way of life. There is not the slightest shame in reading them, nor in placing them, and what's more, some even boast that the small ads are the only thing in Lesbia they read'.[34] The small ads became so important for the journal over the years that they were the subject of a special report in the February 1985 issue, where they were described as a 'pathway to survival' for women who did not frequent the 'lesbian world'.[35] In the same year, a group of lesbians in Grenoble created the journal *Lettres à Sappho* (Letters to Sappho)

(1985–1988), which consisted entirely of small ads for friendly or romantic contacts, jobseekers, various objects for sale, or holiday plans.

Above all, thanks to its national reputation, *Lesbia* provided much more than a forum for contact and up-to-date information about lesbian issues. Indeed, filling the void created by the precariousness – or in numerous regions the absence – of the lesbian movement during the 1980s, the journal took on the role of a support organisation for lesbians who were isolated or facing discrimination. The journal's director and co-founder, Christiane Jouve, recalled this aspect of the work:

> At *Lesbia*, we receive a lot of post. [...] There are all these women who write to us 'you are my last hope'. [...] Lives on paper pile up on the desk, and we figure out what to do with them: legal problems, divorce, child custody or cases where children have been taken away from their mother, these are all passed on to lawyers, but where should we direct the women who live in regions where we have no contacts? Serious psychological problems, depression, suicide attempts, social rehabilitation after a period in hospital: these women phone instead, they ask for nothing more than a few words, just a few little words.[36]

Lesbia's assumption of this supportive function, and its role in the creation of social connections, also entailed the organisation of monthly parties – proceeds from which were ploughed back into the journal – and summer and winter leisure trips, organised by the *Lesbia Evasions* (Lesbia Getaways) service from 1985 onwards: 'I would like to tell the vast majority of our clients that to see them smiling at us, dancing, being happy together, is for us the greatest reward of all', wrote Jouve.[37] In general, the lesbian press informed its readers about all activities aimed at the lesbian community: the establishment of activist groups, activist group meetings, music festivals, parties, international gatherings, holiday trips, the opening of community venues, meetings/debates about recent publications, all of them a helping hand to break down isolation. Finally, it is important to take into account the creation of the journal itself as part of the production of collective belonging. For Catherine Gonnard, editor-in-chief of *Lesbia Magazine*[38] from 1989 to 1998, each step in the production of the journal, from the first reading of the articles to the page layout, printing, packaging and despatch of copies, comprised so many 'moments of working together' through which was forged a 'between-lesbians'[39] that the final product then extended to others.

Lesbia's close relationship with the everyday lives of its readers particularly explains its success: neither a specialist journal nor an alternative zine, *Lesbia* was truly a 'magazine', characterised by a light tone that was at once generalist and professional. The monthly editorials established a direct, friendly relationship between the editor-in-chief and the readers, the magazine's 'initiatives' section enabled lesbians from all walks of life (an electrician, a picture restorer, an IT engineer, etc.) to talk about their mundane, everyday experiences at work, and every month there were special reports on topics as diverse as lesbians and old age, Jewish lesbians or the 'lesbian look'. With *Lesbia*, lesbianism was neither merely a political identity, a membership of a counterculture, nor a stigmatised sexuality. It was a way of living and being alive, a shared experience of the world rooted in the texture of everyday life, which it stamped with its own particular, shifting and idiosyncratic mark.

THE LESBIAN PRESS AS A SPACE FOR THE DEVELOPMENT OF POLITICAL DEBATE

Parallel with the creation of social connections among lesbians, the lesbian press also provided a framework for political debate, as witnessed by the publications' different political orientations. Some, such as the *Journal des lesbiennes féministes*, argued for a lesbian position within feminism. *Lesbia* was distinctive in that it was not produced by an activist group and concerned itself with lesbians' cultural, social and everyday lives, without taking any position on the political issues that occupied the movement: 'To preserve the independence that is indispensable to all forms of the media, we refuse to take one side or another: we take all sides, because lesbians are on all sides'.[40] For other publications such as *Espaces* (Spaces) (1982–1983), which described itself as 'a monthly publication of information and commentary by radical lesbians', their whole *raison d'être* was to champion a radical lesbian approach. This newsletter had its first issue in January 1982, in the wake of the establishment in April 1981 of the *Front des lesbiennes radicales* (Radical Lesbian Front), which had itself been a result of the fight between feminists and radical lesbians in spring 1980. *Espaces* and also *Chroniques aiguës et graves* (Chronic[les] Acute and Severe[41]) (1983–1984), the *Bulletin des Archives Recherches Cultures Lesbiennes* (Lesbian Culture Research Archives Newsletter) (1984–1992),[42] *Clit 007, concentré irrésistiblement toxique* (Clit 007, Irresistibly Toxic Concentrate) (1981–1984) in Geneva, the newspaper *Les Lesbianaires*[43] (1982–1996) produced by the *Centre de documentation et de recherches sur le lesbianisme radical* (Information and Research Centre on Radical Lesbianism) in Brussels, and the quarterly *Amazones d'hier, Lesbiennes d'aujourd'hui* (Amazons of Yesterday, Lesbians of Today) (1982–2015) in Montreal, were the architectonic plates of a nascent radical lesbian discourse in the French-speaking world which opposed alliances with either 'hetero-feminists' or gay men. Lastly, other publications, such as *Quand les femmes s'aiment* or *Paroles de lesbiennes féministes* (Words of Feminist Lesbians) (1980–1981), functioned in particular as newsletters, and provided summary reports on debates at national feminist lesbian gatherings. In this sense, the lesbian press was a privileged space for the politicisation of the lesbian community and the circulation of political debate.

However, as well as being a space for the propagation of political information, the lesbian press was also the place where new political issues and fault lines emerged. By

Front cover of *Espaces*, Issue 10, January 1983. The speech bubbles read: 'If we reduced the space between us' … 'Your place or mine?'.

providing a space for contrasting ideas, the lesbian press enabled journal contributors and readers to interact, and by means of those exchanges it gave strength and reality to the idea of community. One of the most intensely debated issues in the lesbian press during the 1980s was lesbian sadomasochism (SM): '"Authentic liberation" or "imitation of male sexuality" – arguments collide as the battle lines are drawn', as *Chroniques aiguës et graves* summed up.[44] The lesbian press became the principal arena for the clash between different points of view, and the controversy exploded in the second half of the 1980s after the publication in July 1987 of an issue of *Lesbia* that included a special report on lesbian fantasies. Illustrated with erotic and SM photographs of lesbians, it provoked the wrath of numerous readers. In the December 1987 issue, five months after the publication of the controversial report, one reader was still castigating 'the photos that accompanied the July issue's report on fantasies': 'For me, they seemed to be nothing other than appalling sadomasochistic pornography aimed at men'.[45] The row continued to intensify, to a point where the writer and philosopher Françoise d'Eaubonne – a historically important participant in the MLF, and co-founder of the *Front Homosexuel d'Action Révolutionnaire* (FHAR, Homosexual Front for Revolutionary Action) in 1971 – entered the debate with an opinion piece titled 'The female censors', in which she exclaimed: 'I'm sick to death of censorship and repression! I'm sick to death of the witch hunt against fantasy, which has been fertile soil for all forms of creativity since time immemorial! [...] I think I'm going to try writing a critique with the title "Puritanism, a feminist infantile disorder"'.[46]

Moreover, the purview of the lesbian press exceeded the bounds of the strictly 'lesbian', because the political debate extended to the issue of mixed-gender alliances in the homosexual press. *Homophonies* (1980–1987), the 'Monthly Lesbian

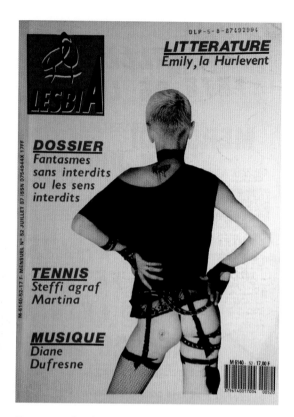

Front cover of *Lesbia*, Issue 52, July 1987, bearing the headline 'SPECIAL REPORT: Fantasies with no taboos and no limits'.

and Gay Publication of the *Comité d'Urgence Anti-Répression Homosexuelle* [Emergency Committee Against Homosexual Repression]', was full of articles on the central problematic issue of mixed-gender alliances, which crystallised in particular around the representation of gay men's sexuality – a point that had already sparked lesbians' departure from the FHAR ten years previously. After the publication of a photograph of male genitals in *Homophonies*, MIEL published an article in the next issue titled 'Enough is enough', in which they denounced the photograph as 'visual assault, sexual assault and psychological rape'.[47] One male contributor replied to MIEL's article, asking:

But what are we doing together, if the symbol and basis of our sexuality is perceived as rape by the women alongside whom we are fighting, *and if that perception cannot be questioned*? Are we doomed, as strange bedfellows, to pursue our activism together out of sheer necessity, and to create an alliance of compromises? Are we doomed to mark out a neutral space where our homosexuality (whether male or female) will drown in unreality, insubstantiality and total insipidity? [...] It is possible to view the world otherwise, such that male genitals are not automatically synonymous with rape, and female genitals are not automatically intended for the male gaze and synonymous with an invitation to rape.[48]

In short, thanks in part to these political interactions, the lesbian press and the mixed homosexual press throughout the 1980s constituted a space for the construction and documentation of the political and theoretical debates of the day, as well as the history of the various lesbian collectives reshaped by the friction these controversies caused. Since in France these debates had no place either in academia (as they did in the United States[49]) or in more generalist feminist journals, the lesbian and gay press is an indispensable tool for retracing the history of lesbian sexuality and activist thought during the 1980s.

Front cover of *Homophonies*, Issue 53, March 1985, bearing the headline 'MIXED ALLIANCES, FEMINIST DEPARTURES'.

FOR LESBIAN WRITING (ÉCRITURE LESBIENNE): THE PRESS AS INTIMATE AND POETIC TERRAIN

Finally, the space of the lesbian press encouraged the birth of a new language beyond the phallic economy, a language that radical lesbian Michèle Causse has called *alphalecte*.[50] Seeking to express intimate lesbian experience, in 1979 a group of lesbians in Lille created the journal *Dire nos homosexualités* (To Speak Our Homosexualities) (1979–1980), which brought together personal accounts and poetic texts where 'the said and the unsaid [...] have their place, and always will'.[51] The language is faltering, hesitant and unsure of itself, but this 'fragmentary mode of writing', the contributors write, 'enables us to attempt elucidations, albeit scrappily, that we have previously only attempted verbally'.[52] This quest for a linguistic and theoretical elsewhere was extended by the journal *Vlasta* (1983–1985), created in 1983 by Suzette Triton following her departure from *Masques* in April 1982. Subtitled 'Amazonian fictions/utopias', this literary, historical and political journal published 'scattered and previously unseen'[53] texts

fictions
utopies
amazoniennes

n.4   60ff

Front cover of *Vlasta*, Issue 4, June 1985.

on lesbianism, through which took shape 'a multiple people, a people of mutants, a people of potentialities that appears and disappears, that is embodied in social, literary, and musical events',[54] to borrow Félix Guattari's formulation. In 1987, in Albi in southern France, Nadine Laroche oversaw *La Grimoire* (The Spell Book), which was published twice yearly from 1987 to 1997 and brought together artistic, poetic, political and literary offerings from contributors all over France; the contributors were the exclusive recipients of copies of the collective journal/artwork thus created. The literary experiments continued in 1989 with the journal *Suite des cris* (Next Screams) (1989–1990) in Paris, and in the journal *Délires et chuchotements* (Cries and Whispers) (1990–1992), created in 1990 by 'women from the South-West and elsewhere', which described itself as 'a selection of texts, collages, drawings and photos, by women and for women, which whisper words of Love and Tenderness, and sometimes cry out in anger'.[55] Indeed, almost all of the lesbian press was peppered with fiction and poetry sent in by readers in search of a space for a writing of their own.

At the turn of the 1980s and throughout that decade, the lesbian press in France did not simply reflect a pre-existing movement, but was rather the place where a sense of collective belonging was invented and took shape. An anchor point for isolated subjects, the lesbian press *made* the lesbian movement. Embodying the moment of fusion of the 'group' where the political subject arises, it thus offered a space for socialisation, politicisation, and intimate and literary experimentation. Much more than a form of traditional news media, the lesbian press – in the same way as lesbian archives, but to a different degree – simultaneously embodied the possibility of dealing with the 'insidious trauma'[56] of lesbian lives through the collective construction of a space of one's own. As the matrix where the lesbian community flourished and took root – illustrated in particular by the longevity of *Lesbia*, which ran from 1982 to 2012 – the lesbian press also demonstrates the centrality of memory by preserving a history of the present as it unfolded. It allowed lesbians to hear an echo of themselves that was not to be found in the feminist press of the 1970s, a 'fantasy echo'[57] that conveys the sound of possible identifications with others like oneself in the present, but also with the history of that quest for others like oneself which shaped the lesbian past and of which lesbians are the heirs, often without knowing it. The joy of discovering these echoes of oneself in the lesbian press is palpable in the words of this young reader, aged seventeen, who, after several fruitless attempts to obtain a copy of *Lesbia*, wrote:

> Yesterday, I went to Boulevard des Italiens to see a film, and on the way out I found myself in front of a newspaper kiosk. I couldn't stop myself asking my eternal question, 'Do you have the magazine *Lesbia*?' – 'Yes, of course.' I couldn't suppress a cry of joy, I was so happy. I would have paid any money for it. […] Happiness was here, in [the] human smile of the newspaper seller, and in the pages of this magazine.[58]

ACKNOWLEDGEMENTS

A French language version of this article first appeared in *Le Temps des Médias*. *Le Temps des Médias* is an academic journal published by Nouveau Monde Éditions, and the SPHM (Société Pour l'Histoire des Médias). It publishes historical research on media, mediations and mediators. It approaches this field in a broad sense including economic, social, political and cultural aspects, means and techniques of communication, production and circulation of information, history of cultural industries, historical sociology of the media, history of audiences or programmes, etc.

All issues are available at: https://www.cairn-int.info/journal-le-temps-des-medias.htm

I thank Louisa Acciari, Catherine Gonnard, Suzette Robichon, Bibia Pavard and the reviewers for the journal *Le Temps des Médias* for their feedback on this article.

NOTES

1. For the feminists who rejected the radical lesbians' critique, the women's movement was supposed to encompass *all* the forms of oppression faced by *all* women in one vast struggle against patriarchy. For the radical lesbians, because feminism presupposed the subject 'women', it thereby reinforced the heterosexual regime within which the categories of sex were produced. According to this logic, only lesbianism – by virtue of its break with heterosexuality – was truly revolutionary.

2. On the history of *Masques*, see L. Pinhas, 'La revendication homosexuelle et l'extrême gauche en France dans les années 1970: de la Ligue communiste révolutionnaire au trimestriel *Masques*', *Dissidences*, 15, 2016, pp. 169–189; L. Pinhas and N. Giguère, 'Presse gaie, littérature et reconnaissance homosexuelle au tournant des années 1980 en France et au Québec: *Gai Pied*, *Masques*, les éditions Persona et *Le Berdache*', *Revue critique de fixxion française contemporaine*, 12, 2016, pp. 5–17.

3. 'Nous sommes 8 fondatrices et collabouratrices à quitter Masques: pourquoi?', *Masques*, 14, summer 1982, pp. 179–184.

4. Translator's note: the word *miel* means honey, and therefore also alludes to the word *goudou* ('dyke'), a reclaimed term of abuse that sounds like *goût doux* (sweet taste).

5. Mouvement d'information et d'expression des lesbiennes, *Être lesbienne aujourd'hui: Le MIEL enquête*, Paris, MIEL, 1986, pp. 15–16.

6. For an exhaustive overview of the lesbian and feminist press from 1970s onwards, see Martine Laroche and Michèle Larrouy, *Mouvements de presse des années 1970 à nos jours, luttes féministes et lesbiennes*, Paris, Editions ARCL, 2009. On the lesbian press, see also Suzette Robichon, 'La presse des lesbiennes: un des moteurs de notre histoire?', *Mouvement des lesbiennes, lesbiennes en mouvement: Dans le cadre des 40 ans du MLF: Actes du colloque et des ateliers*, Paris, Editions Prospero, 2010, pp. 27–38.

7. It is important to neither naturalise nor homogenise the category 'lesbians'. The issue of the material and symbolic conditions of access to the lesbian press and of an interest in lesbian gatherings – conditions such as social class, religion or race – was raised during the 1980s, posing new and difficult questions about the limits of the lesbian subject. This topic is developed at length in my doctoral thesis, *Lesbian Trouble: Feminism, Heterosexuality and the French Nation (1970–1981)*, London School of Economics, supervised by Clare Hemmings, 2018. http://etheses.lse.ac.uk/4041/

8. The expression 'a people who are missing' is borrowed from Gilles Deleuze's *Cinema II: The Time-Image*, London, Bloomsbury, 2013 (English translation of *L'Image-temps*, Paris, Éditions de Minuit, 1985).

9. Translator's note: *le torchon brûle* literally means 'the tea towel [or rag] is burning', but it is also an idiomatic expression for 'the situation is deteriorating'.

10. *Femmes en Lutte, XIIIe*, 'Pourquoi nous ne travaillons plus avec le MLF XIIIe', in Association La Griffonne, *Douze ans de femmes au quotidien: 1970–1981 douze ans de luttes féministes en France*, Paris, La Griffonne, 1981, p. 34.

11. For an in-depth analysis of the Mouvement de libération des femmes' heteronormativity and censorship of lesbian-speaking positions, see my doctoral thesis, *Lesbian Trouble: Feminism, Heterosexuality and the French Nation (1970–1981)*, London School of Economics, supervised by Clare Hemmings, 2018. http://etheses.lse.ac.uk/4041/. See also Ilana Eloit, 'American Lesbians Are Not French Women: Heterosexual French =Feminism and the Americanisation of Lesbianism in the 1970s, *Feminist Theory*, 20(4), 2019, pp. 381–404.

12. The women's movement comprised three strands during the 1970s. The first was the materialist strand of 'revolutionary feminists'. This strand demanded the abolition of the categories of sex, and stood for a feminist movement that was autonomous from other struggles. The second was the differentialist strand organised around the group *Psychanalyse et Politique* (Psychoanalysis and Politics). This strand sought the liberation of women through the affirmation of sexual difference, and it rejected the adjective 'feminist'. The third, known as the 'class struggle' strand, refused to separate women's struggle from the class struggle. It was politically linked to far-left organisations. See Françoise Picq, *Libération des femmes, quarante ans de mouvement*, Brest, Editions dialogues, 2011.

13. M.-J. Bonnet, 'De l'émancipation amoureuse des femmes dans la cité: Lesbiennes et féministes au XXe siècle', *Les Temps Modernes*, 598, March–April 1998, pp. 85–112. http://semgai.free.fr/contenu/textes/bonnet/MJB_emancipation.html

14. Translator's note: the title *Histoires d'Elles* literally means 'stories/histories of them [women]' – or better perhaps, 'herstories' – but it is also a homophone for *histoire d'L* (story of L), and thus a play on the title of Pauline Réage's 1954 erotic novel *Histoire d'O* (Story of O). It may also be a deliberate echo of the 1973 film *Histoires d'A*, a feminist documentary about abortion directed by Charles Belmont and Marielle Issartel.

15. Catherine, *Histoires d'Elles*, 16, October 1979, p. 6.

16. Suzette Triton, 'Le Temps des Femmes n'est pas celui des lesbiennes', *Masques*, 11, autumn 1981, p. 136.

17. 'Le Temps des Femmes: menteuses!', *Le Temps des Femmes*, 13, winter 1981–1982, p. 5.

18. J.W. Scott, *Only Paradoxes to Offer: French Feminists and the Rights of Man*, Cambridge MA, Harvard University Press, 1996 (translated into French with the title *La citoyenne paradoxale* [The Paradoxical Citizen], Paris, Albin Michel, 1998), p. 1.

19. G. Fraisse, *Reason's Muse: Sexual Difference and the Birth of Democracy*, Chicago, University of Chicago Press, 1994 (English translation of *Muse de la raison: La démocratie exclusive et la différence des sexes* [Reason's Muse: Exclusive Democracy and Sexual Difference], Aix-en-Provence, Alinéa, 1989); G. Fraisse, 'La démocratie exclusive: un paradigme français', *Pouvoirs*, 82, September 1997, pp. 5–16.

20. *Des femmes en mouvements*, 2, February 1978, p. 9.

21. B. Anderson, *Imagined Communities: Reflections on the Origin and Spread of Nationalism*, London, Verso, 1983, p. 46.

22. B. Anderson, op. cit., p. 6.

23. D. Eribon, *Insult and the Making of the Gay Self*, translated by Michael Lucey, Durham NC, Duke University Press, 2004, pp. 133–134.

24. The group *Gouines rouges* (Red Dykes), formed in Paris in 1971, was the first lesbian political group in France. The *Groupe des lesbiennes féministes* was formed in Paris in late 1975, and the *Groupe de Lesbiennes du Centre des Femmes de Lyon* (Lyons Women's Centre Lesbian Group) in 1976.

25. *Journal des lesbiennes féministes*, 1, June 1976, p. 4.

26. Translator's note: *Quand les femmes s'aiment* literally means 'when women love each other'. It is also a homophone for *quand les femmes sèment* (when women sow), as in the feminist slogan *quand les femmes sèment, les hommes ne récoltent pas* (when women sow/love each other, men do not reap).

27. 'On a essayé', *Quand les femmes s'aiment*, 1, April 1978, p. 2.

28. On *Lesbia*, see Jade Almeida, *Étude de contenu de la presse lesbienne: Lesbia Magazine de 1982 à 2012*, master's dissertation, Université Paris 1 Panthéon-Sorbonne, supervised by Pascal Ory, 2015.

29. 'Letters', *Lesbia*, 2, January 1983, p. 2.

30. N. Nobili, 'Ici et ailleurs', *Désormais*, 2, July 1979, p. 3.

31. 'Un repas-rencontre des abonnées de Lesbia en Midi-Pyrénées', *Lesbia*, 43, October 1986, p. 8.

32. Ibid., p. 10.

33. Ibid., pp. 9–10.

34. C. Gonnard, 'Dossier: Cinq ans de Lesbia. La face cachée de nos lectrices', *Lesbia*, 58, February 1988, p. 17.

35. M. Goldrajch, 'Dossier: Les petites annonces', *Lesbia*, 25, February 1985, p. 10.

36. C. Jouve, 'Le dernier espoir', *Lesbia*, 50, May 1987, p. 3.

37. C. Jouve, 'Une fête très ordinaire', *Lesbia*, 60, April 1988, p. 1.

38. *Lesbia* became *Lesbia Magazine* in 1989.

39. Interview with Catherine Gonnard, 19 March 2016, and written communication, 6 September 2016.

40. 'L'an 01 de Lesbia', *Lesbia*, 13, January 1984, p. 3.

41. Translator's note: the French word *chronique* can mean both 'chronicle' and 'chronic', yielding the play on words in this journal title.

42. Founded in 1983 under the name *Les Feuilles vives* (Vivid Pages), the *Archives Recherches Cultures Lesbienne*s (Lesbian Culture Research Archives) is a lesbian archive centre, accommodated today in the *Maison des femmes de Paris* (Paris Women's Centre). Originally established on a radical lesbian basis, it soon moved away from that position, but has maintained its commitment to lesbian autonomy as the collective's primary principle.

43. Translator's note: the neologism *lesbianaire* – which could perhaps be translated as 'lesbianary' – echoes *féminaire*, a word coined by Monique Wittig to refer to compendiums of feminist myths and symbols in her 1969 novel *Les Guérillères*.

44. Dolores, 'Un sacré paquet de nœuds', *Chroniques aiguës et graves*, 3, July 1983, p. 37.

45. P. Duncker, 'Resis-stances!', *Lesbia*, 56, December 1987, p. 48.

46. F. d'Eaubonne, 'Les censeuses', *Lesbia*, 60, April 1988, pp. 47–48.

47. MIEL, 'Trop c'est trop', *Homophonies*, 19, May 1982, p. 19.

48. J.-M. Choub, 'Une place pour le corps', *Homophonies*, 23, September 1982, p. 26.

49. In the United States, the 'sex wars' – a huge controversy over sexuality, which sharply divided feminists during the 1980s – took shape at a conference held at Barnard College on 24 April 1982.

50. M. Causse, 'Une politique textuelle inédite: l'alphalecte', in N. Chetcuti and C. Michard, *Lesbianisme et féminisme, histoires politiques*, Paris, L'Harmattan, 2003, pp. 119–130.

51. *Dire nos homosexualités*, 3, 1980, p. 1.

52. *Dire nos homosexualités*, 2, 1979, p. 1.

53. *Vlasta*, 1, spring 1983, p. 6.

54. F. Guattari and S. Rolnik, *Molecular Revolution in Brazil*, Los Angeles, Semiotext(e), 2008, p. 9 (English translation of *Micropolitiques*, Paris, Les Empêcheurs de penser en rond, 2007).

55. *Délires et chuchotements*, 4, December 1990, [n. p.].

56. A. Cvetkovich, *An Archive of Feelings: Trauma, Sexuality and Lesbian Public Cultures*, Durham NC, Duke University Press, 2003, p. 44. Ann Cvetkovich defines 'insidious trauma' as 'the affective nature of everyday experiences of systemic violence' (p. 44).

57. J.W. Scott, 'Fantasy Echo: History and the Construction of Identity', *Critical Inquiry*, vol. 27, 2, winter 2001, pp. 284–304.

58. Isabelle, [untitled], *Lesbia*, 16, April 1984, p. 39.

3 Seeking Acceptance or Revolution? An Overview of the First Italian LGBTQ Magazines (1971–79)

DARIO PASQUINI

If one relied exclusively on available studies of the history of the Italian press, one could conclude that an Italian queer press has never existed: LGBTQ periodicals are not mentioned.[1] This essay addresses this oversight, highlighting the significant contribution that LGBTQ magazines have made to print cultures in Italy.[2] However, it is worth identifying that a queer press emerged relatively late in Italy, only after a homosexual press had been developing, sometimes for decades, in other European countries. This is surprising given that Italy, at least in terms of law, was not particularly hostile to homosexuality in comparison to other countries: antisodomy statutes were stricken from the Italian criminal code in 1890. It is not the aim of this essay to investigate the reasons for this paradox. However, it is important to register in the context of this book the hypothesis advanced by some scholars, according to which collective moral condemnation of homosexuality in Italy proved so effective that it prevented for a long time any kind of public support for LGBTQ people from developing.[3]

This emphasis on moral rather than legal condemnation is clearly identified in an article published in the first Italian 'homophile' magazine.[4] The first issue of *Homo*, which was active in Milan from October 1972 until October 1975, addressed with an article entitled 'Legge e controlegge' ('law and against-law') the differences in attitude toward homosexuality between Italy and other European countries. The author of the piece, an attorney writing under the pen name Alberto Musotto, argues that laws against homosexuality in Northern Europe have the goal to 'repress what social custom was inclined to tolerate, if not to discharge or to encourage.' 'In our country, ' he writes:

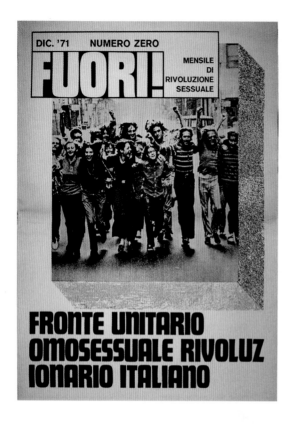

Front cover of *FUORI!*
Issue 0, December 1971.

the law-maker does not intervene because social censure is very strong, merciless, unhuman... [I]n Italy, thus, social reprobation has replaced law in repressing [homosexuality] ... [T]he question is, then, to modify not criminal norms but [the] censorious and punitive attitudes of the Italian society that provoke unspeakable suffering in those members of the other sex [sic].[5]

According to the author, in Italy social stigma against homosexuality was so strong that legislation was not necessary to discourage homosexual people from engaging in any kind of overt, public activity.

It was a year earlier, in December 1971, that the very first Italian homosexual magazine, *FUORI! mensile di liberazione sessuale,* a 'monthly [magazine] of sexual liberation', commenced publication in Turin. The magazine was created as the organ of the first Italian LGBTQ movement, the homonymous, radical Marxist FUORI!, that had also been founded in Turin, in May 1971. *FUORI!* magazine was established by bookseller Angelo Pezzana, the founder of the FUORI! movement, and it was published, though with significant interruptions, until 1982.

FUORI! was a graphically sober yet elegant product, designed in the format of a newspaper with a front page in two or more colours. The magazine consisted mainly of written content but also featured photos, drawings and cartoons. Often these illustrations sought to represent the emotional condition of homosexual people. A drawing by Turin based artist Enrico Colombotto Rosso published on the back cover of the second issue of the magazine, for example, represents 'how we look "in[side]"', alluding to those who are not yet 'out', It is an image of unease, in which faces and bodies of people are compressed within a sphere. Emma Allais – a member of the editorial collective of *FUORI!* – realized a series of strips entitled 'gay flower' (an ironic reference to the slogan 'gay power'). In this cartoon, a gay person is represented as a flower that withers while placed next to the 'thorny' 'love' of members of its own family and of society (all depicted as fat plants) and blooms again if 'hugged' by the genuine 'love' of a fellow gay person.

FUORI! is the abbreviation for Fronte Unitario Omosessuale Rivoluzionario Italiano (Unitary Revolutionary Homosexual Front of Italy). In Italian the word also means 'out', a reference to the act of 'coming out' as LGBTQ people.[6] The inspiration for the

FUORI!

giu. '72

no. 1

mensile di
liberazione
sessuale

fronte unitario
omosessuale
rivoluzionario italiano

Lire 400

Collettivo FUORI!
Omosessualità e Liberazione

Angelo Pezzana
Chi parla per gli omosessuali?

Sanremo
Come si vince contro chi ci opprime

Alfredo Cohen
Contro la psichiatria

Domenico Tallone
Gli stregoni del capitale

La pagina di Fernanda Pivano

**Cuba - Spagna - Femminismo
Soccorso Verde**

Front cover of *FUORI!*,
Issue 1, June 1972.

name came from *ComeOut!*, the earliest US LGBTQ magazine of the post-Stonewall era, whose first issue was published in New York in November 1969.[7] Like the Gay Liberation Front in the US, the FUORI! movement had branch associations in several Italian cities. In 1972 it promoted the first homosexual demonstration in Italy, which took place in Sanremo against an international sexology congress that was organized by the Italian Sexology Association and included panels on alleged therapies (including electroshock treatment) for 'curing' homosexuals. After interrupting the proceedings of the congress with his comrades, Angelo Pezzana used a microphone to deliver a speech, famously stating: 'I am homosexual and am happy about it.' FUORI! was, from its very beginning, a movement interested in exploring identities which the definition of 'homosexual' is not fully able to accommodate. Mario Mieli, one of the most well-known personalities of the Italian LGBT movement and one of the most prominent members of FUORI!, was a pioneer theorist of fluid sexual identities, to which he attributed strong political implications.[8] As FUORI! member Enzo Cucco states in the first article of the magazine dedicated to transgender people, the 'meaning' of the term 'transsexual' that '"we from the movement" [have] always given [is] different from the one commonly used', with transsexual referring to 'the one who is not monosexual in a continuous change of sexual "forms" and "modes", seamlessly.'[9]

FUORI! was edited by a collective of people, coordinated by Pezzana.[10] The 'responsible editor' (*direttore responsabile*) of the magazine, which proudly defined itself as a 'NO COPYRIGHT paper' (i.e. fully reproducible), was the publisher, activist of the Italian Radical Party, and journalist Marcello Baraghini.[11] Only members of the national association of journalists (*Ordine dei giornalisti*) were, and still are, allowed by Italian law to edit a magazine or newspaper, thus being responsible before the law for what is published. In order to circumvent this norm, which he defined as 'Fascist',[12] Baraghini agreed to formally occupy the position as editor of a great number of publications of different political orientations, while in practice not being involved in the job. As a consequence, he was subjected to numerous investigations and trials because of the content various periodicals had published. *FUORI!'*s collective thanked him for making it possible to print the magazine and thus to express the freedom of opinion

FUORI!, Issue 1, June 1972, pp. 8 and 9.

stated in the Italian Constitution.[13] In its first years the magazine's circulation was around 8,000 copies sold per issue.[14]

FUORI!, whose emotional rhetoric and relevant impact on its public I have analyzed elsewhere,[15] published cultural and political contributions such as writings by poets Allen Ginsberg and Fernanda Pivano, writer, performer and singer Alfredo Cohen, who was also a member of the *FUORI!* collective, and philosopher Gianni Vattimo. Personalities such as Pezzana or Mieli provided up-to-date and original political-theoretical elaborations. In their first editorial, the members of the magazine's group highlight a 'fundamental and honestly revolutionary precondition' of their act of coming out, which it is worth quoting from at length:

> We came out with the claim to be ourselves, with the will to find again our vital identity
> in structures in which the OTHER has absorbed, modified, reified every possibility of
> expression of the self... Coming out, for a homosexual, can be everything or nothing,
> the action that makes of the self its own history or [the action] that deletes [the self's
> history]... because coming out can just mean to simply accept one's own role and to live
> it within the grey limbo of those who have renounced to look beyond it, for their own

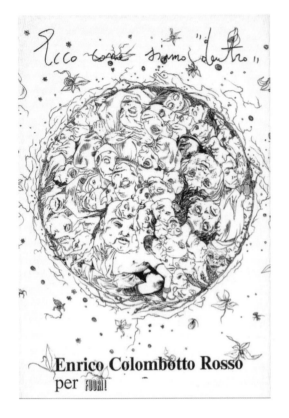

Above left: Back cover of Issue 2 of *FUORI!*, July/August 1972.

Above right: 'Gay Flower' strip in Issue 2 of *FUORI!*, July/August 1972, p.14.

life... Those [who] want to be accepted do not know that acceptance is even offered to them. In some countries, they are allowed to marry. They have not realized yet that the absorption of the man and the restitution of the automaton is in the logic of the capital... Revolution is JOY and it is so in the same moment in which, after overcoming all the barriers of a non vital condition, it becomes LIBERATION... When homosexuality becomes aware of its being the aberrant product of a society of sole production, then... it stands in the centre of a dynamic process whose means is… , right, the destruction of the capitalistic-bourgeois structures, but whose final aim is the re-achievement of the MAN... because the homosexual, who has no gratifying roles to grab in order to hide his own desperation... and to whom his condition as an object, [a condition that] for others is masked, appears in its whole brutal evidence, cannot but unmask every single attempt of exploitation.[16]

In this article the joy of being a fighting, openly homosexual person aquires a crucial role in the battle for liberation. The condition of subordination in which society places the homosexual person becomes, in the words of FUORI!, the key to sabotage capitalism's dehumanizing structures.

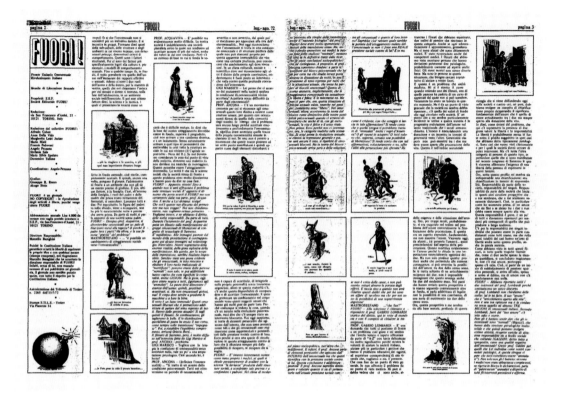

A similar language is used in an article by Mario Mieli, 'I radical-chic e lo chic radicale' published in *FUORI!* in 1973. Starting from a radical Marxist perspective, Mieli harshly criticises what he defines as the 'radical-chic' attitude of many alleged revolutionaries. These individuals, according to Mieli, prove incapable of exercizing 'a constant dialectic with themselves', a dialectic which 'protects from the incessant conditioning [of] the bourgeois ideology' and which allows the 'accomplish[ment of] a more profound practical-cognitive subjectivity.'[17] Mieli argues that 'some puritan could object that, thank God (what am I saying? Thank Marx) this attitude... does not concern... the great majority of heterosexual leftist activists [and] that at the most this is a manifestation of that "bourgeois decadence of that bunch of marginalized lesbians and faggots [*culatoni*]…"' 'But the faggot', Mieli continues, 'being used to being the target of many attacks from many severe critics... has learnt to... suspend judgements and prejudices, having from his side neither a *culture* or "values" that reward oppression but only his own suffering as excluded and untolerated.' Mieli, evoking the 'sensitivity of the faggot's critical thinking', is able to identify examples of 'radical-chic' as a 'counter-revolutionary' force. He mentions the 'acritical exaltation of delinquency as [an] immediate revolt against society' and 'those alleged revolutionaries in 1968' who, after a 'brainwashing [of] supposed

FUORI! , Issue 2, July/ August 1972, pp. 2–3.

Marxism' and 'much Maoism-Stalinism' have become within months 'spokespersons of the most-evil, so-called leftist... reactionary spirit.' Mieli goes even further by attacking for their 'radical-chic' attitude some of his fellow members of the *FUORI!* collective who, 'in order to add lustre...to *FUORI!* strive for filling the magazine's pages with articles signed by "great names" of the *gauchisme* and of the international "counter-culture".'[18]

This article is evidence of an unusual ideological depth for a 21-year-old boy, the age Mieli was when he wrote it. A year earlier, in a letter to Angelo Pezzana, he expressed some considerations about the political strategy to be adopted by the FUORI! movement, juxtaposing personal experiences and ideological analysis:

> Yesterday evening I was in Piazza Duomo [in Milan] in order to drop into the [public] bogs. I arrived just in the depths of the meeting of the Movimento Sociale [the main Italian neo-Fascist party, MSI], with great tricolour flags and people cheering to 'Italy! Italy!'. These days I have been studying the origins of Fascism and I had the impression of a flash back into history... but realizing [*me souvenir*] that we are in full 1972, the year of my 20 years, made me shudder... and I felt terribly lonely... The bogs were empty (out of fear) until the meeting was over, then they were again full of people. Those who claim that in public bogs only sex is going on are superficial. There is a real culture, a real drama, real suffering that comes out of minimal, controlled gestures, of one's elusive look, of the hard and of the soft cock, of the sinuous streetwalker's exhibitionism...
>
> I felt lonely again... with a group of straight friends, of those 'totally open' to homosexuality... [in] the commune where some of them are living ...they were so violent while playing cards...and the revolution will be violent... To be successful [the homosexual movement] should be Communist. But since it is not Communist, it will not be successful. This conclusion is really tragic, isn't it?... In case we will not be able to insert the homosexual minority within the revolutionary masses... what will happen to us during the revolution, at a time in which the weight of the bourgeois ideology will still press heavy on everybody's shoulders?... This is the practical line which I think it is more important to follow: 'propagate' homosexuality among comrades. ... [...] We must convince them to become themselves promoters of the social demands and of the values of homosexuality... Fighting with us means to fight for their own liberty, against the jealousy that harasses them, against their frigidness, self-castration, against their myth of masculinity.

As in the article for *FUORI!*, in this letter Mieli combines an intransigent, communist approach to LGBTQ activism with an urgent need to provoke a change in the mainstream Communist movement, in which 'social demands' and the 'values of homosexuality' should be integrated and thus transform relevant practices, aims and even minds. In Mieli's words, only the homosexual, because of his special condition, has the capability to point the right way toward the revolution.

However, Mieli's hopes for what FUORI! could achieve would soon fade, disappointed by reality. Angelo Pezzana never really shared the Marxist revolutionary approach of Mieli and other FUORI! members such as Carlo Sismondi, even if he always granted them liberty to express their opinions.[19] Even in his editorials for the magazine Pezzana showed that, rather than being inspired by Marxist theories, he was influenced by the experience of the movements for the emancipation of other minorities, mentioning as examples Black and Jewish movements.[20] By 1974, Pezzana and the Turin FUORI! group decided to give up the far left political orientation of the movement and merge with the more reformist Radical Party of Italy. This sparked a harsh debate, not only within the FUORI! groups – since the FUORI! group of Milan did not agree with the decision and eventually declared autonomy – but also in the broader homosexual movement. In the editorial for a new magazine, *Usciamo Fuori!* (Let's go out!), that was published for just one issue, the Milan group represented Pezzana's decision as illegitimate, denying that he, and the Turin group, ever had the leadership of the FUORI! movement or the authority to 'negotiate alliances' with other parties. The editorial defined as 'absurd' the fact that Pezzana had promoted himself as 'leader [of an] assumed base... that has never released any kind of delegation. For what concerns us, we remove from him any (self-granted) authority to speak in our name.'[21] Notably, the editorial also denied that there was any equivalence between the FUORI! movement and *FUORI!* magazine.[22] The magazine, the group wrote, 'represents only the editorial collective which publishes it' while the FUORI! movement was 'a more complex' reality, which the magazine could not mirror.

THE ROLE OF LESBIANS IN THE EARLY HOMOSEXUAL PRESS IN ITALY

Even if most of *FUORI!*'s editors and contributors were men, the magazine made efforts to grant a certain gender diversity with regard to its authors, contents and public. In the magazine's first issue three pages were dedicated to female homosexuality, with articles and poems. In 1974 *FUORI!* published an entire issue, which was named *FUORI! DONNA*, edited by the female members of the editorial collective. This was not the only time that *FUORI!* attempted to reflect perspectives and points of view that lay beyond male homosexual experience. A practice such as transvestitism (which, as I discuss below, *Homo* would treat in a scornful way) was considered by *FUORI!* worthy of discussion. After Monica Galdino Giansanti, who defined himself as a 'homosexual transvestite' who 'does not want to appear as a woman [or] be a woman in order to attract heterosexuals' had sent an enthusiastic letter to the magazine, he was asked to be interviewed and eventually joined the editorial collective of *FUORI!*, publishing a column of letters from transgender readers.[23]

The special issue *FUORI! DONNA* included an editorial alongside a letter, which had been sent to a number of feminist groups all over Italy in order to stimulate a discussion about the topic of homosexuality.[24] Replies were published as well, and those groups which had not replied were mentioned and an empty space left to represent the lack of

Front cover of *FUORI! DONNA*, summer 1974.

Opposite page: *FUORI! DONNA*, summer 1974, pp. 3, 4, 10 &14.

feedback. While some of the replies showed sympathy, others insisted that sexual orientation was a private matter, and for this reason not worthy of discussion. Emma Allais, who was the coordinator of the special issue, worked with much enthusiasm on the project and was protective of the autonomy which had been granted to her. In a letter that she sent to Pezzana she reveals a certain irritation:

PERCHÉ FUORI! DONNA
E COME

Un bell'editoriale fastoso di vocaboli da addetti ai lavori, un FUORI!DONNA pieno di analisi squisite, tanto per scansare l'accusa-ricatto di superficialità? Grazie tante, non abbiamo voluto un numero tutto nostro per fare della kultura lontana dalla nostra realtà presente, l'abbiamo voluto per risolvere, o incominciare a risolvere, alcuni problemi urgentissimi, che ci stanno più a cuore del dell'intellighenzia italiana e dei nostri fratelli radical-chic. Abbiamo detto kultura (giusta la definizione venuta dagli Stati Uniti dove il K è simbolo di razzismo trovandosi per ben tre volte nel la sigla del Ku-Klux-Klan) perché nei consigli di qualche amico vecchio del mestiere, che da buon maschietto nutriva scarsa fiducia nella nostra capacità di fare un "buon" giornale, abbiamo sentito il suono sgradevole di questa consonante: quale si ritrova, vedi la combinazione, nel "Kinder-Küche-Kirche" (bambini-cucina-chiesa) dei compiti della donna non soltanto tedesca. Ma questa volta, pur chiedendo scusa per gli errori di stampa, che del resto non sono mai mancati nei precedenti numeri del FUORI!, non interessa fare un "buon" giornale, ma semplicemente un giornale che ci aiuti a iniziare un dialogo

costruttivo con le femministe e con le omossessuali ancora velate, e le altre indifferenti o peggio diffidenti nei confronti del vecchio FUORI! Che è stato ed è utilissimo, non lo neghiamo, a situare correttamente la rivoluzione sessuale, ma non raggiungeva coloro che, con FUORI!DONNA, intendiamo raggiungere. Se ai nostri fratelli radical-chic questo numero non piacerà (ma perché poi, se ci amano?), pazienza. Le lesbiche sia no noi e intendiamo gestire noi i nostri problemi più urgenti, ferma restando l'adesione all'interpretazione teorica che con loro abbiamo dato della nostra lotta di omosessuali. E se la nostra risposta, a chi ci aveva e sempre ci avrà per amiche affettuosissime e costanti, sembrerà il risultato di una presa di coscienza, ma una sorpresa sgradevole, un tradimento, pazienza. Ma questa volta devono averla loro.

In questo numero, dunque, c'è il risultato del la nostra lettera ai gruppi femministi, ci sono le denunce di alcuni (non tutti, la carta non bastava) aspetti della nostra oppressione. Ma c'è anche la proposta di uscir "fuori" a quante, sentendosi sole, non osavano farlo. Da questo numero devono capire che siamo abbastanza forti per venire alla luce.

La Redazione di
FUORI!DONNA

FUORI! ESTATE 1974 Pag. 3

LA NOSTRA LETTERA
AI GRUPPI FEMMINISTI

Abbiamo inviato questa lettera a tutti i gruppi femministi italiani di cui abbiamo trovato l'indirizzo su EFFE, e altri ancora.

Care compagne,

ci risulta che in certi gruppi femministi l'omosessualità di alcune militanti non solo non è ancora valutata come apporto rivoluzionario di altissimo potenziale, ma subisce oppressioni se non (orrore!) delle emarginazioni.

A questo punto noi donne del FUORI! (che per inciso, come vedrete dai primi dieci numeri del nostro giornale che vi inviamo a parte, siamo sempre state femministe), abbiamo il diritto-dovere di intervenire.

Per aprire un dialogo che non si può più rimandare, per sgombrare il terreno dalle COMUNE orizzonte di femminismo dalla confusione che ancora regna a proposito dell'omosessualità femminile, dedicheremo al nostro dibattito tutto il prossimo numero del giornale, che chiameremo FUORI! DONNA e sarà interamente redatto da donne, omosessuali e non.

Ai gruppi di Torino abbiamo mandato la nostra lettera giusto per sfinfare. Perché in realtà non vi si pratica razzismo nei nostri confronti. Vi siamo sempre state accolte con gentilezza; come vi è siamo grate, amiche di Rivolta! Alcune di noi, approdando dagli errori della provincia alle vostre riunioni, non dimenticheranno mai il sollievo sparso sulle loro ferite dalla vostra premura; e voi, ragazze di Alternativa, ci avete perdonato se non potevamo frequentare le vostre sedute; ci trovavamo alle manifestazioni, gridavamo insieme i nostri slogan; voi avete imposto ai compagni ancora imberbi di falzocratismo in presenza dei ragazzi del FUORI! che qualcuno non volevo voi aveste gridato "La virilità è un mito fascista" dimostrando di aver capito tutto. E a voi, ragazze di Via Lambrano, non fummo il bronzo se, in crisi di crescenza, non avete potuto fare a meno di scaricare su noi, quella sera, la vostra tensione; se suna di voi, ancora credendo alla leggenda che vi vuole invidiose del pene, ci ha gridato "Noi siamo femministe ma non per questo rinunciamo alla nostra femminilità"; né faremo il broncio a te, M.L., se hai smstitto impassibile. Ci vedremo ancora e non ci scanneremo.

Dalle risposte dei gruppi italiani e di alcune omosessuali che vi si rifugiano accuratamente velate, ci constata che la maggioranza è ancora legata a vecchi pregiudizi, ma che non si tratta della totalità; per noi è molti la simo, perché ci conforta nella nostra convinzione che la lotta è comune. Ora si tratta di far uscire "fuori" le omossessuali da un femminismo che potrebbe essere una sublimazione, una fuga (ne abbiamo visto un caso clamoroso a Roma: alla ragazza che ci parlava male del FUORI! non mancava che la pipe in bocca, ma questo negare un'evidenza che non fa che celare il pene, e voi confermare che il mito del fallocratismo in pe in bocca, ma questo negare un'evidenza che non fa un meccanismo che conosciamo bene negli oppressi) un femminismo ianutentico e quindi dannoso a chi lo indossa, ma anche, ahi noi, alla nostra causa. Speriamo che queste scarne parole scarnione le discussioni sono salutari; ma si tratta anche di conquistare alla rivoluzione sessuale i gruppi che si finano so alcuni obiettivi trascurando il primo: la liberazione sessuale della donna, di TUTTE le donne, omosessuali comprese.

Stefania Sala

FUORI! ESTATE 1974 Pag. 4

E tanti altri gruppi di FUORI! DONNA si possono formare, dipende solo da NOI

L'amicizia di Maria e gli articoli del FUORI! stavano davvero contribuendo a togliermi la paura della contraddittorietà, della poliedricità di me e dei miei desideri, delle mie esitazioni.

Una sera, gioielo ho anche detto: "Ora ho anche meno paura a desiderare di fare una carezza, a un uomo come soprattutto a una donna. Ho meno paura anche a farla; non solo a desiderarlo".

Ma questo solo con poche persone; forse a far più di una carezza, di qualche gesto affettuoso, non arriverò mai con una donna.

Non mi importa però molto di cosa in futuro farò o non farò; se sarò sempre eterosessuale o cambierò: mi importa che, pur la definizione, inizio ad esprimermi, a cercare il mio corpo e quello degli altri, a stabilire con loro un contatto meno goffo, meno frustrante.

Da sola non si sarei mai arrivata.

visto ragazze
che non sono poi
così inutile?

Risposta di
Rivolta Femminile
Milano

Risposta di
Anabasi
Milano

Risposte del Collettivo Femminista di Brera
Via Cerva 6, Milano
e del CISA, Corso di Porta Vigentina 15/A
Milano.

L'esigenza primaria per l'essere umano è la libertà. La libertà individuale e conseguentemente quella sociale passa attraverso la libertà sessuale. La prima forma di libertà è quella dello scioglimento dei ruoli.

donna = sesso debole
donna = casalinga
donna = sottomissione
uomo = forza
uomo = responsabilità
uomo = padre-padrone

C'è da dire altro?

Anche la distinzione in omosessuali, bisessuali, eterosessuali è fasulla: fasulla come tutti i ruoli.

Gli uomini danno della "lesbica" ad una donna per vendicarsi della sua indipendenza, della sua autonomia, della sua non-sottomissione, e prescindere dalle preferenze sessuali.

Tutte le donne, in questi momenti di lotta, dovrebbero essere orgogliose di essere tacciate dagli uomini immaturi, impreparati e prepotenti, ansiosi di riaffermare una egemonia, che non hanno neppiù più in nessun senso, di essere "lesbiche", cioè indipendenti, autonome, autogestite.

Quanto ai gusti e alle tendenze sessuali, sono fatti privatissimi, sono compagne, poiché ci diciamo, care compagne, e prescindere dalle preferenze sessuali, hanno il diritto alla libertà di scelta più piena, ed alla coedotta più autonoma.

Tutte le donne capaci di reggersi sulle proprie gambe e di pensare con la propria testa hanno il diritto-dovere dell'autonomia e dell'autogestione.

Adele Facc...

per il CISA, Centro Informazioni Sterilizzazione e Aborto e per il Collettivo Femminista di Brera.

FUORI! ESTATE 1974 Pag. 10

- Ma non ti pare un cimitero?

- E infatti qui giace, aspettando il glorioso giorno della

Risposta della Filf Roma	Risposta di Anna Memnis Cagliari	Risposta delle Nemesiache Napoli
Risposta del Collettivo Femminista di Vicenza	Risposta di Clementina Di Lernia Trento	Risposta di Anna Heiz Napoli
Risposta di Lorenza Fontana Bolzano	Risposta del Movimento Femminista Grossetano Porto Santo Stefano	Risposta del Movimento Liberazione della Donna Napoli
Risposta del Collettivo Femminista Gelese	Risposta del Gruppo Femminista Catanese	Risposta di Licia Cavazzani Urbino
La redazione sotto immane pioggia di proteste caduta		Risposta di Lotta Femminista Venezia

FUORI! ESTATE 1974 Pag. 14

You have to let me make this issue my way... otherwise I would feel once again castrated... [Y]ou tell me to make an issue for only women and I burden myself [sic] because the thing gives me joy: if you then poison this joy for me... by dictating, unconsciously, once again your law, I feel cheated by my friend and fight comrade and I feel a malaise that pushes on my breastbone... Obeying you would be a bad thing for me and for you; for me because my happiness would go to hell [*andrebbe in merda*], for you because you would keep... practising antifeminism, even if an unconscious one... This time you are not going to sign the magazine and I assure you that it will not make a poor impression in comparison to the previous ones... Don't take away my joy of creating.[25]

Another letter to Pezzana from two years earlier indicates that Allais tended to under-value herself ('my friendship is of very little worth because I myself am nothing special') while showing great affection for him ('I love you' [*ti voglio bene*]; 'I will always feel admiration and gratitude [for you]'). At the same time she appeared well aware of the importance of their job for *FUORI!*:

We have to provide high level work, accepting the risk of being absorbed as a cultural phenomenon: but it is these [cultural phenomena] that leave their mark. Maybe you don't care at all to go down in history as the founder of the movement of homosexual liberation in Italy from the pages of your *FUORI!*, but by now you have gone down already with a courage which no one among us would have had.[26]

Yet the cautious and non-enthusiastic replies, along with the lack of answers, from many feminist groups to the initiative of *FUORI! DONNA*, together with the fact that the special issue edited by and for women remained an isolated case in the history of *FUORI!*, are significant. They help to highlight the problematic relations of Italian lesbians in this period to both the homosexual and the feminist movement. Even if no magazine strictly intended for lesbians existed in 1970s Italy, there are other examples of printed content edited by, and addressed to, lesbian women. For example, the first autonomous lesbian group in Italy, the 'Brigate Saffo' from Turin, were granted an autonomous, homony-mous space in the magazine *Lambda* (which I will analyse below in more depth) between 1978 and 1979. When it started out, this represented just a half-page of the magazine but from the end of 1978 until mid-1979 (when the lesbian group dissolved) *Brigate Saffo* became for three issues a real supplement of *Lambda*.[27] In their first contribution to *Lambda*, the Turin-based group attacked a feminist magazine, *Quotidiano Donna*, which in an article had described Brigate Saffo as a mere feminist collective:

We are not a feminist collective, we are a collective of revolutionary lesbian women who fight for sexual liberation but also against everything that oppresses women... Our radio programme is not about 'love!!!' – despite [the fact that] we often and willingly make love, given the fact that we have no problems of birth-control – but it is about topics of general interest such as sex, abortion, work...[28]

The first issue of the supplement featured an interview with acclaimed actress and left-ist supporter Franca Rame, who was the wife of actor, playwright and future Nobel Prize winner Dario Fo and who in 1973 had been raped by a neo-Fascist gang.[29] Just as interesting as Rame's quite embarassed declarations (she insisted that it was the first time she was talking about homosexuality and she feared she would say 'something stupid' [*cretinate*]) are the questions which the interviewer(s) asked her. The discussion started down a slippery slope as Brigate Saffo asked Rame's opinion about 'homosexual males' pose of feminine behaviour, that however is not feminine, of a female stereotype... that we all well know, is a fake image.' Rame's reaction was one of quite sharp refusal:

I find it really fake... deeply wrong... let's leave the politicized male... [as] for him it is a choice, even if a questionable one, to wear high heels... I am talking about the classical transvestite... I find them deeply ridiculous... they lose [their] dignity... there is no contempt... I really don't know... you have caught me off-balance...

After Brigate Saffo asked her if it was 'more or less the same thing also for women... posing as males', Rame replied that 'the woman posing as a male never verges on misery.' However, as Rame started distinguishing between 'physiologically homosexual women' and those women who 'become [homosexual] for a situation, for love', the interviewer added her own opinion, saying that 'it is not because I feel I am a man, I mean... no roles! There is also someone who feels she is a man, but this, in my opinion, is very wrong.' A further question to Rame significantly concerns the fact that 'in many feminist groups [*collettivi*] are women who are in a relationship... but within those same groups this discourse is never raised and actually is in some sort of way banned. [Is it] because it frightens', the interviewer asks, 'or for what reason?'

Brigate Saffo's choice of topics for this interview is interesting, because it confirms what Elena Biagini has pointed out about the condition of Italian lesbians during the 1970s. 'In other European countries and in the United States', she wrote, 'an autono-mous lesbian movement' had been founded almost a decade earlier than in Italy.[30] In this context, lesbians 'continued to have a massive but little visible presence, with some exceptions' in the feminist movement, at least until 1979, while they were 'out' but 'numerically scarce' in the homosexual movement, where the first lesbian group was founded only in 1977. It is noteworthy that after Brigate Saffo's polemical article against *Quotidiano Donna* was published in *Lambda*, *Quotidiano Donna* showed a growing attention toward lesbians. In 1979, the Roman lesbian group Artemide e le Furie was granted an autonomous space, the 'Pagina lesbica', within the magazine. Moreover, in the same year the Coordinamento Donne Omosessuali (Cdo) in Milan also started to collaborate on a regular basis with *Quotidiano Donna*, participating in the Milan editorial office of the magazine.[31]

A CONFRONTATIONAL RELATIONSHIP: *FUORI!* AND THE HOMOPHILE MAGAZINES *HOMO* AND *CON NOI*

The episode between *Quotidiano Donna* and *Lambda* highlights the differing political positions occupied by print journals and how they informed, and argued against, one another. After *FUORI!* launched in 1971, two further homosexual periodicals of a very different sort were founded in 1972: *Homo* and *con NOI*. An important peculiarity of the Italian LGBTQ press is that, unlike in other countries, so-called 'homophile' magazines were founded *after* and not *before* Stonewall. While *FUORI!*, as a post-Stonewall radical homosexual magazine was founded quite early, or at least in line with other foreign counterparts, homophile magazines such as *Homo* and *con NOI* started publication in a period in which foreign homophile periodicals had been active for decades.[32]

Homo, already mentioned above, was published initially as a supplement to the erotic magazine *OS*. *Con NOI* was published in Rome, with interruptions and with other names

Front cover of *Homo*, Issue 1, October 1972.

– *per NOI; NOI…e gli altri; noi insieme per una nuova realtà gay* – perhaps in order to try to avoid the seizures that it suffered at various times across the 1970s. Both *Homo* and *con NOI* were commercial magazines and were far less political in approach than *FUORI!*. A significant attraction for most of their readers surely resided in the pictures of naked men published in both magazines. However, they also included more traditional content such as articles, cultural surveys, editorials and letters to the editor.

The first front page of *Homo* depicts a young man with lipstick on. Partly overlapping with this unconventional image, written advice, which would appear also on the front pages of subsequent issues of the magazine, warns the reader: 'This magazine addresses sexual topics freely. There are specialized pictures and articles that are in relation with a culturally very advanced kind of reader. If you think that these topics might offend your sense of decency please don't buy us [sic].' (In 1973 this warning was replaced by the warning 'Forbidden to minors.') From this notice it is

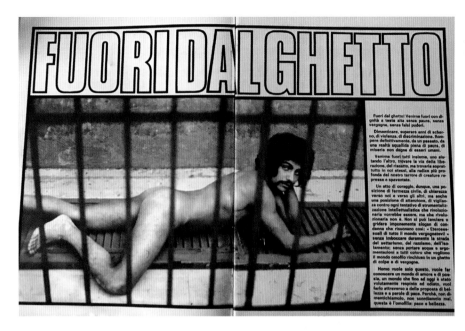

Fuori dal ghetto! Venirne fuori con dignità a testa alta senza paura, senza vergogna, senza falsi pudori.

Dimenticare, superare anni di scherno, di violenza, di discriminazione. Rompere definitivamente, da un passato, da una realtà squallida piena di paura, di miserie non degne di esseri umani.

Venirne fuori tutti insieme, uno aiutando l'altro, trovare la via della liberazione, del riscatto, ma trovarla soprattutto in noi stessi, alla radice più profonda del nostro terrore di creature represse e spaventate.

Un atto di coraggio, dunque, una posizione di fermezza civile, di chiarezza verso noi e verso gli altri, ma anche una posizione di attenzione, di vigilanza contro ogni tentativo di strumentalizzazione intellettualistica che rivoluzionaria vorrebbe essere, ma che rivoluzionaria non è. Non si può lanciare o gridare impunemente slogan di condanna che risuonano così: «Eterosessuali di tutto il mondo vergognatevi» senza imboccare duramente la strada del settarismo, del razzismo, dell'isolamento; senza portare acqua e argomentazioni a tutti coloro che vogliono il mondo omofilo rinchiuso in un ghetto di colpe e di vergogna.

Homo vuole solo questo, vuole far conoscere un mondo di amore e di poesia, un mondo che fino ad oggi è stato volutamente respinto e odiato, vuole farlo attraverso a delle proposte di bellezza e a parole di pace. Perché, non dimentichiamolo, non scordiamolo mai, questa è l'omofilia: pace e bellezza.

'Fuori dal ghetto', *Homo*, Issue 1, October 1972, pp. 4–5.

evident that the magazine did not desire a clash with authorities who, in that period, and in accordance with the highly moralistic approach of the ruling party Democrazia cristiana, were particularly apt to seize media representations with alleged sexual content that might offend public decency.[33] The editorial office of the magazine included some photographers and the published pictures often had a professional and original touch. Eventually some illustrators joined the group, including Vincenzo Jannuzzi, who created cartoons such as one depicting a priest carrying a large candle which is actually his own penis.

The first issue of *Homo* also featured an unsigned editorial next to a large picture of a naked young man who seems to be taking the sun on a terrace. There are some bars dividing the viewer from the young man, and they may refer to the title of the editorial, 'Out of the ghetto!', which alludes to the deprivation of liberty. According to the editorial, whose text contains a number of references to fear, it was important to 'come out of the ghetto', but 'with dignity, with heads held high, with no fears, shamelessly... to forget, to overcome years of mockery, of violence, of discrimination... to come out all together, helping each other, to find the way of the liberation... to find it above all in ourselves, in the deep roots of our terror as repressed and frightened creatures.'[34] 'Coming out', the author of the editorial argues, is 'an act of courage' but is also 'a position of attention and of vigilance against every attempt of intellectual exploitation that aims at being revolutionary, but is not. It is not possible... to scream slogans of condemnation that sound like "heterosexuals of the world, shame yourself", without turning to the road of sectarianism, racism and isolation.' The allusion here is clearly to the FUORI!

movement: the 'homophiles' from *Homo* wanted to make it clear from the very first issue that their approach was different from FUORI!'s Marxist position. Their aim, far from being violent, was simply to 'make visible' the 'homophile world', which had been so far 'closed in a ghetto made of guilt and shame' and which was alternatively framed as a 'world of love and poetry.'[35]

In another article from the first issue of *Homo*, 'Legge e controlegge', mentioned above, the author argues that one of the magazine's main tasks – 'to destroy age-old prejudices and taboos' against homosexuals – was not an easy one.[36] He continues:

> Minorities... have always had a hard life... it is very difficult, if not impossible, to find a solution to the problem on a strictly legal basis, as many homophile circles have often been urging... Homophiles should unite their efforts in order to remove social censure. How?... This magazine has been founded with the aim also to look for, and to pursue, a strategy of protection of the rights of homophily to free expression, by correcting the most evident errors within public opinion, by making alliances with those, among the heterosexuals, who are closer to the homosexuals, as they are closer to oppressed races and exploited classes.

In the editorial of the second issue of *Homo* the condemnation of the political strategy of FUORI! seems suspended:

> Starting a discourse... starting talking about us, about our lives, about our urgencies. But how? Perhaps by accepting revolutionary systems and languages? It can be the right way, it could be the only way to come really out. Or to use a quiet way, let's say a reformist one, which will allow us to be 'accepted' by a society that keeps isolating us savagely?... We are sure that the solution is beyond any bitter controversy... we believe that whoever acts in favour of the homophile ideal is right, is useful... only if we are united will we be successful in transforming our life, in feeling really proud of being homosexuals.[37]

Yet, according to *Homo*, there were some homosexuals who did not act in favour of the homophile ideal. In an interview with a self-declared 'happy homophile', published in the same issue, a twenty six year old owner of a milk store, who is represented in a series of pictures, argues that the right way to 'overcome prejudices and racist discriminations against homosexuals' is not the one chosen by those 'coarse homosexuals, the exhibitionists', whose 'attitude embitters the soul and [purposefully avoids] the solution to the problem of moral recognition and peaceful coexistence.'[38] The interviewer, apparently agreeing with him, adds: 'The transvestites as well...' to which the milk store owner exclaims: 'Please, let's leave them... They are those who more often lay themselves [open] to denigration... people... make huge confusion... homosexuality is... something deeply different.' According to

Homo, then, both 'exhibitionist homosexuals' and 'transvestites' do not behave appropriately and thus damage those homophiles who behave in the right way.

Like *Homo*, *con NOI* and its alter egos published front pages usually featuring portraits of young men in colour. A notice in the magazine invited readers who 'wish to pose for the magazine' to contact the professional photographer in charge by providing a 'photo *al naturale*.'[39] The internal pages were in black and white with a dated graphic style: for example the editorials were framed by decadent decorations in black that would maybe better fit an obituary. The magazine's issue number 0, which was published in November 1972, just one month after *Homo*'s first issue, contains an editorial, which, besides a vague remark about the magazine's desire to avoid 'fashionable riots', does not contain any allusion to *FUORI!*.[40] Rather, it dwells, almost in the form of a poem, on the concepts of happiness and pleasure:

> It is good what brings pleasure. Each lust, which does not damage anybody, should be satisfied. Everybody should first of all make himself happy. Sex is no gnawing demon, nor a raging God. It touches the flesh and the soul. Its diverse exercise does not imply ridiculous distinctions. Natural laws are still mostly unknown. Human laws vary across times and places. May the man love the woman, the woman the woman, the man the man for endless unions at the root of desire, into the present.

A later article, however, presented an open critique of the strategies of FUORI! that closely resembles that made by *Homo*. The author of the text, Massimo Consoli, a leading personality of the Italian LGBTQ movement, had initially joined the FUORI! group, and wrote an article for the first issue of *FUORI!*.[41] Soon, however, his relationship with the Turin movement went cold. In particular, Consoli critiques Mario Mieli's use of the term 'revolution.' Consoli makes clear that 'homosexuality in the present context is naturally revolutionary.'[42] However, he argues that 'the comrades from FUORI! are mistaken when they speak about revolution' because:

> One can promote the most brilliant... theories but when these [theories] bounce back in a limited, closed, sectarian environment... in a real ghetto which one has voluntarily gotten himself into, [then] social structures do not suffer [even] a minimal shake. What effect can 1,000 copies... of a magazine achieve that defines itself as 'revolutionary' and that instead practices the most alienating verbal masturbation?... The homosexual [person] lives her life in permanent contact... with people who are not homosexual... a reality with which we think it is not intelligent to assume an *a priori* position of hostility... our precise function is to liberate the homosexual [person] from two thousand years [of] moral, social and religious prejudices... And this looks like a more than revolutionary action!

In his view, it was much more 'revolutionary' to look for a contact with those who are 'not homosexual', rather than to lock oneself up in a 'sectarian environment' such as that of *FUORI!*.

Returning to the first editorial of *con NOI*, I have noted that it linked sex with desire and pleasure. According to *FUORI!*, too, sex was related to a positive emotion, namely joy. However, the premises and arguments differ widely from *con NOI*'s. *FUORI!* reacted immediately to the attacks published in *Homo* through an article which juxtaposed *Homo* to two erotic magazines that published gay nudes: *OS* (of which *Homo* was a supplement) and *Men*. The article in *FUORI!*, entitled 'The Fake Images', describes the three magazines as instruments of the capitalist market. Regarding *OS* and *Men*, the main argument represents a Marxist condemnation of alleged 'coarse pornography' that is also based on moral considerations. According to *FUORI!* the 'male and female naked bodies' published by *OS* were 'lugubrious and mortifying' in contrast to the idea that 'sex is joy, is life, is above all... a vehicle of affirmation, of recovery of liberty.'[43] In such magazines, the article argues, 'sexuality is reduced, manipulated... by the economic relations of production, which functionalize all human activities to the values of profit and good.' This argument, it continues, also applies to *Homo*. *FUORI!* notes that *Homo* is divided into dedicated sections – 'the page of justice, that of medicine... of religion, of fashion' – that are typical of 'commercial magazines for women.' It concludes that a 'division of subjects' produces 'a divided homosexual', as the '"homophile" homosexual' and 'the "feminine" woman' are 'united on the level of sexual oppression' through those 'entertainments and interests', such as 'fashion... gossip... [and] picture stories', to which they are subjected by the 'male society.' From the very beginning of their common presence within the Italian press, then, a confrontational relationship developed between *Homo* and *FUORI!*. In contrast to the 'noisy' approach of *FUORI!*, *Homo* urged a 'quiet' and 'reformist' strategy to gain society's acceptance. *FUORI!* fought back by disdainfully labelling *Homo* as a magazine for queens that had surrendered to the 'sexual oppression' of the 'male society.'

It is notable that a young reader of *FUORI!* did not fully share in the publication's stigmatization of commercial homosexual or erotic magazines. Enrico G., a 20-year-old boy from Rome, in a letter to *FUORI!* states:

> Until some years ago (3 or 4) I was sure I was sick (!)... Eventually, little by little, I have convinced myself of the contrary and in this, I must say, magazines such as *Homo* and *Noi* [sic], helped me, whose obscene content you rightly point out, in the text more than in the pictures, but which have had the 'merit' to let me accept myself little by little, without desiring anymore to be like 'all the others.'[44]

Another reader of *FUORI!*, a 27-year-old from Genoa, points out that for an 'openly homosexual' man like him, magazines like *Homo*, *OS* or *Men* were useful in order 'to answer personal adverts and to get to know new people.' However, after the distributor of these magazines in Genoa had been arrested, the 'only distractions' were 'cinemas, public gardens and the entrance of the railway station' in order to find some 'chances for a sexual release.' In short, the 'homosexuals from Genoa have had to return to the bogs.'[45] A third reader agrees with *FUORI!*'s sharp condemnation of these magazines (in particular *Homo* and *Men*) which he sees as 'exploiters of others' unhappiness and anguish.' By contrast, he reports that he has spent part of his last Sunday in a 'happy' mood by reading the 'pages of *FUORI!*'[46]

THE END OF THE RADICAL QUEER PRESS

Through an examination of queer print cultures in Italy, this essay has charted the fraught debates taking place between revolutionary and assimilationist positions in the LGBTQ movement in the 1970s. One further episode is of note here, in relation to the homosexual magazine *O-MPO* and its founder Massimo Consoli. Before founding *O-MPO* in 1975, Consoli was a contributor to both *con NOI* and *Men*, and for this reason he was much criticized within the wider LGBTQ movement in Italy. *O-MPO*, which stands for Organo del Movimento Politico degli Omosessuali (Organ of the Political Movement of Homosexuals), was a poorly designed and drafted cyclostyled publication, which was self-published by Consoli with an irregular frequency until 1993.[47] It was not distributed and on sale within the formal market.. Its look was more similar to that of a high school journal than to a classic periodical.

On several occasions, entire issues of *O-MPO* only contained texts that Consoli had previously published elsewhere. Consoli, unlike the group around *FUORI!*, rarely emphasized protest or activism, despite calling himself an anarchist and a socialist. In the first editorial of *O-MPO*, for example, 'ignorance' is mentioned as the main target of the war to be fought in the name of liberation, even before, in order of appearance, 'the prejudices, the bad faith and the persecutions.' This didactic approach is confirmed by another early editorial, in which the 'best weapon' for a homosexual is said to be education.[48]

In the first editorial, Consoli states that FUORI!, whose 'sectarian positions' and 'Marxist analysis of the homosexual condition' he had never shared, nevertheless 'fulfilled an extremely important social and liberating function.' He adds that the 'integrationalist organization AIRDO [the Italian Association for the Recognition of Homophile Rights, founded in 1972] did not succeed... in performing an incisive action directed towards our liberation.' The Political Movement of Homosexuals, by contrast, which aimed at preparing the ground for the formation of a political party of homosexuals, had significant potential, as the homosexuals, Consoli estimated, were 5 % of the Italian population. However, he assured readers, '*O-MPO*'s pages would always be open to those...organizations', as 'whoever fights for the liberation of the homosexual class is our friend, comrade and ally.' It is noteworthy that Consoli, in a letter to his close friend the poet Dario Bellezza from 1970, i.e. a period preceding the development of the Italian LGBT movement, writes: 'I have [been] convincing myself more every day that my mission (please do not laugh!!!!) is the one I had been feeling since I was very young... [i.e.] to help the homosexuals to come out of the ghetto in which one wants to confine them (and in which too often they themselves want to be confined).'[49] In 1970, then, he uses the same expression, 'out of the ghetto', that he would use in his 1973 article for *con NOI*, and that *Homo* in 1972 chose as a title for its first issue's editorial, both mentioned above. This helps us identify that Consoli had the potential to be a significant link between two factions of the early homosexual movement: the radical Marxist groups and those around the 'homophile' periodicals. Consoli's failure in building a structured, durable and 'popular' homosexual political initiative that would try and overcome these differences can be perhaps partly explained by his character, including a certain anarchic and at the same time elitist attitude, as well as by a personal, mutual dislike that developed very early between him and the founders of FUORI!, in particular Pezzana.

In November 1976 the FUORI! movement founded a new magazine, *Lambda*, with the aim of connecting with non-FUORI! leftist gay groups.[50] Initially, the magazine was a supplement to the periodical *Alternativa radicale*. At first it was edited by Angelo Pezzana (the 'responsible editor') and eventually by FUORI! member Felix Cossolo, who was a worker for FIAT, the automobile manufacturer based in Turin.[51] In 1982 the publication would merge with a new magazine, *Babilonia*. In its first editorial, *Lambda* urges a new form of 'intellectual function', that should include 'personal involvement in daily and social life.'[52] 'If a homosexual writer writes about sexuality', the editors argue, 'then he should do it using above all the first person, thus immediately facing his readers. Only [by doing] so will the baronies of culture and the super-stars of the entertainment industry (such as some famous directors who live their own homosexuality by debasing it) cease to exist.' The allusion here is to an unidentifiable film or theatre celebrity (maybe theatre and film director Franco Zeffirelli), who, although homosexual, had never sympathized with the Italian homosexual movement. The same editorial explains that the choice of the name of the magazine was based on the fact that 'lambda' was adopted as a symbol by 'most of the homosexual groups', because it is the starting letter of the Greek verb that 'means to liberate oneself.' In the third issue, Angelo Pezzana, talking both as a member of the Radical party and as founder of FUORI!, clarifies that *Lambda* refuses what he calls a 'reformist' approach, as he and his comrades 'don't care at all to be accepted by the society.'[53] He also attacks those whom he defines as 'homosexual clowns', as he doesn't 'want to call [them] comrades'; they 'run gay dance clubs and shamelessly use the mark [of] FUORI for activities that don't have anything in common with our fight.'[54] The right approach to be adopted, instead, is to avoid 'reproducing... in our movement any traditional organization' and to lead a 'joyful' fight with 'no violence', in order to 'destroy the society that we refuse.'

Only a year later, however, a harsh controversy exploded within *Lambda* itself, after Felix Cossolo published a fictitious interview with Marco Pannella, the charismatic leader of the Italian Radical Party.[55] In the interview, which was not clearly presented as fictitious, Cossolo reported that Pannella had declared he was not a 'faggot' [*frocio*]. In the fictional conversation Cossolo mentions a man in Turin whom Pannella was allegedly 'phoning continously' because he was 'in love with him' and after being asked if this was true, the fictitious Pannella avoids answering. Pannella, who was a member of the Italian Parliament and had sympathized with the homosexual movement, came out as bisexual only in 2010.[56] This article was then an outing to which many reacted angrily. Pezzana withdrew his name as responsible editor of the magazine and published an article in which he stated that the 'fake interview' with Pannella was 'billions of light years away from what I intend as [our] political fight', not only 'because it has attacked in a terrorist way a comrade toward whom I feel profound affection and admiration, but above all because it opens to a "style" in which I do not recognize myself, a cowardly anti-homosexual "style".' As a consequence, most of the FUORI! members left *Lambda*'s editorial office and the magazine was subsequently published as a supplement of the magazine *Re nudo*, whose editor, Marina Valcarenghi, became the 'responsible editor' of *Lambda*. In the following months, despite serious financial difficulties, Cossolo succeeded in keeping the magazine published, by funding it through the organization of the first gay camps in Italy – collective holidays at seaside locations in the South of the country.[57]

The transformation undergone by *Lambda* can be seen as an introduction to the changes that Italian LGBTQ publishing would experience in the 1980s. *Babilonia*, which was based in Milan, was founded by Felix Cossolo and Ivan Teobaldelli. It offered a combination of political and cultural contributions with pop content. It was much less serious and politicized than *FUORI!*, containing interviews with celebrities and pictures of naked men, and was more heavily illustrated and graphically elegant than *Lambda*. Like *Lambda*, *Babilonia* was also financed through the organization of gay camps and its issue No. 0 was presented to the public during one of these events in Apulia.[58] A symbol for this flexible approach, that also implied a commercial component, is the fact that after the second issue the editors changed the subtitle of the magazine – '[a] monthly [magazine] of gay culture and information' – replacing the word 'information' with 'seduction.'[59] Abandoning what Massimo Consoli had labelled a 'ghetto' of radicalism was accomplished at a cost of a certain level of assimilation to the characteristic forms of mainstream print culture.

In conclusion, the development of the first Italian LGBTQ press in the 1970s resulted in the publication of a range of periodicals which were different in terms of rhetoric, style, political orientation and aims. Some of these, in particular the 'homophile' magazines such as *Homo* and *con NOI*, were somehow born already outmoded. Other publications, however, like *FUORI!* and, to a lesser extent, *Lambda* placed Italy at the avant-garde of the international LGBT movement for their often original content, and for their circulation and impact on Italian society. The emotional and political impact of all of these publications can be appraised by the private letters that hundreds of readers submitted to them. 2021 marked the fiftieth anniversary of the birth of FUORI! – a historical anniversary that invites reflection on what that organisation, its associated journal, and the many other print publications that circulated in Italy across the tumultuous 1970s, managed to achieve.

ACKNOWLEDGEMENTS

The editors would like to extend their thanks to Marina Turchetti, Director, Library of the Central State Archive, Rome, Roberto Filippello and Fondazione Sandro Penna for their help in sourcing images to accompany this article.

NOTES

1   Paolo Murialdi. 2006. *Storia del giornalismo italiano: dalle gazzette a Internet*. Bologna: Il Mulino; Valerio Castronovo and Nicola Tranfaglia. 2008. *La stampa italiana nell'età della TV. Dagli anni Settanta a oggi*. Rome-Bari: Laterza; Mauro Forno. 2012. *Informazione e potere: Storia del giornalismo italiano*. Rome-Bari: Laterza; Oliviero Bergamini. 2013. *La democrazia della stampa: Storia del giornalismo*. Rome-Bari: Laterza.

2   On the history of LGBT people and of the LGBT movement in Italy, see Gianni Rossi Barilli. 1999. *Il movimento gay in Italia*. Milan: Feltrinelli; Andrea Pini. 2011. *Quando eravamo froci: Gli omosessuali nell'Italia di una volta*. Milan: Il Saggiatore; Giovanni Dall'Orto. 2015. *Tutta un'altra storia: L'omosessualità dall'antichità al secondo dopoguerra*. Milan: Il Saggiatore; Massimo Prearo. 2015. *La fabbrica dell'orgoglio: Una genealogia dei movimenti LGBT*. Pisa: Edizioni ETS; Elena Biagini. 2018. *L'emersione imprevista: il movimento delle lesbiche in Italia negli anni '70 e '80*. Pisa: Edizioni ETS. Porpora Marcasciano. 2020. *Tra le rose e le viole. La storia e le storie di transessuali e travestiti*, Roma: Alegre.

3   For instance, Giovanni Dall'Orto argues that religion played a crucial role in this context. Giovanni Dall'Orto. 1988. 'La "tolleranza repressiva" dell'omosessualità: Quando un atteggiamento diventa tradizione.' In Arcigay Nazionale. Ed. *Omosessuali e stato*. Bologna: Cassero. 37–57.

4   I am using the term homophile here to indicate those magazines, most of them founded before the Stonewall riots, that focused on homosexual issues without in general contesting society in the name of gay 'liberation'. For the use of the term 'homophile'

within the early US LGBT movement, see Lillian Faderman. 2015. *The Gay Revolution: The Story of the Struggle*. New York: Simon & Schuster. 86.

5   Attorney [avv.] Alberto Musotto [pseudonym?]. 1972. 'Legge e controlegge. Il codice ignora l'omofilia, il costume la condanna.' *Homo*. No. 1 (October). 36.

6   The FUORI! group was perhaps the first to use the term *uscire fuori*, to mean 'coming out'. However, the term did not succeed in entering Italian vocabulary or slang. Even today the English expression is still much used as is the expression *dichiararsi* gay/lesbian/homosexual..., i.e. to declare oneself as being gay/lesbian/homosexual.

7   Angelo Pezzana. 1996. *Dentro & Fuori: Una autobiografia omosessuale*. Milan: Sperling & Kupfer. 54.

8   See for instance: Mario Mieli. 1977. *Elementi di critica omosessuale* (*Elements of homosexual criticism*). Torino: Einaudi.

9   Enzo Cucco. 1979. 'Transessuali.' *FUORI!* No. 21/22. 43. I must point out, however, that in an interview, published as part of the same article, with a young transgender person who states that she has the intention to be operated on in order to change her sex from male to female, Cucco interprets sex changes as a sort of 'slackening' towards society's urge for 'normality', i.e. a clear choice between female and male gender identities.

10 The *collettivo* was intended as a group with a non-hierarchical structure. In this case it refers to a substitute for an editorial office, but it was also the word that many political and social groups of the 1968 and post-1968 movement in Italy used to define themselves.

11 See the statement in *FUORI!*, No. 7. January/February 1973. 2.

12 See Baraghini's statement pubished in *con NOI*, No. 0, November 1972. 1.

13 *FUORI!* No. 7, January/February 1973. 2. See also Marcello Baraghini. 2018. *Manuale per diventare editore all'incontrario*. Imola: Babbomorto Editore.

14 Editoriale Inverno. 1973. *FUORI!* No. 11 (Winter). 2.

15 Dario Pasquini. 2020. '"This Will Be the Love of the Future": Italian LGBT People and Their Emotions in Letters from the FUORI! and Massimo Consoli Archives, 1970–1984.' *Journal of the History of Sexuality*. Vol. 29 No. 1 (January). 51–78.

16 Collettivo redazionale. 1972. 'Omosessualità e Liberazione', *FUORI!* No. 1 (June). 1.

17 Mario Mieli. 1973. 'I radical-chic e lo chic radicale.' *FUORI!* No. 7 (January/February). 16.

18 Above Mieli's article is placed a statement of the editorial collective in which it is stated that 'most of the members' do not share the 'personal opinions' expressed by the author but that they agreed to publish the article in order to open a debate within the magazine. Ibid.

19 Author's phone call with Angelo Pezzana, 4 March 2020.

20 See for example Angelo Pezzana. 1972. 'Chi parla per gli omosessuali?' *FUORI!*, No. 1 (June). 2.

21 *Usciamo Fuori!*, undated [1975]. See also a letter from a reader, and friend, to a member of *FUORI!* magazine, in which the former complains that, after the federation with the Radical party 'the revolutionary homosexuals have become simple radicals.' Gianfranco C. to Francesco Merlini. 17 February 1975. Folder 195, Archivio FUORI!, Fondazione FUORI!, Turin (cited hereafter as AF-FF).

22 *Usciamo Fuori!*, without date [1975], published as a supplement to the magazine *Rosso*.

23 Monica G. Giansanti. 1972. 'Travestirsi e fare la rivoluzione.' *FUORI!* No. 4 (October). 13–15. I must point out that in my essay 'This Will Be the Love of the Future', op. cit., I misread the date of the letter by Monica, which was not from 1978, but probably from 1972 (62–63).

24 La redazione di FUORI! DONNA. 1974. 'Perché FUORI! DONNA e come.' *FUORI!* No. 13 (Summer). 3. The language of the editorial seems to be influenced by Mieli's above mentioned article about 'radical chic'.

25 Emma Allais to Angelo Pezzana, undated [1974], folder 193, FF-AF.

26 Emma Allais to Angelo Pezzana, 18 September 1972, folder 190, FF-AF.

27 Biagini. *L'emersione imprevista*. Op. cit. 55.

28 Brigate Saffo. 1978. *Lambda*. No. 13. 9.

29 'Cinema Italia intervista a Franca Rame prima dell'inizio di 'tutta casa, letto, chiesa', *Brigate Saffo* [supplement of *Lambda*, No. 18/19, 1978], 1–2.

30 Biagini. *L'emersione imprevista*. Op. cit. 51–61, 107, and, specifically with regard to the position of the women members of FUORI!, 40. There were, as Biagini shows, some important exceptions to the low visibility of lesbians in the feminist movement, for example in the Roman *collettivo* of via Pompeo Magno: Biagini, 78–88.

31 Biagini. *L'emersione imprevista*. 66.

32 Homophile magazines such as the US *ONE* and the French *Arcadie*, for example, were founded in the 1950s, while the Swiss *Der Kreis* appeared in the 1930s.

33 See Liliosa Azara. 2018. *I sensi e il pudore: L'Italia e la rivoluzione dei costumi (1958–68); La morale sessuale degli italiani dalla legge Merlin al Sessantotto*. Rome: Donzelli.

34 'Fuori dal ghetto.' *Homo*, No. 1, October 1972, 5.

35 Ibid. It is significant that a similar accusation of 'upside down racism' against 'more or less liberating 'associations'' appears in the first issue of *per NOI*, the 1975 relaunch of the magazine *con NOI*. 'Perché "Per noi"? Il direttore risponde', *per NOI*, No. 1, 1975. 4.

36 Musotto. 'Legge e controlegge'. Op. cit.

37 'Essere omosessuali.' *Homo*, No. 2, November 1972. 4.

38 'Homo intervista: Tony Pietta. Candida conversazione con un omofilo felice', *Homo*, No. 2, November 1972. 5–6.

39 *con NOI*, No. 4, March 1973. 24.

40 La redazione, 'Editoriale', *con NOI*, No. 0, November 1972. 3. *con NOI* 's responsible editor was the same as that for *FUORI!*, i.e. the above mentioned Marcello Baraghini.

41 Luciano Massimo Consoli. 1971. 'Omosessualità e rivoluzione.' *FUORI!* No. 0 (December). 9. On Consoli see Dario Pasquini. 2018. "Uscire dal ghetto': Il ruolo di Massimo Consoli nel movimento LGBT italiano e internazionale.' In Mirco Modolo. Ed. *Nuove fonti per la storia d'Italia: Per un bilancio del secolo breve.'* Rome: De Luca. 154–157.

42 Massimo Consoli. 1973. 'Fuori?' *con NOI*. No. 6 (May). 60–61.

43 Mauro Bertocchi, 'Le false immagini', *FUORI!*, No. 6, December 1972, 3–4.

44 Enrico G. to *FUORI!* and to Francesco Merlini, 12 February 1975, folder 195, AF-FF.

45 Franco A. to *FUORI!*, 14 October 1974, folder 193, AF-FF.

46 Bentivoglio to *FUORI!*, 5 February 1973, folder 190, AF-FF.

47 For Consoli's financial difficulties in publishing *O-MPO* and in running the dance bar and cultural association Ompo's see Victor D. S. to Massimo Consoli, 17 February 1977, and Massimo Consoli to Dino F., 23 August 1978, box 1, Fondo Consoli, Central State Archive, Rome (cited hereafter as FC-ACS).

48 [Massimo Consoli], 'Perché "O-MPO"?', *O-MPO*, No. 1, April 1975; and Frocik [Massimo Consoli], 'Editoriale', *O-MPO*, No. 3 (n.d. [1975]).

49 Massimo Consoli to Dario Bellezza, 14 October 1970, box 293, FC-ACS.

50 Further spaces for the expression of homosexual voices or, at least, addressed to the homosexual public in the 1970s, were *La pagina frocia*, the 'Faggot Page', which was a weekly survey that appeared from November 1979 until May 1980 in the radical Communist newspaper *Lotta continua* and the porn magazine *DoppioSenso*, which was founded in 1977 and proved the most long-lasting gay publication in Italy, shutting down in the early 2000s.

51 For further information on Cossolo, see: Felix Cossolo. 2015. *40 anni in movimento 1975–2015*. Self-published.

52 'Editoriale', *Lambda*, No. 1, November 1976. 1.

53 Angelo Pezzana, 'Sfogo politico infettivo', *Lambda*, No. 3, February 1977. 1–2.

54 The allusion is most probably to Massimo Consoli. See a letter of the same period from Felix Cossolo to Massimo Consoli, in which he states that he is 'really disappointed' at getting to know about the organization of a Saint Valentine party in Consoli's club Ompo's, noting that 'everything is permitted to the detriment of the faggots, even if in this case the exploiters are faggots who should be repudiated', Felix Cossolo to Massimo Consoli, 12 February 1977, box 279, FC-ACS.

55 Felix Cossolo, 'Pannella dichiara: 'Non sono frocio'', *Lambda*, No. 10, 1978, 8.

56 Clemente J. Mimun (interview with Marco Pannella), *Chi*, 12 May 2010.

57 On this experience see Felix Cossolo and Ivan Teobaldelli. 1981. *Cercando il paradiso perduto. Momenti di vita comunitaria gay.* Milan: Gammalibri.

58 Barilli. *Il movimento gay in Italia.* Op. cit. 147.

59 Ibid, 148.

4 Change Always Has to Build: In Conversation With Gail Lewis

TAYLOR LE MELLE

When Gail Lewis and her co-organisers Valerie Amos, Amina Mama, and Pratibha Parmar, were approached in 1984 to edit a special issue of *Feminist Review* focusing on Black women, they sought and received full editorial control of the journal. The group used *Feminist Review Vol. 17 Issue 1: Many Voices, One Chant: Black Feminist Perspectives* to give space to Black and South Asian women writers, poets and activists who articulated their perspectives within a women's liberation movement which often ignored the role of race and class as compounding (and constitutive) aspects of patriarchal strictures of gender and sexuality. Amongst the contributor list were members of the publishing co-operative Black Woman Talk, the Black women's film collective *Late Start*, the women's newspaper *Outwrite* and the Brixton Black Women's Group (BWG), of which Lewis was also a member. In *Many Voices, One Chant*, collectively they noted the 'ongoing need for white women to take note of and act upon Black feminist critiques of the content and form of contemporary British feminism'.[1] Preceding even the table of contents, the issue begins with a roll call listing of Black women's groups and organisations in the UK. It was a process of becoming visible, through print.

Lewis came to *Many Voices, One Chant* as a founding member of Organisation of Women of African and Asian Descent (OWAAD), as well as a member of Brixton Black Women's Group. Her consistent commitment to building intergenerational discourses with writers, educators and artists has made Lewis a vital mentor to students of Black feminist thought and abolitionist thought. A writer, editor, psychotherapist, researcher, educator and activist, Lewis has been active since the 1970s in anti-imperialist and anti-racist groups in London, UK, where she was born and raised. Though she was a member of the socialist feminist Lesbian Left group, her primary focus has been on collective action and resistance against racial capitalism.

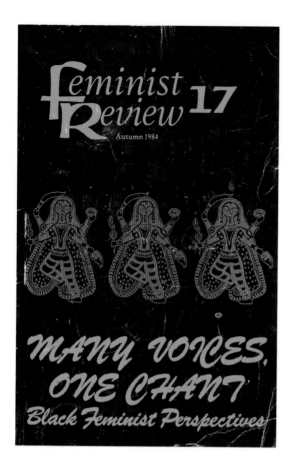

Front cover of *Feminist Review*, Vol. 17 Issue 1 (1984): *Many Voices, One Chant: Black Feminist Perspectives*.

In *Many Voices, One Chant*, Lewis participates in a roundtable discussion, 'Becoming Visible: Black Lesbian Discussions with Carmen, Shaila and Pratibha,' in which the group of women make apparent the inextricable relationship between 'politics and vulnerability'.[2] Their 'development of a Black Lesbian feminist perspective'[3] informed their organising and their 'overall political perspective'[4] while simultaneously their visibility as non-heterosexuals within racial capitalism hindered their viability as paid workers in white feminist organisations[5] and as comrades in the Black Power and Women's Liberation Movements.[6] Still, they named separatist politics as utterly 'facile',[7] resisting any impetus to make 'hard and fast rules' about who a Black Lesbian should organise or sleep with.[8]

'Becoming Visible' explicates the four discussants' feminism as always 'developing' or 'in development', echoing their awareness of a rapidly changing social and political landscape – a characteristic of social and political landscapes, always – and of an intense expansion of the visibility of those politics. One participant spoke to her experiences of social isolation only a few short years before the conversation took place.[9] In the roundtable, the group called out another feminist periodical *Trouble & Strife* for its apparent 'inability' to find Black feminist writers and editors. Lewis, along with other members of the BWG – Melba Wilson and Olive Gallimore – would go on to be interviewed in the Summer 1990 issue of *Trouble & Strife* six years later. In the interview with Agnes Quashie, Lewis discusses in more detail the organisation of BWG and its relationship to both the Black Power movements and the white feminist movements in London. By participating in discussions like those that appeared in *Feminist Review* Issue 17 and *Trouble & Strife* Issue 19, Lewis and her fellow organisers were integral to the documentation of the Black womens' movement in the UK and Europe. Their participation in these printed contexts functioned to stage the relationships that fed the movement and provided a form of self-documentation of the community spaces they worked with and through. This ensured a certain degree of memory could be kept in the archive, about the issues that Black women were facing as well as their organising efforts.

Since then, Lewis has written extensively on a wide range of subjects, intertwining perspectives on citizenship, nationhood, sexuality, psychoanalysis and Black study. Her personal history and early political formations are covered in her essay 'Birthing Racial

Difference: conversations with my mother and others.'[10] In addition to the coupling of politics and vulnerability exemplified by this text, one of Lewis' major discursive contributions to the feminist movement has been the reminder that 'households are not immune from the dynamics of racism'.[11] This equally could and should serve as a guiding principle in the queer social and political landscape as well. The combination of a personal and political anti-imperialism is foundational to her Black, feminist, and queer discourses in print and otherwise, as her analyses traverse psychic, affective and emotional registers because, as she notes, 'politics needs an emotional understanding too'.[12] After finding therapeutic counselling to be an inroad to inform her own understanding of how racism, sexism and homophobia can affect us, Lewis' practice made a watershed shift as she began to incorporate psychoanalytic thought into her practice, training as a psychotherapist at Tavistock Clinic. What is made possible from her combination of Black feminist thought and psychoanalysis is not only an intellectual synthesis of two disciplines, but crucially a possibility of articulating, for example, 'the political power of erotic life-force'.[13]

Becoming Visible: Black Lesbian Discussions

Carmen, Gail, Shaila and Pratibha

As black lesbians in Britain we are growing in our numbers and in strength. The following discussion is a result of eight hours' taped discussion between four of us. It was impossible to reproduce the full text of the discussion due to lack of space. Here we are printing only extracts of our discussions and we hope to publish the full text as a pamphlet in the near future. The process of coming together and talking and eating has been exhilarating and strengthening. When we started out, two of us were unsure and reluctant about being identified by our real names, but towards the end of our discussions, we felt strengthened and supported and decided to be identified. We are all aware of how vulnerable we are making ourselves and putting our lives at risk in many ways, but it is only when we begin to make ourselves visible that we can break the silence about our lives.

Feminist Review No.17, July 1984

Carmen, Gail, Shaila, Pratibha, 'Becoming Visible: Black Lesbian Discussions', *Feminist Review*, Vol. 17 Issue 1 (1984), p.53.

I first came to know Gail through Evan Ifekoya, a London-based artist whose focus – not only in the work they make, but in their daily lived practice – has been to archive and renew interest in Black Queer practice from the 1970s – 1990s. In the few years that I have known Gail, her scholarship, her accounts of the past, and her friendship, have been integral to my understanding of anti-racist efforts in the UK. Usually, we might meet each other for a coffee or drink somewhere in East London to have a conversation but in summer 2020 our only option was to stay in touch via Zoom, which is where the conversation for this volume took place.

While not planned to be, I now feel what we discussed serves as a useful sequel to Gail's contribution, with Clare Hemmings, to *Feminist Theory*.[14] Gail and I pick up the discussion where she and Hemmings ended, addressing the very 'problem' of her work being historicised as 'queer' when its theoretical and political locations are within feminism, race, sexuality but not *homosexuality* in particular. Though she was undeniably 'out' as a Black lesbian by the time of the *Feminist Review* special issue, we discuss to what extent she was writing on 'queer' (or, in the 1970s, lesbian and/or dyke) issues and to what extent queerness is a useful lens to bring to her work because it is part of the 'wholeness' of the author.

Images of Black Women Organizing

Compiled by Shaheen Haq, Pratibha Parmar and Ingrid Pollard

OLD AND COLD— NO MORE! INCREASE PENSIONS

TGWU RETIRED MEMBERS ASSOCIATIONS

BRENDA PRINCE/FORMAT

Pensioners Day of Action, Jubilee Gardens, London, August 1983.

Black Women in Media Conference, April 1984 — music workshop.

SIMILOLA COKER

INGRID POLLARD

'Late Start Film and Video Collective', 1984.

Black Women in Media Conference, April 1984 — video workshop.

SIMILOLA COKER

Shaheen Haq, Pratibha Parmar, Ingrid Pollard, 'Images of Black Women Organizing', *Feminist Review*, Vol. 17 Issue 1, 1984, pp. 90–1.

AN OPENNESS TO A POSSIBILITY

TLM: Should we start by talking about the relevance of queerness as an organising principle? I think examining history, examining things that have come before, and organising that examination around queerness – even though it might not have been organised that way at the time – is useful from an archival standpoint; which is maybe different from my own participation in events, panels, books, or whatever, around queerness. I don't necessarily feel like that 'queerness' summarises how my contribution to 'the forum' is organised.

GL: I suppose if I think about it, and I have to say it's been around in my mind over this last year, because when I did a conversation that was published in *Feminist Theory* with Clare Hemmings, Clare asked me about, or noted that in my work, queerness or sexuality as a site of struggle hadn't been foregrounded. And that is absolutely right.

At one level it's because then, when I was younger and coming out, and then came out as it were… so, you make a declaration as to your own subjecthood, if you like: 'I'm now one of you,' became a point of connection and a claim about development, I guess. 'I was this, then, and now I'm this, now.' And although at a personal level, just in terms of my own sense of me, the struggle to own what we now call 'my queerness,' and to declare it, was inordinately difficult, it was really difficult. I think I've said this before in public forums that there was a period when I truly believed Black women and lesbian did not combine. There was no such thing as a Black lesbian. Then of course Audre Lorde and Barbara Smith declaring themselves, you think "Oh, okay, yeah, it's possible!" A way to be was made possible through those declarations. Coming out stories were important in that sense. And my own struggle with that was difficult and very freeing when I did it. That was in the mid-seventies. Even that whole notion of 'Tell me your coming out story,' I don't even know whether coming out, anyone's coming out story, is part of a conversation of community building, collective building, these days, as it was in the seventies and eighties…

So, that was really important, but as a frame around which to organise politically it wasn't important for me, in a sense. The question of anti-racism, anti-imperialism that was inflected through a form of Black feminism was absolutely the priority. And it was because I felt that those categories – well, two reasons I guess: One is that I had been formed… the idea of who I could be, who I could not be, what I could not be, what opportunities were open to me, what wasn't, was absolutely structured through racism, both micro-socially within the household but also on the larger national stage, and the international stage. And that my politics had within it a kind of class politics and an anti-imperialist politics was the thing through which I wanted to be active. I felt that that was really important. That made more sense to me, psycho-socially. Politically as well, but psycho-socially.

TLM: But actually at the time there *was* a lot of political organising that was centred around queerness and the ability to be out, whether from a legal framework, whether just from a social perspective of being able to walk down the street without being harassed… But that wasn't what was driving you?

GL: Exactly. And there really was. And it's going to be contradictory because there absolutely was. There was the rise of the Gay Liberation movement in the UK, and everything with the Gay Liberation Front that was kind of masculine in some senses, but women were involved. There were the struggles within feminism for lesbian presence, within white dominance feminism for lesbian presence, etcetera, all of that. And I became active within feminism. I was a member of a group called Lesbian Left that was socialist feminists, organising under the identity of lesbian. But there was still something… it wasn't my absolute – it wasn't my home. The issue of an international struggle against racial structuring of the world – racial capitalism as we'd now call it – the importance of that, that's where I felt, eventually, was my

TLM: The clips that you recorded for British Library almost ten years ago, there's a little tag between yours and between Stella Dadzie's interviews.[15] I think that the question the interviewer asked her was about the formulation of OWAAD and whether sexuality had a place within that formulation. And she said something to the effect of, 'I think it was more at the forefront for Gail'.

GL: I think what Stella is pointing to is that obviously I was out as lesbian at the time, and also that sexual identity as the position from which we mobilised our politics was not at the fore in OWAAD. But the tensions around whether or not OWAAD and the Brixton Group – and I don't know about the other groups – could be associated with lesbianism, woman-loving-woman, non-normative sexualities, obviously caused rifts within the movement as a whole.

And of course, for me it mattered because it was about me personally, even while I was still foregrounding these other organising categories, so sets of oppressions and lived experiences, as organising categories for political mobilisation. But also, because we're talking as well about publishing, I did, for the British version of *Our Bodies, Ourselves* that came out in 1978, I am involved in a lesbian conversation, but I'm the only Black woman, the only woman of colour in there.[16] The other three women (is it?) are white women. And then later for *Feminist Review 17*, the so-called Black women's issue, I'm in that as a Black lesbian with other Black lesbians; Black in the old sense.[17]

I mean, it's *Feminist Review*, so in some senses it's an intervention into white dominance feminism, but in terms of the content, the stuff we talk about, it's a published intervention into Black Nationalist organising as well. And so we recognised there was a real importance to put into the frame questions of the control of desire, sexuality, that was being replicated in the Black movement, and the ways in which there wasn't sufficient account of the difference it would mean to be out as a Black or of colour queer (I'm using today's terminology), queer woman or feminine-identified, or lesbian. And at that time, oftentimes the question to declare yourself as dyke would be the one that would, in my mind now, be a naming that would trouble a gendered position. It wouldn't be straightforwardly woman. So, you'd be woman-loving-woman, but you wouldn't be declaring yourself as 'woman.' You'd say there's a complicated relationship to normative ideas of womanhood.

TLM: It's an interesting and efficient language-gesture. So, what then qualified as being out in those scenarios? I think in a 2020 sense, most of that has to do with what would be qualified as performance; not to say that it's fake, but something that is performed or announced in some way, whether that be through social media or any other public digital forum, and at specific moments. Maybe it's Coming Out Day, maybe it's Bi-Visibility Day, but it's a visibility question as well, in terms of using that day to say, 'This thing applies to me'. So that is one way of being out, which I think necessitates a certain degree of performativity that's not really for everyone, no matter what is being performed. But then I also think there is this thing at the level of the social which is having and using and utilising certain vocabularies, being willing to quite literally perform a certain intimacy in public. And actually you're kind of changing my impression as to what we are inheriting in this moment.

GL: Okay, but see, Taylor, this is why intergenerational conversations are so important. It's through intergenerational conversation, not only that we can chart movement, but also that we can, together, create what we might call a third space or a new space which shows us that change always has to build, is always a vision to the future, it's always an uncertain, open... an openness to a possibility that we don't know what it's going to look like, what the outcome's going to be. And we have to be open, politically we have to be open. But the route to that openness, what we can gather on the way that can be helpful, and what we need to let go of, can emerge through the intergenerational conversations because it helps us to change what we think, what we take for granted. It helps us to see what can be achieved by certain modes of being-ness at a particular conjunctural moment, and what modes of being-ness are no longer important.

So, if there was something important in the seventies and eighties – and maybe nineties, I don't know – about a being-ness that was a, 'I've come out! Here's my coming out story!' it's a declaration of saying, 'I refuse a particular categorical nomination that's been assumed about me, and I'm declaring another one. I'm entering into another one'. Of course it's going into another one; we know that, and queer was an attempt to disrupt that.

But now...how old are you?

TLM: Thirty two.

GL: So, you're thirty two, I'm sixty nine. The huge decades between us, and here we are having this conversation. In those thirty years, now we know how to decode modes of presentation in a way to say, "Oh, look, queer, queer, queer, queer, queer, queer, queer."

TLM: I also think what's happened is that we know to a certain extent everyone is queer. And I'm saying that flippantly but like...(laughter).

GL: We do, but that's because of the struggle. The point is, is that both the anti-racist, the sexual liberationist and the feminist, the convergence of those pressures on what was taken to be normatively 'just', 'it just is,' were such to reveal their power but also their penetrability to disrupt them.

Your generation inherit that, including inheriting notions of performativity and all that kind of stuff, and understand that there's a difference – there can be a difference – between subjecthood and our own sense and claim for and fashioning of personhood, those distinctions. Well that's part of the legacy of activism. And now our task is to talk intergenerationally and say, 'Where do we go now? Where *do* we go now?' At what moment is performance itself a kind of oppression and at what moments does it still need to happen?

TLM: I think that is really important that we keep doing that because I feel like we're in a phase of capitalism in which subjecthood and brand is so intertwined.

GL: Yes. And the point is our theoretical resources have expanded so much, so we can think these things differently, we can think with other concepts that push our minds in other directions as well as our practices of self.

CREATIVE WORK IS ALSO THE POLITICAL WORK

TLM: So, with all this in mind, you being who you were then, I'm really curious about not only what sorts of things OWAAD was publishing but also I'm very curious as to what a group that functioned like OWAAD, was born out of the principles that OWAAD was born out of, how was OWAAD using printed matter? I'm thinking about anything from putting up signs to making a zine and all of those gestures that one can make to share an idea with printed matter. And I'm wondering what was your relationship to that? Did it feel like an effective way to galvanize this spirit of anti-imperialism?

GL: There was *FOWAAD* that was what you call a zine, I guess, the newsletter of OWAAD that was produced and there were people involved on the *FOWAAD* committee, people were involved in committees to get work done. Stella was always so important because she was so dedicated to OWAAD and put a lot of labour into that organising. So there was that and that was a newsletter of stuff that was happening around the country; we'd ask for stuff to come in and stuff that was happening internationally, you know just as a

Front cover of *FOWAAD*, the newsletter of OWAAD, Issue 7, November 1980. Ref. DADZIE/1/8/1 (© Stella Dadzie, available at Black Cultural Archives)

newsletter. Including whether it would be advertising of a demonstration or a report on the demonstration or something like that.

Then of course, it was at that time that Suzanne [Scafe], Bev [Bryan] and Stella [Dadzie] got together to do *Heart of the Race*.[18] It was called 'the book project' at the time... And I think initially there was a sense that more people would be involved but they were the three that got it together and did it. The original came out in '85. It was seen as a companion to Amrit Wilson's *Finding A Voice* that had come out in the late seventies.[19] And echoed... I'm not sure whether the Manchester group Abasindi had produced a book, it'll be in the book *Catching Hell*.[20]

So, there'd be all sort of ways in which there were contributions to movement publications, leaflets, newsletters, etcetera. But movement publications would include, for example, publications around the miners' strike up in Yorkshire because there was a couple of Asian women who were really involved in the miners' strike stuff. There was the ways in which women involved in OWAAD – or connected to OWAAD but not necessarily operating from OWAAD – were involved in Black People Support the Miners from London, where it would be 'support the striking miners in Kent' and contributing to leaflets and stuff. So, it's about how the tentacles went out into other publications as much as what was published as *FOWAAD* as an OWAAD publication, or *Heart of the Race* from women within OWAAD producing a thing, you see.

And then, there was of course the stuff that we did in things like *Feminist Review* issue 17, those kinds of stuff. And there was *Charting the Journey* as well that me, Pratibha Parmar, Liliane Landor, Shabnam Grewal and Jackie Kay worked on.[21] We'd all been involved in OWAAD... *Charting the Journey* came out from Sheba Publishers and Araba and Michelle, they'd been connected to OWAAD but they were now in Sheba working with a couple of other white women. So it's more like a rhizomic formation. Melba [Wilson] and I put something in *Trouble & Strife* which was much more of a radical feminist magazine.[22] We did stuff for *Spare Rib*. In a sense you need to have conversations with other women from other groups – because I was still located in the Brixton group – to see where stuff went. And stuff went into film too. So, Pratibha, for example, who wasn't in the Brixton group but had been in OWAAD, became a filmmaker. Dorothea Smartt very much got involved, out of the Brixton group, in publishing and poetry and doing that kind of workshop work and everything. So, you see what I mean? People went in all directions.

TLM: Well, I think one of the things that Black feminism really kind of owns in the discipline of writing – but really knowledge creation – is the huge amount of respect [that it has], for lack of a better word, for poetry, fiction. So you mentioned also Jackie Kay...

GL: And Maud as well, Maud Sulter and of course Lubaina [Himid], doing that work together early on.

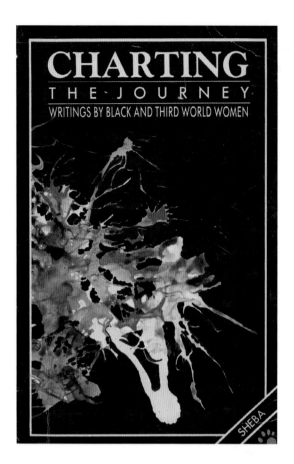

Front cover of *Charting the Journey* (1988).

TLM: And the way that actually fiction and creative writing – creative work – is also the political work. I think that maybe now, again thinking about inheritance, I think there's a lot of pressure to really imbue creative work with politics and really make sure that it communicates politically or maybe actually that creative work is used to kind of represent politics, whereas I think that what you're reminding me of is maybe actually the way in which the politics is already there, it can already be there. I really do see that. I don't think that Black women in the U.K, Dorothea's generation and before that, really get so much credit for using fiction and poetry in that way, in the way that Black American women really do get that credit, the Toni Morrisons, etcetera. I think that's Black Studies, in fiction, really.

GL: Yes I think that's really right because of all the work… the so-called 'non-fiction work' that was produced and was so important and drawing on long legacies, that's the thing. From the continent, from the sub-continent, from the Caribbean itself, long legacies of modes of expression. This is how we express! This is how we've expressed! And it goes back, Taylor, to the thing that we're making the distinction with, the subject positions as those racialised subjects who are full of inadequacy, that position being completely thrown away and just ignored, really, in what we would now call fugitive practices of artistic production, where we name ourselves, where we *be* differently, nowadays we talk about we *be* in Blackness. That was so important. And there was also Hazel Carby's *Reconstructing Womanhood*, a sister who was in the Brixton group as well.[23] She did an important bit of archival recovery work. There was so much! It was an incredibly generative time, a lot of that generative work came from women, dykes (some would define as that but not everybody) but women who were women-loving-women. Some were in heterosexual relationships, many were not.

QUEERNESS AS A BREACH OF CATEGORISATION

TLM: Is it important, other than in any book that's already delineated as a queer archival practice, is it important to acknowledge that? Or why would it be important to acknowledge that? Not to say is it, but *why* would it be important to acknowledge that?

GL: Well, the question probably is, *is* it important? You see, my 2020 head and heart says no, but because you're inviting me to go back to my 1975 head and heart: yes, yes yes! Because we didn't know you existed! Because we thought we could not possibly *be*. There may be loads of colour people who feel themselves to be queer or feel queer is something to do with them, maybe it's not even to *be,* but queer is a nomination that they can inhabit but they don't think they can, then maybe just hearing it again matters. Maybe it matters. I just don't know. Do we need to know that Audre Lorde defined herself as a lesbian and was woman-loving?

TLM: I think we have no choice.

GL: But do we need to know?

TLM: Okay, yeah, this is a great question. With her we have no choice because it is so integral to the arguments that she was making. But for someone for whom that was not the argument that they were making in their writing, that is where I wonder to what importance...

GL: For me, then? For me, does it matter about me, given most of my writing? I don't know! I suppose in so far as it matters at all to have any knowledge of an author, then part of my wholeness would have to be that. I mean, I've been with Liliane for thirty-five-and-a-half years, even if that's all we took, apart from questions of desire, what would it mean to excise that? At the same time, do we need to big it up? I don't know. You tell me, it's up to your generation (laughter). But there is something about the moment, the time frame from which we feel we're speaking; now, no, but then I just assume everybody knows about me, so I don't even have to think about it.

TLM: I think your point about coming to a text with the wholeness of the author, then yes, that is a part of that wholeness. Where my cynicism comes from is actually again, related to this let's say 2020 neoliberal late capitalism issue of the marriage between self and brand. I think race or racial subjecthood has also been very ripe for selling, for monetisation but I also think that queerness is incredibly ripe for capitalising upon... and it's maybe not even monetisation in terms of dollars but a particular social currency which I don't think is ever cashed-in upon by the author, or can be, but is cashed-in upon by the reader, for sure, publisher, maybe, the institution, the organiser. I think that cashing-in on that currency does begin to preclude people actually engaging with the damn text! So what I become cynical about is actually then the most interesting, or the thing that is given the most space of examination in an author like yours' work, would be the queerness over and above anything else that's happening in the work; which I also think happens in relation to blackness as well in different ways. That's my cynicism.

GL: I get that. I suppose just two things. One is to say, it is absolutely right for you to press that point about that coming together of subject and brand, that's really important. Precisely because what it really underscores is the ways in which it is indeed, in these times of racial capital, in *these* times, our very bodies that are captured every time we go into the net and the algorithms decide what we are, and it's us who they want to buy, they don't really care what we buy, it's *us* that they want to buy for their marketing. That's really important and that's the thing, again… So, just as we're thinking about the time, so too that has to be layered into the character of racial capital and its technologically driven character at any particular time. It's really important. In fact, now we should more and more refuse it, in a sense, refuse to be named as subject and refuse it. That links to the second point: Blackness as opposed to people categorised as Black and identifying as Black people in that sense and doing. But Blackness as a mode of living, thinking, feeling, breathing, is, I think, itself a form of refusal and fugitivity. It's not the same and it lives itself differently, so in that sense it articulates with queerness as a breach of categorisation, as a breach of those things. And it lives itself through a being-ness that isn't a subjecthood, or at least it's in struggle with subjecthood, of course because they are so powerful but those moments of living differently feel so important.

TLM: I think what that necessarily means is that to either preserve that fugitivity or to embody or live that fugitivity as opposed to representing it – I think that there's an overdevelopment of representation that we are dealing with right now that I think makes a very interesting relationship to this kind of archival work of going back to particular times where representation was really important, right? I think in order to embody this fugitivity, this is flippant but – I'm like 'no more talks.' To me that's what that means, right? No more talks, no more anthologies, it's breath-work and therapy now, and other things that don't have a constituent aspect of speaking to the forum.

GL: Yeah, I know what you mean. At the same time, I guess… I guess I'd want to say, take everything that you've said, which is in many ways a deep extending of the debates that were going on in the late eighties, early nineties around the question of Black representation and the critique of positive images and all that kind of stuff. Which is to say these questions have been around for a while just at the moment at which we declare a presence we're also saying 'Well what does that mean? Is that something that's represented then? And what does it mean?' And we know, absolutely how white supremacist neoliberal media wants to have, in order to tick their diversity boxes – don't really want our presence as staff in their agencies, I don't think they do want that – but they do want us to be present in a particular mode of good-boy-and-girlness, to tick their modes of representation, 'see look we've got X percent of our magazine for that year was people of colour' or you know.

Why I'm saying you're right to push that point now is to remind us is because it carries forward those earlier debates, it really condenses them, I mean deepens them! I think we're at a time where they press even more urgently. And at the same time (and this probably really is because of my generation, my kind of chronological generation, although I think I change through time) I want us to be able to convene into forms of collectivity in order to press beyond the individual and the atomisation that would happen – especially as that's an atomisation premised on notions of property and self-possession, we need to be self-possessed which is central to racial capital – and I want us to convene into collectivities that can move with the question that you pose and the serious doubt and the kind of rejection of representation, if you like. I want us to go with that in order to press together to see what other vista might open up that can… I don't want to say open onto a vista but make it feel like we can recognise each other and ourselves otherwise.

I want us to be able to recognise ourselves and recognise a constant process of *becoming* otherwise that I think can only happen through communing collectively but has to not be representation as we've known it. And I don't know what that would be. It comes back to where we spoke at the beginning, it's an openness, a radical openness to the unknown but we need to remain open. So, I want to go with your question and not close it down but use it to open up.

AN OPENNESS TO BE ABLE TO COMMUNE COLLECTIVELY

TLM: I think there's another thing about us gathering in this moment that I want to know: what do we need to be ready? To be in community in this way, to have these conversations in a way that opens out, goes out onto this vista, right? I do have this sense that we all need to… everyone who gathers in that group also has to be ready to go there, no?

GL: Yeah! Maybe I can join up my response to that question with something I wanted to say at the end of what we last talked about and that question about a radical rejection of the notion of representation, but still wanting to have an openness to be able to commune collectively. I think maybe that has implications for the question of publishing as writing and maybe, I really don't know, it's about my own ambivalence about writing, but maybe writing – you know, you were saying no anthologies and all that – close down too much. Maybe they fix too much. And maybe the mode of publishing needs to not be in the written form. Or at least not only in the written form. That there can be writing along with other registers of publishing, other modes of publishing.

And then, I think the question of writing in response to 'what do you/we need to be ready for?', well, one thing certainly is not to think that reading-writing prepares you for too much (chuckles). The reason why knowing what's in the books is not enough and not to think that can solve us, help us – is because what we need to know and what we need to be ready for and able to do is hold ourselves and each other open to *really* seeing the hurt, the harm, the damage and also really *seeing* the potential that collectively we have to heal. I mean it's not going to be without scars, there's scarification. It's not going to be without scars but to heal together in a way that's never complete, never once and for all, is always going to have to keep happening! It's an onward, onward journey. So, it's that, but that then involves a capacity to be in the space together with our differences.

TLM: Can the spaces – and by space I mean the programmes, talks, events, the anthologies, etcetera – can all of those things that I think do a very valiant, intellectual work of unarchiving, which I think we are revealing is at the very least concurrent with a healing work – can these spaces actually or usefully be co-opted into legitimate healing spaces?

GL: Well, that would be part of the work. It's not like 'if we paint it blue, does that make it ok?' It's part of the work of continually re-forming the spaces and working out what shape the space needs to be in order to contribute to the process of healing. Because it is a process, it's an unending process of keep going on, we have to see that we have to attend on all fronts. If it becomes an anthology, for example, and that's a space, and people come into it as people called readers and maybe become reading groups to think about it or take it into another forum, all of that is about continually re-working the words into another iteration; either because the reading group says, 'This is what I got from it', or 'I found that a bit limiting but it helped me to understand something'. The healing comes when something called understanding isn't just an intellectualised abstractedness but is a way, a mode of practicing self in connectivity, in connection with others, that says, 'And I can stay open to and stay with as long as necessary the feelings evoked in me or in others in the room'. We have to be able to stay with the feelings and not run too fast away from them.

This particularly comes up in relation to abolition work; abolition is such a vast and deep concept. So often we can move into a kind of intellectualisation which is a bit like getting up at a rally and coming out with a slogan and not staying with 'what the fuck! I don't know what to do with this because, yes, I don't think people should be in prison, but that bastard that did that to me and my sister, my mum, my grandmum, I wanna kill them!'. And staying with it. And we can read and read and read but we have to stay with 'what are the implications of that?' How is that an emotional expression of a carceral logic that could change or not. And when we face the realities… just on the TV the other day there was something I didn't know about until recently but in January of this year, three Black women were walking home in Kilburn where I grew up, you know, leaving a club and just got savagely beaten by a group of white men and the police covered it up and to this day nothing happened.[24] It's come back in the news. The harms of that, that reality about the ways in which a body called 'Black woman' can be totally abused because she is Black and not a woman, if you see what I mean, in the classic sense of [Black] women don't get to be women – What do we do with that? That's what I mean about the spaces. So then, the logic of that is: how do we give ourselves and each other permission, as well as capacity but the first step has to be permission, to stop and stay with that pain, those differences between us because it's going to evoke all sorts of differences of opinion and stay with it, in order not to revert to some simple so-called representational project or an anthology or a slogan.

TLM: Or an artwork.

GL: Yeah, whatever. As important as all those things will be in the assemblage but in the *moment* because you asked me to come at this through a therapeutic lens; how do we stay with it? How *do we* stay with it? And after all, isn't that what Toni Morrison – because we called her up there – was trying to address in *Beloved*?[25] How do we stay with it? In order to take our dead with us and live with that, to take the scars on the back, to know they are a tree and are not a tree and move forward into something, the outcome of which we don't know. It has to remain open, it *has* to remain open. That's what I think.

TLM: Yeah, Ok. [Both laugh]

GL: If we were to have a reconvening of this I might have another view.

TLM: What I feel like we need, generally and really is exactly that; practice with staying with it. I even think that the moment that you have to make an advert of any sort to gather people together, I just think none of this can actually legitimately be connected to our writing, to our artwork, as that writing and that artwork is circulated in a professional sense. The minute that you have to finish that piece of writing toward a deadline or you have to close that event toward the end of the advertised end of the session… I think this can only happen, for me (and maybe this is just for me), this can only happen at that level of who I can touch, who I can get my hands on without an advert. That's the scale.

GL: Yes, I get that. But perhaps that's to accord to the object – the artwork, the anthology, the film, the poem, whatever it is – too much because what it can do is stimulate something that then lives its life in this other space and then it's done some work, it's done some of its work because it's stimulated a question, a set of conversations, a feeling that then goes somewhere else and convenes for a moment. And we do the work. That's why it's about the assemblage of objects too.

TLM: Ok, so we're not cancelling the act of writing just yet?

GL: No! We're not cancelling any of those things out. We're saying they're important objects but they're not everything and we need to think of them as items in an ongoing iterative process.

TLM: Got it!

NOTES

1 Valerie Amos, Gail Lewis, Amina Mama and Pratibha Parmar (eds), *Feminist Review*, Volume 1, Issue 17: *Many Voices, One Chant: Black Feminist Perspectives*, Autumn 1984.

2 Carmen, Gail, Shaila and Pratibha, 'Becoming Visible: Black Lesbian Discussions', in *Feminist Review*, Volume 1, Issue 17: *Many Voices, One Chant: Black Feminist Perspectives*, Autumn 1984, 55.

3 Ibid. 61.

4 Ibid. 62.

5 Ibid. 57–8.

6 Ibid. 64–5.

7 Ibid. 60.

8 Ibid. 61.

9 Ibid. 56.

10 Gail Lewis, 'Birthing Racial Difference: conversations with my mother and others', *Studies in the Maternal* Vol. 1(1), 2009, 1–21.

11 Gail Lewis in Brenna Bhandar and Rafeef Ziadah (eds), *Revolutionary Feminisms: Conversations on Collective Action and Radical Thought*, London and New York: Verso, 2020, 57.

12 Ibid. 59.

13 Foluke Taylor and Gail Lewis, 'Confer: Black Feminisms in the consulting room' [Available online at: https://www.youtube.com/watch?v=qjJvNqk4tME, accessed 31 March 2021]

14 Gail Lewis and Clare Hemmings, "Where might we go if we dare': moving beyond the 'thick, suffocating fog of whiteness' in feminism', *Feminist Theory*, Vol. 20(4), 2019, 405–421.

15 Stella Dazdie interviewed June 2011 for Sisterhood and After: The Women's Liberation Oral History Project, available at the British Library.

16 Boston Women's Health Book Collective, Angela Phillips and Jill Rakusen (eds) *Our Bodies, Ourselves*, Harmondsworth: Penguin and Allen Lane, 1978.

17 Lewis discusses the category of 'political blackness' and coalition work in the UK in the 1980s at length in her interview with Clare Hemmings, "Where might we go if we dare': moving beyond the 'thick, suffocating fog of whiteness' in feminism', 409.

18 Beverley Bryan, Stella Dadzie and Suzanne Scafe, *The Heart of the Race: Black Women's Lives in Britain*, London: Virago Press, 1985.

19 Amrit Wilson, *Finding a Voice: Asian Women in Britain*, London: Virago Press, 1978.

20 Abasindi Cooperative, *Catching Hell and Doing Well: Black women in the UK*, London: Trentham Books, 2015.

21 S. Grewal, Jackie Kay, Liliane Landor, Gail Lewis, and Pratibha Parmar (eds), *Charting the Journey: writings by Black and Third world Women*, London: Sheba Feminist Press, 1988.

22 Agnes Quashie, 'Talking Personal; talking political: Interviews with Gail Lewis, Leba Wilson and Olive Gallimore about the Brixton Black Women's Group', *Trouble and Strife: A radical feminist magazine*, Issue 19, 1983, 44–52.

23 Hazel V. Carby, *Reconstructing Womanhood: The Emergence of the Afro-American Woman Novelist*, New York: Oxford University Press, 1987.

24 Richard Watson, 'Racist attack investigation reopened by Met Police', 21 October 2020. Available at https://www.bbc.com/news/uk-54622169 [Accessed 8 November 2020]

25 Toni Morrison, *Beloved*, New York: Alfred A. Knopf Inc., 1987.

Part 2

MATERIALS AND MAKING

5 The Sexual Revolt in Spain in the 1970s Through Its Publications: Ideas, Fears and Aesthetics

ALBERTO BERZOSA AND GRACIA TRUJILLO

In the early 1970s, opposition to the Franco regime in Spain underwent a process of radicalization that revealed, among other things, the increasing levels of conflict in factories and the virulence and everyday actions of the student commandos acting inside and outside university campuses in the main cities. Anti-Franco radicalization at this time was not only evident in terms of intensity, but also in the growing number of causes for political organization. In this regard, the emergence of social movements with issues related to gender and sexuality placed at the centre of their protests, as was the case with the incipient Homosexual Liberation Movement, is particularly notable. Within the ecosystem of political resistance in the 1970s, this movement acted alongside others such as the neighbourhood and feminist movements, maintaining some points in common, such as the establishment of alliances with the main political actors (workers and students), and developing their own vindication strategies. This led them, among other things, to oppose laws such as the *Law on Dangerousness and Social Rehabilitation* (*Ley de Peligrosidad y Rehabilitación Social*, LPRS), and hetero-patriarchal traditions inherent to the nationalist/Catholic morality staunchly defended by the Franco regime. The LPRS was a piece of legislation used by Francoist lawmakers to criminalize, persecute and put homosexuals (among other social groups, like prostitutes and homeless people) into psychiatric hospitals and jails. The aim was to 'cure' and rehabilitate, that is, to correct homosexual desires and sexual practices, which were considered an illness.

The first attempts by the movement to organize social protests in Spain were framed in the terms of gay liberation as it was understood in France, Great Britain and North America. The transition from dictatorship to democracy was a period of social and political euphoria spurred by the possibility of achieving lost freedoms and rights under Franco's fascist regime (1939–1975). It offered new opportunities for social mobilization, which, in the case of sexual and gender dissidents, resulted in the creation of the so-called Homosexual Liberation Fronts. The term 'fronts' echoed Marxist ideas on collective organization. These groups were organized not only in the main cities of the country, Madrid and Barcelona, but also in Bilbao, Valencia and Seville.[1] The gay and lesbian liberation movement had an essentially radical ideology that called for combative mass mobilization. It described itself as a revolutionary force, embedding a discourse on sexual politics in larger narratives about social change.

Another characteristic of the anti-Franco political resistance, which emerged in the early 1970s and would remain throughout that decade, was an independent activist media. An important activist documentary of the time entitled *El cuarto poder* (*The Fourth Estate*), directed by Helena Lumbreras and Lorenzo Soler in 1970, insisted precisely on that point as one of the main efforts that organized citizenship should undertake, not only to combat manipulation and the lack of news diverging from the official discourse, but also to build mechanisms for expression and organization of the interests of social movements. This political commitment had a clear aesthetic implication, since the means of production of the magazines were precarious and the conditions of exception and illegality required urgent and non-systematic forms of work, that created the circumstances in which these kinds of publications were produced. Self-publishing meant working with cheap materials, without a clear and coherent structure from one issue of the magazine to the next, and without an aesthetic unity.[2] In return, the authors enjoyed a great deal of creative freedom that allowed them to articulate complex imaginaries with widely varied references, mixing classical elements with current ones from popular culture, which they decoded and appropriated. They also combined photography and illustration in an original and dynamic way. In short, these publications were a unique and special product, which had a bomb inside, given its forceful political content: an ensemble of information, provocation, criticism and continuous calls for political activation. Often they were not regular magazines, but zines with a short shelf-life. The finish was unimportant. Craft-like, with a limited number of copies produced on very rudimentary equipment, these magazines were both manageable to produce and easily distributed.

The fundamental need for communication was partly fulfilled by organizations that mobilized in favour of sexual liberation throughout the period of underground activity and continued with greater stability during democratic times. In the following pages, we shall review some of the most noteworthy publications of the movement in terms of their historic, political, and aesthetic relevance, specifically those produced by the Movimiento Español de Liberación Homosexual (MELH), the Coordinadora de Col·lectius d'Alliberament Gai (CCAG), Euskal Herriko Gay Askapen Mugimendua (EHGAM), and the Grupo de Lluita per L'Alliberament de la Lesbiana (GLAL) of the Barcelona Feminist Platform.

PIONEERS AND RADICALS

At a time when gay liberation in Spain existed merely as an echo from abroad and the official legislation toughened its repressive nature with the approval of the already mentioned LPRS (1970), the MELH was created. This pioneering group came into being in 1971, founded by a group consisting mainly of moderate lawyers and inspired by the gay-friendly French collective Arcadie. Only a few months after its foundation, the collective started editing and distributing the newsletter *Aghois* (*Agrupación Homófila para la Integración Social* [Homophile Association for Social Integration]), the first ever publication aimed at a gay audience produced in the Spanish State. This began as clandestine material and had no significant network of readers or editors to sustain it. As a result, the first editorial team – composed of Armand de Fluvià, Francesc Francino, Antonio de la S., Xavier-Daniel, and Biel Moll – sought help from Arcadie's founder André Baudry for legal, logistical, and editorial support. Baudry provided, among other things, a list of subscribers to the *Arcadie* magazine in Spain, a mailbox in France, and also allowed them to establish themselves as a supplement of the magazine for a Spanish audience. This allowed *Aghois* to remain active for two years, with a total of eighteen issues published.[3]

The first issue appeared in January 1972 and continued monthly throughout that year. From January 1973, it became increasingly irregular and the issues ceased after January 1974. The bulletin was sent from France to a number of subscribers until the Spanish Minister of the Interior, López Rodó, managed to get his French counterpart to suspend publication and shipment to Spain. From the outset, *Aghois* offered interested readers a variety of homosexuality-related news and editorial features. It included discussions on history, medicine, religion, politics, books, poetry, film, counter-chronicles of current events related to sexuality, such as congresses and commentaries in generalist Spanish newspapers such as *ABC* or *La Vanguardia*, and advice regarding how to talk about homosexuality within the family. All of these factors turned this magazine into one of the first mechanisms to articulate a conscious, mainly male, gay culture, which would develop further later in the 1970s. In ideological terms, the publication evolved along the same lines as the MELH itself, from more moderate reformist positions – evident in the 'homophile mottos' collected in Issue 6, written in a naïve tone and a nearly obsolete language even at the time (homophile/heterophile) – to more radical postures incorporating elements of more leftist French associations, such as the Front Homosexuel D'action Revolutionnaire (FHAR) and Argentina's Homosexual Liberation Front.[4] The publication adapted its discourse to the general tone of anti-Franco militancy thanks to the Marxist ideas brought forth especially by the militant Amanda Klein beginning with Issue 13.[5]

Aesthetically, the publication was characterized by what we could describe as underground aesthetics. It featured a sober presentation of materials and binding, consisting of pages stapled together in one corner, with no illustrations inside and irregular ink

Aghois magazine, No. 6,
Movimiento Español de
Liberación Homosexual,
June 1972. (Centro
de Documentación
Armand de Fluvià)

blotches and stains caused by the mimeograph reproduction. The exception to this thriftiness came in June 1972, when Issue 6 included photographs on the cover for the first time. These images of 1970's first Gay Pride Day parade in New York were used for documentary purposes, but they also defined the objectives sought by the movement in Spain: the occupation of public spaces by gays and lesbians, which in 1972 seemed utopian. In fact the cover was a reproduction of a page from the American magazine *QQ*. The composition of the images is very simple: a dozen photographs juxtaposed side by side making different levels until the surface of the page is covered. There is no narrative intention, nor of sketching a dialogue between the images through opposition. They all provide the same information: you can go out on the street to celebrate diversity. Their effect among Spanish readers in 1972 must have been shocking since these were likely the first images they saw of gays, lesbians and trans people demonstrating in freedom.

In Issue 12, published in December the same year, there is another illustrated cover. In this case, the image is a reproduction of the movement's first poster in the Spanish context. Created by Lluis Cobas, the graphic became a recurring icon in certain circles of militancy, as is evident in the 1977 documentary *Abajo la Ley de Peligrosidad!* (*Down with the Danger Law!*). In the film, director José Romero Ahumada used the image to lay out the movement's history from its inception to its first demonstration, which took place that year in Barcelona.[6] The design of the poster is elegant and minimalist. A frame with firm but wavy forms contains the ambiguous face of a young person with long curly hair looking to one side. The drawing does not clarify the gender of the individual in a deliberate way and the symbols that flank the head allude to a tension between the masculine and the feminine that is not resolved. Very few elements are needed to refer in this way to a certain sexual indeterminacy which, as we have pointed out, became an early icon of the movement. Everything about *Aghois* is ground-breaking in the context we are looking at, but one key reason it was exceptional is that it was the only graphic material developed for public distribution before Franco's death in 1975. In the following years, the situation would change: militant collectives multiplied and, with them, publications and graphic materials.

The proliferation of publications after 1975 did not lead to a complete abandonment of underground aesthetics, although there was undoubtedly a larger variety of content and a general improvement in terms of design. There were as many newsletters published as there were collectives. If we refer here only to publications by mixed collectives, we can highlight *Gay Hotsa* by Euskal Herriko Gay Askapen Mugimendua (EHGAM), the most important political collective in the Basque Country; the Madrid-based *La ladilla loca* by the Castilla Homosexual Liberation Front (FLHOC); *Debat Gai* by the Barcelona-based

Aghois magazine, No. 12, Movimiento Español de Liberación Homosexual, December 1972. (Centro de Documentación Armand de Fluvià)

Front d'Alliberament Gai de Catalunya (FAGC), or *La pluma* by the Coordinadora de Col·lectius d'Alliberament Gais (CCAG), also from Catalonia. The latter deserves greater attention given the radical nature of its political positions and aesthetic originality.

LA PLUMA OR BEING CAMP IN THE 1970S

The CCAG was established in 1978, following a split in the FAGC, which was founded two years earlier and was the first and largest collective after Franco's death. The FAGC started as a radical, Marxist group. In its *Manifest* (1977), they called for the end of social classes and the invention of new social relations,[7] positioning themselves somewhere between the mottos of workers' parties and mass organization of the time and Michel Foucault, who called for friendship as a way of life.[8] Nonetheless, it soon focused its energies on developing militancy through lawyers' offices and legal reforms, trying to attain its fundamental objective of revoking the LPRS and legalizing the collective. This 'state focus' did not convince its most radical members, who ended up leaving and founding the CCAG. This was not the only issue underlying the split. For these activists, political militancy also had a playful and an aesthetic component, which conflicted with orthodox formulas or short-term political ends. Luis Escribano, a militant of the FAGC and the CCAG, explained that the differences within the FAGC were that 'some people wanted to be serious and others not, some wanted *locas* to be inside and others, outside.'[9] These statements reveal a more profound disagreement, which opposed political positions such as integration versus difference and normalization versus the defence of identity freedom, which also led to a quarrel regarding the role of transvestites in the movement. Some FAGC elites were opposed to their presence at the front of demonstrations because they considered them contrary to their investment in normalization. In contrast, the more radical militants positioned transvestites as revolutionary subjects. These ideas were gathered in CCAG's Manifesto (1978) upon its creation, and they defined the editorial line of its magazine, *La pluma*, of which six issues – 0 to 5 – were published from 1978 to 1980.

La pluma stood out among the media outlets of the time because of its radical content and its decisive defence of a set of basic principles, which it upheld in all of its issues. A review of the magazine's editorials reveals that among its main objectives was to foster autonomy for homosexuals, to call for collabouration with other groups of socially marginalized people, to promote a firm opposition to the capitalist system, male chauvinism and authoritarianism, to reject the idea of normality and the processes of normalization offered by the system, such as the commercial ghetto, and to stand against the efforts to mask the repression of gays and lesbians during the first years of the transition through, for example, the Constitution or the repeal of the LPRS. In ideological terms, *La pluma* called for autonomy and did not conform to any clear political orthodoxy. In general terms, two consistent struggles can be recognized: a libertarian tendency, even though they did not hesitate to criticize anarcho-syndicalism when it exhibited hints of authoritarianism,[10] and an interest in breaking away from consensus and confronting political reformism.[11]

La pluma had an audacious and courageous attitude, giving space to the most controversial topics and voices within the Spanish sexual liberation movement of the time. Its articles revolved around varied topics, from the situation of homosexuality in the neighbourhoods to its links with the army or the new forms of repression under democracy.[12] There was also cultural news, book reviews, short stories, and poems. Dossiers were central to *La Pluma* and were included as pull-outs in each issue. They included special reports on topics of historic interest, such as 'History and meaning of the International Homosexual Liberation Day,' published in Issue 1; political wagers that distinguished them from other collectives, such as the double dossier dedicated to 'Transvestites and Transsexuals' in Issue 2 and 3; and polemics on topical issues such as 'Homosexuality and Teaching' in Issue 4, which was evidently influenced by French theories of perverted pedagogy articulated by René Schérer, or 'Ghetto Trash' in Issue 5. The predominant limitation of the publication in its role as the voice of the sexopolitical vanguard was the absence of articles exclusively devoted to lesbian topics. Lesbians were often cited together with gays and transvestites as allies in the struggle for sexual liberation, but, differently from the latter, lesbians were not valued in such an evident manner, even though they were also in a situation of marginalization, defencelessness, and social invisibility. The abolition of the LPRS did not have the same impact on gays and lesbians. The latter experienced it as a political victory rather than as something that transformed their lives at the personal level at the time.[13]

Graphically, *La pluma* was characterized by a free and imaginative design, close to the lo-fi aesthetic of fanzines. Each issue experimented with chromatic variations and different fonts and included a large number of illustrations, photographs and posters in the central pages as well as an illustrated back cover for each issue, some of them veritable exercises in political satire. Its pages were full of references to Aubrey Beardsley's modernism and the associated resonances of Oscar Wilde's homoerotic universe, mixed with more topical features and adverts promoting subscription. All of this, together with a fresh and aggressive language resulting from a conscious appropriation of

La Pluma magazine (back cover), No. 4, April–May 1979. (Colección José Romero Ahumada)

Above left: *La Pluma* magazine, No. 3, October 1978. (Colección José Romero Ahumada)

Above right: *La Pluma* magazine, No. 5, 1979. (Colección José Romero Ahumada)

offensive terms, marshalled a balanced and attractive style for those familiar with the moment's counterculture. In addition, there were references to the imaginaries of other social movements, such as on the cover of Issue 5, which alluded to the slogans of anti-nuclear organizations, exchanging the 'Nuclear? No thanks' for 'Faggot? Yes, thanks.'

The magazine's use of sexually ambiguous imagery is particularly noteworthy. Examples included the illustrations that accompanied the dossier on transsexuality, in which an aesthetic that lies between punk and glam came to the fore, or the parodies of well-known icons such as Uncle Sam who now pointed his finger to involve the reader in the struggle for sexual liberation, dressed as a man with a big moustache who also wears a lady's hat. The most striking instance was the illustration on the back cover of issue 3. The humorous cartoon caricatures the scene of the annunciation of the Angel Gabriel to the Virgin Mary. The angel appears carrying a band in which we can read 'Constitución,' to link its message with the Spanish Constitution approved in 1978 in the midst of the democratic Transition. Around the figure are a series of cherubs wearing bands sporting the initials of the political parties of the time. In front of them, Virgin Mary is kneeling, portrayed as the saint of fags; she wears a luxuriant beard and has visible hair on her arms. Mary is a transvestite dressed in a cape with the symbol of the inverted triangle and the letter lambda, symbols of international and Hispanic sexual liberation. Behind the Virgin there is a pile of books with the initials of the parties, representing the 'commandments' which are their political doctrines. The cross-dressing Virgin seems impressed and submissive before the angel Gabriel who, according to the lower legend of the image, asks the representative of the fags of the Transition to be good and to join the social and democratic normality of the new times. The yielding Virgin answers in the affirmative. The illustration offers a critical view of the passive attitude of many gays, lesbians and trans people during the Transition who assumed without resistance any proposal of integration into society, and the consequent loss of their queerness. The pink ink, the religious context, the political criticism and the reference to transvestism and fluid identities contribute to the force of this drawing, which emblematises the radical attitude of *La Pluma* and the CCAG.

LESBIAN IMAGINARIES

In the active years of the transition to democracy, libertarian ideology was the protest frame in the Fronts of Homosexual Liberation, where lesbians and gay men mobilized together. As Trujillo has previously explained in an article dedicated to butch representation in Spain, such ideologies also influenced:

> the configuration of lesbian identity with its critiques of social labelling and the existence of homosexual identity (understood as difference). Lesbian political groups, however, defended the need to name themselves as such although images of masculine lesbians, or lesbians with *pluma*, were not elaborated or used by these groups. The context of control, repression and social and political hostility in general was too tough to be able to expose themselves like that.[14]

The function ascribed to mobilization in Spain was revolutionary: the key ideas that emerged at that

Top: 'Nuestra lucha es tu lucha' ('Our Fight is Your Fight') in *La Pluma*, No. 2, July–August, 1978. (Colección José Romero Ahumada)
Above: *La Pluma* magazine (back cover), No. 3, October 1978. (Colección José Romero Ahumada)

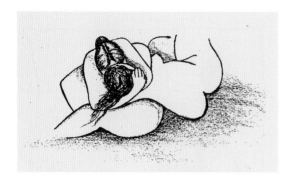

Two women in
La ladilla loca, Frente de
Liberación Homosexual
de Castilla (FLHOC),
1980. (Fundación
Salvador Seguí)

time called for a classless society, the abolition of the family and the elimination of all those structures that maintain and feed heterosexism and *machismo*. Lesbian autonomous groups were created within the movement as early as 1977, sharing with their gay colleagues the fight against a series of urgent social and legal discriminations based on a different sexual option. The first Pride march was organized in Barcelona in 1977, when lesbian and gay groups had not yet been legalized.[15] The emerging discourses of lesbian political collectives in these years can be found in internal organisational documents (gathered, for example, in dossiers, meeting minutes, records of seminars, collective communiqués and some activists' writings), as well as in publications such as *Gay Hotsa* by EGHAM that included political writings, illustrations and poems by ESAM (Emakumearen Sexual Askatasunerako Mugimendua), the lesbian political group that was part of the Basque Front. Another example are materials published in Madrid by FLHOC's Women's Group in the collective publications *La ladilla loca* (1980) and *Aquí el FLHOC* (1980). The constant presence of sections dedicated to lesbians in the press of the Fronts of Homosexual Liberation, whilst minor in comparison with their gay counterparts, are the result of the political persuasion that lesbian activists carried

*Mujer, libera tu deseo
lésbico* (Woman, Free
Your Lesbian Desire),
Rampova, 1982.
(Colección Santiago
Gregori)

out to convince their comrades of the importance of giving space and visibility to lesbian issues, representations and discourses. This was not only an issue of (political) justice but more importantly of gaining a wider social impact for the gay and lesbian liberation movement. In some of these publications, like *La ladilla loca*, not very sophisticated (and not very sexual) images that had some significance for lesbian imaginaries in those years were included. There is quite a contrast if we compare them with the illustrations created just a few years later by Rampova.[16] Her drawings show a significant leap in political terms thanks to the combination of very direct lesbian slogans with the re-appropriation of mass culture icons such as Patti Smith or Marlene Dietrich. In Rampova's work, the insinuations, veiled portraits and floral allusions are definitively left behind.

In those early days of lesbian political organizations, however, the most important publications were created far from the capital. Groups such as the Bilbao-based ESAM independently published an anthology of political texts and topics of interest for the collective, *Dossier on lesbianism* (1979), as did the Col.lectiu de Lesbianes de Valencia, part of MAG-PV (Moviment per L'Alliberament Gai al Pais Valencià). These publications circulated in activist networks, serving to share texts by each organization for the purposes of collective debate. As with *Aghois*, the materials and the bindings of these publications were simple, consisting of sheets stapled on one corner, with very few or no illustrations, and imperfections resulting from print processes. In the *Dossier* published by Col.lectiu de Lesbianes de

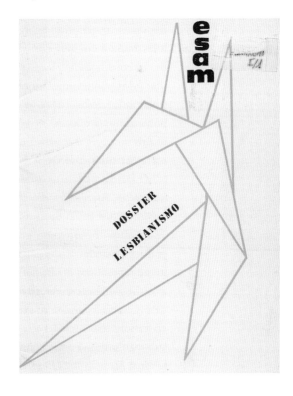

Dossier sobre el lesbianismo, Emakumearen Sexual Askatasunerako Mugimendua (ESAM), 1979. (Emakumeen Dokumentazio Zentroa)

Valencia, the group of activists collected texts such as 'Contradictions between gay militancy and family life', which they wrote for the First National Conference of Lesbians in Madrid (1980). In this text they expressed concerns with the fact that their families did not know they were lesbians, something that, as they explained, changed as a result of writing and discussing the document between themselves. Other texts gathered in the publication included 'Women's alienations', 'The use of the body' and 'Possessiveness and jealousy'. The *Dossier* contained only a couple of blurry photographs, one drawing, and two poster reproductions.

Another significant collective working at the time was the Grup de Lluita per L'Alliberament de la Lesbiana (G.L.A.L.) of the Coordinadora Feminista de Barcelona (Barcelona Feminist Platform), formed in February 1979. This group functioned as a nexus in the Barcelona feminist and lesbian political and cultural sphere, in which there were already active projects like the publishing house and bar, La

Papers Gais,
No. 0, Moviment
d'Alliberament Gai del
Païs Valencià, 1980.
(Archivo Casa de la
Dona, Valencia)

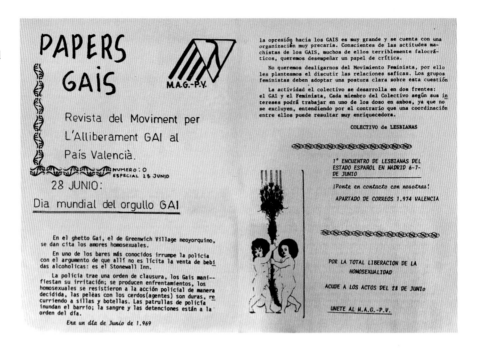

Sal. This collective, the G.L.A.L, published a newsletter a year later, which had a correspondence section allowing readers to communicate with the editors. This procedure was common not only during those years, but up to the second half of the 1990s, until the internet became more commonly used. Even then, the issue of anonymity meant that print publications continued to use mailboxes in the late 1990s and early 2000s (such as the lesbian fanzine *Bollus Vivendi* [1999–2001]). The transition from print publications produced by political groups to digital platforms lies outside the scope of this essay yet it is worth noting that the shift impacted the diversity of discourses, representations, and visibility.

G.L.A.L's newsletter took its title from the name of the collective that produced it: *Boletín informative del GLAL*. Between 1980 and 1982, the group managed to publish six issues, at first on a monthly basis, with the final issue appearing after a one year hiatus. The attention-grabbing logo of the political group was well known in the politicized circles of the gay and lesbian liberation movement since it was commonly found reproduced in circulation printed on stickers during those years. The simple but effective design features a central circle with a flower with open petals inside and is clearly a sexual allusion to the vagina. The representation follows a tradition in western art history that includes the works of the US artist Georgia O'Keeffe, and in Spain, although utilising a more abstract language, the pop works by the Spanish artist Mari Chordá made in the 1960s such as *The Great Vagina* (1966). Around the logo's flower

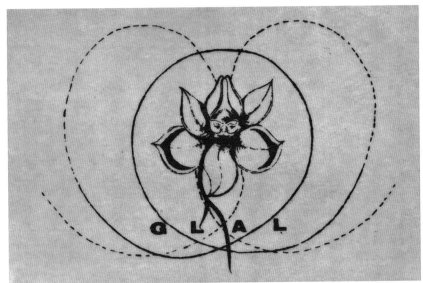

G.L.A.L. sticker, *c.* 1978.
(Colección José Romero
Ahumada)

La gran vagina (*The Great Vagina*), Mari Chordà,
1966. (Museo Nacional
Centro de Arte Reina Sofía)

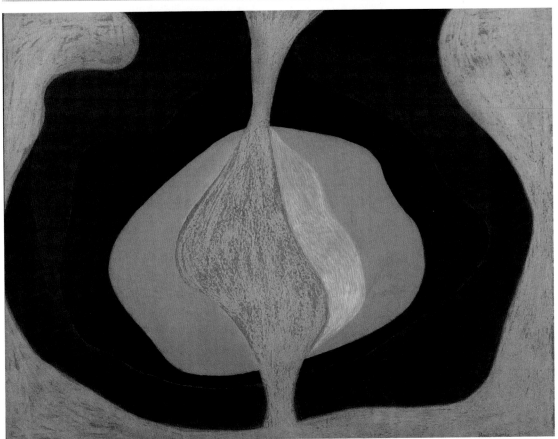

BOLETIN INFORMATIVO DEL G.L.A.L.(GRUP DE LLUITA PER L'ALLIBERAMENT DE LA LESBIANA) DE LA CORDINADORA FEMINISTA DE BARCELONA, apartat 'e correus 2493

editorial

ompañeras: Después de un es-
rado y merecido descanso es
ival aqui estamos de nuevo,
n la brecha, abriendo un nue
o curso de actividades femi-
istas/gai, que para nosotras
esbianas feministas, son la
ase de nuestra lucha diaria;
igualdad de derechos para el
mbre y la mujer y el reco-
cimiento del lesbianismo
omo una variante de la sexua
dad de la mujer.

s complace recordaros que
guen progresando los prepa-
tivos para la 2a. Conferen-
a estatal de lesbianas a
elebrarse en Valencia y la
. Conferencia internacional
lesbianas, que se celebra-
en Amsterdam y que falta
cidir la fecha. Los detalles
concretos de estos en-
entros se facilitarán a tra-
s del boletin a medida que
s vayamos recibiendo.

problematica de la mujer
sbiana, sin embargo, no es
go que atañe solamente a la
sbiana. Es un problema social
que como tal atañe a toda
sociedad. El sentimiento
mosexual es universal; no
a desviación patológica co-
se ha pretendido hacernos
eer. Sólo unos intereses
ncretos, los de nuestro
stema Patriarcal, han ocul-
do y distorsionado esta
alidad. No es casualidad

seguido, salvo raras excep-
ciones, una trayectoria para
lela.

La humanidad se ha debatido,
atraves de los siglos, entre la problematica de la supervivencia de la especie en
la conquista de su medio ambiente, y la evolución de la
mente hacia conductas más hu-
manas. Desafortunadamente se
ha producido un desequilibrio
al inclinarse más hacia los
primeros objetivos.

El método adoptado por el
sistema Patriarcal para ase-
gurar la supervivencia de la
especie es la heterosexualidad
forzada. Los derechos del indi
viduo quedaron sacrificados en
beneficio de la especie. La
matanza de seres humanos en
las guerras, provocadas por
el ansia ciega de poder, se
ha podido mantener a costa
de leyes opresoras y explota
doras de la mujer que se ha
utilizado como fuerza repro-
ductora. La represión de la

Sin embargo, hoy podemos con-
templar como, paradojicamen-
te, esta defensa irracional
de la especie se ha converti-
do en un verdadero peligro
para nuestra supervivencia.
Vivimos en ciudades superpobladas. Inmersos en el
miedo casi terror, de la
extinción de nuestros recur-
sos naturales; expuestos a
la contaminación del medio
ambiente (derrames radioac-
tivos, gases, deshechos indus
triales, etc.), con la amena
za de una guerra nuclear y
aun así, la hipocresía de
una "moral" represiva sigue
en vigor; se condenada toda
manifestación humana que no
conforme con las normas del
Sistema que nos está destru-
yendo como individuos y como
especie, el que ha creado
las ciudades superpobladas,
contaminadas, claustrofóbicas
llenas de gentes marginadas
que son una denuncia constante
de la incongruencia de un sistema opresor que, a costa de

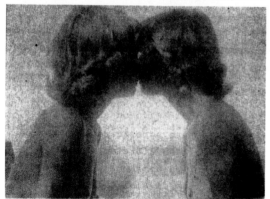

G.L.A.L. magazine (and detail), No. 1, Grup en Lluita per l'Alliberament de la Lesbiana, September–October, 1980. (Biblioteca Nacional de España)

are oval shapes rendered in a finer stroke that seems to dissipate towards the frame and might refer to legs parting. The acronym of the group underlines the design. The allusion to lesbian bodies and desires appears obvious today. In the 1970s and early 1980s, when non-heterosexual people were more than accustomed to read between lines and to look for (mostly veiled) references to homosexuality, it was surely understood with similar clarity.

In the first issue of the 'news bulletin', GLAL established an aesthetics and content that was reproduced throughout following issues. The September–October 1980 issue opens with an editorial addressed to the *compañeras*, where the collective states that their aims as lesbian feminists are 'equal rights for men and women and the recognition of lesbianism as a variant of women's sexuality.' They later explain that 'the lesbian problem' is not something that affects only lesbians, but society as a whole. The repression of homosexuality and the denial of women's rights, they argue, have similar origins and follow parallel trajectories. The bulletin, which was printed in colour (in purple, another wink to the shared subcultural language of femi-nism) on larger pages than usual and employing a format more similar to a formal publication than a simple compilation of texts like those discussed above, includes a couple of photographs of two women, one on the cover and the other illustrating a text on 'Self-repression: a real problem of lesbian women'. In both cases, the figures appear in profile, with only their faces visible. It is probable that these photographs came from a foreign publication, a common feature (together with, in general, a lack of explicit sexual content) of the vast majority of lesbian print publica-tions of the time and throughout the 1980s. It was not until the early 1990s that more sexually explicit illustrations, photographs, and graphic materials created by Spanish lesbian queer activists began circulating in Spain, rather than being imported from other contexts. It is this that differentiates lesbian feminism of the 1970s and 1980s from succeeding lesbian queer representations.[17] As well as the photographs, the central

pages of the first issue of GLAL's newsletter featured a summary of the meeting held by COFLHEE (the Platform of Sexual Liberation Fronts, that coordinated political actions at the national level) in Euskadi in July 1980. This text was accompanied by a photograph of GLAL's activists standing behind a banner at a demonstration and holding posters with slogans such as 'Lesbianes. Volem ser', ('Lesbians: [we] want to be') a key political and impassioned declaration reflecting the oppressive context experienced in those years and the struggle to change it.

Issues 3 and 4 of the bulletin retain the combination of, on the one hand, photographs taken from other publications to illustrate political and informative contents, and, on the other, more erotic images. The latter hardly ever show explicitly sexual gestures and scenes, in contrast with most of the mixed press in which there were many sexualized images of gay men, sometimes with a humorous tone too.

Issue 3, from January and February of 1981, is dedicated to the International Lesbian Conference held in 1980 in Amsterdam. The cover of the issue reflects the DIY aesthetics that characterise the publications discussed throughout this essay. The logo of the conference occupies the centre of the design. Around it, illustrations and photographs are organised in a simple collage that shows several aspects of the Dutch city, such as

Above left: *G.L.A.L.* magazine, No. 3, Grup en Lluita per l'Alliberament de la Lesbiana, Jan–Feb, 1981. (Biblioteca Nacional de España)

Above right: *G.L.A.L.* magazine, No. 4, Grup en Lluita per l'Alliberament de la Lesbiana, Mar–Apr, 1981. (Biblioteca Nacional de España.)

clogs and a windmill. The arrangement also includes a drawing of a woman playing saxo-phone, which alludes to the more ludic part of the conference. Above the composition are the words 'Amsterdam with love,' a naïve formulation that reflects the significance of talking about desire and love in those complicated years of repression, silences and closets, but also gatherings and other forms of (political and daily) resistance. Within the issue, comments address the topics of being together, sharing, taking care and support-ing each other. In fact, in the pages of the bulletin there are plenty of images of women hugging in an affectionate way.

The cover of issue 4 also addresses the notions of care and fellowship, mixing three different references: two intertwined hearts, to illustrate the second anniversary of the Collective; three figures of a model or female dancer who poses with sinuous positions and gestures and a golden and very tight dress; and lastly, a naive drawing, again, of three embracing women who scream *¡Jo, qué bien lo pasamos!* (Wow, how much fun we had!). Once again, this early lesbian imaginary underlines the idea of feminist fel-lowship and solidarity as tools that allow the expression of affective (and, sometimes, sexual) bonds from which to think political strategies.

FINAL OBSERVATIONS

In the 1970s and early 1980s, the Spanish streets were filled with written words and images that overlapped, changed, were pasted up then torn off or written over. It was one of the common ways for the ideas and imaginaries of the anti-Franco resistance to circulate quickly. For those who participated in the struggles of sexual and gender dis-sidence in this period, it was also a way to occupy public spaces and generate a common identity, the sense of a shared fight. Whether clandestinely under Franco, or more openly in the, no less repressive, transition period, lesbians and gays administered their own press and through it created an iconography that functioned as an element of political action. The publications coordinated mobilizations and fuelled debates. It is noteworthy how, from the various activist sensibilities, the groups sought out certain aesthetics to express specific political positions, as can be seen through the fanzine aesthetic and the ambiguous representations of gender of *La Pluma* or the use of colour in G.L.A.L.'s bulletin. These magazines and bulletins exist today in personal collections and independent or institu-tional archives and are evidence of the passage of pioneers of the Homosexual Liberation Movement through the Spanish streets. They are part of material culture that, through recuperation and scholarship, not only registers the central discourse and issues of the time, but also provides insight into the ways that activists expressed their tastes, the forms and colours through which they recognized themselves. At the same time, the dispersion and difficulty of access to these materials promotes reflection on the precarious structures that, since the 1970s, archives of social mobilizations have inherited.[18] We hope that this changes in the near future.

NOTES

1 Armand De Fluvià. 1978. 'Los movimientos de liberación homosexual en el Estado Español.' In Martin S. Weinberg and Colin J. Williams, eds, *Homosexuales masculinos: Sus problemas y adaptación*. Barcelona: Fontanella.

2 This is with the exception of clandestine political groups that had artistic organizations within them. A major example of this were the publications of the People's Union of Artists (UPA), which included a number of artists linked to the PC (m-l), a radical Maoist party. Their publication *Viento del pueblo* (*People's Wind*) demonstrated a coherence and a very avant-garde aesthetic. See Noemi de Haro-Garcia. 2019. 'La Familia Lavapiés: Maoism, art and dissidence in Spain.' In Jacopo Galimberti, Noemi de Haro-Garcia and Victoria H. F. Scott (eds). *Art, Global Maoism and the Chinese Cultural Revolution*. Manchester: Manchester University Press. 187–212.

3 Armand De Fluvià. 2003, *El moviment gai a la clandestinitat del franquisme*. Barcelona: Laertes. 50–56.

4 Ibid. 62.

5 Amanda Klein is the pseudonym of one of the first and main political activists in the MELH. Although we have little detail on her biography and the position she occupied within the collective, we do know that she led the line of thought with a Marxist base in the internal debates that conditioned the policies of the movement and also the contents of *Aghois*. For more information, see De Fluvià, ibid. 104–108.

6 Alberto Berzosa. 2017. 'Sexopolíticas del cine marginal de los años 70 en España.' *Arte y Políticas de Identidad*. No. 16. 17–36.

7 FAGC. 1977. *Manifest*. Barcelona. 38.

8 Michel Foucault. 1981. 'De l'amitié comme mode de vie.' *Gai Pied*. No. 25. 38–39.

9 De Fluvià. 2003. Op cit. 157.

10 Uno que caga para adentro y le gusta!!!!. 1979. 'CNT = Anarquía mal entendida.' *La Pluma*. No. 4. 21.

11 La Pluma. 1978. 'La homosexualidad ante la constitución.' *La pluma*. No. 1. 3.

12 The links between the army and homosexuality in the Spanish context of the time oscillated between homoerotic imaginaries, where comradeship could be understood as a form of close and sentimental relationship between men – as occurs in some war films such as *¡Harka!* (Carlos Arévalo, 1941) or *A mí la legión* (*Follow the Legion*, Juan de Orduña, 1942) – and the criticism of the cruelty of compulsory military service, the so-called 'mili', which was a kind of training in military routines to which all men had to submit, except those who proved to have a physical or mental handicap to do so, and which was normally a threatening space for gay or trans people.

13 Gracia Trujillo Barbadillo. 2008. *Deseo y resistencia. Treinta años de movilización lesbiana en el Estado español*. Madrid: Egales. 88.

14 Gracia Trujillo Barbadillo. 2014. 'Butches excluded: Female Masculinities and their (Non) Representations in Spain.' In Rafael M. Mérida-Jiménez (ed.). *Hispanic (LGT) Masculinities in Transition*. New York: Peter Lang. 35.

15 See Trujillo. 2008. Op. cit.

16 Rampova was a pioneering artist and activist on the Valencian scene since the 1970s. She founded the political cabaret group Ploma 2 together with Clara Bowie, Greta Guevara and Amadora Von Stenberg in 1980. She was also the author of many stickers, comics and illustrations in which she creates a world where Bertolt Brecht, Rosa Von Praunheim, and Rita Hayworth are mixed. She was a member of radical Valencian groups such as the Moviment per l'Alliberament Gai del Pais Valencià (MAG-PV) and the Kollectiu Alliberament Sexual (KAS).

17 See Trujillo. 2008. Op cit.

18 See Gracia Trujillo Barbadillo and Alberto Berzosa. (eds). 2019. *Fiestas, memorias y archivos. Política sexual disidente y resistencias cotidianas en España en los años setenta*. Madrid: Brumaria.

6 Sexual Difference and Queer Subjectivity in Slovak LGBTQ Print Periodicals

VIERA LORENCOVA

Print media production was initiated by Slovak gay, lesbian, bisexual and transgender (LGBT) activists in the 1990s with the aim to encourage authentic self-representation, facilitate intra-community interaction, and disseminate accurate information about LGBT rights advocacy that was largely absent from the mainstream media. In November 1989 the transition of power in Czechoslovakia marked the beginning of unprecedented changes that resulted in a series of profound political, economic and cultural transformations. By 1990, the state-controlled media system was replaced with a decentralized free market media model effectively dismantling the practice of heavy-handed censorship. The principles of participatory democracy and respect for – and protection of – human rights and freedoms, including the freedom of thought and expression, were at the forefront of these reforms. In the early 1990s, the lives of LGBT people in Czechoslovakia also started to change. The first LGBT organizations in Czechoslovakia emerged in 1990, and with them, the first community-based print media. In 1993, when Czechoslovakia split into two separate countries, the Czech and Slovak LGBT rights advocacy groups started to forge two separate paths.

The first, and for several years the only gay and lesbian organization in Slovakia was Ganymedes, founded by Marián Vojtek and Ivan Požgaj in Bratislava in June 1990. As Ganymedes crystallized into a community of a growing number of primarily gay-identified men, a desire to establish a separate lesbian organization materialized in 1993 when Hana Fábry founded Museion. By the beginning of the new millennium, a small but growing network of Slovak LGBT activists helped to establish their community presence in six locales: in Bratislava (Ganymedes, Museion, Altera, H plus, and HaBiO), Banská Bystrica (Museion-stred, Altera, CKKISM, HaBiO and Podisea), Žilina (HaBiO), Košice (Ganymedes and HaB), Trenčín and Handlová (Ganymedes). In May 2000, activists from Slovak LGBT organizations formed the coalition *Iniciatíva inakosť: Spolužitie bez diskriminácie sexuálnych menšín* (The Initiative difference: Coexistence without discrimination of sexual minorities) and intensified campaigning efforts for the legalization of same-sex partnerships, and legal protection from discrimination on the basis of sexual orientation under the Equal Treatment Law. In the following decades, new LGBT rights groups and organizations joined the coalition, including QLF, Nomantiles, and TransFúzia.

This essay maps the trajectory of six print periodicals published in this context in Slovakia between the years 1993 and 2020: *Aspekt, L-listy, Séparé, Atribút g/l, Q archív,* and *QYS magazine.* It aims to highlight the importance of do-it-yourself and community-based print media as sites of self-representation and cultural production of counter-hegemonic representations of gender and sexual difference that have contributed to the disruption of heteronormative cultural norms, and mobilization of the nascent LGBT activism in Slovakia. Mapping the trajectories of these print periodicals, my analysis unfolds in response to the following questions: What were the initial motivations, modes of production and distribution of these print periodicals? What formats, genres, themes, aesthetics and politics of representation of sexual desires, pleasures, practices and identities characterized each of them? In what ways have these periodicals reflected and shaped the agendas of LGBT rights advocates in Slovakia? What did these periodicals accomplish?

ASPEKT 1/1996: LESBIAN EXISTENCE

In 1993, a handful of Slovak feminist activists, writers, academics and artists launched the feminist journal *Aspekt* (1993–2004). The journal's production process was coordinated by its two chief co-editors, Jana Cviková, a professor of German and Comparative Literature at Comenius University in Bratislava, and Jana Juráňová, a writer of fiction books, columnist, playwright, translator, and a former reporter for Radio Free Europe.[1] Cviková and Juráňová were the founders of Aspekt, the first Slovak feminist organization devoted to education and publishing, which was established in Bratislava in 1993 'from the initiative of women who thought it was time to take ideas about equality, democracy and liberalism seriously and apply them in the everyday reality of women in Slovakia'.[2] The same year they put together a pilot issue of *Aspekt,* the first and, for the following ten years, the only explicitly feminist journal disrupting the patriarchal and heteronormative status quo of Slovak literary and academic discourse. In the first editorial titled 'A Letter from Bratislava: Towards a Post-socialist Feminism', Cviková introduced the ambitions of the new journal as follows:

On the one hand we would like to, immodestly, attract women of many interests, through shifts in a wide spectrum of themes [...] On the other hand we are modestly trying to avoid speaking in the name of all women. Our goal is rather simple: an option of more free choice of social roles, which should not be strictly predetermined by gender. We are experiencing a huge societal change, which brings along insecurity and the shaking of social roles [...] Old social roles are falling apart and we are trying to find our place in the new ones. Despite all the changes, the life of a woman in our country continues to be significantly more gender determined than the life of a man [...] The space in which a person searches for the right life alternative is, for a woman, narrowed by her gender. And because of this we chose a feminist view as the most meaningful and effective [...], as a possibility for women who wish to play the role of a subject in their lives.[3]

Production was funded from grants secured by Cviková and Juráňová and the pilot issue was published with the financial assistance of the Swiss foundation Pro Helvetia. Writing, translating, editing, design and layout were done by experienced professionals on a volunteer-basis. In the following years, the journal's production costs were funded by the German foundations Frauenanstiftung and Henrich Böll Stiftung. Additional grants from funding agencies and donors made it possible for Aspekt to build a library, and to organize literary evenings, art performances, seminars, and conferences. As well as publishing a journal, Aspekt became the first Slovak publisher of fiction and non-fiction books with a specialized focus on gender and feminist issues.

Aspekt's ambition to 'stimulate women's search for a sense of identity across all social, educational, professional, and ethnic groups' was a particularly challenging task in the postsocialist cultural milieu, characterized by a historical absence of grassroots organizing promoting women's self-reflection and empowerment, an embryonic stage of a culturally specific feminist and queer activism, and the gradual introduction of Northern American and Western European feminist and queer theory amidst the ongoing social, political, and economic transformations.[4] Proudly self-identifying as 'a thorn in the foot as well as a thorn in the eye of the patriarchal society and its politics,' *Aspekt* established itself as an interdisciplinary feminist journal with an ambitious theoretical, literary, and artistic content and format, aspiring to uncover, deconstruct and challenge the deeply-rooted androcentric and heteronormative patterns of dominant academic and literary discourses.[5] The long-range aspiration of *Aspekt*'s founders was to initiate paradigmatic shifts in the thinking and everyday lives of women and men in Slovakia.

Between 1993 and 2004, *Aspekt* published 21 monothematic issues, ranging between 92 and 334 pages in length. Its sophisticated design, original artwork, and subdued colour printed with a matte finish in A4 format evoked the visual esthetic of a literary magazine. The journal printed between 1,200 and 3,000 copies per issue that were distributed to individual and institutional subscribers, independent bookstores and libraries nationwide. The content of *Aspekt* ranged from original and translated analytical and literary essays and excerpts from books, to interviews, book reviews, short stories, poems, and visual art. One of *Aspekt*'s defining features was a commitment to present a wide variety of feminist concepts, viewpoints and theoretical approaches; each issue was organized around a particular theme (e.g. The Beauty Myth; Motherhood; Women's Writing; Lesbian Existence; Fears and Barriers; Human Rights; Violence; Patriarchy; Dramas and Women's Stories) explored from diverse feminist perspectives.[6]

In its attempt to map the complexity of women's experiences, the journal's critical exploration of the forms and sources of women's marginalization also included examination of non-normative gender and sexual identities, desires and practices. *Aspekt*'s seventh issue (1/1996) set out to examine the theme of 'Lesbian Existence' and represents the first explicit introduction of feminist writing on gender and sexual difference in the realm of Slovak literary and academic discourse. The editorial and essays featured in this issue offer analytic tools for conceptualizing women's non-normative sexuality, invite readers to explore what it means to be a lesbian, and call for a culturally specific analysis of heteronormativity and the sources and forms of homophobia in Slovak culture. While *Aspekt*'s key ambition was to introduce its readers to the pluralism of feminist theorizing, the seventh issue went beyond surveying a variety of feminist perspectives by outing the deeply closeted experiences of lesbian-identified women in Slovakia. One of the co-editors, Anna Daučíková, a Slovak fine artist whose art work was featured in *Aspekt* 1/1996, described the conceptual framework of this issue in the following words:

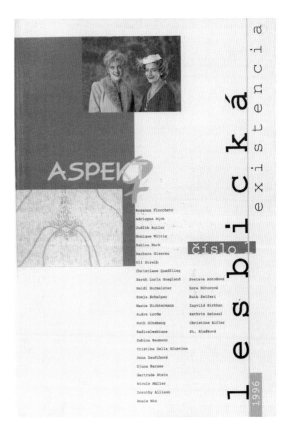

Front cover of *Aspekt*, No. 1, 1996, that includes a photograph 'Coming Out – Coming Home' (1995), co-created by Anna Daucikova and Christina Della Giustina.

> When I started [to work on the issue] I felt "divided," because our conceptual framework was going in two directions. On the one hand, there was a need to increase societal tolerance and appeal to the heterosexual population to formulate and articulate their views [towards the gay population]. […] On the other hand, I was feeling unhappy about the situation in our lesbian community, that we don't know almost anything about ourselves. Many of us depend only on the realm of our own experience, and don't have any knowledge to reflect on our existence. Each is left at the mercy of her own problems, and if she does not happen to be in a happy partnership, her life is almost unbearable. We, lesbians, are exiled to the worst kind of loneliness – without any positive role models.[7]

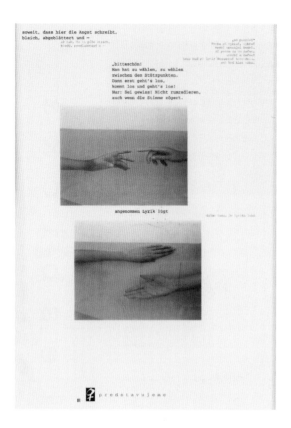

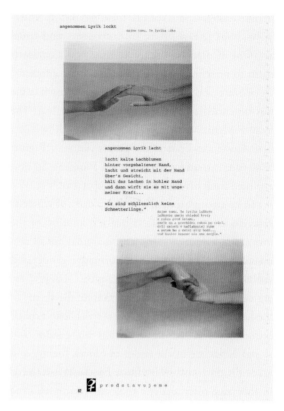

Aspekt, No. 1, 1996, pp. 81–2. Reproduction of video stills from an experimental video and performance *Acquabelle* (1995), co-authored by Anna Daucikova and Christina Della Giustina.

In addition to the personal reflections on 'lesbian existence,' *Aspekt* 1/1996 featured descriptive and factual narratives about lesbian activism and politics in Slovakia, the Czech Republic, Poland and Germany, alongside classics of lesbian theorizing including the first Slovak translations of Audre Lorde's 1978 essay 'Uses of the Erotic: The Erotic as Power', Adrienne Rich's 1980 essay 'Compulsory Heterosexuality and Lesbian Existence', and excerpts from Judith Butler's 1990 book *Gender Trouble: Feminism and the Subversion of Identity,* among others.[8] Analytical essays, empirical studies and literary reviews were interspersed with sensual representations of homoerotic desire in poetry, fiction, and visual art aimed at initiating self-reflection for lesbian-identified women, offering potential identification models, and de-stigmatizing sexual difference in the eyes of the heterosexual majority. Unlike both the previous and following issues of the journal that primarily (though never exclusively) explored the experiences of heterosexual women under conditions of patriarchy, the seventh issue explicitly invited its readers to question the regimes of power that keep the heteronormative status quo in place, to explore the complexities of homoerotic desires, and to examine the pluralism of sexual identities.[9]

It is important to emphasize that the lesbian issue of *Aspekt* was the first collection of texts about 'lesbian existence' available to Slovak readers, and, for the very first time in the history of the journal, all 1500 copies of the issue sold in a relatively short time. Throughout the decade in which it operated, *Aspekt* remained unique as the only feminist journal in Slovakia and the only source that invited Slovak readers to engage in theoretical explorations of gender and sexual difference from the perspective of feminist and queer theory. *Aspekt's* regular readership consisted primarily of university-educated readers interested in theoretically hybrid feminist discourse, many of whom regularly attended public lectures, conferences, talks, and discussions with authors, the organization of which was and continues to be a regular part of Aspekt's activities. In 2004, the closure of the journal was experienced as a significant loss in Slovak feminist academic and literary circles. However, given the journal's anthology format, old issues continue to serve as study material in gender studies and feminist theory courses. The complete ten volumes of the journal are archived in Aspekt's library,[10] which is open to the public. Aspekt continues its mission as the only Slovak independent publisher of feminist and gender-themed books, both fiction and non-fiction. Its publishing and educational activities clearly demonstrate its editors' determination to challenge the patriarchal and heteronormative discourses of Slovak literary and academic canons, and their ability to thrive as an intellectual force that fosters critical thinking about gender and sexual difference.

L-LISTY (1995–1999)

From the moment she founded the first Slovak lesbian organization, Museion, in 1994, Hana Fábry was determined to establish an accessible community-based periodical 'by and for lesbians'. According to Fábry, the organization strived to fight for equality of sexual minorities in all areas of public and private life; advocate for the institution of same-sex partnership; and provide assistance with establishing clubs, helplines, publications and counseling centres for lesbians.[11] *L-listy*, the first community-based lesbian newsletter circulating in Slovakia, was launched in 1995 out of a need to provide access to information and to facilitate contacts within the growing community. It was produced by volunteers from the lesbian organization Museion-stred (a regional branch of Museion) that was established in Banská Bystrica in 1995 by Zuzana Kiripolská and Marielle Doms. The name of the newsletter, *L-listy* (L-letters in the English translation) denotes its original letter format, typed initially on a typewriter, copied and distributed by regular mail among a small group of lesbian-identified women participating in Museion's activities. Using the capital letter L (that signified, without a doubt, the identity marker "lesbian") was considered safer than using the word "lesbian," since the newsletter was circulated also among women who were concerned with being outed against their will if it was found in their possession.

In 1996, a grant from the foundation Zdravé mesto Banská Bystrica enabled technical improvements in the production process of *L-listy*: a typewriter was replaced by a computer, the format changed from the larger A4 to a smaller A5 publication, photographs and illustrations were added, and the number of pages grew. However, out of necessity to keep production costs down to a minimum, Kiripolská and Doms preserved the newsletter's xeroxed-and-stapled image, which gave the newsletter its distinctive do-it-yourself aesthetic.

The primary goal of the newsletter was to circulate announcements about local activities organized by and for lesbian-identified women interested in outdoors activities (e.g. hiking, biking, and camping). Invitations to such community happenings were geared towards newcomers, who faced isolation and had no other means of accessing information about activities organized by the local lesbian community. Later, *L-listy* also included announcements about Museion's social events, such as Zlet čarodejníc (Gathering of the Witches), geared towards participants from all regions of Slovakia. The newsletter also had a limited circulation in the neighboring Czech Republic, and, as a result, some of the advertised activities and events provided an opportunity to connect with the Czech lesbian community, for example during hiking trips in the Tatra Mountains, or when Slovak lesbians travelled to Prague to join their Czech sisters at the annual music festival Apríles. In addition to the announcements, the newsletter published important contact information (a P.O. Box and a help-line phone number), and miscellaneous articles on health, body, same-sex relationships, and lesbian parenting, among other topics. The editors regularly invited the readers to contribute with their original short stories, poetry, illustrations or photographs, and suggestions for community events, and the published contributions continued to further cultivate the newsletter's characteristic do-it-yourself aesthetic.

L-listy was published irregularly, in monthly to quarterly intervals, and had a limited circulation that never exceeded three hundred copies per issue. It was distributed by mail, free of charge to all members of Museion and any interested non-members willing to cover the postage, or in person by several volunteers. Most readers discovered *L-listy* during their first contact with Museion; others found out about it from their friends, who either participated in or knew someone who participated in Museion's activities, and who gave them a free issue or told them where they could obtain one. Upon reading the first issue, most opted to subscribe, even if they were not able to participate in the activities promoted or reported on in the newsletter. It was common for each issue of the newsletter to be shared among several readers, and therefore the number of readers well exceeded the number of subscriptions.

In 1998, when the editors Kiripolská and Doms moved to the Netherlands, the production of the newsletter was divided between four women in two different geographical locations, Slovakia and the Netherlands. The last issue of *L-listy* was published in 1999, when it became increasingly difficult to sustain its production due to a lack of funding, and as Museion-stred underwent organizational transformation into a new organization, Altera. *L-listy* represents a unique and valuable artifact of a pre-political stage of the formation of Slovak lesbian community in the second half of the 1990s. Despite its irregularity, vernacular content and visual aesthetic, do-it-yourself publishing, and limited distribution, it is important to acknowledge its significance, considering that until the late 1990s, for lesbians, especially in the rural areas of Slovakia, the newsletter was the only source of information about local activities, resources and events for lesbians, and, at the time, the first print publication that had set out to facilitate intra-community interaction among lesbians in Slovakia.

SÉPARÉ (1999–2000)

In spring 1999, the community-based newsletter *Séparé* (1999–2000) represented a new attempt to initiate interaction among lesbians in Slovakia. Its founder, Anna Daučíková (the co-editor of the 1996 lesbian issue of *Aspekt*), hoped that *Séparé* might initiate what she had been, for years, longing to be a part of: a regular dialogue among lesbians in Slovakia. She envisioned *Séparé* becoming an 'imaginary space,' a symbolic meeting-place of the emerging lesbian community, as she wrote in the first editorial:

> Lesbians in Slovakia don't have any space, meeting-place, club, teahouse or a pub, and since it is unlikely that anything like that will exist in the nearest future, we decided […] to create this imaginary space, which will allow us to be in touch with each other, to discuss, to argue, to become friends (and maybe even lovers, wow!) – via mail, through this new 'insider-publication' done by ourselves for ourselves.[12]

Séparé's primary goal was to facilitate connections among Slovak lesbians, who were forced into isolation by the heteronormative society. As Daučíková put it:

> Don't be afraid of the freaky separatism… after all, we already are separated, so many of us don't even know about others, we are spread all around the republic, in some places more thickly, in other places only sparingly. Some of us are separated even into the neighboring streets, as we recently have discovered, and we didn't know it for so many years.[13]

In addition to embodying the separated, isolated and invisible existence of lesbians, the name *Séparé* could also be interpreted as signifying a desire to establish a symbolically autonomous (separate and thus safe) space, inspiring lesbian-identified women towards self-reflection, self-representation, and the formation of a visible lesbian community:

> Our *Séparé* thus could become our niche, a smoky or freshly aired, cozy, mental club that would allow us to learn mutually about our opinions on this or that, what we each know, what we are gifted with, what is happening, and what should be happening, and even what has been happening in our past lesbian cultural history.[14]

Séparé's production and distribution process did not significantly differ from *L-listy*. However, the magazines pursued a slightly different mission: while the primary goal of *L-listy* was to circulate announcements and contact information, *Séparé* aspired to cultivate self-exploration and intra-community interaction. While it has never been referred to as a "zine" by its producers, the amateur production process and appearance of *Séparé* (and by the same token, also *L-listy*) fits the *Factsheet Five* working definition of a zine as 'a small, handmade amateur publication done purely out of passion'.[15] *Séparé*'s do-it-yourself ethic and production process, its mission, tone and appearance is comparable to zines such as *Bikini Kill*, *Thorn* and *Slant* informed by the Riot Grrrl underground feminist punk movement that emerged in the US in the early 1990s. It is interesting to note that while *zine* had no place in the vocabulary of most Slovak language speakers in the 1990s, many were familiar with a D.I.Y. production process of dissident amateur publications produced clandestinely during the years of socialism known as *samizdat*.[16] Despite their similarities (the low-budget production process and limited circulation), there are some notable differences between a *zine* and *samizdat*. For one thing, the degree of risk that has been associated with the production and circulation of *samizdat* in an oppressive political context does not typically apply (or not with the same intensity) to the production of most zines; however, some zinesters are known for being targeted for their political views, just as dissidents were under socialism. In Czechoslovakia, throughout the 1970s and 1980s, *samizdat* epitomized a form of resistance to the state's suppression of the freedom of expression; their distribution was illegal, risky, and possible only through underground networks. Emerging in the context of Western liberal democracies in the 1970s and 1980s (e.g. US, Canada, UK, Western Europe), zines, perhaps not unlike other genres of amateur cultural production, exemplify an innovative form of self-expression that has often been interpreted as an attempt to overcome alienation. *Séparé*'s focus on authentic self-representation (rather than political opposition) and on facilitating community formation, are visions that it shares with other feminist and queer zines.

How do zines contribute to community? How do they help to overcome a feeling of alienation? In his book *Notes from Underground: Zines and the Politics of Alternative Culture*, Stephen Duncombe points out that zines are important sites of both community formation and self-expression. 'People create zines to scream out "I exist", they also do it to connect to others saying the same thing'[17]. As Green and Taormino put it 'among other things, zines are sites for communication, education, community, revolution, celebration, and self-expression'.[18] The four issues of *Séparé* (1999–2000) embody all of the above. *Séparé* started as a personal attempt to disrupt an experience of alienation, a desire to form a club of her own, a search for validation in the absence of media representations of oneself, an effort to initiate interaction among women who have never met but share something in common and, ultimately, a project to create a visible lesbian community.

The first issue of *Séparé* emphasized the desire for the periodical to function as a medium of self-expression as well as interaction, characterized by non-conformity, humour, creativity, daring, and mutual support:

> It would be good if we felt free [here in *Séparé*], without feeling an inferiority complex, to draw, scribble, write about, or take photos of anything that comes to our mind... We would like to speak in *Séparé* about many things, about lesbians and non-lesbians, about life, happiness, partnership, pain, love, erotica, hate, loneliness, in short, about everything. We will also try to have fun with it, give each other courage, look at things with humor, to feel better, and to do something for it. And so, I hope we will find out what is happening with Altera, what has been started and ended by Museion, what are the plans of Museion-Stred, the women's section of Ganymedes, and hundreds of other lesbian communities all around the world.[19]

Like many zines, *Séparé* was envisioned as 'a place to walk to...a free space: a space within which to imagine and experiment with new and idealistic ways of thinking, communicating, and being',[20] but also, on a more pragmatic level, a space that would facilitate an exchange of information about and among lesbians in Slovakia. In 1999, *Séparé* was the only printed outlet (briefly) informing about and reflecting on the events in the emerging lesbian community: for example, local and national gatherings of lesbian-identified women; the first photo exhibit of lesbian photographers in Slovakia; the fifth gay and lesbian film festival in Slovakia; the International Gay and Lesbian Youth Organization (IGLYO) conference attended by Slovak lesbian, gay, and bisexual youth; and the participation of Slovak athletes and fans at the 1998 Gay Games in Amsterdam, Netherlands. Information was mixed in with short stories, photos, poems, transcribed conversations, personals and invitations for letters and contributions. *Séparé* encouraged inter-community interaction by inviting its readers to join the first Slovak and Czech LGBT internet forum launched on the Sophia web page, and to listen to the first Czech radio broadcast for lesbians and gays.

Despite the explicit acknowledgement that *Séparé* was produced by the Club of Lesbian Authors (KLA), the bulk of the work was done by Anna Daučíková, Hana Fábry and Vanda Teocharisová, who produced and mailed, free of charge, four issues, averaging 150 issues per print-run. Daučíková took on *Séparé*'s production with a fierce determination to promote lesbian visibility. She was not your typical zinester; as a faculty member at the Fine Arts Academy in Bratislava, Slovakia, specializing at the time in photography and experimental video production, she was fully occupied with her art projects and teaching. Part of a vanguard of emerging feminist and lesbian activism in Slovakia, Daučíková was a co-founder and co-editor of *Aspekt* between 1993–6, a coordinator of the lesbian section of the Slovak gay organization Ganymedes in 2000, a co-founder of the coalition *Iniciatíva inakosť* (The Initiative Difference), and a founder of QA/DIC, the queer documentary and information centre that published a print periodical *Q Archív* from 2002 until 2003, which I go on to discuss later in this essay.

While *Séparé's* existence was short-lived, in many ways the zine accomplished what it set out to do: to initiate authentic self-expression and collabourative identity exploration. A low-budget, community-based print publication made by and for lesbians, *Séparé* was limited by a lack of resources; it was produced with no outside funding, relying on free xerox-copying and volunteer labour. In the Spring of 2000, Daučíková decided to quit *Séparé* and put her energy into becoming a spokesperson for the coalition *Iniciatíva inakosť* (2000–2001). Fábry, too, joined the coalition, and went on to become an editor of a new monthly print magazine *Atribút g/l*. As Daučíková recounted to me, *Séparé* ceased to exist after one year for the following reasons:

> (1) I lost the opportunity to print for free; (2) I stopped writing, because of my realization that lesbians [in Slovakia] are not ready for a dialogue at the level that I was envisioning; (3) two existing lesbian organizations [Museion, Altera] were not able to do anything to prevent this publication from being anything more than an underground publication without any outside financing; (4) finally, out of my frustration that followed, however, it appears that it [the disappearance of *Séparé*] also mobilized some women to become involved in *Atribút g/l* [a new monthly magazine of gays and lesbians launched in 2000].[21]

ATRIBÚT G/L (2000–2002)

In May 2000, soon after the production of *Séparé* came to a close, *Atribút g/l,* a new monthly periodical for gays and lesbians, the first of its kind to be distributed and sold at the newsstands nation-wide was launched in Bratislava. Its trajectory differs from the print periodicals that preceded it. Behind *Atribút's* initial conceptual idea was HaBiO (The organization for homosexual and bisexual youth), whose coordinator, upon securing funding from the Netherlands Embassy in Slovakia, started to seek volunteers to launch the project. At first, a number of HaBiO members committed to work on the magazine's production but the task proved to be more difficult than they originally envisioned. After several months of fruitless attempts to get the new periodical underway, they turned for help to Hana Fábry, the coordinator of Museion, who agreed to take over the project. Pressed by the deadlines of grant agencies, she reached out to fellow LGBT activists, including Ivan Požgai, Jozef Gréč and Vanda Teacharisová, quickly threw together a team of volunteers, and by May 2000, the pilot issue of *Atribút g/l* began to circulate among readers nation-wide. In the magazine's first editorial, Fábry introduced *Atribút g/l* as:

the first official Slovak medium that creates a serious space for those of us who are DIFFERENT, [who are] homosexual, bisexual, transsexual. Finally, we are starting also in Slovakia to publicly speak and write about ourselves in the first person. We don't need any psychologist or sexologist to do it for us – we are healthy. A priest does not have to speak about us anymore with his pointed finger and his eyes turned to the sky – there are some believers among us, too. A nun does not have to feel sorry for us – there is no reason for pitying us. And our parents don't have to start to cure us. We don't want that! We are here. We are here with our own attribute […]. We are who we are, normal, comfortable and happy the way we are. We make our own decisions, and where the system does not allow us to do that, that's exactly the target of our activities, that's where *Atribút g/l* is heading. Its ambition is to bring to the minds and vocabularies of our community, as well as other open-minded members of our society, words such as "difference," "sexual minority," "tolerance." To fill these words with a specific positive content. Not to be afraid of the word *teplý* [gay]. Not to be afraid to be *teplý* [gay]. It is not derogatory. If we won't feel inferior, we will not be seen as such by the public.[22]

Atribút's sixteen black-and-white pages with a blue monochrome cover, printed in A4 format on recycled paper, were filled with announcements, interviews, commentaries, short stories, original and translated articles, photographs, and contact information. The pilot issue had no display of advertisements or personals and was distributed for free. Along with the mission of the newly established LGBT coalition *Iniciatíva inakosť*, the first issue published an open letter which readers were encouraged to sign and mail to the Vice Chairman of the Committee for Human and Minority Rights and Regional Development, Pál Csáky. The goal of the letter was to express support for LGBT activists in their efforts to lobby for same-sex partnership legislation and to put pressure on Parliament to implement anti-discrimination legislation. The editorial promised to keep its readers informed about the efforts to 'eliminate discriminatory legislative norms from all spheres of life', and asked for feedback and original contributions.[23] 'I am sure I don't have to remind you how anxiously we are waiting for your reactions. […] *Atribút g/l* is a coming out of homosexuals in Slovakia and coming out is an attribute of society's normal life. *Our* life!', as Fábry put it.[24]

Three volumes of *Atribút* had a relatively consistent format and content presented in fifteen regular sections: *editoriál*, *rozhovor* (interview), *história: déjà vu, déjà vécu* (history – already seen, already lived through), *akcia sk* (LGBT events in Slovakia), *akcia cz* (LGBT events in the Czech Republic), *homomonitor* (media monitor), *celebrity, homix* (a mixture of comics, cartoons, satire and critical commentary), *poviedka* (short story), *infoinzert* (information and ads), *zoznamka* (classifieds), *tip Atribútu* (*Atribút's* recommendation), *kinohit* (film picks), *pel-mel g/l* (LGBT world news), and links to Slovak LGBT web sites (e.g. *inak.gl*), among others. With the exception of the section *déjà vu, déjà vécu* that consisted of reprints of articles published during the 1960s until the 1980s in the Slovak media, *Atribút* focused on contemporary issues, ranging from reports on events organized by Slovak LGBT activists to interviews with LGBT activists and political allies to critical commentaries on parliamentary debates.

The signed editorials had a personal tone and focused on the most recent events in Slovak LGBT activism and politics. In February 2002, *Atribút* carried a rather unusual editorial written by Milan Ištván, the MP for the Social Democratic Left party, who presided over the first ever parliamentary discussion of the proposed legalization of same-sex partnership – an historic occasion in the Slovak Parliament – and encouraged further mobilization of sexual minorities and their collabouration with politicians in the struggle for gay rights:

> The last day of January in the Slovak Parliament was devoted to homosexuals. For the first time in history, the Slovak Parliament carried out a discussion about a quality of life of a minority that was, until now, on the margin of interest of our society. The reason [for this discussion] was the same-sex partnership bill […] The members of the homosexual minority must not get scared, must not become discouraged after the first defeat in Parliament. They should continue to lobby, particularly in the third sector and in the media […] Our politicians include and, I believe, will continue to include, people who are not hypocrites and morons, people who are principled, and who will do everything to secure respect for this minority. It is not going to be easy. There is a lot of work ahead of us. I want to ask for patience and collabouration. We have to be long distance runners, and [be able to] visualize our finish-line. We have to know what we want. We want a tolerant society, a normal life, not a life with double standards.[25]

In addition to the editorial, this issue of *Atribút* included a detailed account of the debate, the results of a vote initiated by the MP Alojz Rakús that prematurely ended the debate, and a public statement issued by the LGBT coalition *Iniciatíva Inakosť*. *Atribút* was the only media source in Slovakia that published the whole parliamentary speech presented by the MP Ištván, along with a critical reflection on the first tangible results of years of lobbying for same-sex partnership law.

The reprints of old articles previously published in the "socialist" media, included regularly in *Atribút*'s section *déjà vu, déjà vécu* represent authentic examples of dominant discourses on homosexuality that on rare occasions appeared in Slovak media prior to 1989. After decriminalization of homosexuality in Czechoslovakia in 1961, the task of disciplining homosexuals was handed over from legislators and law-enforcement to psychiatrists and the media. The nuances of this shift are clearly exemplified in the article 'Dnešné problémy homosexuality' (Today's problems with homosexuality) originally published in 1975 in the magazine *Zdravie ľudu* (People's health), and republished in *Atribút* 9/2002. Representing the views shared by many of his contemporaries in the 1970s, psychiatrist Ernest Guensberger argues that homosexuality, while no longer considered a criminal act in Czechoslovakia, is a sexual aberration that leads to isolation and societal ostracizing. As he put it:

> Homosexuality is perhaps the most common sexual aberration. […] Not long ago, homosexuality was not only criminalized but it also led towards isolation of afflicted individuals and towards their "societal death." The homosexual was marked, and thus excluded from the society. Why? Sexually normal people feel a deep repulsion towards all aberrations. This repulsion was supported also by religious views, according to which homosexuality is immoral, a result of decay, sinful already in the stage of thoughts.[26]

The author concludes by suggesting a connection between drug addictions and 'various forms of perversions, including homosexuality,' and warns that 'this increases the danger of active psychic contagion'.[27] Paradoxically, the article includes a photograph depicting large graffiti sprayed on the wall of a metro station in Paris that reads: *Contre la repression de l'homosexualitee* (Against the repression of homosexuality), with the following commentary:

> Here we should mention that already before the introduction of new laws that decriminalized homosexuality, there has been a movement of homosexuals fighting for their rights. Today, there are also such activities as are portrayed in the photograph from the Parisian metro. Any affiliations of such kind are misguided. Even though they offer a certain substitute for societal self-realization, simultaneously they separate homosexual individuals from normal collectivity. Therefore, it is pertinent that in our society we do not limit ourselves only to offering medical help, but that we treat as many cases as possible. This is the only solution to how to incorporate afflicted individuals into the environment that would be acceptable to them, and to create adequate conditions for their existence. Also, those who are not suitable for treatment might be able to live in a normal environment, if they succeed to overcome certain barriers.[28]

What are we to make of this conclusion? While the author acknowledges the existence of gay rights activism, he is quick to emphasize that any such affiliations are "misguided". It is clear that his primary message is to reinforce the imperatives of heteronormativity, in tune with other advocates of the medical sickness model of homosexuality. Republishing this article in 2002 served as a reminder of how little has changed in the attitudes of some Slovaks (lay people and psychiatrists alike) towards homosexuality, a point implied also by the name of the rubric – *déjà vu, déjà vécu*.

Front cover of *Atribút g/l*, No. 5, 2001.

While *Atribút* was open to displaying advertisements (and also personals, which were published free of charge), the periodical did not succeed in finding commercial sponsors, did not sell well at the newsstands, and made no profit. Thus depending on grants provided by various foreign donors (The Netherlands Embassy, Open Society Foundation, the United States Agency for International Development) to cover its production costs, *Atribút* remained in circulation for thirty months. In 2002, its volume grew (it was "doubled" twice when published bi-monthly in 2002), and its name was changed to *Atribút* – a monthly for gay men and lesbians (the abbreviation *g/l* was dropped). *Atribút* was the first and, at that time, the only LGBT periodical that was nationally distributed and sold on the newsstands across Slovakia. It was relatively easy to obtain for those who resided in Bratislava; however, in rural areas, the most common way to learn about it was by word-of-mouth, since the magazine was very rarely displayed on newsstands and, in most instances, one had to ask for it and then wait until the salesperson searched through the piles of unpacked periodicals hidden under the display. In some places, it was simply not available. Some readers received free copies of *Atribút* upon their first contact with one of the local LGBT organizations, some found free copies in gay clubs or in student dormitories, while others learned about *Atribút* from its editors, and became regular subscribers and sometimes also contributors.

Even though *Atribút* failed to attract a wider readership, its closure was perceived as disappointing by many of its regular readers. In its last issue (11/12 2002), *Atribút's* editors reassured their readers that they were not ready to give up: 'We love *Atribút*, it is our media-baby, and we want it to live'.[29] Unable to secure adequate funding, the editors decided to archive the magazine and make some of its content available through the *ganymedes.sk* web domain. [30] In the years following *Atribút's* closure, Fábry continued to write and share her blog posts, photographs, and information about LGBT activism on *Lesba.sk* [31] and *Changenet.sk*[32] websites, and as of 2005, also on *L-Blog*.[33] Her *L-Blog* explicitly encouraged participatory knowledge-production; in addition to inviting comments from readers and other bloggers, it was interlinked with other weblogs devoted to LGBTQ issues, and its archives also included guidelines and templates for those who wanted to create their own weblogs.

Q ARCHÍV (2002–2003)

In January 2002, during fieldwork in Bratislava, I observed the launch of Q archív – Documentary and Information Centre (QA/DIC), the first LGBT archive in Slovakia. When I returned to the field in the summers of 2002 and 2003, I searched through QA/DIC's collections and participated in its video screenings, workshops and discussions. I realized I had been observing not only the growth of the first public space in the context of Slovak culture explicitly designated as 'queer' but also (and perhaps foremost) a community in its making. In the course of several months, QA/DIC became a popular place that attracted on a weekly basis dozens of visitors, including those who were not previously affiliated with any of the LGBT organizations. In addition to the group of volunteers who worked on archiving miscellaneous artifacts (cataloguing selected articles from mainstream print media, compiling queer print periodicals, books and video materials, creating databases and so on), Q archív also organized lectures, discussions and weekly video screenings, and published a monthly newsletter. The project was conceptually developed by Anna Daučíková, who secured startup funding for the project from the European Community (Phare Access Programme Grant), and coordinated all

Below left: Front cover of *Q archív*, No. 1, 2002 (lesbian).

Below right: Front cover of *Q archív*, No. 1, 2002 (gay).

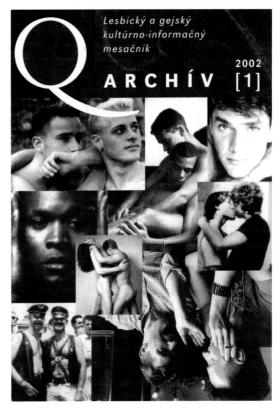

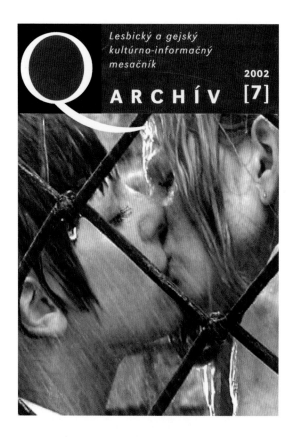

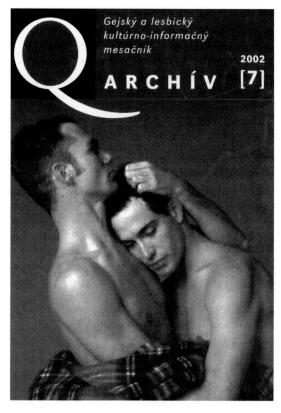

Above left: Front cover of *Q archiv*, No. 7, 2002 (lesbian).

Above right: Front cover of *Q archiv* , No. 7, 2002 (gay).

of QA/DIC's activities. The main goal of the project's multiple activities, according to Daučíková, was community development that 'started with building this space, to offer opportunities for personal reflection, and for acquiring and sharing knowledge about our history and our present situation'.[34]

In June 2002, I observed QA/DIC's growing audience, comprised predominately of young people who gathered on a regular basis to watch and discuss LGBT-themed films, to share their personal experiences, to donate collections of various artifacts, to browse through books and periodicals, and to coordinate activist projects. The visitors included regulars, who took part in all of QA/DIC's activities; occasional visitors, who socialized mostly outside of the archive's premises; and often a handful of newcomers, among them one-time visitors or questioning friends, some of whom quickly transformed from curious guests to regulars. The funding from the EC Phare Programme provided the finances to sustain the centre for fifteen months; the grant was used to pay the rent on a furnished office space, to purchase two computers, a printer, a scanner, a xerox-machine, two VCRs, a TV set, a phone line, an internet connection, and miscellaneous software and office supplies. A portion of the grant was used to partially compensate for the work of the archivists, lecturers, editors, and project coordinators, and to finance the bilingual publication (Slovak and English) of *Report on Discrimination Against Lesbians, Gay Men and Bisexuals in Slovakia*. The remaining portion of the grant was used for financing the production of the monthly newsletter *Q archív*.

In comparison with *L-listy, Separé* and *Atribút g/l, Q archív* has a sleek aesthetic, achieved through a dynamic layout and more sophisticated graphic design, enhanced with high-quality glossy paper that visually distinguished the newsletter from all previous lesbian and gay print periodicals. All fourteen issues have a consistent format and structure; they are printed in A5 format and each consists of twenty-four pages with three bimonthly issues containing forty-eight pages. Each print run averaged 500 copies per issue.[35] *Q archív* gained a regular readership mainly among the visitors of QA/DIC, who attended film screenings and discussion series organized between March 2002 and March 2003. It was distributed free to all QA/DIC visitors, in gay bars, in the hallways of Comenius University in Bratislava, and via mail to the coordinators of all Slovak LGBT organizations.

The newsletter's editors, Hana Púčiková and Roman Martinec, were responsible for the content of the two halves (lesbian and gay) of the newsletter respectively, mirroring the organizational division of the archive into gay and lesbian sections. The

Below left: Front cover of *QYS* magazine No. 1, 2016.

Below right: Front cover of *QYS* magazine No. 3, 2017.

newsletter's simultaneous reinforcement of binary identity categories and its discursive gesture towards overcoming the limits of binary identity categorization symbolized by the letter Q (the initial of the term *queer*) in the newsletter's title and the archive's name seemed incongruous. The binary categorization was also evoked on the upper right corner of every page of the newsletter: the pages were marked as part of either the *lesbian* or *gay* sections, with a separate *gay* and *lesbian* table of contents, editorials, and monthly schedules of QA/DIC events designated for gays and lesbians. The reinforcement of the binaries seemed paradoxical considering that some articles published in *Q archív* paid explicit attention to the question of terminology – for instance, the etymology of the clinical term *homosexuál*, the political dimension of the terms *gej* (gay), *lesba* (lesbian), *trans/transka* (trans) and *kvír* (queer) within the emerging Slovak LGBTQ community, and the limits of identity categories.

To promote QA/DIC's activities, the newsletter published dates and times for planned discussions, lectures, and video-screenings, interspersed with updates on archiving efforts and media monitoring, film and book reviews, commentaries and short interviews with LGBT activists. For the most part, *Q archív* offered very limited information about the activities of other Slovak LGBT organizations, with the exception of publishing their contact information (phone numbers, addresses and web pages) and occasional announcements. It also included short articles on the history of and contemporary issues relating to LGBTQ activism in different parts of the world. The newsletter featured photographs taken during QA/DIC's discussions, lectures, street rallies, and gay pride marches. Many visuals, however, including photographs that appeared on covers, were downloaded from the internet; these included portraits of LGBT activists and theorists; performers, film directors, actors, authors and book covers mentioned in the texts; various logos and symbols of gay pride and LGBTQ activism; and miscellaneous illustrative stock photos.

The newsletter's initial aspiration – mapping the history and present of Slovak LGBT activism – was quickly replaced by less programmatic and more spontaneous content, shaped mainly by the editors' personal interests. The editors both acknowledged that the content reflected, in part, their limited choices of original texts and visuals; they both worked actively on soliciting contributions in order to diversify the content, however, only a few contributors came forth with publishable materials. While the newsletter fulfilled its goal of informing its readers about QA/DIC's activities, *Q archív* lacked a substantial discussion of the politics of sexual difference, and offered only a fragmented reflection on Slovak LGBT rights activism. As Ivan Požgai, the co-editor of *Atribút* (2000–2002), pointed out with a good dose of sarcasm, *Q archív* paid more attention to film reviews and LGBT characters from the films screened at QA/DIC than to the efforts of Slovak LGBT activists and/or pertinent Parliamentary debates. [36] In their defense, the editors of *Q archív* argued that their focus on film was intentional; had they focused on the coverage of Parliamentary debates, they would have been, inevitably, repeating information that was at the time routinely covered by *Atribút.*

The last issue of *Q archív* was published in March 2003, when the EC grant expired, and no follow-up funding materialized. In spring 2003, the archived materials collected by QA/DIC were divided between the NGOs Ganymedes and Altera, who agreed to continue maintaining and updating the archived collections in their respective office spaces in Bratislava. In the absence of resources needed for the production of print periodicals, Slovak LGBTQ-themed web pages, online newsletters (*Ganymedes infomagazín*; *Alterácka A4*), forums, internet discussion groups, blogs, webzines (*Lesba.sk*) and social media sites (Queer Leaders Forum, Duhovy PRIDE Bratislava, Iniciatíva Inakosť, TransFúzia, Nomantiles divadlo, LGBT Professionals Network, Dúhový rok) began to proliferate and gain regular followers.

QYS MAGAZINE (2016–)

When the first issue of *QYS magazine* came out in July 2016, some of its readers were too young to remember *Aspekt, L-Listy, Separé, Atribút g/l* and *Q archív*. In the years that elapsed since *Q archív* terminated publishing, Slovak LGBTI activists, especially media-savvy millennials, gradually established their presence on social media platforms that afforded free, instantaneous and interactive experience between the users. In 2009, a group of activists from Queer Leaders Forum took the lead in reinvigorating LGBTI rights advocacy in Slovakia by launching a campaign for the rights of same-sex couples to marry, adopt children and seek IVF, in addition to promoting community outreach programmes of the newly established Q-centrum, and organizing and cross-promoting *Dúhový Pride* Bratislava (The Bratislava Pride Festival) via social media.[37] From 2010, LGBTI activists from *Iniciatíva Inakosť* started to use social media to promote their campaigns, educational workshops and events that aim to contribute to the visibility of LGBTI people in Slovakia. *TransFúzia*, the first Slovak organization 'for the empowerment of transgender, including transsexual, gender non-conforming, genderqueer and other non-binary people, as well as people with trans history and experience'[38] established its social media presence as of 2011. In the absence of queer print media, Slovak LGBTI organizations have come to rely on social media networks to inform the public about their activities, to facilitate intracommunity interaction, and to mobilize support for LGBTI rights advocacy in Slovakia.

Launched thirteen years after the newsletter *Q archív* ceased to exist, *QYS magazine* acquired a special distinction as the only print periodical with an explicit focus on the lives of LGBTI people in Slovakia. Printed on a quarterly basis in A5 format and full colour, on high-quality paper with a glossy finish, the magazine features articles about queer art, literature, theatre, film, history, research, LGBTI rights activism, projects and events. Produced by a team of ten to fifteen writers, editors, photographers, graphic designers and other contributors, each issue focuses on a particular theme that is explored through editorials, interviews, essays, reports, and reviews that are supplemented with original photographs and illustrations. Between July 2016 and July 2020, *QYS magazine* published fifteen issues, ranging from 28 to 89 pages, that explored the following themes: Visibility of LGBTI People (Summer 2016), LGBTI in Schools and Education (Fall 2016), I am a Lesbian and I am Ok (Summer 2017), Partnerships (Fall 2017), LGBTI in Workplace (Spring 2018), Queer Film and Theatre (Fall 2018, 2019), Queer Culture (Winter 2017, 2018, 2019), Queer Visual Art (Spring 2019, 2020), and Pride (Summer 2018, 2019, 2020). The magazine is published simultaneously in print and online. What fuels the desire to create a print magazine in the era dominated by digital media platforms and social media? As Andrej Kuruc, one of the co-founders and editors of *QYS* put it, 'the main reason why we have decided to launch *QYS magazine* in print is because we believe that Slovak LGBTI community deserves to have one'.[39]

QYSko, as the magazine is colloquially referred to by some, has an estimated readership of 600 to 1,000 readers, most of whom read the magazine online. [40] The complete volumes of *QYS magazine* are made available on Issuu, an electronic publishing platform that enables the creators to share the content digitally for free. Its circulation in print is limited; 150 copies of every issue are distributed in print to regular subscribers that include LGBT organizations, cultural centres and libraries. Twenty to thirty copies per issue are sold in two independent bookstores (Artforum and Martinus). Every January, the Winter issue of *QYS* is typically launched in the form of an event in a local LGBTI bar that gives readers the opportunity to converse with authors and invited guests, such as people interviewed in the given issue. Free copies of *QYS* are distributed to all attendees, between thirty and forty at each event.[41] Promoted well in advance through social media, these events aim to serve a dual role – to carry out the magazine's mission to enrich the lives of LGBTI people in Slovakia, and to create publicity for *QYS*. The Summer issue of *QYS* typically prints 500 copies to create more robust publicity for the annual Rainbow Pride Festival that takes place in Bratislava and Košice. Every new issue is vigorously promoted on social media and on its official website.[42]

Simultaneous production and distribution of the print and online editions of *QYS magazine* is not the only feature that distinguishes the magazine from its predecessors. Conceived in the context of a larger project, *Podpora mladých* LGBTI *ľudí* (Support for Young LGBTI People), the magazine received financial support from the Slovak Ministry of Culture (2016–2018), the Fund for Art, and the Slovak Ministry of Justice (2018–2020).[43] *QYS magazine* is part of the series of activities and events known as *Dúhový rok* (Rainbow Year) that include the annual LGBTI Pride Festival, Queer Film Festival, and "Drama Queer" Festival that are unique in the Central European context.[44] The sheer fact that these projects and events are happening, and that they are made possible with the financial support from the Slovak governmental agencies, reveals how much has changed in Slovakia in the past three decades, and how much is being accomplished by LGBT rights advocates. And yet, expressions of homophobia, transphobia and anti-LGBTI attitudes are, at the time of writing, becoming more militant in response to the increasing visibility of LGBTI people in Slovakia, who are 'unafraid to come out and be proud of who they are,' as the editor Andrej Kuruc points out in the first issue of *QYS* (1/2016).[45] While the younger generations of LGBTI people are the magazine's primary target audience, as is implied by the magazine's full title *Queer Youth Slovakia*, the editor Veronika Valkovičová expressed her hope that its readership will not only include LGBTI readers but also parents, educators and others, who affect the lives of young LGBTI people.[46]

Over the course of four years the magazine has gradually lost its initially didactic, and, at times, sentimental tone, its textual content has become more substantial and thought-provoking, and its design more coherent and impactful. The Summer 2020 issue of *QYS Magazine* that featured highlights from the FAR Agency's report on the status of LGBTI people in the European Union, Serbia and Macedonia, several in-depth interviews, stories about the hurdles with organizing Pride Bratislava during the COVID-19 pandemic and how queer couples coped during the quarantine, poetry, an invitation to a multi-genre exhibit about 100 years of queer history titled Loading: Love, reviews of LGBTI-themed performances, films, television series and music, along with a generous inclusion of illustrations and photographs, demonstrates clearly the magazine's growth. Its commitment to authenticity and creative exploration of gender and sexual difference in the context of contemporary Slovak culture shines through every page.[47']

This essay creates a blueprint for the lesser known history of queer print media in Europe. While these vignettes about *Aspekt, L-listy, Séparé, Atribút g/l, Q archív,* and *QYS magazine* offer only imperfectly encapsulated glimpses into the context and content of six relatively short-lived print periodicals published between 1993 and 2020, their significance should not be overlooked. Together, they comprise thousands of pages of texts and visual representations that represent a rich archive of feelings, voices, desires, bodies, politics, pleasures, events, experiences, failures, accomplishments, dreams, and hopes of several generations of LGBT people in Slovakia. They have the potential to serve not only as valuable artifacts of LGBT rights activism and queer community formation in Slovakia, but also as an inspiration for all those who seek authentic representation, and who consider queer media to be a meaningful form of cultural production and an indispensable part of life.

NOTES

1 In 1991 Jana Juráňová co-edited the first publication of feminist literary texts in Slovak language that appeared in the special issue of a literary journal *Slovenské pohľady na literatúru a umenie*, Vol. 107, No. 11, 1991. In 1993, Juráňová became one of the co-founders of the feminist journal *Aspekt*.

2 See <http://www.aspekt.sk/>

3 See *Aspekt* 1/1993:3. My translation.

4 *Aspekt's* ambition was to improve 'the social and political situation of women through purposeful educational work and publicity, to promote women's self-confidence and self-awareness.' See Jana Cviková, *Prelude: New Women's Initiatives in Central and Eastern Europe and Turkey.* Hamburg: Frauen-Anstiftung, 1995: 33.

5 See <http://www.aspekt.sk/>

6 Between 1993–2004, *Aspekt* published the following monothematic issues: The Beauty Myth (1/1993), Motherhood (1/1994), Feminisms (2/1994), Witches (3/1994), Women's Writing (1/1995), Women and Power (2–3/1995), Lesbian Existence (1/1996), Fears and Barriers (2/1996), Human Rights (1/1997), Woman's Body I , II (2–3/1997), Women's Thought (1/1998), Women's Spaces (2/1998), Violence I, II (4/1998, 1/1999), Personal is Political (2/1999), We Are not Born Women, We Become Women (1/2000), Patriarchy (2/2000 – 1/2001), Dramas (2/2001), A Body Became a Word (1/2002), and Women's Stories (1/2003–2004). Many articles from the journal were regularly assigned in the courses offered by the Philosophy Department, and the Gender Studies Program, FFUK, Bratislava.

7 See 'Rozhovor Aspektu', *Aspekt* 1 (1996): 113. My translation.

8 The first Slovak translation of *Gender Trouble* was translated by Jana Juráňová and published by Aspekt in 2003 under the title *Trampoty s rodom: feminizmus a podrývanie identity.*

9 The task is to 'discover our own sexual identity, the uniqueness of our autoeroticism, our narcissism, and distinctiveness of our lesbianism,' as Luce Irigaray put it. See Fiochetto, Rosanna, 'Nebeská milenka,' *Aspekt* 1 (1996): 11. My translation.

10 See <http://www.aspekt.sk/category/kniznica/aktuality-kniznice>

11 See <http://www.lesba.sk>

12 See *Séparé* 1/1999:2. My translation.

13 See *Séparé* 1/1999:2. My translation.

14 See *Séparé* 1/1999:2. My translation.

15 See Karen Green and Tristan Taormino. 1997. *A Girl's Guide to Taking Over the World: Writings from the Girl Zine Revolution.* New York; St. Martin's Press, xi.

16 *Samizdat* is a compound word, adopted from Russian, meaning "done by ourselves" that is used in Slovak and Czech in reference to the dissident press. For more on the history of the samizdat and the dissident press in Czechoslovakia, see Marketa Goetz-Stankiewicz (ed.). 1992. *Goodbye Samizdat: Twenty Years of Czechoslovak Underground Writing.* Evanston, Illinois: Northwestern University Press.

17 See Stephen Duncombe. 1997. *Notes from Underground: Zines and the Politics of Alternative Culture.* London and New York: Verso, 44.

18 See Green and Taormino (1997: p. xiv).

19 See *Séparé* 1/1999:2.

20 See Duncombe, op. cit., 195–6.

21 Email correspondence with Anna Daučíková, 6 February, 2001. My translation.

22 See Fábry, Hana. "Editoriál", *Atribút g/l* 1/2000: 3. My translation.

23 *Ibid.*

24 *Ibid.*

25 See 'Editoriál', *Atribút* 2/2002: 3. My translation.

26 See Ivan Požgai, 'Déjà vu, Déjà vécu', *Atribút* 9/2002: 6–7. My translation.

27 Ibid, 7.

28 See Ernest Guensberger, qtd. in Požgai, Ivan, "Déjà vu, Déjà vécu." *Atribút* 9/2002: 7. My translation.

29 See *Atribút* 11/12 2002: 9. My translation.

30 See <www.gaymedes.sk>

31 See <www.lesba.sk>

32 See <www.changenet.sk>

33 See < http://www.lesba.sk/blog/>. *L-blog* was established on December 6, 2005.

34 Interview with Anna Daučíková, January 23, 2002, Bratislava, Slovakia. My translation.

35 *Q archív*'s first issue was published in March 2002, the last issue came out in March 2003. It was published on a monthly basis, with the exception of three double-issues: 5/6 2002, 9–10/2002, and 13–14/2003.

36 See Ivan Požgai, 'Editoriál', *Atribút* 11–12, 2002: 3. My translation.

37 See <https://www.facebook.com/pg/DuhovyPRIDE/about/?ref=page_internal>

38 See <https://www.facebook.com/transfuzia>

39 Interview with Andrej Kuruc, June 2, 2018, Bratislava, Slovakia. My translation.

40 Online correspondence with Andrej Kuruc, September 28, 2020. My translation.

41 Online correspondence with Andrej Kuruc, September 28, 2020. My translation.

42 See <https://qys.sk/>. The website also offers the option to order a print copy of the magazine (5 EUR per issue, 15 EUR per annual subscription).

43 Between 2018–2020, the production of *QYS* was possible thanks to the Fund for Arts and a grant programme provided by the Slovak Ministry of Justice that aims to promote, support and protect human rights and prevent all forms of discrimination, racism, xenophobia, antisemitism and other forms of intolerance. See <https://qys.sk/donori/>

44 See <https://duhovyrok.sk>, <https://qys.sk/o-nas/o-magazine/>and <https://queerslovakia.sk>

45 See Andrej Kuruc. 'Viditeľnosť LGBTI ľudí v spoločnosti'. *QYS* 1 2016, p. 2. My translation.

46 See Veronika Valkovičová. 'Uvodník'. *QYS* 2 2016: 3. My translation.

47 See *QYS* Summer 2020 <https://issuu.com/nomantinels/docs/qys_magaz_n_leto20_>

7 Revolt Press, Pornography and the Development of Gay markets in Sweden

TOM CUBBIN

In a letter sent to Swedish tobacconists and newsagents in 1972, Revolt Press owners Michael Holm and Geurt Staal attempted to persuade shopkeepers to stock their publications because it would attract new demographics to their business:

> Did you know that there are over 300,000 homosexuals and around 1 million bisexuals in Sweden alone? These people want to be informed. REVOLT provides this information. Revolt is Sweden's only magazine for homo- and bisexual men and women... If you include Revolt in your range and advertise it from the start, you will immediately attract new customers. Customers will not only buy Revolt, but other products too.[1]

The letter gives a clue as to a shift in the development of queer publishing that extended beyond campaigning organizations towards the expansion of gay male culture that incorporated increasing awareness of international gay styles and consciousness. Sweden's reputation as a pioneer in the field of sexual rights was partly due to the success of organizations set up to campaign for education and equality: RFSU (est. 1933) focused on sex education and family planning, while RFSL (est. 1950) focused on sexual equality, particularly for homosexuals. The decriminalization of homosexual sex between adults in 1944 marks Sweden out as an early legal reformer in this respect. Sweden's large geography, however, meant that its homosexual populations were dispersed, while the social democratic cultural construction of 'folkhemmet' (people's home) was largely constructed around ideas of family life.[2] For many homosexuals across Sweden, Revolt publications were their first contact with gay life and, as the letter indicates, tobacconists and kiosk owners might be the first to take advantage of this significant market.

The influential magazine *Revolt: mot sexuella för-domar* (*Revolt: against sexual prejudice*) ran from 1969 (initially as *Viking*) to 1986 and included a mixture of politics and porn for the Swedish domestic market. The magazine included serious articles on gay rights, cultural reportage, contact ads, erotic fiction and photographic pornography as well as 'how to' guides that might expand the sexual repertoires of its readers. It was primarily targeted at men but included occasional articles and photoshoots about lesbian issues. From their base in Åseda, a village on the edge of the 'bible belt' in the South of Sweden, Holm and Staal developed an international business that took advantage of Sweden's liberal laws that allowed the publishing of many types of pornography considered obscene in other countries.

Mirroring a general trend towards fringe market segmentation,[3] Revolt also quickly started to produce more specialist magazines such as *Toy* (from 1973), and *Mister SM* (from 1974), which were published in Swedish, German and English and catered to sado-masochists and fetishists across northern Europe.

An early issue of *Revolt* magazine (1971), which indicates it was formerly known as *Viking*.

From 1971–1986, they published over 15 separate magazines for different niches.[4] Revolt Press was known internationally as the publisher of Tom of Finland's *Kake Comics* during the 1970s. A number of magazines published by the press were targeted to paedophiles,[5] as some sex-liberals saw paedophiles as a sexual minority equally deserving of sexual pleasure alongside groups like sadomasochists and fetishists.[6] Dutchman Guert Staal, who was the businessman in the operation, also imported pornographic films and sold a range of small items such as jock straps and lubricant via mail order under the name Revolt Produkt. They also established Revolt Shop in Hamburg, the first sex shop in Europe aimed at gay men, although this was quickly taken over and run by a local couple.[7]

This hive of commercial activity in the forests of Småland played a key role in the development of gay culture and rights in Sweden and Europe. As historians of sexuality have long argued,[8] commercial ventures such as bars and magazines have been crucial for providing infrastructures that have enabled rights organizations to flourish. Most recently in his book *Buying Gay*, David K. Johnson has shown how American physique magazine entrepreneurs who were willing to fight court cases, but also maintain mailing lists and defend the interests of their clients, participated in important pre-Stonewall forms of activism.[9]

The taboo of combining sex and business was a common topic of discussion in social democratic Sweden in the 1960s and 1970s. Michael Holm lamented in an early issue of *Revolt*, 'Why is the word "commercial" usually pronounced with a distinct disgust?'[10] The explosion of Swedish pornography in the 1970s was sharply criticized by leftist feminist groups who sought limitations on what could be published on moral grounds,[11] which was partly seen as due to the dominance of men in the promotion of sex liberal ideas.[12] As historian Jens Rydström neatly summarizes:

> The contradictory picture of Sweden as a liberal country with lax morals on the one hand, and as a country of disciplined citizens and subtle coercion on the other, is part of its history. Nowhere else in the world could students of the controversy of normalization versus sexual radicalism have a better field of study.[13]

Two studies have already positioned Revolt within this tendency: Hanna Bertilsdottir Rosqvist has identified *Revolt* magazine as a source for detecting a shift from a sex liberal discourse to one centred around homosexual identity,[14] and Klara Arnberg collected valuable data about Revolt Press and other publishers in her economic history of the Swedish pornographic press.[15] While demonstrating that commercialism was taboo for some sexual equality campaigners, the authors' focus on discourse and economics does not address the centrality of images across Revolt's publications. Although discussions on potential negative aspects of commercialization of gay life may have been of concern to some activists, it is difficult to know how the magazines were read by the majority of their subscribers, and how hybrid publications featuring debate articles and pornography influenced different consumers. In this essay I address the need to simultaneously understand pornography as object and practice – a commodity whose production and consumption are also sexual acts.[16] Following from this, we can start to ask about the influence that pornography has had on sexual styles in Swedish society.

As will become clear, the production of gay pornographic magazines must also be considered within a broader transnational context as the flows of images and ideas were informed by travel and trade across national borders. In this essay, I therefore examine how the gay pornographic press in Sweden was reliant upon pre-existing international networks – both to secure magazine content, but also to have a basis for developing a Swedish idea of liberation for sexual minorities. This can be seen in the production of photographic pornography for a specifically Swedish market. Conversely, the privileged legal position of the Swedish pornographic press following the abandonment of practically all censorship for pornography in 1971 enabled Revolt to play an important role in the coherent development of European leather and sadomasochistic communities and business networks. The experience of buying and selling equipment that emerged in leather and fetish scenes also opened the way to new product markets, which were in turn opened to Swedish consumers. I will therefore focus on two main questions: How did Revolt Press develop gay economic markets in Sweden? How did these developments influence the sexual styles of gay men, both at home and abroad?

REVOLT PORNOGRAPHY AND EUROPEAN NETWORKS OF GAY EROTIC IMAGES

Revolt Press emerged as a result of encouragement and support from Axel and Eigil Axgil – the Danish gay rights activists and publishers who were key figures for Scandinavian homosexual rights movements. The Danish organization Forbundet af 1948 was important across Scandinavia and provided the vital infrastructure for members to form the Swedish organization RFSL (then known as the Swedish Federation for Sexual Equality), in 1950.[17] Holm's entrance into gay publishing was through acquaintance with the Axgils in the late 1960s when he worked as a correspondent for the TT News Agency in Malmö.

In 1969, he moved across the Öresund to Copenhagen where he started the magazine *Viking*, which was the second commercial homosexual periodical aimed at a Swedish market (the magazine *HOMO* had been published between 1966 and 1969).[18] At this time, the only regular gay newsletter available in Swedish was *Följeslageren* published by RFSL. In a period when the popular press in Sweden aligned homosexuality with prostitution and petty crime, the editors of *Följeslageren* had been keen to use the publication as a 'tool for tolerance and understanding' that frequently focused on emphasizing respectability to a heterosexual majority.[19] This included a refusal to publish contact announcements that included non-normative sexual practices such as sadomasochism and transvestism.[20] To read and submit such ads, many RFSL members subscribed to the Axgils' magazine *Vennen*, which included erotic photography alongside articles on gay politics and culture, making it an important model for Holm.

The decision by RFSL not to reference sexual practices outside of what might today be called 'vanilla monogamy' was a source of ire for sex liberals who had been influenced by Lars Ullerstam's 1964 book *The Erotic Minorities* (De erotiska minoriteterna). The book, which was translated into nine languages, took an absolutist view on sexual freedom, arguing for the removal of punishments for paedophilia, incest and exhibitionism, and for the relative harmlessness of sadism, masochism, voyeurism, transvestism and necrophilia.[21] As a self-identified sex-liberal,[22] Holm would attempt to create space within Revolt publications for the representation and discussion of the interests of such minority groups.

However, the logistics of sourcing enough editorial and visual content for a new Swedish magazine would have been a challenge. By initially locating the magazine in Copenhagen, Holm was able to tap into transnational networks of erotic photo studios with which the Axgils had been closely involved. While much is known about the history of physique photography in the US due to the efforts of the Kinsey Institute in archiving and preserving material, little research has been undertaken about the practices in

Europe, even though magazines such as *Physique Pictorial* regularly featured images and advertisements from physique studios based in Western Europe and particularly London. It is clear that the Axgils played a coordinating role in the circulation of pornographic images in Europe through their company International Modelfoto Service which led to their imprisonment for distributing illegal materials in 1955.[23] As distributors, the Axgils formed a node in pornographic distribution networks that had expanded rapidly in the inter-war years and included homosexual practices, as well as fetish and BDSM imagery.[24]

In his pioneering work on British pornography in transnational networks prior to 1945, Jamie Stoops has demonstrated that unlike mainstream film and literature of the period, 'pornographic materials displayed features such as female-dominant sex, equitable power dynamics between genders, homosexuality and the acceptance of extra-marital and non-monogamous sexuality',[25] meaning such materials were not only sexually explicit, but offered entirely distinct models of sexuality and gendered interaction.[26] If producers and photographers in Europe before 1945 rarely created pornography solely for distinct heterosexual or homosexual markets,[27] the advent of Danish magazines like *Vennen* played a key role in assembling and directing material towards a homosexual audience, something which was continued in Sweden through Revolt Press.

While there were localized disturbances such as the arrest of the Axgils, the development of transnational networks of pornography distribution 'resulted not only in shared cultural dialogue and exchange, but in overall stability within the system.'[28] In the late 1960s, the process of publishing photographs in pornographic magazines consisted largely of selecting images from catalogues of producers within transnational systems. This is evident in the Danish magazines *Eos* (from 1958) and *Coq International* (from 1969), which included material shot by independent studios in Europe, North America and occasionally northern Africa. Such images were selected from catalogues and royalties were paid for their usage. However, pornographic images produced in one context would not necessarily retain their meaning in another, and one of the main tasks for Revolt Press was to interpret a wide range of sexual styles for a Swedish audience.

DOMESTICATION OF GAY PORNOGRAPHY

While international collabouration was essential for *Revolt* magazine to flourish, Holm and Staal did not have the financial means to locate the press in a major city such as Stockholm where international contacts may have been easier to come by.[29] 'A little red hut in the woods deep in the forests of Småland'[30] was announced as the new headquarters for the press in 1971. The magazine also changed its name from *Viking* to *Revolt* because when they tried to register the title with the Swedish Justice department, the name *Viking* had already been taken by a sailing magazine.[31] As the business grew, they relocated offices to the former glassworks at Åseda, a town whose name became known among gay men as the site of the foremost publishers of Swedish gay magazines.

While little changed for gay people in the town itself,[32] the location of Revolt Press outside of major urban centres is significant because of its connection to provincial Swedish culture. For example, journalist Robert Sandström remembers that many priests living in the countryside subscribed to *Revolt* magazine. In a 1978 article, Holm reflected on how after initially raising a few eyebrows, the magazine was tolerated by a town glad of the employment:

> Nobody reacted negatively as far as we know. In the time we worked with Revolt the town has been run by both social democratic and conservative parties. All parties have been equally supportive of the company and have helped to secure good conditions for our work. The Evangelical churches have been more cautious, but even among the Baptists there are some who greet us as normal in the street. You can therefore be gay and have a great life in a small Swedish town. Sometimes you can even be positively surprised, like the doctor who was happy to have *Revolt* in the waiting room. 'It's Åseda's only magazine, and it's no worse than *Playboy*, is it?'[33]

However, the ideological motivations for printing pornography in Åseda had little in common with the kinds of lifestyle promoted at the *Playboy* mansion. Although there are several possible reasons why they named their company *Revolt*, Holm and Staal's engagement with the Swedish sex-liberal discourse of the 1960s means it is likely that they were familiar with the concept of Revoltpornografi. This is a reference to the controversial 1965 'sex issue' of the Swedish cultural magazine *Ord och Bild*.[34] In his article 'Pop and Pornography', Lars Bjurman proposed a distinction between a passive or narcotic 'medhårspornografi' (frictionless pornography) and 'Revoltpornografi', which he describes in the following way:

> Revolt pornography is defined by its being outside of, and in principle, against society. It is therefore anarchistic rather than revolutionary, and the term includes the notion that its social threat is individuated. Its function is to be sharply morally offensive in any given society. It follows that society can disarm it through allowing its publication. However, this can't happen without society itself being altered, and that is the point. Whether it intends to or not, revolt pornography works for sexual liberation [*sexuell frigörelse*], which frictionless pornography, even in the best case, stalls.[35]

A functional Revolt pornography would not have been possible by simply reproducing images from international networks and Danish porn catalogues. Much of the imported photography included rent boys and styles of photography that failed to communicate an image of sexual liberation. While the magazine took no stance against sex workers (debate articles on the topic were regularly featured in the magazine), it was important to find

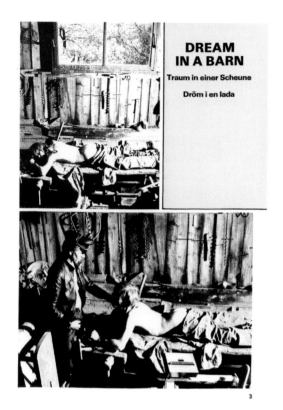

**DREAM
IN A BARN**

Traum in einer Scheune

Dröm i en lada

'Dream in a Barn'
photo-story, featured
in *Mister SM* , No.9,
1974.

ways of depicting how sexual liberation might *look* in Sweden. Furthermore, reproduction rights were a significant expense for magazine entrepreneurs – and cutting costs in this area was key. According to publisher Jon Voss, who began his career working with *Revolt*, an entire photo catalogue was obtained from a rival Danish publisher as part of a settlement following a copyright infringement where they published Tom of Finland images to which Revolt Press owned the rights.[36] For a time, the company even printed *Din Del,* a local business directory and phone book that they used to boost their income.[37] By producing their own erotic photography, the press could lower costs while creating images that could relate more closely to the experience of Swedish homosexuals.

A case in point is the pornographic photo-story 'Dream in a Barn', published in *Mister SM*, although similar stories were featured in *Revolt*. The story is simple – a boy lies on a work bench in a barn. Behind him are some tools, augers for excavating holes for fence posts that don't quite speak to the magazine's macho title. In the second photo, a man arrives in a leather jacket and Muir cap. The barn looks like a typical shed at a Swedish *landställe*, or country cabin. There is a sense that some friends have dressed up to play after a midsummer feast. Even in black and white, it is possible to tell that the leather is poor quality. Two more young men arrive in cheap leather, and a minor orgy is staged for the camera. Despite the promises of the magazine's title, the sex is quite vanilla and the result is rather endearing.

The barn in which the dream shoot took place was probably also the nearest available 'studio.' Peter Appelqvist, the magazine's editor who also undertook much of Revolt's design work frequently invited young men from across Sweden, and also from Hamburg for photoshoots.[38] In this particular example, the inclusion of leather iconography associated with the image of the American gay outlaw is brought into a Swedish setting. But what is at stake in the introduction of leathersex into a context that is legible as specifically Swedish?

The engagement of pornographic imagery with notions of everyday life in Sweden, and particularly the Swedish countryside, could provoke curiosity and amusement. Most infamously, the heterosexual film *Come and Blow the Horn* (*Fäbodjäntan*, dir. Joseph W. Sarno, 1978) features the use of a Falukorv (a traditional Swedish sausage) as a dildo in the Swedish national heartland of Dalarna. As Mats Björkin has shown, the Swedish barn (fäbod) has a long history of eroticization: it was a space where women tradition-ally took care of cattle following a law from 1616 that prohibited men from working as herders due to the fear they would commit sodomy.[39]

A number of scholars have drawn attention to efforts made by pornographers to create gay pornography that is legible along national lines. This has the effect both of distinguishing a locally made product from an international gay visual style that became particularly prominent by the 1980s,[40] and of locating gay desire within a national idea.[41] Behind the analysis of gay male pornographic settings is the idea that in male-to-male sex, the social and spatial location in which it occurs is somehow differently indexed to that in male-female porn. As Cante and Restivo explain in relation to film:

> In staging any sex scene for the camera, a moving-image text invariably indexes social space. In making that action 'take place', it thus indexes fantasy space too. When the action is male-male sex, the spaces in which it transpires can never constitute neutral backdrops. This results from the fact that the acts themselves are non-normative.[42]

In 'Dream in a Barn', not only is male-male sex made visible in a demonstrably Swed-ish space, but American leather culture is made Swedish. While leather fetishism has a European history that goes back at least until the 1920s, the individuals in this shoot are styled as American leathermen – particularly evident through the presence of the Muir leather cap. Swedishness is frequently announced through the material setting of place rather than specific references to the nation. In this sense, the tools, and the feel of wood in the barn re-locate exotic sexual styles for a national audience. By importing a gay pornographic narrative into daily life, a strategy that is common to most pornography,[43] Revolt played a key role in enabling Swedish gay men to see themselves engaging with a range of gay styles. The image of the US leatherman symbolized an urbane gay style that included sexual practices as well as developed forms of socialization and community through bars and motorcycle clubs. This specific mixture of sexual and social contact in an eroticized masculine setting depicted in this photo-shoot makes the story more than a simple sexual fantasy: it argues that something like American leather culture could be possible in Sweden too.

Holm's diverse international contacts in leather and fetish communities provided some of the mechanisms to introduce US leather culture into a Swedish context. For example, Larry Townsend, author of *The Leatherman's Handbook* frequently wrote arti-cles and erotic short stories that were translated into Swedish in Revolt publications. Holm also attempted to explain cultural phenomena such as SM to an audience who were uninitiated. The earliest article to cover SM in *Revolt* was called 'It's nice…when it hurts' (1971), and draws attention to the fact that SM 'relationships' could be achieved through contact ads, but that at that time the nearest club was in Germany. The article ends with a note that expresses the small and informal nature of the infrastructure available at that time:

> Revolt's editorial staff will gladly help readers who are interested in S/M, rubber, leather, chains etc. to get in contact with companies who have the right paraphernalia for satisfying games. Just write what YOU want.[44]

The informal nature of networks at this time meant that personal correspondence was an important way for Swedes to become involved in them, but it was also part of Holm's mission to get Swedish men into kink by popularizing it to a broader section of gay society. Holm frequently provided free advertising space to leather clubs[45] and actively attempted to support the scene.

The domestication of different styles of pornography – but in particular leather and fetish – was therefore coupled with attempts to support clubs and businesses to provide infrastructure for alternative types of gay identity and sexual styles. This would have been impossible without using contacts in Germany, the UK and the USA to provide equipment and knowledge for the young Swedish leather scene. The distribution of *Revolt* magazine provided a strong subscriber basis to enable such networks to develop. However, Revolt Press would also make an important contribution to publishing for sexual minorities in the rest of Europe.

SM AND FETISH PORNOGRAPHY

The Swedish language *Revolt* magazine would have been impossible to finance without the revenue generated from publishing pornography marketed to specific niches abroad, in particular, the larger West German market.[46] Revolt Press produced two magazines aimed at the leather and fetish market in West Germany, the UK and Northern Europe in general. *Toy* focused on leather, rubber and uniforms and 'STUDS with dynamite cocks.' The magazine was the closest European equivalent of the American *Drummer* magazine aimed at US leathermen. *Mister SM,* on the other hand, could not be legally distributed in West Germany. Holm explained to a reader frustrated by the lack of articles in German that 'German gay magazines cannot write about s/m or accept s/m ads due to the censorship there.'[47]

One of the logistical challenges for Revolt Press was therefore the question of how to smuggle such magazines from Sweden to West Germany. According to Jon Voss:

> They had a German transgender woman who packed it into huge suitcases… She took the bags on the boat from Trelleborg to Sassnitz, drove through East Germany and into Berlin and distributed it to the shops there.[48]

Leather in the Swedish countryside features on this cover of *Mister SM* from November 1975.

Such stories are difficult to corroborate and leave open many questions, such as: how did East German customs officers react? Did they not intervene because the final destination was West Berlin? Was bribery involved? Furthermore, along with other Swedish pornographers during the 1970s, Revolt produced paedophile magazines which, like *Mister*

SM, were legal in Sweden but not in West Germany. Titles such as *Ganz Junge Knaben* indicate that they were produced with the German market in mind.[49] Were these also part of the smuggling operation? Such questions highlight the need for further research into networks of European pornography distribution in the twentieth century in relation to the changing legal status of various materials.

Part of the role of *Mister SM* and *Toy* was to publish material about sexual interests not deemed profitable elsewhere in Europe. Containing a mixture of erotic fiction, pornographic photo stories, a lively letters page and contact announcements for men in Europe (and a few in North America), *Mister SM* was a more specialist magazine that solicited content from its readers that would highlight various sexual practices as well as zones of controversy within the scene. As well as SM, this included images and articles defending role-play in Nazi and SS uniforms,[50] as well as stories (both written and visual) that included scat (shit) porn. *Toy* and *Mister SM* also promoted various social and correspondence clubs which could be joined by writing to Revolt in Åseda. These included organizations such as Scat Club Europe, Rubber Men's Club and SCAB – the Society for Cruelty and Brutality.

Crucially, the networks of business contacts that developed through running magazines like *Mr SM* and *Toy* were a precursor to more mainstream developments in a gay consumer culture. Regular advertisers included Walters Leder Boutique in Munich, RoB in Amsterdam, the British company KCS who imported leather Muir caps, and Stig Wollbrecht who ran a small leather business in Gothenburg (though he was renowned for bad quality and using thin leather to wrap plastic). Later issues included both adverts and content produced by Jim Stewart who ran Fetters, the world-renowned bondage gear producer in London.[51] *Toy* included similar advertisements, but its larger circulation meant that it also attracted advertisements from US firms offering mail order such as The Trading Post in San Francisco or R.F.M. based in Los Angeles.

Toy magazine could be legally sold in Germany due to the absence of sadomasochism and focus on leather, rubber and uniform fetish. In the second half of the 1970s, the magazine was relaunched with a focus more clearly on fetish markets.

While known as the publishers of Tom of Finland's *Kake Comics,* another significant contribution of *Toy* to gay men's sexual styles in Europe was the promotion of the American artist Bastille (a.k.a. Frank Weber) whose scenes of post-industrial perversity, sharing of bodily fluids through tubes and machines, created a zone of sexual fantasy that spoke to the developed rubber and latex scenes in Europe.[52] Bastille's depiction of skinheads in rubberwear partly drew on British rubber and skinhead fetishism and expressed a sense of submission to pleasure that was an alternative to the posing associated with the leather 'clone' look.[53] Through the magazine and in publishing *Toy* 'specials' that featured erotic artwork, Revolt Press promoted visual artists who pushed the boundaries of sexual fantasy and taste, thus upholding Bjurman's concept of revolt pornography. Bastille served as an inspiration to a range of fetish-wear designers including London's Recoil.557[54] and his

Cover of *Toy* magazine, Issue 6 after its fetish rebrand, 1977.

influence is felt today in stores such as Berlin's Butscherei Lindinger. Since the early 1980s, the Scandinavian Leathermen Club in Stockholm has produced elabourate parties that attempt to recreate Bastille's artwork through decoration and strictly monitored dress codes.

Toy and *Mister SM* therefore played an important role in giving coherence to the European leather and fetish scenes. Part of this process related to the promotion of businesses who could produce and source appropriate equipment for such activities. Like the American magazine *Drummer*, the magazines worked to legitimize niche sexual interests – however they were much less concerned with promoting a leather style or look. It is curious to note that by the mid 1970s, it was primarily fetish publications in the Revolt Press range that could be seen as an avenue for promotion of a broad range of products and services that indicated gay markets which extended beyond pornography and bars. Revolt's other publications primarily focused on pornography as their main commercial offering to the gay market until a wider range of products became available at the end of the decade.

REVOLT AND THE PRODUCT MARKET IN SWEDEN

The market for clothing, lube, condoms, bondage devices and novelty objects expanded greatly in the US and Northern Europe throughout the 1970s, and Sweden was no exception. However, the reception of such products in Sweden was greatly influenced by the long history of education in sexuality. Concerns relating to the arrival of more sexual products can be seen in the development of new product ranges by RFSU (Swedish Association for Sexuality Education), who had actively campaigned for abortion rights, availability of contraception and sex education in schools since 1933. The marketing of RFSU products speaks to some of the idiosyncrasies of the Swedish market for sex items in the early 1970s, which was split between sex shops known for low quality products, and RFSU products such as contraceptive devices and sex aids which were thought to be of high-quality, but lacked sex appeal due to plain packaging and functional design. In the 1970s, RFSU also increased its provision by expanding into clothes and attempting to attract a younger demographic to its products through 'Flowers and Bees' shops. Just as there was an increasing discussion about the commercialization of sex through the opening of some small gay venues, so too was there controversy surrounding the transformation of an educational organization focused on education and family planning into one which could grow through addressing new markets. A 1972 article in the cultural magazine *Ord och Bild* included an interview with RFSU's director who explained:

> Our customer base consisted mainly of older women buying compression stockings and steady middle-aged family men who bought safe RFSU condoms. You never saw young people in our stores. To get closer to the 15–25 target group we decided to place less emphasis on safety as a selling point and to imbue the products with a spark of excitement.[55]

The development of gay product markets by Revolt Press must therefore be understood in the broader context of what was happening in Sweden which was slowly transforming into a more consumer-oriented society.

The products sold through Revolt Post Order provide insight into the development of a consumer gay market in Sweden. 'Is it sore?' (är det motigt?) asks a back page advert on an early issue of *Revolt*. The advert, for an RFSU-gelé, a lubricant produced by the Swedish Association for Sexuality Education appears in plain, medicinal looking packaging. The advert was accompanied by an announcement for 'P.soap: for daily penis hygiene' (P.tvål för daglig penishygien), and promised that 'your partner will value it.' The objects in this advertisement came from the category of health items which fit with RFSU's designation as an organization focused on health, education and safety. The pairing of lube with a hygiene product seems to emphasize its functional-

Full-page postal order advertisement for Penis soap and 'Gelé' lubricant, in *Revolt mot sexuelle fördomar*, 1971, No. 2. The main text reads: 'Hygiene is important … for your health, for your safety. And believe us, your partner will value it.'

ity – while the lack of a specific product for gay men implies, in this publishing context, an unintended, secondary use. The RFSU products sit awkwardly within the magazine's broader visual mission of legitimizing desire among its readership.

It is only in 1979 when an advert for a lubricant aimed at the gay market appears in *Revolt* magazine – many years after products from leather and fetish suppliers were sold by post order. 'Revolt Press introduces a new lubricant that is made by gays for gays', proclaimed the announcement. In the meantime, the magazine's circulation had grown significantly due to the inclusion in 1977 of *Revolt* in the national newspaper distribution system run by Pressbyrån.[56] This meant that newsagents would be required to stock *Revolt* if they wanted to carry other magazines,[57] thus ensuring the magazine's availability outside of urban centres.

Made from vegetable oil, LUBE promised to be 'scentless, tasteless and water soluble'. Possibly imported from the US, this appears to be the first example of a mail order lubricant for gay men in the Nordic countries (it was also distributed to Norway and Finland). The wide shape of the pot makes it easier to scoop up lube, which is of use when fisting a partner. Being scentless and tasteless contrasts with general cultural understandings of the anus as an abject organ,[58] while the jar itself displays one word: 'natural.'

The move from distributing RFSU's products to the promotion of a lubricant specifically for the gay market is a small clue as to how homosexual markets in Sweden

Advertisement for lube featured in *Revolt mot sexuelle fördomar*, 1980, No. 1. The text reads: 'NICE NEW LUBRICANT: Revolt Press introduces a new lubricant made by gays for gays. The lubricant is called LUBE and is a 100 percent vegetable-based product, based on vegetable oil. It is tasteless, odourless and water-soluble. Flecks can be removed with soap and water. LUBE is sold in 4oz jars (113.4 g) and costs 40 SEK/DEK, 50 NOK, 36 FIM.'

NY SKÖN GLIDSALVA

Revolt Press introducerar en ny glidsalva, som är gjord för bögar - av bögar. Glidsalvan heter LUBE (loob) och är en 100-procentig vegetabilisk produkt, vars bas är vegetabilisk olja. Salvan är smaklös, luktar inte och är vattenlöslig. Fläckar tas lätt bort med tvål och vatten. LUBE säljs i burk om 4 OZ (113,4 g) och kostar skr 40:- dkr/nkr 50:- fmk 36:-

REVOLT PRESS AB, Box 4, 360 70 Åseda. ORDERTEL 0474/114 77
Porto och expeditionsavgift skr 5:- dkr/nkr 6:- fmk 4:- tillkommer.
För postförskott (endast inom Sverige) tillkommer skr 5:-

developed during the 1970s to enable new practices of consumption based on gay styles. The imported lube – specifically designed for 'natural' anal sex and fisting – overcomes the wretchedness of an object like RFSU gelé that must be employed for a secondary purpose.

On the one hand, this simply mirrors the emergence of a gay product market in the West. However, in promoting gay interests through marketing products alongside politics and pornography, Revolt Press drew on a wide range of cultural practices to introduce alternative sexual styles to a broad Swedish readership. While the identification of emerging subjectivities among gay men in Sweden during the 1970s and 1980s is well documented,[59] the role of commercial print pornography in introducing and promoting new gay styles as part of gay popular culture in print has been underestimated.

CONCLUSION

The success of Revolt Press ultimately lay in its strategies of engaging Swedish print culture in international networks and fostering inclusive discussions, however bounded by the implications of a sex-liberal approach and their overwhelmingly male subscription base. In showing and promoting a plurality of ways of being, Holm and Staal played a key role in balancing the pursuit of the interests of sexual minorities and subcultures and connecting business and politics that provided a foundation for modern gay culture in Sweden. The ambition of including a range of editorial and political opinions (as long as they were not deemed too puritanical) shows a clear attempt to produce a magazine that would reflect a sex-liberal culture and foster forms of free speech among Swedish homosexuals. In a 1985 article, Holm remembered how 'Sex liberalism was part of a broader anti-authoritarian political movement. We believed (and believe) in people's ability to develop their sexuality in their own way.'[60]

The sale of new products marked the introduction of more confident sexual identities and initiated a shift towards a greater focus on culture and lifestyle in Swedish gay publishing. For the next generation of Swedish gay publishers such as Jon Voss and Dodo Parikas (whose first publishing venture *Magasin Gay* ran from 1983–1984 with the support of Revolt Press), it was pop culture rather than pornography that was to be the hook for gay cultural expression. Increasingly, pornographic and pop culture content was segregated as gay and queer identities became stronger and less defined by sexual behaviour.

Don Kulick has argued that Sweden's reputation as a sexually liberal country was gradually eroded from the late 1980s, whereby conceptions of 'good sex' rejected the combination of sex and commerce in particular settings. [61] The forced closure of gay bathhouses in the wake of HIV/AIDS in 1987 was followed by a number of laws enacted after the adoption of feminist policies by parties across the political spectrum that were geared towards the regulation of sex and pornography.[62] The 1991 law that forbade the production and consumption of pornography considered 'violent' (including depictions of sadomasochistic sex and fisting), and the law prohibiting the purchase of sexual services (1999), show that Holm and Staal's vision of a sex-liberal Sweden was comprehensively defeated.

Yet, Holm and Staal's explorative approach to markets and styles in the early years of the post-Stonewall era was crucial for men in Sweden and Europe to discover a range of attitudes towards sex, sexual politics and gay culture. Their legacy, of using magazines to represent minority sexual interests with the intention of making them intelligible, if not necessarily accepted, should be seen as an important contribution to the historic development of gay men's sexual styles in Europe.

ACKNOWLEDGEMENTS

Many thanks to Jon Voss, Robert Sandström and Johan Falk, all of whom took the time to tell me about their experiences of working with Revolt Press.

Research for this chapter was financed by Riksbankens Jubileumsfond as part of the project *Crafting Desire: An international design history of gay male fetish making*.

NOTES

1   Letter from Geurt Staal sent to Swedish tobacconists in November 1972, 'Revolt Press AB samling av trycksaker', National Library of Sweden, Stockholm. This and all other translations by the author.

2   See Martin Andreasson. 2000 (ed.). *Homo i Folkhemmet: Homo och bisexuella i Sverige 1950–2000*. Anamma: Göteborg.

3   David K. Johnson. 2019. *Buying Gay: How Physique Entrepreneurs Sparked a Movement*. New York: Columbia University Press. xii.

4   Other titles listed in the National Library of Sweden Database include *Magasin Gay, Hot, Man-to-man* and *Killen*.

5   These included the titles *Hokon* (1972), *Miniboys* (1974), *Chicken* (1973–79), *Bambino* (1974), and *Teenangels* (1975–1983). Klara Arnberg makes the point that some of these had additional German titles, where it was not legal to sell or distribute child pornography. Klara Arnberg. 2010. *Motsättningarnas Marknad : Den Pornografiska Pressens Kommersiella Genombrott Och Regleringen Av Pornografi I Sverige 1950–1980*. PhD thesis, Umeå University. 264.

6   Holm penned a number of articles in defense of paedophiles and child pornography during the 1970s, but according to those interviewed for this essay, this haunted him later in life. See Hanna Bertilsdotter-Rosqvist. 2012. 'Desiring Difference, Desiring Similarity: Narratives on Sexual Interaction between Boys and Men in the Swedish Homosexual Press 1954–1986.' *Sexualities*. Vol. 15, no. 2. 117–138. On the relationship between legislation and the commercialization of child pornography in Europe, see Tim Tate. 1990. *Child Pornography: An Investigation*. London: Methuen.

7   See Bernhard Rosenkranz and Gottfried Lorenz. 2006. *Hamburg auf anderen Wegen: Die Geschichte des Schwulen Lebens in der Hansestadt*. Hamburg: Lamda-Ed. 177–181

8   John D'Emilio. 1993. 'Capitalism and Gay Identity.' in Henry Abelove, Michèle Aina Barale, and David M. Halperin (eds.). *The Lesbian and Gay Studies Reader*. London: Routledge. 467–476; Jeffrey Escoffier. 1998. *American Homo : Community and Perversity*. Berkeley: University of California Press; Amy Gluckman and Betsy Reed. 1997. *Homo Economics: Capitalism, Community, and Lesbian and Gay Life*. London: Routledge.

9   See Johnson, *Buying Gay*. Op. Cit.

10   Michael Holm. 1971. 'Käre Vän och Läsare.' *Revolt*. No 2. 1–3.

11   See Petra Östergren. 2006. *Porr, Horor Och Feminister*. Stockholm: Natur och kultur.

12   Don Kulick, 2005. 'Four Hundred Thousand Swedish Perverts.' *GLQ: A Journal of Lesbian and Gay Studies*. Vol. 11 no. 2. 211.

13   Jens Rydström. 2001. *Sinners and Citizens: Bestiality and Homosexuality in Sweden 1880–1950*. Chicago: Chicago University Press. 2.

14   Hanna Bertilsdotter-Rosqvist. 2011. 'Att Berätta Bögberättelser: Från Sexliberalism till Homoidentitetsretorik I Svensk Homopress under 1960–1980-talet.' *Lambda Nordica* 16:1. 9–40.

15   Arnberg. *Motsättningarnas marknad*. Op. cit. The complementarity of these perspectives is clear in a co-authored essay which explores how controversies around commercial venues were constructed in discourse during the 1980s surrounding gay male spaces such as Stockholm's Viking Sauna and the offices of sexual rights organization RFSL. See Hanna Bertilsdotter-Rosqvist & Klara Arnberg. 2015. 'Ambivalent Spaces: The Emergence of a New Gay Male Norm Situated Between Notions of the Commercial and the Political in the Swedish Gay Press, 1969–1986.' *Journal of Homosexuality*. Vol. 62 No 6. 763–781.

16   Jamie Stoops. 2018. *The Thorny Path: Pornography in Early Twentieth-Century Britain*. Montreal: McGill-Queen's University Press. 5.

17 Stig-Åke Petersson. 2000. 'En svensk homorörelse växer fram: RFSL 1950–2000.' In Martin Andreasson (ed.). *Homo i Folkhemmet: Homo- och bisexuella i Sverige 1950–2000*. Göteborg: Anamma. 11–19.

18 Hanna Bertilsdotter-Rosqvist. 2016. 'Bad Sex, Good Love: Homonormativity in the Swedish Gay Press, 1969–86.' *GLQ: A Journal of Lesbian and Gay Studies*. Vol. 22 No. 1. 38.

19 Andréaz Wasniowski. 2007. *Den Korrekta Avvikelsen: Vetenskapsanvändning, Normalitetssträvan Och Exkluderande Praktiker Hos RFSL, 1950–1970*. Umea: Holzweg. 184–186.

20 Ibid.

21 Lena Lennerhed. 1994. *Frihet Att Njuta: Sexualdebatten i Sverige På 1960-Talet*. PhD Thesis, Stockholm University. 153.

22 Michael Holm. 1985. 'Flumliberaler tankar.' *Revolt mot sexueller fördomar*. No 5. 7–10.

23 Wilhelm von Rosen. 1999. 'Pornografiaffæren i 1955.' *Zink*. No 4. 14–18. Archival records are shown for International Modelfoto Service in the Danish National Archives, however the author was unable to access the documents due to Covid-19 travel restrictions.

24 See Chapter 2 in Stoops, op. cit. See also Robert Vincent Bienvenu II. 1998. *The Development of Sadomasochism as a Cultural Style in the Twentieth-Century United States*. PhD Thesis, Indiana University.

25 Stoops. Op. cit. 93.

26 Ibid. 94.

27 Ibid. 130.

28 Ibid. 68.

29 Interview by author with Robert Sandström, May 2020.

30 Michael Holm. 1971. 'En röd liten stuga i skogen.' *Revolt mot sexuella födomer*. No 10. 2.

31 Ibid.

32 Interview with Robert Sandstöm, May 2020.

33 Michael Holm. 1978. 'Bög i Åseda.' *Revolt mot sexuella födomar*. No 9. 6.

34 Arnberg (163) and Lennerhed (196) both draw attention to this article, but the connection between Bjurman's 'revolt pornography' and the name of Revolt press is not made.

35 Lars Bjurman. 1965. 'Pop och pornografi.' *Ord och Bild*. No 3.

36 Interview by author with Jon Voss, August 2020.

37 Interview with Robert Sandström, May 2020.

38 Interview by author with Johan Falk, May 2020.

39 Mats Björkin. 2005. *Fäbodjänten: Sex, Communication and Cultural Heritage*. In Olle Edström and Alf Björnberg (eds.). *Frispel: Festskrift till Olle Edström*. Skrifter Från Institutionen För Musikvetenskap, Göteborgs Universitet. 165–173.

40 Peter Rehberg. 2016. '"Männer Wie Du Und Ich": Gay Magazines from the National to the Transnational.' *German History*. Vol. 34, no. 3. 468–485.

41 Dan Healey. 2010. 'Active, Passive, and Russian: The National Idea in Gay Men's Pornography.' *Russian Review*. Vol. 69 No. 2. 210–230.

42 Rich Cante and Angelo Restivo. 2004. 'The Cultural-Aesthetic Specificities of All-Male Moving Image Pornography.' In Linda Williams (ed.). *Porn Studies*. Durham, NC: Duke University Press. 142.

43 Ibid. 147.

44 Michael Holm. 1971. 'Det är skönt när det svider: Litet om sadomasochism.' *Revolt mot sexuella fördomar*. No. 4. 18.

45 Interview with Johan Falk, May 2020.

46 This was mentioned in my interviews with Jon Voss, Robert Sandström and Johan Falk.

47 Readers' Letters. 1980. *Mr SM*. No. 25. 15.

48 Interview with Jon Voss.

49 Arnberg. *Motsättningarnas Marknad*. Op. cit. 264.

50 *Mister SM*. 1980. No. 23. 22–23.

51 See Tom Cubbin. 'Fetters and the Cultural Origins of some Bondage Objects.' *Journal of Homosexuality*. Forthcoming.

52 I speculate that the relative strength of the European leather scene compared to the US was partly due to British precedents such as John Sutcliffe's AtomAge clothing and publishing business, but also due to the institutionalization of leather in the US as a symbol for the homosexual sexual outlaw. Clubs and societies upheld leather as the primary expression of fetish and were therefore more resistant to other material fetishes during the 1970s and 1980s.

53 See Martin P. Levine. 1998. *Gay Macho: The Life and Death of the Homosexual Clone*. New York: New York University Press.

54 See Marc Martin. 2017. *SCHWEIN: Bastille Traces*. Paris: Agua.

55 Lotte Möller. 1972. 'Från frihetsrörelse till varuhus i sex.' *Ord och bild*. No 3. 95–106.

56 Michael Holm. 1977. 'Sex är alltid bra.' *Revolt mot sexuella fördomer*. No 6. 1.

57 Arnberg. Op. cit.

58 Tomasso Milani. 2018. 'Is the rectum a goldmine? Queer theory, consumer masculinities, and capital pleasures.' In Paul Baker and Giuseppe Balirano (eds.). *Queering masculinities in language and culture*. Basingstoke: Palgrave Macmillan. 19–42.

59 See Bertilsdottir-Rosqvist, 'Att Berätta Bögberättelser.' Op. cit.

60 Holm, 'Flumliberala Tanker'. Op. cit.

61 Don Kulick. 'Four Hundred Thousand Perverts.' Op. cit.

62 Kulick argues that the 'sex wars' that took place among US feminists were largely absent from the Swedish discourse. Instead, as 'feminism' was promoted within the political system during the 1970s, markers of 'good sex' as promoted by organizations like RFSU came to be used as a guide for legislation against activities such as pornography, prostitution and erotic dancing. Ibid. 211–212.

8 *Mietje:* In conversation with Gert Hekma and Mattias Duyves

BENNY NEMER

On a beautiful summer day in August of 2018, my boyfriend Bastien and I visited Amsterdam-based scholars and activists Gert Hekma and Mattias Duyves to talk about their involvement in *Mietje*, a radical gay journal published in the late 1970s. It was Bastien's birthday, which increased the already festive feeling I experience whenever visiting the couple's fabulous home. For the fastidiously preserved back issues of *Mietje* that Gert had taken out in advance of our conversation are but a fraction of the trove of publications of queer historical importance that fill the bookshelves of Gert and Mattias' apartment. Their home is a giant library housing more than seven thousand books, journals, and art catalogues collected over forty-five years of passionate activism and scholarship: books on the Marquis de Sade and his legacy; sexual liberation movements; masturbation; male prostitution; and the intersections between sex and crime. There are a few books on werewolves. There is a shelf devoted to child sexuality and intergenerational love. A section on urinals and the culture of gay sex in public toilets. First edition copies of the earliest German sexology books. Shelves filled with ethnographic studies of sexual difference around the world. Every issue of *BUTT* magazine.

And while books make up the main collection that dominates the visual experience of their home, the library co-exists with other objects and artefacts that have been collected, preserved, and organised in similar ways: plants, vases, artworks, and other unclassifiable objects and paraphernalia that mix and mingle into a maximalist archive of the couple's lives and times. Indeed, the concept asserted by numerous theorists that the defining characteristic of a queer archive is its fragmentary, incomplete nature, replete with gaps and absences, seems momentarily suspended in Mattias and Gert's world, which overflows with material, populated with a cast of characters whose words and images call out to the visitor like a mass choir.[1] The two men have lived in this apartment

Cover of *Mietje* No. 6 & 7, 1979. Courtesy of Mattias Duyves and Gert Hekma.

since 1979, and over the years, their collections and lives have spilled over into other spaces within the building: they occupy another book- and plant-filled apartment above this one, along with students and friends. When we visited, the queer activist and social anthropologist Renaud Chantraine was staying for a few days in a diminutive bedroom where the eminent queer philosopher Guy Hocquenghem once stayed during a visit to the couple in the 1980s.

Mattias prepared a pot of tea, which he placed on a large, square table in the salon where Gert and I were busy arranging the flowers Bastien and I had brought as an offering. The table is covered with a thick piece of clear plastic film, under which the couple maintain an ever-evolving collection of paper ephemera: pictures and texts cut out of newspapers and magazines, exhibition invitations, letters, and other print material, a kind of mood board of the current moment. The effect that day was one of a three-dimensional collage, with the couple's current arrangement of paper below the plastic covering, and the copies of *Mietje*, the parrot tulips, and the tea cups above. The table is positioned beside a wall of large windows that look down at the summery activity of the Oudezijds Voorburghwal: tourists and pleasure-seekers wandering the Red Light District, ogling sex shop displays, taking photographs of the thirteenth-century Oude Kerk, getting high, and alternately marvelling at or using the curvaceous nineteenth-century urinals that dot the canal.

Mietje was a large-format newspaper produced by a group of Dutch gay activists from 1977–1979, many of whom were members of the Nijmegen-based radical gay activist group the Rooie Flikkers, or Red Faggots. The newspaper offered readers a full range of content, from political news to Dutch translations of gay political thought from France and Germany; poetry and song lyrics; film criticism and essays on gay history; sexy photo spreads, cartoons, and wild collages promoting or documenting parties and live music events. *Mietje*'s aesthetic was joyful, experimental, visibly created with care and consideration. The pages were printed in bright, saturated colours that – at least on Gert and Mattias's copies – have not faded over time: deep purple, hot pink, royal blue, carmine. It featured a range of typographical styles, combining typewritten passages, headlines in a variety of Lettraset typefaces, and florid handwritten texts, including a custom-designed logo font that vaguely conjures penises in a range of exuberant positions. The summer 1977 issue lists eighteen contributors, among them Gert and Mattias.

I spent the afternoon flipping through *Mietje*'s colourful pages while discussing its history with Gert and Mattias. To ask them a question about a book in their library or an event from the past is to initiate a long discussion of the entangled webs of relationships and overlapping histories that make up their involvement in activist life, queer thought, and the evolving political and intellectual cartographies of Amsterdam, the Netherlands, and Europe. They each carry a seemingly infinite amount of knowledge and information about queer lives and practices that they wish to impart, and they do so using the same

Mattias Duyves, Benny Nemer, and Gert Hekma discussing *Mietje* in Duyves and Hekma's home. Photograph by and courtesy of Bastien Pourtout.

oblique lines of logic as their library, tracing links between people and places, ideas and events; sifting through memories of parties and protests, arguments and love affairs. Bastien took photographs and eventually wandered into the labyrinth of the couple's home, lured by the call of the books, the plants, and the idyllic balcony garden that extends towards the tower of the Zuiderkerk, whose bells ornamented our conversation by chiming every fifteen minutes.

GH: For us it was very interesting to work on *Mietje* but we also, at the same time, had our parties going on. So for example, [when we lived in a flat on] Weesperstraat, we hired the university students' canteen for an evening, and there we had a party with all the music that we liked.

MD: Here you can see the first posters [for that event]. 'Rooie Flikkers bring you a night full of screaming faggots – *nichten*.'

BN: Because *nichten* is another word for faggot, isn't it? It means something like a niece.

GH: Yeah.

BN: That leads me to a question about the title, *Mietje*. A few friends have told me their interpretation of *mietje*, as another term for an effeminate man or a faggot. In 1977, when the first issue came out, how would a Dutch person understand that word? Instead of something like the word *flikker*, which was already being used quite a bit by the [Dutch gay activist group] Flikkerfront, what would *mietje* mean to a reader? Does *mietje* have a more intense charge?

GH: It has a very negative charge. [We used both *mietje* and *nichten*] in the Red Faggots, but only amongst ourselves.

MD: All of these words were completely forbidden to use in open discourse, or in a journal. The words have pejorative associations. To me the word *mietje* is much more identified with Nijmegen, that part of the Netherlands.

GH: *Mietje* comes from the word *sodomiet*.

BN: It derives from *sodomiet*, so it's like *sodomietje*. 'Little sodomite'. So why were the Rooie Flikkers based in Nijmegen? What made Nijmegen an important centre for gay political activity?

MD: Nijmegen is the most northern city of Limburg, the most traditional Roman Catholic province. It produced many, many Jesuits, to give you an example, because all the major institutions for the Jesuits were there. And then overnight in the sixties, many of these so-called Jesuit students radicalised, and they became Marxists. Nijmegen University became the most red university, along with Tilburg and other universities in the south – a much more red university than in Amsterdam, so very radical. And in this very radical student milieu where everything was contested there was a little group of gay men who started to create [the journal] *Flikkerkrant*, and they were really in debate with the student movement of Nijmegen. And the student

Below left: Front cover of *Mietje* No. 2, 1977. Courtesy of Mattias Duyves and Gert Hekma.

Below: Back cover of *Mietje* No. 2, 1977. Courtesy of Mattias Duyves and Gert Hekma.

Above: *Mietje* No. 2, 1977, page 13 (detail). Courtesy of Mattias Duyves and Gert Hekma.

Above right: *Mietje* No. 2, 1977, page 14 (detail). Courtesy of Mattias Duyves and Gert Hekma.

movement of Nijmegen had the best publishing house, it translated all the major books from Germany and also from the French structuralists, so from Paris and Berlin. I was studying there for a year, but then I said to myself I should go to Amsterdam for sex, for study, and for the city. And I found out that here is where all the interesting media production was, not in Nijmegen. Many things in Nijmegen went unnoticed in Amsterdam because Amsterdam was always busy with itself, like today, you know how capitals are. That's why I moved to Amsterdam.

BN: When you came together as a group to start *Mietje*, was it especially important for you to create a newspaper and a kind of political presence that was in very clear contrast to what some of your contemporaries were doing, to have an alternative forum? Did *Mietje* have a kind of manifesto?

MD: Yeah. We had a poster [announcing that] *Mietje* was [about to be] published, which also served as a manifesto. Here's the text: 'Our consciousness has been demolished. We are so demolished that only a few gay people will understand how necessary it is to organise as gays, as flikkers. And to know that already there's a hundred-year-old flikker struggle going on—

GH: That's a reference to [the early 20th century German gay rights activist] Magnus Hirschfeld.

MD: 'Our history is silenced, is hidden. And that's why we think that many of our sisters think they are the only ones, or that they are just a casual minority. But we don't want to believe that any longer. We want to take control of the word ourselves because nobody else will do it for us. To tell about parties, about sex orgies, about failures, about long wild nights, and about our paranoia when we leave the door as an open faggot, as a screaming faggot. Our paranoia on the streets, at our work, and what we can do against it.' And it goes on and on and on.

GH: It was very important to us, as a political issue, that private life should become public. And there were two other main issues we always had: that we faggots were separate from the normal homosexuals, who didn't want to stand up and make their private lives public; and that we were separate from the leftist people – there was a very strong feeling that the leftist people had no interest in gay/queer issues.

MD: Here's another quote: 'What we do not want is to integrate homosexuality next to heterosexuality, as if heterosexuality could ever be our yardstick. Heterosexuality needs to be crumbled because it terrorizes all other forms of sexuality.' We proposed political allegiance between the marginalised: 'women, transvestites, pederasts, sado-masochists, whores, lesbians, children, flikkers, and male misfits…'

GH: It was very important for us to do things like making this journal, organising film festivals, making books – making history, making our own culture.

MD: Because nobody else will do it for you.

BN: So I guess at the time when some fag on the street would see a poster like this, they would recognise that language as being in contrast to the language of the COC[2] and their politics of integration.

MD: Yeah, definitely.

BN: Was *Mietje* a forum where different ideas and opinions and forms of expression were welcomed, or did everything have to conform to a certain political agenda in order to make it into the pages?

MD: No, the content was completely diverse. And it was not an academic paper at all. I think it was a dump for all kinds of ideas that were racing through our minds. I always had a penchant for song texts, for lyrics. When we made *Mietje* I always said, 'Who can make a composition? We should produce songs about Amsterdam and gay life!' But I couldn't do it.

BN: But there is a real feeling of poetry and music to the paper, even on an aesthetic, typographical level. Thinking of *Mietje* as a dump, in the most positive connotation of the word, rings true because you have a sense of a group of people who are out, active, curious, finding things, collecting them, bringing them together, translating them, sharing them. Like, here's a poem, and here's a drawing of Constantine Cavafy, and here's a little report on a film festival in Hamburg —

MD: Yeah, it was like that. It was like redeveloping and rediscovering pieces of forgotten culture or hidden culture.

GH: Some people contributed specific things. For example Leo Dullaart was very much into the Frankfurt School, but he also wrote song texts. Mattias wrote about poetry, I wrote a lot about history and about films, but I also wrote about perversion. Charlotte [Paul Geraedts] discussed paedophilia. Everybody had a role to play. Some people wrote about conceptions of beauty, and about [whether identities are socially and culturally] conditioned.

MD: I would never write about sexual acts, to give an example, because I'm simply not really interested in another person's sexual acts, although I always say you should do what you want. But Gert, he's much more interested in the act of sexuality. I was more interested in the art of sexuality.

BN: Because you were both students at the time, did *Mietje* become a forum for the scholarship you were doing at university to be explored and expressed? For example, perversion was already emerging as a scholarly theme for Gert at that time.

GH: [Scoffs] No, no, no. It had nothing to do with university. It was part of the Red Faggots, and we wrote for the Red Faggots. I didn't do it for students at my university, but I guess I was inspired by the Red Faggots to work at university on gay and lesbian issues. So, later on, I did my MA on the anthropology of homosexuality.

MD: At the end of the 1970s, I was a student in sociology and whenever sexuality was discussed it was always part of social psychology or social psychiatry. It was about deviation and to what degree something was deviant or not. And what we discovered, independently, was that there was a whole history of queer activism: as the manifesto I was quoting from noted, there was 'a hundred years of gay struggle.' That was so brand new to us! I remember very well the very first time I saw a pink triangle. All my youth in the Netherlands I had been raised learning about Jewish stars and concentration camps. I'd never heard of gays, I'd never heard of European Roma in concentration camps. So we re-discovered history, or to say it in a different way, I think we were a part of that generation that transgressed the so-called private biography of the homosexual, 'This is your life and you have to live with it.' We transgressed into a more collective, cultural biography, a new horizon.

GH: Which had public dimensions.

MD: A new horizon that really transgressed the private restraints and limits of life. That is what we were doing. And that's why I think it was a kind of playground for Gert to navigate more and more into the study of history. Thijs [Maasen], another guy who contributed to *Mietje*, he's a psychologist, but he also rediscovered the history of certain psychological ideas about homosexuals.

BN: In one of the final issues, there's quite a long, multi-page essay on perversion that was written by Thijs.

MD: He wrote a dissertation on related topics as well and became a well-known psychologist for gay people. He was a radical psychologist; not saying, 'your deviation is a medical or psychiatric deviation,' but inviting the gay to question, 'What kind of gay are you? What kind of gay do you want to be?'

GH: We also had contributions from Martijn [van Kerkhof], the lover of Thijs, who was also a singer. He was part of Tejde & the Flikkers, a sort of radical punk group. And he was very bold and provocative in his statements. He would say: 'I'm a whore. I'm a gay whore.' And 'throw the prime minister out of the window.'

MD: No, he said, *flikker hem uit het raam*, 'throw him out of the window', it's a word game with the word flikker. I think he was one of the Rooie Flikkers par excellence. Because he really lived it, he didn't simply say, 'We should unite whores and flikkers and others.' No, he said 'I will become a whore myself.'

GH: I guess what's also important to say is that *Mietje* was about pleasure. Not only about sexual pleasure, but about the pleasure of meeting and coming together and organising parties and the journal.

BN: It's also clear in the heterogeneity of materials and information that appears in *Mietje*, that the Rooie Flikkers were rather well connected to gay activist communities in other countries. You were translating texts by foreign thinkers such as Guy Hocquenghem, there are pictures of members going to Hamburg for a film festival—

GH: We included material about Muenster—

MD: Copenhagen—

BN: There were articles written about Berlin and about the FHAR[3] in France. I'm curious how *Mietje* circulated. There's a separate question about commercial circulation, because I know you had subscriptions and even a special price for bookstores. But my question is more about the Rooie Flikkers: how did you find out about other radical faggot groups and about what was happening elsewhere in Europe? And how did you maintain relations and dialogue with them?

GH: I remember that Mattias organized Flikkerkamp in Montaigu-de-Quercy, close to Cahors, and Frank Arnal came. Frank was later the head editor of *Gai Pied* magazine in France, the best gay weekly I would say. And the first day he came, I met him because I spoke the best French among the people in the Red Faggots. He talked to me about the gayness of Deleuze and Guattari, Guy Hocquenghem and everything happening in France. After we had this meeting in Montaigu-de-Quercy, we went to Paris, they came to Amsterdam. So there was a circulation. We often went to Paris. And it was cheap because we had friends in Paris who we could stay with, and we had a car, and we had four or five people driving in this car to Paris and back again. They organised film festivals, we organised parties, and there was always curiosity from both sides. Frank Arnal gave me a free subscription to *Gai Pied* for the whole time it existed, more or less. Through Frank we made connections with academics too, such as Michel Maffesoli, a Professor of Sociology at the Sorbonne.

MD: Our networking also involved putting contact advertisements in certain journals. *Libération* was a new journal in those days; back then it was really the porte-parole for everything marginal. I wrote a contact advertisement saying that we were going to organise a summer holiday camp. We put another similar advertisement in [German gay publication] *Schwuchtel*. And here is an answer from a person from Belgium saying, 'Yeah, we read your advertisement and we from the Red Butterfly Collective from Antwerp really want to visit your summer holiday thing, and we want to come with seven people, and we will be very glad when your central committee will acknowledge our request.'

GH: [laughs]

MD: Which we found very funny, because the last thing on our mind was to have a central committee. But that's how the networking operated. People from Copenhagen, and people from Italy got in touch. It made us aware of where our limits were, because we didn't have Italian speaking persons in our milieu. Today, in Amsterdam, you could find in five minutes a person who speaks Italian or Spanish but in those days the city was not that internationalised, not even the university.

BN: I think it's easy to forget the way in which communication and correspondence took place amongst queers in the 1970s.

MD: Yes, but I think the whole movement in those days was always organised along those lines.

GH: Gay people also knew, for example, that you could go to the COC and see what kinds of journals you could get hold of from Germany and Italy and France.

MD: And in those days you already had gay maps available from several cities.

GH: *The Spartacus Gay Guide* [founded in 1970] was a vital source of information.

MD: But a lot of the communication was really improvisation, not unlike the ways in which information circulated in relation to the squats.

BN: I remember even for myself coming out in the early nineties, I moved to Toronto and I just walked around the city in search of the neighbourhood 'where men held hands.' I was intent on finding that neighbourhood, and then chanced upon a gay newspaper. And there was no way for me to find out that information without just going and living it. The ways that the Rooie Flikkers made themselves visible, and how other organisations in other countries, in other languages, made themselves visible to each other and communicated in the 1970s, seems somehow miraculous.

MD: And it was based on person-to-person contact. And this is without considering all the people that we missed, that could not find us and we could not find them! We organised a European summer camp and there were about eighty people. I'm sure

if you did it today through Facebook or whatever you would have to prevent eighty thousand turning up.

BN: To return to questions about commercial circulation: I noticed in the third issue of *Mietje* that there's a list of subscription prices, how much it costs for a back issue and what it cost in the bookstores.

GH: It was very cheap.

BN: How large was the circulation?

GH: I guess at most 500 copies per issue.

BN: And do you remember how many subscribers you had more or less?

GH: No, I have no idea. But I remember taking the journal to the communist bookstore of Amsterdam. And I asked the owner, a gay guy, whether he wanted to sell the journal and he said, 'No, because we don't sell journals.' And I said, 'Well, I see many journals on your shelves,' because the shop was full of communist journals. And then he said, 'Well, we don't sell journals that discuss "bedroom" issues, only political issues.'

BN: If the communist bookstore wouldn't carry it, what bookstores were carrying *Mietje*?

GH: The leftist bookstores and the more culturally liberal ones.

MD: Van Gennep, a more intellectual store, was one. Athenaeum Boekhandel.

Above left: Front cover of *Mietje* No. 5, 1978. Courtesy of Mattias Duyves and Gert Hekma.

Above: Back cover of *Mietje* No. 5, 1978. Courtesy of Mattias Duyves and Gert Hekma.

RAVISSANT

Zaterdagavond 25 februari waren we te gast in het Winterhuder Fährhaus, waar door het BROHWARM-KOLLEKTIV het tweede, jaarlijkse BALL-BROHWARM werd gehouden. Onze eigen GOLDIE presenteerde de zang en -dansvoorstellingen in de grote zaal (1). In de andere zalen werden films en BLUTSTURZ, een autobiografische diashow van Peggy von Schnottgenberg vertoond. Tussen de voorstellingen van de Rooie Flikkers werd LEONARDA, een van de MONTEVERDI toonkunstenaars vlak voor zijn optreden door Hamburgse MATHIAS betoverd (2).
Uit Luilekkerland waren de aldaar beroemde BELLY-SISTERS naar Hamburg gekomen. Deze Sisters, die zich de bevrijding van de buik uit het slanke keurslijf van de homosexualiteit ten doel stellen, flitsten in opwindende BELLY-LOVE scènes over de bühne en zijn nadien op streng dieet gegaan (biefstukken) (3) Dat niet alleen buiken bevrijd moeten worden, toonde ons deze zuster door haar baard met strikken te tooien en de harige borst fier uit het dékolleté te steken (4).
Uit Berlijn was o.a. de beeldschone WIELAND, die met Mann-O-Mann en het winkeltje HULAHUP (Belzigerstr. 23) waar Schmuck, Federn, Glitzer und Tee verkocht worden, bezig is, naar het Fährhaus gekomen.(5) De nacht voordat zij haar grote liefde zou ontmoeten was ROLF, de Brusselse zangeres, die regelmatig nichtenfeesten in de provincie met welluidende en zwoele liederen opvrolijkt, in prima stemming aanwezig (6).
In de wandelgangen, bestemd voor importante zaken, liet de Luxemburgse Markies PIERRE PESCATORI zich op de gevoelige plaat vastleggen in gezelschap van zijn secretaris Prof. BERNHARD ZONNEBLOEM, een belangrijk wetenschapper, die op zoek is naar de echte waarheid en alle problemen daaromtrent (7). In de gevorderde ochtend stond HANS KOK, die sinds kort deel uitmaakt van de Rotterdamse Kunstflikkers, klaar om elke bobbel te registreren (8).

erica & axebelle

HAMBURG

Mietje No. 5, 1978, page 15 (detail). Courtesy of Mattias Duyves and Gert Hekma.

GH: That one was important to us.

MD: They wanted to excel in having every printed zine in the Netherlands in their shop, and it didn't matter what it was about. They had everything, including the most marginal!

GH: But there were also bookshops in Groningen and Maastricht and many other places where we could sell *Mietje*.

MD: And each bookstore would take ten or fifteen copies.

GH: We also had our demonstrations and meetings where we sold *Mietje*.

BN: Were journal sales the major source of income? Because I wonder, especially when I see these beautifully colour-printed copies, how the project was funded. It was clearly not a zine: it doesn't feel like a zine, it feels like a very carefully-assembled, highly-designed, beautifully printed publication. Clearly it's printed on good paper if forty years later it's in such great condition.

MD: It was. I think production choices were driven by what the cheapest thing was that we could find. And the discussion we had about the design was always about how many colours we could include. The first duplications were in black and white. And then if you wanted to add another colour it required another journey through the printing machine, and then it was a little bit more expensive.

GH: We also got money from the parties and the film festivals we organised, as they were always quite successful.

MD: The entry fees for those events were always extremely low. I always said we should charge as low a fee as possible because otherwise the students will not come.

BN: So there wasn't a patron or someone who was a member of the Rooie Flikkers with a lot of money who funded the whole project?

MD: No. Maybe there was someone who now and then put some extra money in. I've got here some of our finance records. The entrance fee to our parties was five guilders which is about two and a half euros.

BN: The graphic design of *Mietje* feels quite special and experimental. Was there one person who was the designer? Or was it also kind of a collabourative project?

MD: I think it was really the art of improvisation, the art of amateurism. I consider *Mietje* extremely amateurist.

BN: But you designed your own typeface that's used throughout.

MD: Yeah.

BN: There were clearly lots of aesthetic experiments being conducted. As the issues go on, it looks like somebody is trying out different things. Were there other newsletters and newspapers that you were reading that were inspiring you aesthetically?

MD: If you went in those days to Athenaeum's magazines section you would see a number of publications with a similar amateurist aesthetic. *Mietje* was rather rich because we had different colours. This one, for instance, has a bold use of green and red. There were pages that I really designed for myself, for my own pleasure. I always liked paintings that include letters. That aesthetic became more and more important to me than simple images. We also had design input from Martijn [van Kerkhof] and Erik Latour. And we had some aesthetic guidance from a designer, Peter van Werkhoven.

BN: What do you mean when you say amateur?

MD: These are not people who went to art school or who were professional.

BN: But still, there's good quality photography in the journal. It's very carefully composed, and the arrangement is very considered. It's not some random thing. So many other zines are black and white, photocopied, but you had a much more developed design aesthetic and were much more ambitious when it comes to colour and print quality.

GH: Erik de Keizer, who was the photographer for the Red Faggots, did contribute, and he did a very good job with his photos.

MD: He made many of the pictures that you see in the issues; today there are students who like to see his pictures because they think his style is 'authentic'. He was there like a fly on the wall, taking spontaneous pictures. Crucially, he had a camera. Most people in our network didn't have a camera in those days.

BN: It seems that the last issue is this double issue from Winter '79, and then it's followed in 1980 by a few journal issues that seem more like festival programmes, like this one, with the title 'Mietje Pietje'.

GH: Yeah, these are festival programmes.

BN: So why did *Mietje* stop being published?

Mietje Pietje, 1980, page 10. Courtesy of Mattias Duyves and Gert Hekma.

MD: Well, it was rather intensive getting the text, organising the texts, assembling the text together… We would say to a group of people, 'Okay, we're going to make the next issue of *Mietje* at the weekend, now you make a text, and you make a text, everybody make a text.' They would submit all of these typed texts. We would use an electrical machine to fit the texts into the page format. We used to do all of this in a beautiful school building that we could use because we knew a teacher who would allow us access. But the guys from Nijmegen would come to Amsterdam when we were putting an issue together, and of course they also wanted to go out at night. They came to Amsterdam ostensibly for working on *Mietje*, but the experience became a little bit intense.

GH: At the time of the last issue of *Mietje*, we were also involved in organising a festival: it was called Festival Mannen Nietwaar. This was a festival to indicate the end of the Red Faggots. We said, well, we should also finish producing *Mietje* at the same time. So this was a double announcement: the end of the Red Faggots and the end of the journal.

BN: So both the journal and the group ended at the same time?

MD: Yeah, exactly. It was a short-lived group.

GH: And there were other groups at the same time coming up in Holland: artist groups and activist groups in Eindhoven and Groningen who would continue this story. A few years after starting things up, we stopped them. A younger crowd took over.

BN: So the end of *Mietje* wasn't because of some kind of conflict or internal struggle?

GH: No.

MD: It's just that things evolved, people moved on, grew away from each other.

BN: What's interesting is that so much gay activism and so many publications flourished in the 1970s, and I guess I have this simplified image of AIDS happening in the early eighties and stopping everything. So it's interesting to see *Mietje* emerge and end in its own sort of natural way, without the intervention of AIDS. It's just a nice reminder of how things emerge and dissipate and transform.

MD: Exactly.

NOTES

1   See Ann Cvetkovich. *An Archive of Feelings: Trauma, Sexuality, and Lesbian Public Cultures*. Durham, NC: Duke University Press, 2003; Elizabeth Freeman. *Time Binds: Queer Temporalities, Queer Histories*. Durham, NC: Duke University Press, 2010; John Potvin. *Bachelors of a Different Sort: Queer aesthetics, material culture and the modern interior in Britain*. Manchester: Manchester University Press, 2014.

2   COC Nederland is an organisation founded in 1946 that advocates for the rights of lesbian women, gay men, bisexuals and transgender people.

3   FHAR, the 'Front homosexuel d'action révolutionnaire': a Parisian activist movement founded in 1971, resulting from a union between lesbian feminists and gay activists.

Part 3

GENERATIONAL INTERACTIONS

9 'This too is Polish culture': In Conversation With Karol Radziszewski

ALEKSANDRA GAJOWY

Karol Radziszewski is a Polish multimedia artist based in Warsaw. In his practice, Radziszewski explores expressions of queerness and is interested in reclaiming radical faggot culture as an anti-assimilationist stance against institutionalised gayness, particularly in Poland where the terms LGBT and queer are often all too easily employed interchangeably. LGBT history and politics designate communities supportive of institutionalised activism, largely following Western models of gay liberation, shaped predominantly in the US since the Stonewall riots of 1969 and often whitewashed. Queer communities, however, have preferred to embrace radical countercultures, anti-assimilationist and antisocial strategies, and to reclaim such homophobic slurs as *pedały* (faggots) or *cioty* (fairies, or, in literal translation, aunts).

Radziszewski frequently works at intersections of Polish culture and history, religious imagery, strategies of appropriation, archives, as well as print cultures. Since 2009, as one strand of his practice, Radziszewski has worked with the activist Ryszard Kisiel, the founder of one of the first gay zines in communist Eastern Europe, *Filo*. Through an ongoing exploration of Kisiel's archive, which houses diverse materials dating back to the 1960s, Radziszewski has developed a fascination with the queer archives of Central and Eastern Europe (CEE), particularly queer cultures and communities in communist Europe before 1989. Continued research has informed his practice. In 2005, Radziszewski founded *DIK Fagazine,* a magazine addressed to 'everyone interested in arts and men.' While initially focused on queerness in contemporary Polish culture, since 2009 *DIK* has gradually become a queer journal dedicated to Radziszewski's travels across CEE and a collection of oral histories and conversations with individuals who remember the experience of being queer in socialist countries. In November 2015 Radziszewski founded Queer Archives Institute (QAI), which aims to distribute, promote, curate, and make available the materials from this expanding archive and to foster collabourations between artists, activists, and researchers interested in queer histories. Some of the recent exhibitions of materials hosted by QAI include *QAI/CEE* at Centrala in Birmingham, UK (2017) and the Multimedijalni kulturni centar in Split, Croatia (2019), as well as *QAI/CO* at the Fundación Gilberto Alzate Avendaño in Bogota (2017). Delving into unexplored, fragmented archives, and bearing witness to largely forgotten and very scarcely documented stories of queer lives in the CEE, Radziszewski's practice is an important contribution to the queer cultures of Central and Eastern Europe. It functions as an informed and deliberate reclamation of anti-assimilationist expressions of queerness beyond institutionalised gayness, which often overlooks the complexities of local histories and contexts in favour of activist strategies imported from the West.

Radziszewski is a queer artist who is simultaneously preoccupied with ideas of Polishness, conceptualisations of Central and Eastern Europe, as well as political activism and the public sphere. His is an important voice in the current political landscape of homophobia, transphobia, misogyny, and patriarchal nationalisms on the rise across CEE, and notably in Poland where the leading far right-wing party Prawo i Sprawiedliwość (Law and Justice) asserts a politics of state-sanctioned discrimination. Radziszewski's work crucially sheds light on the recent histories of queer people in Poland, foregrounding communal activist strategies employed in the recent past that continue to be important and continuing these community-building efforts by nurturing affective connections across time.

Homosexuality was never a criminal offence in Poland, unlike in other CEE countries: in the Soviet Union and Romania, for example, homosexuality was decriminalised in the early 1980s, and in Belarus as late as 1994. However, the dominant social attitudes were predominantly those of ignorance and fear. In the 1970s, the subject hardly entered the public realm though notably, the first article on homosexuality in Poland, Tadeusz Gorgol's 'Homoseksualizm a opinia' ('Homosexuality and opinion'), appeared in 1974 in *Życie Literackie (The Literary Life)*. Gorgol argues that while *pedały* (faggots) – a pejorative term commonplace at the time – are 'mostly people of maybe even high intellectual sophistication, but very often […] deviating from the norm […], also psychological, [they are also] oversensitive people, with many complexes.'[1] Gorgol was convinced that every homosexual man (he does not mention lesbian women) 'understands he is different and fears exposure, and, when exposed – discrimination, [and] he is susceptible to neurosis and depressive states.'[2] Finally, he argues, 'homosexuals make peace with their destiny. They accept poor substitutes for love as real love, with the aid of an element of dreaming and fantasising, [a tendency] which is more popular among these people than among heterosexuals.'[3] While this emphasis on isolation and loneliness as conditions inherent to queer life in Poland continued into the following decade, with the crises surrounding HIV/AIDS in the mid-1980s the question of homosexuality became more pervasive in public discourse.

Perhaps it was this public political response to HIV/AIDS that framed Operation Hyacinth, a nationwide wave of arrests and interrogations of thousands of gay men in November 1985. The reasons for, and scope of, Hyacinth remains largely unknown as there is no access to the so-called Pink Files, the archive of the operation which consists mostly of personal information collected on the arrested men. As Hyacinth was the first instance of openly targeting gay men in Poland, it had a galvanising effect on queer communities across the country, giving rise to first activist efforts (of which Kisiel became one of the central figures) to spread information on the HIV/AIDS epidemic, safe sex practices, and to the gradual fostering of networks of support and community. By February 1990, this collective work allowed for the registration of Lambda, the first LGBT organisation in Poland. The fall of the Soviet Union in 1989 and the end of censorship in Poland in 1990 also contributed to a shift in the 1990s including the founding of a number of gay periodicals and the gradual rise in visibility of queer people in Poland (the first ever Pride March was held in Warsaw in 2001). This progress has not been straightforward and in 2005 the right-wing Law and Justice party won the general election for the first time. In the same year, the then-President of Warsaw, Lech Kaczyński (whose twin brother Jarosław is the leader of Law and Justice), attempted to prohibit the Pride March in the capital, which took place despite the ban.[4] Over the next fifteen years, Law and Justice have largely remained in power and during that time repeatedly placed LGBT and women's rights under attack.

What follows is an edited version of an interview that took place between Radziszewski and myself in Berlin in April 2018. In the years and months since, the political situation in Poland has further transformed. In July 2019, the first ever Pride in Białystok, Radziszewski's hometown, was violently attacked by neo-Nazi counter-demonstrators accompanied by a delayed reaction of the police.[5] In October 2019, the police found a homemade bomb made of gas canisters and fireworks, brought to the Pride March in the city of Lublin by counter-protesters.[6] The general election held later in October 2019 saw another overwhelming triumph of Law and Justice. Campaigning ahead of the election, Jarosław Kaczyński responded to a supporter's question about how the party would handle Pride marches if elected: 'if it were up to me', he said, 'it would all be obvious.' He continued that 'the courts will repeal my bans, because they are totally under the influence of the [LGBT] ideology. It needs to be restricted differently, quietly.'[7] The deeply disturbing narrative of violence, silencing, exclusion, and persecution of queer people in Poland, indicated by these instances of blatant homophobia, which are openly perpetuated by the governing party and the Catholic Church, also dominate the media – in Poland and abroad – and, as a consequence, represent the prevailing narratives of what it means to live in Poland as an LGBTQ-identified person.

It now appears as though the circumstances may be growing ever more dire as I write this introduction in the midst of the COVID-19 global pandemic. In Eastern Europe, particularly in Poland and Hungary, the media coverage of the health crisis and social distancing measures rendering public protest near impossible has demonstrably proven the flourishing of new opportunities to place human rights under attack. In April 2020, the Hungarian government announced new legislation which will end legal recognition of trans people in the country.[8] In Poland, controversial anti-abortion legislation, abandoned after it had caused countrywide mass protests in October 2016, was again discussed in the parliament in April 2020.[9] Leading up to the Polish presidential election in July 2020, Andrzej Duda ran a blatantly homophobic re-election campaign, claiming that 'LGBT is not people' but a 'different neo-Bolshevik ideology' forced upon children.[10] When Duda won the election by 2% of the votes, the slimmest margin since 1989, violence against LGBTQ communities in Poland escalated even further. In August, the non-binary activist Margot Szutowicz was arrested, illegally detained, and refused a lawyer after she defaced a truck driving in Warsaw propagating homophobic slogans such as 'What homolobby wants to teach your children,' and urging people to visit a website to 'see connections between sex education and paedophilia.'[11] Szutowicz's arrest provoked mass protests in Warsaw, across Poland, and abroad, resulting in 48 people being arrested on the first day of demonstrations, and many more assaulted as police brutality quickly got out of control. By August 2020, it appeared as though a crackdown not dissimilar to Hyacinth might be underway.[12]

Under such circumstances, Radziszewski's work on queer archives from CEE is crucial. Not only does it reveal to us little-known histories of queer lives under communism, it is also an important reminder that while we cannot ignore the grim circumstances of communities who find themselves under attack, there is a message of radical resistance and courage in these histories for those who perhaps find themselves without hope today, for those who might recognise themselves in these histories and find their footing in recognising, in the archives accumulated by Radziszewski, their communities, their families, and affective attachments forged across time and space. It is, crucially, a message of militant hope that Radziszewski recognises in the histories to which he bears witness.

QUEER PRINT IN COMMUNIST EASTERN EUROPE

AG: We have been asked to talk about queer print culture in Eastern Europe since the 1970s, but it seems that there wasn't much material and the first print publications only appeared in the 1980s. Could you talk about the few publications you do know about?

KR: There weren't any dedicated queer magazines in the 1970s. Conversations I have had with people point instead to mainstream magazines – particularly in former Yugoslavia – that at times mentioned sexuality, dating and so on. Sometimes they would have queer-themed articles, too. There is an article about this in my *DIK Fagazine: Homosexualité Communiste* [No. 11, 2017] looking at the context in Croatia. The graphic designer I spoke to, Željko Serdarević, said that journalists who were more liberal or happened to be gay tried to smuggle queer themes into the magazine. Serdarević mentions *Start* (1969–1985), which was something of a

DIK Fagazine,
Number 11, 2017.
Courtesy of Karol
Radziszewski.

Playboy equivalent. The journalist Vladimir Cvitan worked for *Start* and managed to include articles in a coded language. And that's all, really, when it comes to the 1970s. Later, publications appeared in the 1980s, virtually all in relation to the HIV/AIDS epidemic or in the 1990s, when the communist system was collapsing.

AG: On the other hand, there were plenty of magazines smuggled from abroad, which certainly contributed to the development of queer print cultures in Poland and Eastern Europe. Ryszard Kisiel, the activist you have worked with for many years now, has talked about these international exchanges. Let's talk about Ryszard first, because he's arguably the most significant person in relation to queer print publications in communist Poland. How did your collabouration with Ryszard start and develop?

KR: I founded *DIK Fagazine* in 2005, which initially looked at masculinity and homosexuality in contemporary Poland, but I soon realised there wasn't too much material out there. I am interested in the past, so I started looking also into possibilities of telling stories of the past. Someone told me there used to be this magazine, *Filo* – I'd never heard about it before – founded by Ryszard Kisiel who's still alive and lives in Gdańsk. I used my contacts to get in touch with him, I think it was 2008 or 2009. Finally we managed to talk on the phone and set up a meeting in Gdańsk, and this is where the first interview took place, later published in *DIK Fagazine: Before '89*

Ryszard Kisiel in his apartment, 2018. Photograph by and courtesy of Karol Radziszewski.

[No. 8, 2011]. It mostly focused on *Filo*. In his flat, Kisiel showed me the mock-ups, and I saw it was much more than I'd imagined. This interview in *DIK*, and the issue overall were a starting point of my interest in archives, and I decided I'd keep meeting with Ryszard and continue our work. It turned into a series of meetings. Train journeys between Warsaw and Gdańsk took ages, but Ryszard didn't want me to take anything out of his flat, so my time for research was very limited. On one occasion Ryszard said 'Oh, I also have something like this,' and took out a bag from under his bed. It was around three hundred slides in labelled boxes, with photo sessions he [and his friends] had done. I started looking at them against the light and understood it was a sensational discovery, but I couldn't really see them, they weren't arranged, and I couldn't take them away. The negotiations went on, and eventually I bought my own scanner, took it back and forth to Gdańsk, and managed to see what the slides contained, and arrange them with Ryszard. In the meantime, I filmed a conversation with him, which made me realise that I wanted to make a film about his archive, which could take the form of a documentary.

DIK Fagazine, No. 8, 2011. Courtesy of Karol Radiszewski.

Regarding the transnational flows of queer print magazines – we're already in the 1980s here – Kisiel lived in Gdańsk, a major Polish seaport, and many of his friends were sailors. They would bring the magazines – mostly from Germany, but also Canada. Kisiel doesn't remember it all, but he mentioned specific titles like *Du und Ich* (1969–2014), a mainstream German magazine; *HIM: Homosexuelle International Magazin* (c. 1971–76), also from Germany. There was also the Canadian *Blue Boy* (1974–2007). Actually, these flows could have been going on already in the 1970s…

AG: Did these influence the magazines later published in Poland, like *Filo?*

KR: In the 1980s, *Filo* largely relied on reprints of information from all over the world. The *Filo* editorial team looked for students who could translate, rewrite, edit. Part of the material was taken from international magazines, but *Filo* was also very locally oriented since the international press was very detached from the Polish context. For instance, foreign magazines reviewed films that were not released in Poland, so instead, *Filo* monitored local media and tried to find any traces of queerness. Then,

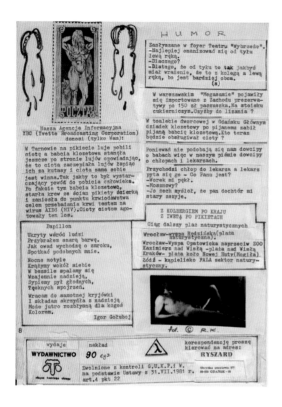

Filo mockup, 1980s.
Courtesy of Ryszard
Kisiel.

there were many texts written by Kisiel and his collabourators, mainly sharing information on HIV/AIDS, health, safe sex, and so on. There were also a lot of drawings, jokes, and stories which were completely local in their character. Kisiel told me that they had heard about Stonewall and its aftermath, about activists fighting for gay rights. They talked about this in the 1970s, about gay liberation, activism, and wondered whether it would work in Poland. Strangely, they didn't know what they would fight for, since homosexuality had been decriminalised in Poland in 1932, and unlike other countries of the Soviet Bloc, it wasn't re-criminalised, so officially that wasn't an issue. The problem was the invisibility of queer people, which meant homophobia was very difficult to contain. It's striking that they had a conversation about there being nothing to fight about, you know? This was the reason why gay activism in Poland only developed in the late 1980s.

Filo started in November 1986 as a direct response to Operation Hyacinth. Hyacinth was a military police action, carried out allegedly to protect 'homosexual environments' in Poland, mostly from a 'criminal element' – HIV/AIDS was barely mentioned. Mostly, though, it was about creating the so-called Pink Files – a database of homosexual men in Poland kept in local police stations. This is why the archives of the operation are very scattered and have never been researched. The Pink Files are an interesting example of a print culture. It's an archive of sorts, but dispersed, invisible, and still politically dangerous. It's inaccessible because there is a possibility that the files include personal details of prominent public figures. Operation Hyacinth also sought to blackmail gay men. Police would ambush them in private flats, offices, schools, and threaten that they would be outed to their family and employers if they didn't agree to cooperate. The collabouration involved signing the so-called 'Homosexual Card,' a form which required them to declare their homosexuality, the kinds of sexual practices they engaged in, how many partners they had had, and – this was the trick – that they had had no sexual encounters with minors. This last statement was allegedly for the men's protection. Really the form was a formal confirmation that they had had sex with men – they declared themselves homosexual. Then, many men were blackmailed to cooperate with the Security Service. Kisiel's reaction was

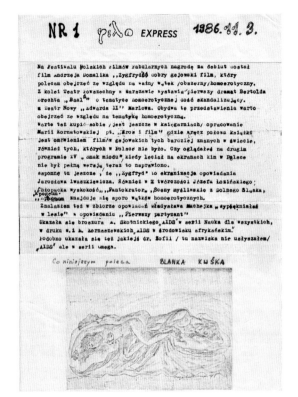

very different. He said that since the police had arranged a coming out for him, then he might as well come out. I think of Operation Hyacinth as an equivalent of Stonewall of sorts, an event that formed consciousness and a community – finally there was an understanding that gay people's rights were being abused. The Warsaw Homosexual Movement appeared in 1987 as a direct outcome of Hyacinth. Up till then, the news coming from the West had been too abstract, I think.

Kisiel thought of starting a magazine because he had been sending many letters to friends and ended up copying them. He wanted to share information he had collected. Generally, he was interested in sharing. In the late 1970s and early 1980s, he travelled the whole country by train, went to over twenty cities in Poland, but also Hungary, Czechoslovakia and Romania, among others, and took photos for a project he called the *Polish Gay Guide to Socialist Countries.* It was a scrapbook of sorts with a printed cover – Kisiel worked in a printing house – which he systematically updated with information about different gay spots around the countries of the Soviet Bloc. There are notes about where to go to a sauna, how much towel rental was, which entrance to take to which toilet at which station… He took photos of all these places – they are mostly undeveloped, in negatives. It's a kind of cruising compendium.

Above left: *Filo,*
No. 1, 1986.
Courtesy of Ryszard
Kisiel.

Above: *Filo,* No 2,
1986. Courtesy of
Ryszard Kisiel.

Ryszard Kisiel, *Polish Gay Guide to Socialist Countries*, 1980s. Photographs by Karol Radziszewski. Courtesy of Kisiel and Radziszewski.

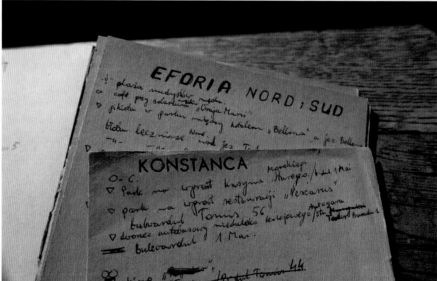

AG: And he shared this with his friends?

KR: Yes, he would make a few copies and send them around. Mostly, the developed photos seem quite boring, like a picture of a park from a distance. Kisiel was documenting his way of getting there: the photos had a very practical purpose. It also helped to develop a network between members of what I call a queer proto-community. It was too early to talk about an actual community, but there was definitely some circulation of information. Kisiel copied these letters and sent them to more and more people. These mail-outs became more elaborate and evolved into a zine. Officially, there were under a hundred copies of each issue, as publication of up to a hundred copies could avoid censor checks, but in fact there were many more in circulation. *Filo* was mostly circulated by post, through Kisiel's PO Box. Subscribers would send envelopes and stamps to receive the zine. Then some people xeroxed those, and *Filo* ended up being distributed across Poland. Some of the issues were reprinted later on, but they are still considered originals because they are printed from the original mock-ups, which were collages of texts, photos and drawings. This was the first thing Kisiel did for each issue and then xeroxed it to a smaller size. Until the fall of the Soviet Bloc in 1989, *Filo* existed in underground circulation, and for a while continued in this form in democratic Poland. It was later officially registered and changed its title to *Facet (Guy)* (1991–1994), when Kisiel's collaborator took over and turned it into a more commercial title, available in newsagents.[13]

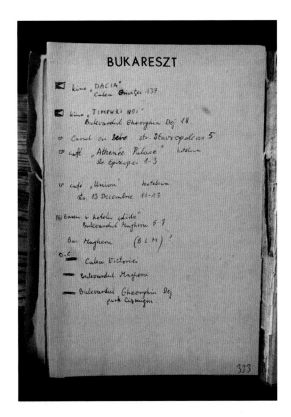

Ryszard Kisiel, *Polish Gay Guide to Socialist Countries*, 1980s. Photograph by Karol Radziszewski. Courtesy of Kisiel and Radziszewski.

AG: What about publications and print materials in other countries of the Soviet Bloc – after the 1970s?

KR: There was *Viks* (1984–85) in the former Yugoslavia, in Slovenia. It came out in 1984 in a zine form. The first gay club in Ljubljana opened the same year. There was this cool lifestyle magazine in Zagreb, *Polet* (1976 – c.1985). They sent this straight photographer Mio Vesović – he was considered very cool at the time – from Zagreb to Ljubljana, to take photos of this newly-opened club. It's very unusual – it's 1984, and he is in Ljubljana, taking explicitly gay photos – an almost naked ass with someone's hand on it here, two guys kissing there. These images were published in this straight magazine in Zagreb. It shows how the queer culture developed at different speeds across Eastern Europe, and also how different publications can be queered. This same photographer also did a project for *Polet,* taking naked pictures of a then very famous Croatian footballer. It became a huge scandal because he had posed naked, and the magazine issue was censored and withdrawn from circulation. Yet the photo editor, Goran Trbuljak, was a well-known Croatian conceptual artist. In the following issue he printed the layout identically, with all the photos replaced by black blocks. It's very interesting as far as print is concerned; you had the complete layout of the original article, but instead of the original there was a text denouncing censorship, and the photos all black, conceptual. It's so beautiful. And then the footballer retracted, he said he hadn't known, that it was all accidental – well, the photos were all full-frontal! He stands there with his dick out, professionally lit, and then gets scared and says he didn't know.

In [the former Czechoslovakia] the first magazine, *Hlas (Voice)* (1931–34), came out in 1931. It was edited by people moving in intellectual circles, and was largely text-based. They wrote a lot about legislation – for instance, about the prosecution of Oscar Wilde. It was a time when Wilde was a universal reference point. It's amazing that this magazine appeared so early on! During communist times, Czechoslovakia was much more restrictive than Poland, so another queer publication – *Lambda* – only appeared in 1990 in Prague. It looks almost exactly like *Filo* – it's also made out of xeroxed collages of texts and images, prepared by a group of enthusiasts. The contents are similar: a selection of both local news and reprints from the international press, lots of information on HIV/AIDS. Also like *Filo, Lambda* was published for a few years, but their circulation was bigger, up to a few thousand copies. It was typical of the sudden optimism of the early 1990s, but it failed because there was no audience.

Another example is Belarus. It's a fascinating case. In Belarus, homosexuality was a criminal offence until 1994. Anything could become evidence of a crime – every photo, a note with a phone number, every little bit of information. There are virtually no queer archives in Belarus except for official criminal records or psychologists' medical reports. People had to destroy every trace or not produce any material queer culture. The first queer magazine came out in 1998 when Belarus regained its independence. Not unlike in Poland, independence was promptly followed by registration of the first LGBT rights group and the first magazine, called *Forum* and later *Lambda Forum* [together, published between 1998–2002].

QUEER PRINT IN RADZISZEWSKI'S PRACTICE

AG: I want to talk about queer print culture also in the context of your own practice. How do you work with print and how do you think of it as queer?

KR: I find queer print culture fascinating. However until recently I only thought of it in the context of zines and magazines. Now I recognise it's much broader and more fluid: for instance, is queering mainstream magazines through smuggling in queer themes part of queer print culture? I would definitely include all sorts of leaflets; all printed publications around HIV/AIDS regardless of the form; and posters, especially those about concerts, clubs... everything that was related to queer culture but announced in printed form. Still, a magazine for me is the core of queer print culture, since it requires arranging these haphazard things into a conceptual narrative. I think that the real queer print culture in Central and Eastern Europe appeared out of necessity to spread information about HIV/AIDS. In terms of my practice… having travelled around, I became familiar with both mainstream and alternative queer cultures from places like the Netherlands, France, and the UK. In the early 2000s, I noticed the tendency to return to queer or faggot-y, rather than gay, print culture. It was about the quality of print itself – the difference between reading online and a paper magazine – but also about telling a story, a curated narrative and layout. I was very excited about this and it encouraged me to start my own magazine. I didn't know about *Filo* at the time, or anything that had previously existed in Poland. It was only when I interviewed Kisiel that I found out about my predecessors.

AG: Do you think of *DIK* as a continuation of *Filo* of sorts? Can you describe the process of how *DIK* has developed?

KR: I wish I could say it's a continuation of *Filo*, but I found out about it too late to be able to fully claim that. I think of *Filo* as my ancestor because it had a different approach. In the early 1990s there were seven gay publications in Poland, and their ambitions were more mainstream, even if they didn't work out. *Filo* was a zine, it was humorous and alternative. But *Filo* was also a bulletin gathering information – something we now have the internet for. So in this sense, some activist online portals probably have similar contents. *DIK* is in principle an arts magazine, it was founded as such. As it coincided with my coming out, I thought it could be a magazine focusing specifically on homosexuality, but also masculinity, the idea of being a man in Poland, in this part of Europe. At first there were interviews about current things, for instance with Michał Witkowski, who had just published his novel *Lubiewo (Lovetown)* (2004) and was on *DIK*'s editorial team for a bit. Then this idea about archives and extending the scope of *DIK* to Eastern Europe came at one point, but I also understood, because of Kisiel, that there was a chance to find things I had never imagined existed. He gave me an entry point to start looking, and once I did, the narrative kept growing. In fact, the magazine is only a curated, printed summary, a closure of specific strands of research. The fact that I decided to include the whole region means that there are many monographic issues around specific countries – Romania, Ukraine, and Czechoslovakia. Poland drifted into the background a bit, but I return to it now, also in relation to the Cruising the Seventies project.[14] The magazine has since its beginnings relied on long interviews and almost literal transcriptions. Sometimes there were stories and articles, photos, and different contributions by various artists around the main subject. *Filo* is my ancestor I refer to in terms of ideas, independence, as something that is queer and non-heteronormative rather than gay, rainbow-y, or LGBT-centred.

A note on terminology in *DIK*: I say, for the English reader, that it's queer, but in fact it is thought out as a magazine about men, about masculinity and homosexuality in CEE. I'm interested in the culture of faggots and queens. Although at first lesbians and trans* people weren't mentioned at all, it was not a gay magazine either. I refer to this tradition of, after Douglas Crimp, 'queer before gay,' rather than a historical or academic meaning of queer.[15] I wanted to relate to non-heteronormativity from before the word 'gay,' associated with emancipation and activism, entered the Polish language [in the late 1980s]. We can also debate whether 'queerness' equals 'faggotry' – I'd say yes, in the English context anyway. Then there's 'fags,' still distinct from the Polish 'pedał,' but it works in the context of queer resistance. It's not assimilationist but working through provocation and difference. *DIK,* rather than focus on LGBT activism, is more about people and personalities presented in full. This was something of a rule, but it's been changing lately. It's been nearly twelve years, and I learned how to write better. Since you can't always get to people, or record them, I started to add more extensive descriptive notes, introductions to interviews and to different issues of the magazine, and I have begun to treat it as a travel journal and emphasise my subjectivity. For instance, the issue on former Czechoslovakia is a reportage-like collection of interviews. I write from my perspective – where I arrive, how much time I have, whom I meet, that one person sends me to another. If you read it cover to cover, it's a mini-reportage introduced through interviews.

AG: Let's talk about the aesthetics of *Filo* and *DIK*. *Filo* had a very specific aesthetic. *DIK* is a whole different thing. How do these aesthetic choices change and evolve, and how do you see them as an editor and artist?

KR: *Filo* was quite distinct from what I associate with zines in the West, which were usually a collection of photos. Kisiel edited the whole issue, *Filo* had its fixed sections and they made up a narrative. *DIK* is similar in that respect. However, aesthetically, *Filo* had the typical 1980s character of a zine – typewritten texts, photos, and drawings are printed in a collage form, mostly prepared by amateurs, without a consciously designed composition, definitely not a professionally planned layout. In *DIK*, there have been three graphic designers, two straight women and one gay guy and their different approaches were interesting to me. One of the women I've worked with would often influence my choice of photographs… well, she would get rid of dicks (laughs). It allowed me to see *DIK* in terms of graphic design through someone else's eyes. It was beyond artistic choice, because she knew what would work well in terms of design. I stress that *DIK* is an arts magazine about masculinity and queerness, and its aesthetics is a signal of sorts. If you think about *Replika* (2005–),[16] for instance, a regular Polish activist magazine, there are rainbows everywhere and plenty of short text blurbs – it looks more like a website layout – it's more of a commercial aesthetic, right? *DIK*'s aesthetics ask you to spend more time with it, in the context of art and politics, but not explicit activism – it's coded in how it looks.

AG: *DIK* is a combination of your roles as an artist, a curator, and an editor. How do you negotiate between them, and how do you see your role in how *DIK* is going to evolve?

KR: My initial idea was to publish a magazine which was not mainstream, but not a zine either. *DIK* is experimental graphically and has a curated narrative. I envisaged a magazine with a clear structure that unfolds if not as a conceptual, then an organisational and thematic entity. At first, I brought together a more or less permanent editorial team. This included [the writer and political activist] Michał Zygmunt, [the Polish literature translator and journalist] Stefan Ingvarsson from Sweden, who lived in Poland at the time and was an important commentator on the Western context, [the curator and journalist] Marcin Różyc and [Radziszewski's partner] Paweł Kubara. The writer Michał Witkowski [author of the 2004 gay novel *Lubiewo (Lovetown)*] was part of the team for a while, too. There was space for artists' contributions, not in a haphazard, collage-like form, but in a permanent section. I took on a role of a classical editor-in-chief, who came up with the overarching concept, and then we looked for suitable content. They were mostly interviews, rarely articles. I have been, still am, the founder and the funder of the magazine. Everybody works for free, but I cover printing costs and then distribute the magazine. The sales income covers the production costs, or not… From the start there have been a lot of parties and other promotional events around the magazine, which contributed to the fringe of queer culture in Poland in that moment.

We initially printed a thousand copies because I wanted to reach a wider audience, which I perceive as an artistic practice beyond the gallery context I have been involved in on many fronts. To me, as far as independent queer culture is concerned, the key is to ensure that it is as widely and democratically accessed as possible. If a magazine is too expensive, you can still see it, share it – use it in a different context than a painting in a gallery. Of course, there's the internet, so the question is to what extent print cultures in the twenty-first century are sentimental, and to what extent they actually work. Still, the physicality of the magazine is important to me. That's why I have worked with outstanding graphic designers. We experimented with layout also to convince people to interact with this paper object as an exhibition of sorts. Later, I became interested in archives and the editorial team has dissolved. I work pretty much on my own now. I expanded *DIK*'s contents to countries beyond Poland, so I travel more. We still worked as a team on the Ukraine issue, but later I was the only one to go travelling. I also decided to get more personal then. As a result, *DIK* became more private, emotional, and a complete narrative curated by me. In that sense, it became more part of my own artistic practice, but it is also an outlet to publish and arrange some of the archives I use for different projects. *DIK* is thematic, monographic, an ongoing project and the core of my practice.

AG: You mentioned that the interviews in *DIK* are largely unedited, transcribed almost verbatim. Has this been an important strategy for you?

KR: At first I didn't edit at all, because I was just learning about being an editor, a publisher, a journalist, a photographer... I didn't want to get rid of things I thought could be important. When I am interviewed as an artist, it annoys me when the edits almost change the meaning of my words. Besides, I was always interested in strategies Warhol used in his work: his films, his magazine *Interview...* This was partly an inspiration to start my own magazine as an artist. The interviews Warhol did were printed verbatim. Warhol's book *A* (1968) is a literal transcript of a twenty-four-hour-long recording, including coughing etc.[17] Later on, I made a conscious choice to not edit so much, because I have been learning about oral history, and understood the significance of testimony. Particularly if it is not edited too much, not manipulated, my work can become a useful resource for academics. I decided I can allow myself to print these long, almost unedited interviews in *DIK*, which can function as primary research material rather than my artistic creation.

QUEER PRINT AS POLITICAL

AG: Do you think queer print materials can effectively infiltrate mainstream culture?

KR: Well, they are often so niche that they only function in parallel to the mainstream culture. The queer culture in Poland in the 1980s didn't influence the mainstream at all. In the early 1990s, the 'gay phenomenon' was a totally new occurrence, regardless of what had been already there, like Kisiel's archive. Things like his were only re-discovered a few years ago, and are still very rare in Polish visual culture. Back in the 1980s his archive didn't change anything – it's only affecting things now, retroactively. To me, it turns thinking about non-heteronormativity in Poland upside down. Things like Kisiel's archive affect thinking about the past, and so do these niche queer publications.

AG: Are there identifiable tensions between official and queer culture in Poland?

KR: There isn't always an independent queer culture. In Poland, there is mostly a focus on activism which copies Western models – the fight for gay and lesbian rights and the right to marry, the rainbow, the legacy of Stonewall. There are fewer local things and more adapted patterns. In one of the first issues of *DIK* I conducted interviews with famous Polish straight male artists such as Artur Żmijewski, Wilhelm Sasnal, Rafał Bujnowski or Zbigniew Libera. It was an interesting intersection of the official culture placed in a queer space. I wanted to queer these artists, the contexts of masculinity, the body, homosexuality to different extents. It was about inserting these straight artists into *DIK* to queer them – and every single one of them, well, it's not that they had a problem with it, but it was very unusual for them, like they made a deliberate choice to allow themselves to be presented in this way. But also, in many cases it was the first time for them to be interviewed about their lives rather than their work. How is a man who is a straight artist different from another straight man who is not an artist? Is he more open-minded, more susceptible to the malleability of gender?

AG: You mentioned the materiality and physicality of *DIK* as an important aspect. How do you situate its importance?

KR: I'm interested in a relatively egalitarian access to print culture. Now, *DIK* is circulated in 500 numbered copies. It was my conscious gesture to accentuate that it's supposed to be collected and kept, rather than read and thrown out. It's also part of my artistic practice – for instance, the issue about Belarus [*DIK* issue 12] contains many of my photographs, some of which will only ever appear in the magazine. You can access them privately, go back to them, share with others – it's all important to me. That's why I don't really mind that *DIK* isn't available online. Perhaps it should be both, so everyone can read it online, but buying a paper copy allows you to have that physical contact with the magazine.

Another thing is that when you read *DIK*, you can do it wherever, you're not limited to a gallery. Particularly with archival material, it would be impossible for me to share all the information, texts, and contexts in an exhibition. The magazine provides a certain order, offers an accompanying narrative, my suggestion of how the presented material can be viewed. For instance, the Belarusian issue begins with my very personal introduction, then there is an extensive interview with an activist who talks about history and archives going back as far as possible; then, there's another, less structured interview about the 1990s and 2000s, and we gradually return to the present; finally, there is a section on the contemporary moment and art. I lead the reader through this narration, constructed by a specific layout.

AG: You talk about queer print being an egalitarian form, but what are its limitations, of the name itself or as practice?

KR: For starters, practically all bookshops have a shelf or a corner for publications that are queer or about sexuality. It introduces a certain order and makes it easier to find for those who are already interested, but many people just stay away from these shelves – so if *DIK* ends up on a shelf like this, its audience is defined by default. On the website of the Polish bookshop that distributes *DIK*, though, there are hardly any other queer publications, so *DIK* is in the arts section. This gives it a chance to spark interest as an arts magazine – because of its graphic design, its layout and nice photos – in contrast to a magazine with naked guys on the cover…

AG: How do you think about *DIK* in political terms?

KR: I know, more or less, where *DIK* is circulated, in which countries. I prepared an exhibition in Columbia through my friend – I have never been there myself – and

DIK issues never reached them from Warsaw. They managed to find a collector in Bogota. This wouldn't have happened with a painting – so the distribution is much wider, even if very specific. This issue of access is very political to me, the question of how widely a message can be delivered, and of when private becomes political.

Another aspect is that while *DIK* may be advertised at New York Art Book Fair, or be included in a mainstream exhibition, it works as a political statement: 'this too is Polish culture.' And then, inside this culture, it's tracing archives and positions. I look for local languages and vocabulary, and create orientation points – Hyacinth rather than Stonewall, for instance. I attempt to collect private histories which contribute to different readings of Solidarność, the fall of communism, and different chronologies. I build an alternative narrative through what I define as queer – not assimilation but provocation; marking difference through proposing new elements of visual and textual culture; evoking queer characters from the past to provide different points of reference; talking about sex and sexuality in a way different than expected by the conservative majority and Catholic morality. In the Polish context, assuming the queer and radical position is the political aspect of *DIK*.

AG: You talk about queering the past in *DIK*, and you often combine this with contemporary contexts. How do you see past, present, and future affecting one another in *DIK*, and how do you think about it in terms of queer temporalities?

KR: I'm not interested in nostalgia or fetishising the archive. Of course, I'm super excited about archives, but I try to avoid locking them in a time capsule where they no longer affect the present. The queer past is political and affects the present and future on a few levels. Firstly, the more we expand the queer sphere of CEE in terms of historical figures, events, and material culture, the more it affects the here and now, the more it provides us with a background and an orientation point to continue this narrative – so gathering, showing and writing about these materials is already political and introduces the temporal context. Secondly, it is raw material for researchers and academics who can analyse this material I make available to them. Ideally, I would like to see this research entering future textbooks and school curricula. I know that some of this is already happening – I know of two people who wrote about my work for their A-level exams – and, limited as it may be now, I really believe that this queer culture will gradually become more popularly known. This is a political and activist task of thinking how the past can affect the future. This is also why I decided to be less explicit in *DIK* and go more into exploring the archive. It seems less confrontational, but this is where the practical aspect of this strategy can be the most effective. Thirdly, it's about inspiration for people now by presenting to them the stories of dissent from the socialist times. If Kisiel can take a train from Gdańsk to Warsaw in drag in 1978, this knowledge perhaps can be helpful to someone who's afraid to go out in a colourful outfit now.

NOTES

1 Tadeusz Gorgol. 1974. 'Homoseksualizm a opinia' ('Homosexuality and opinion'). *Życie Literackie* (*Literary Life*). No. 17/18. 12.

2 Ibid.

3 Ibid.

4 Lucia Kubosova. 2017. 'Poland's ban of gay parade ruled illegal.' *EUObserver*. 4 May. https://euobserver.com/social/23995

5 Renata Kim. 2019. 'Nienawiść w Białymstoku. Wstrząsająca relacja z Marszu Równości' ('Hate in Białystok. Shocking reports from the Equality March'). *Newsweek*. 21 July. https://www.newsweek.pl/opinie/marsz-rownosci-w-bialymstoku-relacja/xg3f8rq. Accessed November 1, 2019.

6 Sandra Wilk. 2019. 'Skąd ładunki wybuchowe na Marszu Równości w Lublinie?' ('Where did the explosives at the Equality March in Lublin come from?'). *Polityka (Politics)*. 2 October. https://www.polityka.pl/tygodnikpolityka/spoleczenstwo/1926920,1,skad-ladunki-wybuchowe-na-marszu-rownosci-w-lublinie.read. Accessed November 1, 2019.

7 Jakub Sobieniowski. 2019. 'Kaczyński pytany o marsze równości' ('Kaczyński asked about equality marches'). *Fakty TVN24 (News TVN24)*. 12 August. https://fakty.tvn24.pl/ogladaj-online,60/jaroslaw-kaczynski-o-lgbt-sady-sa-calkowicie-pod-wplywem-tej-ideologii,960595.html. Accessed November 1, 2019.

8 Shaun Walker. 2020. 'Hungary prepares to end legal recognition of trans people.' *The Guardian*. 26 April. https://www.theguardian.com/world/2020/apr/26/hungary-prepares-to-end-legal-recognition-of-trans-people. Accessed May 13, 2020

9 Shaun Walker. 2020. 'Concerns over Polish government tightening abortion laws during Covid-19 crisis.' *The Guardian*. 14 April. https://www.theguardian.com/world/2020/apr/14/concerns-over-polish-government-tightening-abortion-laws-during-covid-19-crisis. Accessed May 13, 2020.

10 Tomasz Dereszyński. 2020. 'Media światowe zauważyły słowa prezydenta Dudy' ('International media noticed President Duda's words'). *Polska Times (Times Poland)*. 14 June. https://polskatimes.pl/media-swiatowe-zauwazyly-slowa-prezydenta-andrzeja-dudy-ze-ideologia-lgbt-jest-gorsza-niz-komunizm-jest-reakcja-prezydenta/ar/c1-15025414. Accessed 25 June 2020

11 Queer PL team. 2019. 'Czy ciężarówki z homofobicznymi hasłami przestaną jeździć po Warszawie?' ('Will trucks with homophobic slogans stop driving around Warsaw?') *Queer.pl*. 6 December. https://queer.pl/news/203795/ciezarowki-z-homofobicznymi-haslami-przestana-jezdzic-po-warszawie. Accessed August 24, 2020.

12 Kaela Roeder. 2020. 'Poland's LGBTQ activists confront growing crackdown.' *Washington Blade*. 14 August. https://www.washingtonblade.com/2020/08/14/polands-lgbtq-activists-confront-growing-crackdown/. Accessed August 24, 2020.

13 Ryszard Kisiel was interviewed by Karol Radziszewski and Paweł Kubara in *DIK Fagazine. Before '89* (Warsaw; self-published, 2011). In the interview, he mentions that although Poland was already democratic, *Filo* remained an underground publication until the abolition of state censorship on 15 June 1990. The date also marks the last underground issue of the zine, which then continued in official distribution.

14 See this book's introduction, and the website www.crusev.ed.ac.uk.

15 Douglas Crimp. 1999. 'Getting the Warhol We Deserve.' *Social Text*. No 59 (Summer). 64.

16 *Replika* is promoted as 'the only bimonthly publication in Poland concerned with LGBTQ issues.' It has

appeared since December 2005 and is distributed through LGBT-friendly bars and via post. For more information, see the website replika-online.pl

17 See: Lynne Tillman. 2005. 'The Last Words Are Andy Warhol.' *Grey Room*. No. 21 (Fall). 38–45; and Lucy Mulroney. 2012. 'Editing Andy Warhol.' *Grey Room*. No.46 (Winter). 47–71.

10 Queer Memory in (Re)constituting the Trans Lesbian 1970s in the UK

NAT RAHA

Titled *Lesbians Come Together*, the January 1972 issue of the UK Gay Liberation Front's (GLF) newspaper *Come Together* (Issue 11) is an important textual moment in the herstory of lesbian and transgender social life and organising of the early 1970s. The issue, the second produced by women and in this case by the Faraday Road women's commune,[1] opens with a statement that affirms the intent of its editors to 'publish in this issue all the articles that were submitted':

> We have not edited or censored anything. This is not simply an act of blatant Sisterhood, but a conscious attempt by us not to ape the values of heterosexual society.[2]

The issue contains half a dozen articles alongside photographs, graphics and an open letter calling for women to attend the 29th January Gay Women's Think-in. The articles include pieces on feminist collective housing (rosily describing life in the Faraday Road commune), the need for a GLF Women's Centre, ongoing GLF trials and the national think-in, the GLF Transvestite, Transsexual and Drag Queen Group (GLF TS/TV Group), and a piece about going out in drag as a woman for the first time. In Lisa Power's reading, the issue makes important arguments for lesbian separatism.[3] The texts provide a sense of the meetings and discussions ongoing at the time between non-trans and trans lesbians, and other gender non-conforming people, developing radical, political consciousness of their situations. For instance, the article addressing the need for 'A Woman's Place...' or a 'gay women's centre' within the context of the GLF specifically addresses the need for somewhere to socialise and build common cause among gay women:

Front cover of *Lesbians Come Together*, January 1972.

Women's projects would develop organically out of a situation in which we could get to know each other and discover our common problems as women, particularly as gay women: lesbians, bisexuals, transvestites and transsexuals.[4]

The article goes on to describe potential uses and possibilities for the women's centre, envisioning a 'central place where women could get together and rap' (that is, discuss life and issues). The space could be used to hold meetings, for street theatre rehearsals, workshops and classes to share knowledge, and for parties and discos; to undertake 'art and craft work' and produce printed matter such as 'papers, magazines, posters and leaflets'; for childcare and 24-hour 'advice, emotional support, information' for 'sisters from abroad, from prison, in domestic crises etc'; where some could live communally and the GLF Women's Group could be co-ordinated; a place generally to 'Do things to raise bread'.[5] Signed by Frankie and Edith, the article brims with the possibilities of self-organisation, presenting the potential of developing projects, dialogue and consciousness for and by women while centring diverse gay women within the context of a feminist, separatist collective space. The proposal foresees opportunities for solidarity and support, creativity and self-expression, discussing oppressions, sharing knowledge and organising.

REMEMBERING A TRANS LESBIAN SEPARATIST '70S?

This essay undertakes a reparative reading of fragments of print media from the archives of the UK Gay and Women's Liberation movements, addressing the contributions and memories of those who self-defined as trans lesbians (transsexual lesbians and transvestite lesbians) at the time. By centring the countercultural writing along with memories of trans and non-trans women (from the 1970s to the 2010s), reflecting on their experiences within the movements and moments of solidarity and sisterhood between women, I present a liberationist vision of trans life that explicitly emerges from a feminist revolution and from lesbian separatism. With a focus on the London GLF's TS/TV Group and two of its members Rachel Pollack and Roz Kaveney, the essay approaches this material as providing an alternative worldview to that of white progressivist transgender histories that have emerged recently such as that of Christine Burns' *Trans Britain*,[6] and personal accounts including those of celebrities from the period such as Jan Morris and April Ashley.[7] The essay concludes by addressing reflections on the trans 1970s in radical trans print from the 1990s and work by socialist feminist and sociologist Carol Riddell. This essay emerges from an intergenerational public conversation between writer, poet and activist Roz Kaveney and myself, held as part of *Between the Sheets: Radical Print Cultures before the Queer Bookshop*, in Glasgow, Scotland, in February 2017.[8] Parts of Kaveney's recollections from the event on trans organising and cultural production in the queer seventies are cited in this text.

While queer histories and queer memories may at times seem to operate in distinct ways, my work here follows Laura Doan's elucidation that these two practices 'continually rub up against the other', in a manner that may be fruitful for critical historians.[9] I account for moments in the archive where memory is seemingly presented as history, delegitimising and effacing marginal herstories in the process. The essay demonstrates and counters the structuring role that transphobia and transmisogyny play in the memory and historicisation of Gay Liberation in the UK. These forms of oppression enact processes that produce what Charles Morris and K.J. Rawson, following Berlant and Warner (1998), describe as an 'amnesia archive', whereby particular memories and presences of queer people are erased – erasures that, as in this case, may be 'bequeath[ed] and enact[ed]' by queers ourselves.[10] As transfeminist scholar Finn Enke describes, the recovering of histories, in the context of disciplinary functions and 'purifying purges' of collective memory, 'creates portals and connections and communities across time, a possible antidote to alienation and abjection'.[11] The essay thus provides a 'portal' into scenes of trans and feminist sisterhood in the seventies, in which trans lesbians played significant roles in the liberation movements. These are scenes representative of what Abram Lewis describes as the 'eccentric and recalcitrant qualities' of trans archives,[12] moments that the collective memory of gay liberation casts as improbable, rendering their claims to queerness and lesbian sisterhood as inassimilable to that collective memory. These trans lesbian portals are spaces of solidarity that, by the accounts of its participants, would within a few years seem foreclosed.[13]

Numerous scholars have emphasised that collective memory may tell us more about its own present than the past.[14] Erasures or purges within the archives and collective memory carry considerable affective force,[15] and they occur alongside (and potentially supplement) trauma and active processes of forgetting by the subjects who have experienced harm.[16] In an ongoing context of anti-trans political backlash from the far right and transphobic feminists, the stakes of transfeminist herstory and stories remain significant. However, queer memories of trans life in the seventies are by no means lucid. Processes of remembering and historicising key contributions to Gay Liberation by transsexual women and men, drag queens and kings and other gender non-conformists have been active since the late 1980s and early 1990s – most notably in the recovery of Sylvia Rivera, Marsha P. Johnson, Storme DeLarverie and Miss Major as key figures in the Stonewall riots who were also interconnected with Black and Third World Liberation movements.[17] The material precarity, marginalisation and at times the excesses that marked lives of poor trans people in the seventies are infused into both the archive (or the lack of it) and into the bodies that remember. Memory is, as Kaveney attests, an assemblage built from documentation, other people's stories, health and the 'random cells of the brain that you suddenly learn to access again',[18] and it interfaces with the traumas experienced through marginalised bodies and lives and their access to healthcare (or the lack of it). These two factors materially affect these bodies.[19] The traumas of transphobia and transmisogyny (as lived 'historical truths') forge what Dipesh Chakrabarty describes in another context as a 'historical wound' – a 'mix of history and memory' formed dialogically– that exists within both trans collective memory *and* historical bodies.[20] This historical wound makes the prospect of trans lesbian lives blooming within lesbian separatism seem historically improbable, and moreover difficult to bear in the memory of those who lived it. Documentary fragments and traces of trans lesbian life within the Gay Liberation archive, which exist

Lesbians Come Together, 1972, pp.17–18.

in the first place due to moments of sisterhood and solidarity in publishing practices, are a means to hold up and affirm what was experienced, lived and what might have become. Though seemingly few, it is due to lesbian (and) feminist praxis in print and publishing that the materials I discuss exist in the first place.

While the focus of this essay is primarily on trans and non-trans lesbians, it is important to acknowledge that the spaces discussed overlap with spaces inhabited by trans masculine people and trans men.[21] One significant example is Stephen Whittle's involvement in radical, lesbian separatist groups in the mid-1970s. Whittle describes how, after attending the 1974 Women's Liberation National Conference in Edinburgh as part of a Lesbian Collective, he announced to the collective that he 'was in fact a man'.[22] While expecting to face ostracisation, Whittle's self-definition was supported by the group: 'I was listened to, I was given gifts of shirts and ties out of the back of "formerly identified as butch" women's wardrobes', and he was introduced to clubs frequented by trans people.[23] Whittle describes the experience as 'confirming' his then-belief in radical separatism.

DISPATCHES FROM THE GLF TS/TV GROUP

Citing Holly Woodlawn of Warhol's Factory in the title, the article 'Don't Call Me Mister, You Fucking Beast' in *Lesbians Come Together* details the development and experiences of the GLF TS/TV Group.[24] The article opens noting that around forty people have attended the group, all of whom are described as transvestite (or transsexual) women, and the article itself has nine signatories including Rachel Pollack and Roz Kaveney.[25] It is written in a tone that holds the undercurrents of serious harm (including medical treatments such as Electro-Convulsive Therapy or ECT, and getting kicked out of one's house for wearing feminine clothing) alongside moments of possibility and humorous relief. It anticipates and challenges many of the subjects that have dominated public discourse around transgender identities and expressions for the forty-eight years since it was written. The article addresses issues around trans stereotypes and narratives, accessing medical treatment, discrimination and street harassment, and questions of trans pride, 'passing', gender roles and solidarity between diverse women. It details statistics (or the lack of them) of the number of trans people in the UK and problems around medical treatment for trans people, including access to sex hormones; and discusses challenging isolation around trans expression and the need to unravel stereotypes of transgender narratives. In debunking stereotypical conceptions of transsexuality while offering an alternative perspective of consciousness, the group writes, 'No one in the group has ever said, "What horrible trick of nature has me a woman trapped in a man's body?" *We just don't think that way*'.[26] Furthermore, they highlight that compared to 'The psychiatrists who electro-shock us [and] think we're pathetic and tragic', there is much enjoyment in being transvestite.[27] They emphasise the cross-class character of those who have attended the group, their various senses of dress, and discuss the specificity that transvestite and transsexual experience can bring to the wider discussion of gender roles playing out in the Gay Liberation movement at the time:

> Some of us are opposed to roles because they can limit self-discovery. We don't want to discard the male role just to take on the female role. Others think that transvestites can show people that roles can be fun, if you're free to take the ones you want and discard them when you don't want them any more. The most important thing is, no one should tell you, as a man *or* a woman, this is the role you have to play, and you have to play it all the time.[28]

The article here expresses a multiplicity of what can be done with gender roles – it points towards the play and possibility in the performativity of gender.[29] With the refusal of one's limited gender role as assigned at birth, and furthermore refusing to merely be reassigned to a limited female role under the terms of socially conservative and sexist psychiatry, the authors underline the potential pleasure in a free 'play' of gender roles.

The Group's discussion of gender roles resonates with, as DM Withers describes, the Women's Liberation movements' 'sustained revolt "against natural laws"' and its use of the word 'gender' to 'emphasise the repressive aspects of social conditioning, rather than foreground[ing] gender's liberatory potential'.[30] However, the Group are also interested in trans gender expression as a means to joy as part of a politic of liberation. This is juxtaposed with the difference between going stealth – i.e. not disclosing one's trans history, a common demand of Gender Identity Clinics (GICs) after changing gender as an aspect of social assimilation[31] – and the pride in being out as trans. 'One sex-change said she's torn between two desires, one to disappear and be accepted as a regular woman after struggling so many years, the other to shout up and down the street how beautiful it is to be transsexual'.[32] The authors suggest that the 'young' seem the most militant: 'Those who came out long ago are often the proudest [...] But they also know that if you pass you're treated as a human being'.[33]

With self-exploration and group consciousness-raising as important elements of group activity and discussion, a 'more central question' that emerged for the group was 'how to relate to other women' and build solidarity with the Women's movement.[34] 'When we talk about our hopes and fantasies, it becomes apparent that what we want above all is to be accepted as women, primarily by other women.' This attests to what cárdenas describes as trans desire or 'gender longing',[35] where resonances within social worlds open up to political practices, here rooted in a desire for social acceptance by other women. The article explicitly envisions and imagines a coalitional, intersectional Women's movement – after pointing toward the forms of pride developed by Black women and gay women, the group write:

> Think how much more inspiring and beautiful the women's revolution will be when it joyously includes all women. Think of a Holloway [Women's Prison, North London] demo with transvestite, transsexual and drag-queen women, gay women and heterosexual women, black, yellow, brown and white women, mothers, daughters, poor women, rich women, working women, housewives and career women.[36]

Indeed, the issue of *Lesbians Come Together* represents a dialogue that was then occurring between non-trans and trans women within spaces such as the Faraday Road women's commune, where these women met under one roof, a utopian vision from within which such coalitions may not have seemed farfetched.[37] As the opening statement of the issue valorises, a multiplicity of points of view and expressions, including 'polarisations, conflicts and arguments', are 'good' and can have the effect of enriching understanding and resilience within a movement.[38] The sense of possibility contained within the pages of the issue read, in the context of how queer history and lesbian and trans herstory have unfolded, as a utopian 'queer world-making' project,[39] imagining the forging of a sisterhood that struggled to be. The struggle for transsexual women to be accepted by the Women's movement would flare up significantly by the end of the seventies, in particular with the controversy created by Janice Raymond's *The Transsexual Empire*.[40] Yet the GLF TS/TV Group's article represents a discursive space to consider one's 'hopes and fantasies', within which a nascent imaginary of trans liberation was emerging with the promise of potential political practices that could be forged within a wider Women's movement, such as being present at demonstrations in solidarity with incarcerated women. The issue of *Come Together* was published in the month preceding the decision of the women of the London GLF to split from the gay men of the organisation in February 1972, and included indications that the movement was already 'split anyway', the article by Frankie and Edith on 'A Woman's Place…' noting that 'we need better liaison with the brothers, […] but we're fragmented amongst ourselves – we could be so much stronger together'.[41]

REMEMBERING TRANS LONDON 1971

Rachel Pollack started the GLF TS/TV Group in 1971, the same year that Pollack and Edith (Edie, her partner) had moved to London from the USA and in which Pollack came out 'as a woman and a lesbian'.[42] In a recent essay, 'trans central station', reflecting on her life, activism and highlights of her career as a renowned science fiction author, Pollack describes the transformative effect of the Women's and Gay Liberation movements on her life and on the lives of those in the spaces that she and Edie created:

> They [the movements] gave me models of how to trust your own experience rather than society's rules and stereotypes. When Edie and I moved to London in 1971 we joined GLF but also sought out trans groups. At first, I found this frustrating. I was looking for a political consciousness, a framework of ideas. The groups that existed seemed, well, light. And then I realized something. The liberation groups took everything very seriously, constantly arguing, theorizing. The trans group liked to have *fun*. And that was when I understood that being trans was *about joy almost more than anything else*.
>
> That did not mean I gave up on the idea of a group dedicated to consciousness raising. If one didn't exist, I would start it myself. Edith and I began to host weekly meetings in our flat in the Notting Hill section of London. My desire to discuss theory never got very far, but something important happened. We provided a place where people could *be*, and explore, themselves, at whatever level seemed comfortable.[43]

The weekly meetings of the GLF TS/TV Group created a social, political and affective space for trans expression and consciousness raising, rooted in a feminist principle of 'trust[ing] one's own experience'. The group enabled the exploration of selves and desires among its members, and the opportunity for them to collectively share trans joy. Pollack here juxtaposes this space to the 'seriousness' of discussions and theorising among other

Liberation groups. She describes a few members of the group, including Roz Kaveney and an unnamed Japanese trans woman who features as a character in Pollack's short story 'The Beatrix Gates' in a brief scene set in 1971 London.[44]

GLF meetings and groups played a significant role in consciousness-raising: the transformation and politicisation of one's perspective about one's own life, experiences and oppressions. For instance, in *A Life in Three Acts*, actor and drag queen Bette Bourne recalls both the somatic and psychological effect of attending GLF meetings.[45] Bourne describes how 'suddenly when you become conscious it affects your whole body' and how it is a 'thrilling' affective experience that fundamentally changed his outlook, leaving Bourne feeling '[r]ipped off' about his previous life.[46] In the context of the GLF TS/TV Group and perspectives undergirding their article in *Lesbians Come Together*, consciousness raising played a role in enabling 'self-discovery', developing positive affect in relation to self-expression across genders and beyond limited gender roles, while growing one's own awareness of one's body. As Pollack describes of her own coming out, 'I realized I was in exactly the *right* body, for my body told me what it – what I – wanted'.[47] This perspective developed through what Pollack describes, citing the words of Nor Hall, as an 'abandonment to the body's desire' that is 'in itself a form of revelation'.[48]

Kaveney discusses meeting Rachel and Edie during the period, after receiving their telephone number from the GLF and calling from a phonebox. She describes Pollack as 'one of those people that changes your life':

> Rachel and Edie were amazing. It never occurred to me that people could identify as trans and not be straight. It was totally gratifying to meet people that were actually writers, because I had this terrible concern that maybe if I was trans it meant that I wouldn't be able to be a writer, because the only trans writer I'd ever heard of was Jan Morris.[49]

While Pollack remembers the importance of her flat and the group for Kaveney, then still in the closet, to 'explore her secret self',[50] Kaveney emphasises the importance of Pollack as a role model as a trans science fiction writer and a lesbian, engaged in the spinning of new worlds while lampooning the moralities and stereotypes of the dominant one. The latter is crystallised in Pollack's satirical article 'The Twilight World of the Heterosexual', published in *Ink* and reprinted in *Come Together* (Issue 12). Kaveney describes how Pollack, compared to the psychiatrists running the Gender Identity Clinics, provided an alternate worldview on trans, which 'got me over myself to quite a remarkable extent'.[51] She recalls how this was '[i]n large part because of Rachel and [her] "bad attitude", because she was American and no damn British shrink was going to tell her what to do.' She adds that Pollack played a pivotal role in assembling networks and building community, 'finding people who wanted to be found'.

TARNISHING THE MEMORY: AGGRESSIVE MISGENDERING IN THE GLF ARCHIVE

These memories of life trans-formed, of alternative worlds and possibilities of life and writing, are met with the harsh historical truths of violent transphobia and transmisogyny in the archive and memory of the Gay Liberation movement. In the public memory of the GLF, the tensions around trans people in general within gay liberation appears to have been amplified by gay men and radical queens. Cloud Downey, a radical queen who briefly attended the GLF TS/TV Group, notes that the 'big clashes' were between transvestites and 'the men'.[52] In comparison, lesbians within gay liberation – such as those of the Faraday Road commune – primarily seemed to have a problem with practices of drag rather than having problems with transsexual women. Discussing radical drag in the context of an offending incident at a gay liberation ball, Lisa Power claims that 'Drag or transvestism as an issue was always clearly separated from transsexuality in the minds of most GLF women. Indeed, for much of the life of the GLF women's group, transsexuals were welcomed by many lesbians and seen as less problematic politically than straight transvestites'.[53] In one of the two oral histories within Power's book that comments on trans lives, Nettie Pollard discusses how transsexual women attended the women's group, describing their different gender expressions and the mix and dynamics of (non-trans and transsexual) women at the Faraday Road commune.[54] Pollard describes her ambivalence as someone both welcoming of transsexual women, while recognising differences in experience between trans and non-trans women. She 'felt extremely torn on the subject myself because I felt that transsexuals were perfectly valid, and didn't feel that they should be excluded, but at the same time I realized that their history wasn't entirely the same as women'.[55] Furthermore, she remembers an anecdote about Rachel Pollack and Edith attending the Women's Think-In at All Saints Hall, where discussions on whether Rachel should be allowed to attend evolved when a straight, drunken man aggressively misgendered Rachel, leading the women to throw the drunken man out in 'a nice bit of solidarity': '[W]e think we'll have our differences to ourselves but if a straight man comes in we're not taking it from him'.[56]

Transphobia and transmisogyny permeate two of the significant accounts of Gay Liberation in Britain: Aubrey Walter's 1980 introduction to the *Come Together* anthology, and Stuart Feather's more recent *Blowing the Lid: Gay Liberation, Sexual Revolution and Radical Queens* which provides an account of the London GLF.[57] These accounts are replete with aggressive misgendering of trans women, which Pollack subsequently describes as 'either a deliberate insult or something worse, a casual obliteration of the person's identity'.[58] While discussing the London GLF's split in February 1972, and its seeming inevitability given the development of feminist consciousness among the GLF's women and the ongoing 'ego tripping' and 'chauvinism of many gay men', Walter's 1980

Come Together introduction consigns the fate of the GLF TS/TV group to a footnote. The footnote includes a graphic denunciation of one transsexual woman, over and above a substantiation of the perspective of the group:

> The impact of the very just critique of male chauvinism made by the women at this time was confused by the actions of the Transvestites and Transsexuals group, who insisted that they were doubly oppressed within GLF, by the women as well as the men. One transsexual actually handed round photos at the meeting of himself (sic) with both male (sic) genitals and breasts. From the feminist point of view, they were simply playing the game of the chauvinist men.[59]

The concept of 'double oppression' alluded to by Walter had currency in the seventies, describing the intersections of sexist and homophobic oppressions as experienced by gay women, or the intersections of anti-Black, racist and sexist oppressions as experienced by Black women and other women of colour.[60] Rather than considering its terms as claimed by the members of the GLF TS/TV Group – here seemingly unrecoverable from the archive – Walter anecdotally undermines the idea that transsexual and transvestite women could experience double oppression. A classic move of transmisogyny via an epistemological disqualification as described by trans historian Susan Stryker, whereby the 'radical potential' of the knowledge rooted in 'antinormative bodily difference' is 'circumscribed' and rendered 'merely subjective',[61] trans subjectivity itself is here casually obliterated.[62] The 'actions' of the GLF TS/TV Group are stripped of agency, rendered as 'simply playing' a game determined by '*the* chauvinist men' from *the* feminist standpoint, presented as a singular perspective. Indeed, GLF women challenge this claim to a singular feminist standpoint: in her account of the GLF split, Elizabeth Wilson recalls that David Fernbach and Aubrey Walter 'made this totally disingenuous argument. *The feminist line* was that women should meet separately, that women should not meet within the GLF but separately, period. That was *their* radical feminist line'.[63]

While Walter seems unable to cognise the possibility that the members of the GLF TS/TV Group might develop a different feminist standpoint rooted in their particular experiences as described in *Lesbians Come Together*, he is quick to follow this footnote with the development of the politics of the GLF's radical queens. The radical queens were 'Fem gay men' who challenged masculine gender roles and male privilege through practices of radical drag both public and domestic (such as in the Notting Hill drag commune, where there was a practice of sharing clothes), and politically identified with Women's Liberation and its struggles.[64] Invoking a sense of consciousness developed in response to the Radicalesbians' influential 'Woman-Identified Woman' manifesto, Walter describes these Fem gay men as making political identifications 'from the position of being psychically and emotionally more woman-identified than man-identified', adding that they were 'definitely seen as a fifth column in the male sex, working to undermine its privilege and masculinity'.[65] Walter is quick to valorise those working 'within' the male sex to bring about its demise, while dismissing transsexual and transvestite women who refuse to be defined by it.

Walter's transmisogyny and transphobia, coupled to an affirmation of the radical queens, is not alone in the memory of Gay Liberation in the UK. The recent, sizable account of the London GLF by Stuart Feather (who was a radical queen) includes a chapter on transvestites and transsexuals, and reproduces the GLF TS/TV Group's article in *Lesbians Come Together* alongside writing by Rachel Pollack and Julia B from *Come Together* (Issue 14) ('Coming Out as a Transsexual'). Feather's chapter begins with graphic, deprecating descriptions of three trans women in the GLF, aggressively misgendering them and using 'he'/'him' pronouns alongside offensive language.[66] The three women are the same as those described by Nettie Pollard – whose oral history account in *Power*, cited above, is also cited by Feather following his own descriptions – and Feather's account may be read as attempting to revise the memory of these three women. Furthermore, Feather 'stresses' that the GLF TS/TV Group 'never visited or came out at the all-London meetings'.[67] Having claimed that the GLF TS/TV Group article, with its nine signatories, was written by Pollack alone, he says that 'Pollack is not enlightening' on the 'subject' of transvestites and transsexuals.[68] In this regard, Feather's primary concerns are defining and separating these labels from each other, reinstituting the primacy of medical models of transsexuality and undermining Pollack's identity as a lesbian woman.[69] Feather is however invested in challenging a binary system of gender roles, and is interested in theoretical accounts written by Bob Mellors and Mario Mieli.[70] Having both refused trans lesbian identities and claimed that transsexual women such as Julia B are socially conformist, Feather claims he is 'certain [...] that transsexuals, just like homosexuals, challenge the immoral and undemocratic, offend the moral and the aesthetic standards of the hegemony, and will be part of the new'.[71] Reasserting a separatist position around building liberation, '*the* feminist line' discussed above, he writes 'transvestites and transsexuals must fight their oppression for themselves'.[72]

While Feather appears to have missed any developments in transgender or LGBT coalitional organising in the time between 1972 and the publication of *Blowing the Lid*, the aggression and ignorance of his account of trans life and organising within Gay Liberation are impactful – Feather's account reflects and embodies transphobia and transmisogyny as historical sentiments. Such accounts have purchase on the memory of trans people in Gay Liberation broadly, salting historical wounds that affect the work of trans activists and scholars involved in remembering or unarchiving trans presence in the movement. The flash of political possibility of a liberated trans lesbian consciousness witnessed in the work of the GLF TS/TV Group, and the potential feminist solidarity leave an afterimage, a queer memory of a trans seventies that doesn't seem to reappear until the tail end of the decade. This is a seventies that scholars in the nineties sought to recover.

RADICAL DEVIANCE: TRANS '90S SEEKS THE '70S

In the pages of *Radical Deviance: A Journal of Transgendered Politics* (initially incarnated as *Genderfuck* zine), published and co-edited in the mid to late 1990s largely by UK-based trans theorist and activist Kate More, is located the beginning of a counter-memory to the transmisogyny of the gay men of the GLF. This emerged at a moment when remembering the contributions of trans people to the UK Gay Liberation movement gained a new political importance. Moreover, the significance of *Radical Deviance* itself appears to have been glossed over in the history of trans studies, although a portion of its theoretical content is reproduced in the first trans studies anthology *Reclaiming Genders: Transsexual Grammars at the Fin-de-Siècle* (1999/2016), co-edited by More and Stephen Whittle. The journal was produced in Middlesbrough, England and connected to the Gender and Sexuality Alliance (G&SA); its contributors included More and Whittle alongside key contributors to trans and LGBT politics and culture in the '90s, such as Clare Hemmings, Roz Kaveney, Surya Munro, Zach Nataf, Zoë-Jane Playdon and Riki-Ann Wilchins.[73] The journal included trans theory; trans legal and cultural news, including detailed accounts of contemporary trans cultural events and conferences; updates from organisations including Press for Change and on activism such as pursuing provisions for trans people from Rape Crisis Centres; and interviews with leading poststructuralist feminist thinkers, including Judith Butler and Hélène Cixous, and activists.

The trans counter-memory of Gay Liberation is demonstrated in an issue of *Radical Deviance* published on the eve of London Pride 1996, the first London Pride where 'transgender' was explicitly included in the constitution and celebrations of Pride, as part of the development of 'LGBT' coalitional politics. As *Radical Deviance* attests, this move of inclusion came on the back of counter-narratives of the Stonewall riots that highlighted the key roles of lesbians and trans masculine people, alongside drag queens. This was also a period of the development of concepts, culture and politics under the banner of transgender in the UK. An article by Diane Morgan that discusses this moment of inclusion and the development of the term 'transgender' itself as an umbrella term, connects the contemporaneous moment to aspects of transgender history. Transgender is here conceptualised to include drag queens and kings alongside transsexuals and transvestites, which in turn brings (back) together people who may identify as LGB or straight.[74] It thus works to overturn historical conflicts and boundaries between people of different modes of gender expressions and experiences. As More states elsewhere, transgender is 'an umbrella term' that includes a historical sense of conflict: 'in fact the whole gamut of "gender complex" people fighting together instead of against each other'.[75]

Emphasising the importance of drag queens and radical drag within the GLF and the Pride marches and celebrations initiated by the group in the UK, Morgan gives significant space to More's comments on Gay Lib.[76] More argues that 'the lack of alternative readings [of the British GLF] means the writing on TG [transgender] involvement offends a lot of people', and states that 'this is getting better: last year's book by Lisa Power on the GLF, *No Bath But Plenty of Bubbles* may have included almost nothing about TVs and TSs, but does cover much of the "radical drag"'.[77] The issue of *Radical Deviance* includes a discussion between Kate More and GLF activist and lesbian feminist Angela Mason (née Weir), who was then director of Lesbian and Gay rights charity Stonewall UK. Stonewall had just published *Queer Bashing*, their first report on lesbian and gay hate crime in the UK. Pressed by More to discuss transgender issues, given that organisations like Stonewall and Outrage 'seem strangely silent about the issue', Mason admits that she doesn't know much about transgender politics, while also referencing numerous significant flash-points of the trans '70s. She comments on the existence of the GLF TS/TV Group; that 'Rachel Pollack lived with us at one point'; and that she was friends with Carol Riddell in the Women's movement.[78] She notes the fraughtness of the GLF, and that Kaveney 'felt very excluded in GLF'.[79] Discussing the lack of discussion of transgender hate crime in *Queer Bashing*, Mason describes walking with Pollack while she faced 'a constant stream of abuse' as a visible, lesbian transsexual woman in the early seventies.[80] Mason's testimony represents an attempt to attest to and reconcile historical wounds in the memory of the GLF, forging solidarities in this new coalitional queer moment. *Radical Deviance* functions as a discursive space to trial and address the possibilities and pitfalls of queer and feminist coalitional politics in the context of an emergent transgender culture and politics, addressing gaps and posing difficult questions to the historicisations and accounts of the queer seventies that were emerging in the nineties.

CONCLUSION: SISTERHOOD AMID A DIVIDE

This essay has elucidated particular moments within the Gay Liberation movement where solidarity among trans and non-trans lesbians enabled the spread of radical consciousness and perspectives in printed matter, through a then-emergent politic of lesbian separatism. I have shown how the memory of trans lesbians articulates a counter-narrative to transphobic and transmisogynist historicisations of the London GLF, memories that emerged through feminist dialogues in print and in public between the '90s and the 2010s. To conclude, I turn briefly to an important text by feminist socialist trans lesbian woman Carol Riddell. Riddell, a 'radical professor of sociology at Lancaster University',[81] was active in the Women's Liberation movement across the 1970s, presenting papers at Women's Lib and socialist feminist conferences, contributing to *Spare Rib*, living in women's housing co-operatives, and playing keyboard in the Northern Women's Liberation Rock Band.[82]

Alongside co-authoring a sociology textbook with socialist feminist Margaret Coulson,[83] Riddell's critical writing outlined structural critiques of patriarchal capitalism focused on women's role in social reproduction, lesbian perspectives on the Women's

Front cover of *Divided Sisterhood*, 1980.

movement, and her important, early transfeminist text *Divided Sisterhood*.[84] A rebuttal of Janice Raymond's *The Transsexual Empire*, *Divided Sisterhood* was published by News From Nowhere, Liverpool's feminist bookshop, in 1980,[85] and reprinted in Stryker and Whittle's *The Transgender Studies Reader*. The text interweaves a critical review, poems, and an excerpt of an unpublished novel, connecting a politics of 1970s transsexual women's experience to the structural critique of patriarchy while extensively challenging the claims and modes of argument made by Raymond, arguing that Raymond's attempts at denouncing transsexual women through 'ideological purity' are harmful to feminist culture at large.[86] While the critique of Raymond itself is not my interest here, and an account of Riddell's work in the '70s remains to be undertaken, it is important to note that, like other trans lesbian feminists at the time, Riddell's critical analysis and theory emerges from *within* the context of lesbian separatism and living a separatist life. Her writing and ideas from this period emerged from dialogues within the Women's movement, circulating through its publications and forums. Discussing the unlearning of patriarchal cultural values that feminists undertake, itself a significant aspect of consciousness-raising groups, Riddell writes:

> The separation adopted by some women to undertake this struggle is a result of the degree of sexual oppression, intentional and unintentional, shown by men in our societies. But trans-sexual women's transformation in the same way is not incompatible with that of other women, who, as separatists, are able to accept, and work with transsexual feminists.[87]

In this comment, as a response to an oppressive patriarchal context, separatism provides an opportunity for unlearning and forging 'the condition of female humanness'.[88] Such a condition entails a personal 'struggle' that must involve others – intentional communities and groupings between women can enable this work. Speaking from her own experiences in the Women's movement, Riddell understands that transsexual and non-trans women are able to work together on such endeavours.[89]

The possibilities in working together – collabourating and co-operating, printing each other's words, building coalitions and new forms of feminist understanding – emerged tangibly under the roof of the Faraday Road women's commune in 1971, producing *Lesbians Come Together*, and within the Women's movement through the work of transsexual feminists like Riddell. Such possibilities re-emerged in part in feminist organising in the eighties and nineties in groups such as Feminists Against Censorship and in organising against Section 28. Queer and feminist print media from across these decades, driven by radical editorial ethos, reflect the heterogeneous perspectives of trans and lesbian feminisms. The result of the editorial decisions, such as in *Lesbians Come Together* to print all submissions to the issue, is visible traces of trans and non-trans lesbian life and solidarity. These are documents of the politics and discussions inaugurated with Gay Liberation and Women's Liberation and of active dialogues that challenged the elision of trans people in these movements and in the memories of them. Riddell's defence of trans lesbian life in the seventies forms the tip of an iceberg of what was already lived and experienced, and what may yet be unarchived, reconstituted and remembered.

NOTES

1   In an article on feminism and squatting in 1970s
    London, Christine Wall includes a comment from
    GLF member Lee Nurse on 'women-only housing',
    naming the Faraday Road commune as 'the first
    women's house, lived in by women who were in the
    GLF, and before they split from the men in GLF. It
    was a very odd concept actually at the time and all
    the ideas around it seemed really radical […] that
    house became a very important lesbian separatist
    house'. Christine Wall, 'Sisterhood and Squatting in
    the 1970s: Feminism, Housing and Urban Change in
    Hackney', *History Workshop Journal* 83, no. 1 (Spring
    2017): 79–97, https://doi.org/10.1093/hwj/dbx024.
    Citations are from online version, which does not
    contain page numbers.

2   All citations from *Lesbians Come Together* are from
    its reprint in Aubrey Walter (ed.), *Come Together: The
    Years of Gay Liberation 1970–73,* London and New
    York: Verso, 2018, 156.

3   Lisa Power, *No Bath but Plenty of Bubbles.* London:
    Cassell, 1995, 233.

4   Walter, *Come Together,* 158.

5   Walter, *Come Together,* 158–159.

6   Christine Burns (ed.), *Trans Britain: Our Journey from
    the Shadows.* London: Unbound, 2018, 31–38.

7   For a discussion of the contemporary significance of
    Morris and Ashley's memoirs in the context of the
    transsexual memoir genre, see Georgina Juliet Buckell
    (Jacques), *Variations: Transgender Memoir, Fiction and
    Theory.* Doctoral Dissertation, University of Sussex,
    2019. In Burns' *Trans Britain,* Carol Steele provides a
    personal account which discusses the Manchester TS/
    TV Group of the mid 1970s (68–81); and Adrianne
    Nash also provides a personal account that discusses
    aversion 'therapies' including Electro-Convulsive
    'Therapy' (ECT)(39–50).

8   Roz Kaveney in conversation with Nat Raha and
    Jonathan Bay, part of *Between the Sheets: Radical print

cultures before the queer bookshop, 23–24 February
    2017 CCA, Glasgow, Scotland. Hereafter cited as
    'Kaveney et al, *Between the Sheets'.* A live transcription
    of the event by Nicola Osborne forms the basis of my
    citations of the conversation.

9   Laura Doan, 'Queer History/Queer Memory: The
    Case of Alan Turing.' *GLQ* 23, no. 1 (2017), 116.

10 Charles E. Morris III and K. J. Rawson, 'Queer
    Archives/Archival Queers.' In *Theorizing Histories
    of Rhetoric*, by Michelle Ballif (ed.), Carbondale &
    Edwardsville: Southern Illinois University Press, 2013,
    84.

11 Finn Enke, 'Collective Memory and the Transfeminist
    1970s: Towards a Less Plausible History.' *TSQ:
    Transgender Studies Quarterly* 5, no. 1 (2018), 9–10.

12 Abram J. Lewis, '"I Am 64 and Paul McCartney
    Doesn't Care": The Haunting of the Transgender
    Archive and the Challenges of Queer History'. *Radical
    History Review*, No. 120 (2014), 14.

13 Rachel Pollack, whose organising work and memories
    I discuss in the next section, describes quitting the
    women's movement and moving to Amsterdam in
    1973. Rachel Pollack, *The Beatrix Gates.* Oakland,
    CA: PM Press, 2019, 60. In an American example,
    Enke narrates the important work of Beth Elliot in
    1971–73, including her role in the San Francisco
    chapter of the Daughters of Bilitis. Enke, 'Collective
    Memory'.

14 Doan, 'Queer History/Queer Memory'; Enke
    'Collective Memory'.

15 Lewis, 'I Am 64 and Paul McCartney Doesn't Care',
    15.

16 Kaveney et al, *Between the Sheets.*

17 These accounts were seemingly disappeared from
    the collective memory of the Stonewall riots until
    David Isay, *Remembering Stonewall.* Radio Broadcast.
    Storycorps. Weekend All Things Considered, July 1,
    1989, https://storycorps.org/stories/remembering-
    stonewall/ and Martin Duberman, *Stonewall,* New

York: Dutton; Plume, 1993, in which Sylvia Rivera actively represents herself as an agent within the uprising. For contemporary readings of this legacy, see the work of Tourmaline including the film *Happy Birthday Marsha* (2018) and Tourmaline [Reina Gossett], Eric A. Stanley and Johanna Burton (eds), *Trap Door: Trans Cultural Production and the Politics of Visibility,* Cambridge, MA and London: The MIT Press, 2017.

18 Kaveney et al, *Between the Sheets.*

19 At *Between the Sheets*, Kaveney discussed that the number of anaesthetics she had undergone in the 80s, to address medical problems arising from her gender confirmation surgery, had impacted on her memory of the 1970s and 1980s (Kaveney et al., *Between the Sheets*). For an account of the relation between queer memory and historical trauma, in the context of post-Soviet 'postness', see Ana Hoffner, *The Queerness of Memory,* Berlin: b_books, 2018.

20 Dipesh Chakrabarty, 'History and the politics of recognition.' In *Manifestos for History*, by Keith Jenkins, Sue Morgan and Alun Munslow (eds), Abingdon, Oxon and New York: Routledge, 2007, 77–78.

21 In their *Come Together* piece, the GLF TS/TV Group recorded that no transvestite men or transsexual men were attending their group (Walter, *Come Together,* 165).

22 Stephen Whittle, 'Where Did We Go Wrong? Feminism and Trans Theory – Two Teams on the Same Side?' In *The Transgender Studies Reader*, Susan Stryker and Stephen Whittle (eds), New York: Routledge, 2006, 195.

23 Whittle, 'Where Did We Go Wrong?', 195.

24 Walter, *Come Together,* 164–167.

25 Walter, *Come Together,* 164, 167. The article's signatories are Roz, Paula, Rachel, Della, Edith, Susan, Perry, Patty and Christine. The article is quick to define (transsexual and transvestite) 'women' as 'people born males who live as women, or more commonly, dress as women whenever they get the chance.' They add that 'transvestite men – people born female who live or dress as men (if the language confuses you it confuses us too, its not meant to include us) have so far not come forth' (Walter, *Come Together,* 164–165). These definitions notably combine the terms transsexual and transvestite – this discursive move ought to be considered historically in the context of social divisions discussed below.

26 Walter, *Come Together,* 165, emphasis added.

27 Walter, *Come Together,* 165. In her personal account of seeking trans-specific healthcare across the 1950s to the 70s, Adrienne Nash describes being offered and refusing ECT as aversion therapy by Dr John Randell at Charing Cross Gender Identity Clinic in 1971 (Burns, *Trans Britain,* 45–48). In 1975, on being referred again to Randell, Nash recalls how Randell had bought up her prior refusal of a then-discontinued treatment, noting that it didn't work and had been withdrawn. ECT was widely challenged within the Gay Liberation, Mental Patients' Liberation and Anti-Psychiatry Movements in the UK and North America – an important early critique was made by Don Jackson in 'dachau for queers', originally published in *Gay Sunshine* (No. 1, Issue 3, November 1970), and reprinted in *The Gay Liberation Book*, Len Richmond and Gay Noguera (eds), San Francisco: Ramparts Press, 1973, 42–49. For an account of the London GLF's Counter-Psychiatry Group, see Lucy Robinson, 'Three Revolutionary Years: The Impact of the Counter Culture on the Development of the Gay Liberation movement in Britain', *Cultural and Social History* 3 (2006), 458–463. I discuss the violence of ECT and Gay and Mental Patients' liberation activism against it, in the context of 1960s and 70s Massachusetts, USA in my Doctoral Thesis. Natalia Raha, *Queer capital: Marxism in queer theory and post-1950 poetics.* Doctoral thesis (PhD), University of Sussex, 2019. For a recent critique regarding the ongoing use of the practice in North America, see Don Weitz, 'Electroshock: Torture as 'Treatment'.' In *Mad Matters: A critical reader in Canadian Mad Studies*, by Brenda A. Lefrançois, Robert Menzies and Geoffrey Reaume (eds), Toronto: Canadian Scholars' Press, 2013, 158–169.

28 Walter, *Come Together,* 165–166, original emphasis.

29 As DM Withers describes, the modern sense of gender, first used by Ann Oakley in her 1972 book *Sex, Gender and Society*, was 'appropriated' from research undertaken by psychiatrists on transsexual and intersex people, DM Withers, 'Laboratories of gender: Women's Liberation and the transfeminist present.' *Radical Philosophy* 2, no. 4 (Spring 2019), 4.

30 Withers, 'Laboratories of gender', 4, quoting Sally Fraser and Amanda Sebestyen, 'Going Orange' in Amanda Sebestyen (ed.), *'68, '78, '88: From Women's Liberation to Feminism*, Bridport: Prism Press, 1988.

31 Critically addressing the small scale of GICs in the 1960s and 70s, Carol Riddell writes that the GICs 'strove to justify themselves by their conformity – hence all the ghastly gender-amendment training which trans-sexuals have to suffer'. Carol Riddell, 'Divided Sisterhood: A Critical Review of Janice Raymond's The Transsexual Empire.' In *The Transgender Studies Reader*, by Susan Stryker and Stephen Whittle (eds), London & New York: Routledge, 2006, 151.

32 Walter, *Come Together,* 166–167.

33 Walter, *Come Together,* 167.

34 Walter, *Come Together,* 166.

35 micha cárdenas, *Trans Desire,* New York and Dresden: Atropos Press, 2010, 26–27.

36 Walter, *Come Together,* 166.

37 Nettie Pollard describes the Faraday Road commune as a space where 'there might be ten transsexuals and about twelve women', although she points towards their differences in experience. She suggests that some of the transsexuals were at the 'very early stages' of self-exploration, and describes these meetings as becoming 'like a mixed group' (Power, *No Bath*, 244).

38 Walter, *Come Together,* 156.

39 Lauren Berlant and Michael Warner. 'Sex in Public.' *Critical Inquiry*, Vol. 24, No. 2, 1998: 547–566.

40 The controversy around Raymond's book is canonical and in the interest of building a supplementary historical account of the 70s, I do not address it here. For detail, see Riddell, 'Divided Sisterhood'; Sandy Stone, 'The Empire Strikes Back: A Posttranssexual Manifesto,' In *The Transgender Studies Reader*, 221–235; Susan Stryker, *Transgender History*, Berkeley, CA: Seal Press, 2008; Cameron Awkward-Rich, 'Trans, Feminism: Or, Reading like a Depressed Transsexual.' *Signs: Journal of Women in Culture and Society* 42, no. 2 (Summer 2017): 819–841. It ought to be noted that the publication of *The Transsexual Empire* in the UK by The Women's Press also raises questions around criticality and feminist publishing practices.

41 Walter, *Come Together,* 160.

42 Rachel Pollack, *The Beatrix Gates,* Oakland, CA: PM Press, 2019, 50.

43 Pollack, *The Beatrix Gates,* 59. All emphases in this quote are added.

44 Pollack, *The Beatrix Gates,* 60.

45 Bourne was a resident of the Notting Hill drag commune around this period, and involved in assembling *Come Together 15* (Spring 1973). Bette Bourne and Mark Ravenhill, *A Life in Three Acts.* London: Methuen Drama, 2009, 15.

46 Bourne and Ravenhil, *A Life in Three Acts,* 15, 16.

47 Pollack, *The Beatrix Gates,* 50.

48 Pollack, *The Beatrix Gates,* 50. Countering the medical narrative of being 'trapped in the wrong body', Pollack adds: 'No, I was not trapped in the wrong body. I was trapped in the wrong universe. In order to become who I was, I had to break the world open' (*The Beatrix Gates,* 50). She describes science

fiction as one of the important means to do this world-breaking and world-making.

49 Kaveney et al, *Between the Sheets.*

50 Pollack, *The Beatrix Gates,* 60.

51 Kaveney et al., *Between the Sheets.*

52 Power, *No Bath,* 244.

53 Power, *No Bath,* 243.

54 Power, *No Bath,* 244–245. Pollard describes the gender expressions of Claudia, Bobbi and Rachel Pollack.

55 Power, *No Bath,* 244.

56 Power, *No Bath,* 245.

57 Stuart Feather, *Blowing the Lid: Gay Liberation, Sexual Revolution and Radical Queens,* London: Zero Books, 2015.

58 Pollack, *The Beatrix Gates,* 54.

59 Walter, *Come Together,* 32.

60 Iris Morales, *Through the Eyes of Rebel Women: The Young Lords 1969–1976.* New York: Red Sugarcane Press, 2016.

61 Susan Stryker, 'Transgender History, Homonormativity, and Disciplinarity.' *Radical History Review*, Issue 100, 2008, 154.

62 I discuss Stryker's conceptualisation of transmisogyny at length in my essay 'Transfeminine Brokenness, Radical Transfeminism', connecting it to the devaluation of the labour power of trans women and trans femmes. Nat Raha, 'Transfeminine Brokenness, Radical Transfeminism.' *South Atlantic Quarterly* 116, no. 3 (2017): 632–646.

63 Power, *No Bath,* 240, emphasis added.

64 Walter, *Come Together,* 33. For an account of the Notting Hill drag commune, see Bourne and Ravenhill, *A Life,* 22–23. For a historical account of the 1972 actions of the radical queens, also known as the Rad Fems, see Robinson, 'Three Revolutionary Years', 469–471.

65 Walter, *Come Together,* 33.

66 Feather, *Blowing,* 319–320.

67 Feather, *Blowing,* 321.

68 Feather, *Blowing,* 321, 323.

69 Feather, *Blowing,* 329–330, 323–325.

70 For an analysis of Mieli's theory of transsexuality and his radical politics of transvestitism, see Roberto Filippello, 'On Sequins and Shit: The Epistemology of Radical Dress in Mario Mieli's Transsexual Utopia', *Third Text*, Vol. 34, *Third Text*, Vol. 35 no. 1, 2021, 130–144.

71 Feather, *Blowing,* 332.

72 Feather, *Blowing,* 329.

73 The mid '90s saw the publication of two influential books from these contributors: Zachary Nataf's *Lesbians Talk: Transgender,* London: Scarlett Press, 1996; and Riki Anne Wilchins' *Read my lips: sexual subversion and the end of gender*, Ithaca, NY : Firebrand Books, 1997.

74 Diane Morgan, 'Le[T'S]sbigay Together', *Radical Deviance: A Journal of Transgendered Politics* 2, no. 2 (1996), 51.

75 Morgan, 'Le[T'S]sbigay Together', 51. More's definition of transgender, in her introduction to *Reclaiming Genders*, in full reads: 'an umbrella term including all cross-living and cross-dressing people, in fact the whole gamut of "gender complex" people fighting together instead of against each other. In the past we have raised all sorts of dubious boundaries: drag queens and kings were cast out as homosexual perverts, transvestites were fetishists, and perhaps most destructive, transsexuals were raised close to sanctity (unless they were gay or enjoyed sex or something). Transgender's pluralist politics – based on coalition, bringing in the gay community for the first time – offers something seriously to look forward to', Kate More and Stephen Whittle (eds), *Reclaiming Genders: Transsexual Grammars at the Fin de Siècle* (first published 1999), London: Bloomsbury Academic, 2016, 2–3.

76 Morgan, 'Le[T'S]sbigay Together', 50.

77 Morgan, 'Le[T'S]sbigay Together', 50. In her

introduction to *Reclaiming Genders*, More refers to the importance of the political and intellectual contributions of the GLF, as remembered *by* Stuart Feather in *No Bath But Plenty of Bubbles.* She describes this as 'One of the reasons for this book' and its consideration of the relationship between trans-activism and trans-theory (More and Whittle, *Reclaiming Genders*, 1). This is suggestive of the stakes of transmisogyny and transphobia within queer memory – there may be neither a bath nor a baby to negotiate, but the offence it causes can have both lasting and unintended consequences.

78 Kate More and Angela Mason, 'Coalitions, Common Issues, & Hate Crime', *Radical Deviance: A Journal of Transgendered Politics* 2, no. 2 (1996), 48.

79 More and Mason, 'Coalitions', 48.

80 More and Mason, 'Coalitions', 48.

81 Susan Stryker and Talia L. Bettcher, 'Introduction: Trans/Feminism.' *TSQ: Transgender Studies Quarterly* 3, no. 1–2 (2016), 10.

82 Carol Riddell, 'Divided Sisterhood', 158; Women's Liberation Music Archive, 'N', Online at https://womensliberationmusicarchive.co.uk/n/ (accessed 8th June 2020).

83 Margaret Coulson and Carol Riddell, *Approaching Sociology: A Critical Introduction*, London: Routledge and Kegan Paul, 1972.

84 Carol Riddell, 'Notes, In Lieu of an Editorial,' *Socialist Woman*, May–June (1973); Riddell, 'Divided Sisterhood'.

85 In a 2016 interview with Combined Academic, a member of the News From Nowhere co-operative emphasises the importance of solidarity with the political movements of the late 70s and early 80s. While there are no comments on the Bookshop's own publications, the piece points out that the Bookshop became a women's co-operative in 1981. Combined Academic, 'News from Nowhere: The Co-operative Bookshop run by Women', *Verso* blog, 2nd March 2016, https://www.versobooks.com/blogs/2532-news-from-nowhere-the-co-operative-bookshop-run-by-women.

86 Riddell, 'Divided Sisterhood', 157.

87 Riddell, 'Divided Sisterhood', 153.

88 Riddell, 'Divided Sisterhood', 153.

89 Riddell, 'Divided Sisterhood', 153.

11 Uses of the Past: Sexuality, Self-image and Group Identity in German Lesbian Magazines in the 1970s

JANIN AFKEN

n 1975 – proclaimed the International Women's Year by the UN General Assembly – two magazines published explicitly by lesbians and for lesbians appeared in West Berlin for the first time: *Lesbenpresse* (*LP*, Lesbian Press) and *Unsere kleine Zeitung* (*UkZ*, Our little Newspaper). The aim of both magazines was to promote networking for lesbian women in Germany and to act as a feminist medium of publication by women, for women. Although *UkZ* and *LP* were similar in this regard, the way in which they worked to achieve this intention was in many ways diametrically opposed.[1] *UkZ* was primarily a revival of the traditions and culture of the Weimar Republic whereas *Lesbenpresse* sought a separatist, lesbian counterculture and society for women. To achieve this aim, *Lesbenpresse* was not only eager to follow in the footsteps of a lesbian history and past, but also it tried to make space for lesbian-matriarchal myths and legends in articles.

The fact that both magazines appeared only a few weeks apart in February 1975, were both from West Berlin, and originally arose from the networks of Homosexuellen Aktion Westberlin (HAW, Homosexual Action West Berlin) invites a comparative analysis. First, I will discuss in this essay the aesthetic and narrative mediation of the concepts of and references to the past. How do *LP* and *UkZ* differ in terms of their aesthetic presentation and style and how can these be read in terms of their respective references to the past? Then I will turn to the contexts surrounding the emergence of each magazine and the composition of the groups who produced them. Concentrating on the first few issues of each magazine, since *UkZ* appeared once per month and *LP* was published irregularly, I will go on to explore the way that the past is conceptualised in both magazines. Here I am interested in the representation and understanding of the past, whether it is a closer past that can still be traced – in the example of *UkZ* – or a more distant, mythical past. In what ways is the past constructed, and what function does it serve, in the context of the 1970s? In the case of *Lesbenpresse,* references to the past are also connected with alternative concepts of life and society, which, as utopias, are to be considered together with a possible alternative future rather than merely an alternative past.

Previous research on German lesbian magazines is sporadic and usually only available in the form of unpublished final papers by students that concentrate on topical thematic approaches. These include, for example, the outstanding masters thesis by Franka Fieseler as well as its condensed summarized results in the article 'Vernetzte Netze – vielfältige Foren ('Networked Networks – A Wide Range of Forums: The history of lesbian-feminist magazines in Germany') from 2008. In her masters thesis on Lesbian Action Center (Lesbisches Aktions Zentrum, LAZ), Lara Ledwa also discusses *Lesbenpresse,* as does Lisa (now Lorenz) Weinberg's masters thesis, which examines the sexuality discourse on butch and femme, among other things, in *UkZ* and *Lesbenpresse.*[2] Finally, a paper by Naemi Eifler on anti-semitic thought patterns in lesbian magazines, in particular in *UkZ* and *Schwarze Botin,* is also relevant.[3] Various reviews have been published of the individual magazines *Lesbenpresse* and *UkZ* and the organisations that founded them, L 74 and LAZ. Some of the earliest research in this area appears in Ilse Kokula's 1983 monograph, *Formen lesbischer Subkultur. Vergesellschaftung und soziale Bewegung (Forms of Lesbian Subculture: Socialization and Social Movement),* which discusses the emancipation groups LAZ and L 74 and their respective press organisations. There are also self-portrayals of the *UkZ* publishers, as well as articles by the former publishers Helga Trachsel and Eva Bornemann, in the trailblazing anthology of lesbian history *In Bewegung bleiben. 100 Jahre Lesbenbewegung (Keep Moving: 100 Years of the Lesbian Movement),* edited by Dennert, Rauchut and Leidinger in 2008. A section dedicated to *Lesbenpresse* appears in an article authored by Evelyn Kuwertz and Ulrike Stelzl, 'Der ästhetische Anteil innerhalb der Publikationen der Neuen Frauenbewegung' ('The Aesthetic Proportion Within the Publications of the New Women's movement'), published with an editorial written by Silvia Bovenschen and Peter Gorsen in the magazine *Ästhetik und Kommunikation* in 1976. This article aimed to scrutinize new forms of aesthetics and communications within the Women's movement, hinting toward new approaches to the exchange of information that these publications enabled.

UNSERE KLEINE ZEITUNG (UKZ, OUR LITTLE NEWSPAPER)

UkZ was simple in design and similar to a newsletter in the readership it intended to reach. In its first few years, and largely for financial reasons, the magazine was produced using the simple dot matrix method. The texts were typed on matrices with a type-writer and printed without adding any colour. These lo-fi production methods reflect an aesthetic similarity to the Weimar period, and are markedly different to the colourful, psychedelic aesthetics of the 1970s. In particular, the cover of *UkZ* draws on aesthetic borrowings from the 1920s and '30s. The lettering of the title on the cover uses an unknown font, but its simplicity is reminiscent of the typography used in modernism. In particular, the abbreviation *UkZ*, which is graphically distinct, can be read as a clear aesthetic reference to the 1920s.

Front cover of *UkZ – Unsere kleine Zeitung* No. 10, October 1976.

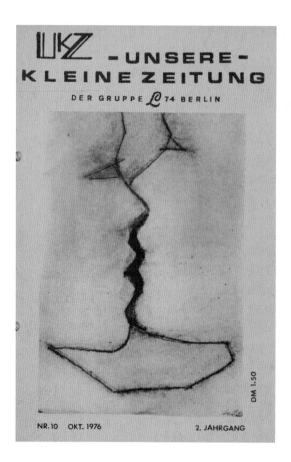

For the first three years of publication, Gertrude Sandmann's illustration *Liebende* (*Lovers*) adorned the newspaper on each cover. A Jew, Gertrude Sandmann survived the Holocaust in a hideout in Berlin. She was a painter and graphic artist taught, in the 1920s, by Käthe Kollwitz. Sandmann's sketch *Liebende* shows two profiles, identifiable as female, kissing tenderly. It is reminiscent of works by Koll-witz, but also of Jeanne Mammen, both of whom were famous in Weimar Germany. (Jeanne Mam-men even produced paintings about the Weimar queer subculture). During these first three years of production, small individual drawings by Sandmann appeared alongside articles she wrote on the themes of women and art and on the resonance of the 1920s in the present. In the second issue, Sandmann herself explains why she considers publishing the drawing *Liebende* in *UkZ* to be appropriate:

> I have provided the drawing *Liebende* for the title page of *unserer kleine zeitung* because I believe it expresses the characteristic of lesbian love: Tenderness. Tenderness makes people happy – both those who give it and those who receive it. Where there is no tenderness, even the wildest sexuality cannot separate people from their loneliness.[4]

Here, tenderness is played out against sexuality and used as a motive against loneliness and for lesbian

AUS DEM INHALT

	Seite
Aus unserer Gruppe	5
Das Jahr der Frau	7
Kulturecke	13
Frauen im Beruf	17
Alltagsgeschichten	23
Allgemeines	24
Literaturverzeichnis	30

Titelbild:

"Liebende" von Gertrude Sandmann.

AUS UNSERER GRUPPE

Lesbos

Entwicklung der "GRUPPE 'L' 74 BERLIN"

Aus eigener Erfahrung weiß ich, wie schwer es ist, Kontakt zu anderen homosexuellen Frauen zu finden.

Bisher war ich weder in einem Kreis lesbischer Frauen, noch kannte ich Adressen derartiger Gruppen oder Lokale.

Erst durch die TV-Filme: "Nicht der Homosexuelle ist pervers, sondern die Gesellschaft in der er lebt" (Rosa v. Praunheim) und: "Wir nehmen uns unser Recht!" (HAW), erfuhr ich vom Vorhandensein homosexueller Gruppierungen wie H A W (Homosexuelle Aktion West-Berlin) und A H A (Allgemeiner Homosexueller Arbeitskreis).

Da Mitglieder dieser Organisationen (HAW) vorwiegend j u n g e Frauen sind, war ich als ältere Lesbierin daran interessiert, eine Gruppe homosexueller Frauen ab ca. 30 Jahre zu bilden, weil ich aus eigener Erfahrung die Probleme der homosexuellen Frau kenne und verstehe.
Der erste Versuch einer Frau der HAW war gescheitert, also ging ich selbst an diese Aufgabe. Einen am 8.11.74 verfaßten A u f r u f sandte ich an Frauen, deren Anschriften mir – freundschaftlicherweise von der HAW (LAZ) genannt wurden.

Um ein Treffen zu ermöglichen, stellte uns der AHA in Berlin 10, Behaimstr. 18 einen Raum unentgeltlich zur Verfügung,
w o f ü r   w i r   h e r z l i c h   d a n k e n !

Zielsetzung unserer Gruppe:

Anknüpfung menschlicher Kontakte,
Aussprachen über unsere speziellen Probleme als
homosexuelle Frauen

2 3

love and happiness. Tenderness becomes an indicator of lesbian love and emphasises an emotional relationship between women, rather than one marked by sexuality and desire. The general restraint of the magazine, especially in the first years, which reveals itself on the front cover in relation to sexuality and women's love, seems to express a continuity of a more careful, restrained culture of exchange, which communicated via codes and ciphers.[5] Although Weimar Germany is better known for licence and debauchery, rather than restraint, debauchery could only take place in safe and hidden places like the homosexual clubs with their fixed system of admitting members. In magazines and within the public sphere, lesbians mostly had to conceal their identity and their desires. They played safe, as did the women of the L 74 group and the cover of their magazine.

The analysis of the title page of *UkZ* and the remarks by Gertrude Sandmann suggest that there was no heightened interest in lesbian sexuality, the sexualised body and/or sexual practices in *UkZ*. Rather, the focus of the magazine was on community, partnership, work, culture and community life, with integration with the main concerns of the women's movement emphasized several times. It should be stressed that I am referring

Double-page spread of *UkZ – Unsere kleine Zeitung*, No. 1, 1975, pp. 2–3.

here to the earliest editions of *UkZ* and the first years of *UkZ*'s existence. Discussions around sexuality as well as questions of sexual practices and sexual role behaviour were intensively discussed in *UkZ* from the mid-1980s onward, partly because the generation of its members had changed.[6]

Unsere kleine Zeitung was published by the group L 74. It appeared every month from February 1975 to 1987, then every two months and for the last time in May 2001. At its peak, the magazine reached a circulation of 1,300 copies; it started out with 200 editions.[7] From the outset, *UkZ* was posted to addresses in Berlin as well as throughout West Germany.[8] The magazine advertised itself through other feminist journals such as *Lesbenpresse*, *Courage* (1976–1984), *Emma* (1977–) and *Lesbenstich* (1980–1993). It was also possible to subscribe as a reader. *UkZ* played an important role in communication and networking, especially in rural regions where there were no lesbian groups.

The name L 74 refers to the year the group was founded, 1974, and the L stands for Lesbos. L 74 was founded on the initiative of Käthe (Kitty) Kuse, at the time a seventy-year-old lesbian who, as a member of Homosexuellen Aktion Westberlin (HAW), regretted not meeting lesbians of the same age but only young female students. The call for a group of lesbian women to network and collabourate in November 1974 started by Kuse explicitly addressed older and employed lesbians. Early on the group decided to publish a magazine with the first edition ready three weeks later in booklet form. Along with Kitty Kuse, the founding members included the communist Hilde Radusch (1903–1994) and the painter Gertrude Sandmann (1895–1981). All three had experienced the Weimar Republic and its lesbian culture.

In *UkZ*, then, there are many connections and references to the Weimar Republic. Some poems and short stories by both nearly forgotten and well-known authors and artists from the 1920s and 1930s are reprinted in the first editions of *UkZ*. The first issue of the magazine includes, under the heading 'Kultur-Ecke' ('Culture Corner'), a reprint of the poem 'Auf einen Café-Tisch gekritzelt' ('Scribbled on a café table') by Mascha Kaléko as well as biographical notes on the author. There is also an article by Eva Rieger containing a reference to the female composer Chris Baumgarten, who was born in 1910 in Berlin. This article points out the importance of remembering female authors and composers, because they were quite rare in the 1930s and also in the 1970s. According to Rieger, both Mascha Kaléko and Chris Baumgarten represent exceptions. It was also necessary to draw on texts (literary and theoretical), themes and key players from the Weimar past because in West Germany, until the first publication of the magazine in 1975, there were very few texts containing lesbian feminist themes and content. Sigrid Weigel explains this, saying that, until the mid-seventies, there was a 'pre-literary phase of the women's movement.'[9] Although Weigel is referring only to feminist literature, I would suggest broadening her approach to include feminist *and* lesbian literature. This is because the women's movement can't be separated from the lesbian movement. For

Weigel and her contemporaries, there was a strong feeling of needing a specific feminist literature which fulfilled feminist demands that was connected to the women's movement. Such a feminist literature came to life with the publication of Verena Stefan's *Shedding* in 1975, which drew on cultural products from the Weimar Republic period and successful female artists and authors from the time. The re-publication of poems and short stories from authors of the 1920s also answered a desire for feminist cultural products. For the same reason, *Lesbenpresse* resorted to texts, lyrics, and players from the US, where the lesbian movement had formed as early as the 1960s.

The influence of the past upon the present becomes tangible through the revival of knowledge from the Weimar period. For example, an article entitled 'Vor 50 Jahren' ('50 Years Ago') in the seventh issue of *UkZ*, dated August 1975, quotes a section of Magnus Hirschfeld's contribution to the book *Sexualkatastrophen* (*Sexual Catastrophes*), edited by Ludwig Levy-Lenz and published in 1926.[10] In his contribution Hirschfeld discusses the nature of homosexuality. The article reflects on Hirschfeld's research on homosexuality; it emphasises that 'the topic "homosexuality" has [not] only become current recently', but can be traced back to the 1920s.[11] It is particularly important to the authors of the article in *UkZ* to note 'that findings were published fifty years ago that should be common knowledge today!'[12] Here, a clear connection to the knowledge and tradition of the Weimar homosexual culture becomes evident.

The group name L 74 Berlin, which was mostly used in its abbreviated form and is also found in this form on the cover of *UkZ*, is also inscribed with a temporal dimension. The name refers to two of the group's core obligations: firstly, despite being close to Weimar tradition, they were primarily committed to the present ('74) and to the city of Berlin. Secondly, the reference to the island of Lesbos also marks a link to a distant, mythical past, namely ancient Greece and the famous poet Sappho. The story of Sappho from Lesbos is considered to be the origin myth of lesbian love, particularly in the western hemisphere.[13] The name of this figure became a popular codeword, which was used in the Weimar Republic in addition to other terms such as *Freundinnen* (female friends) or *wilde Veilchen* (wild violets).[14] The fact that the word 'Lesbos' in the group name is only referenced by the letter L together with the numbers 74 is part of this tradition of using codes. Although the Weimar subculture is legendary for its extravagant parties, clubs were usually secret, not noticeable to outsiders, and could only be attended by members. In some clubs, such as Klub Monbijou, you could only join via the recommendation of a current member. Accordingly, the name of the group marks a cautious, almost defensive use of the word 'lesbian' and thus recalls the customs of the Weimar Republic, according to which mentioning words such as 'homosexuality', 'homosexual' or 'lesbian' in public, in newspapers, on the radio, and so on, was unthinkable.[15]

The choice of the magazine title illustrates a clear reference to the Weimar Republic, which can be read as a direct link to its lesbian and emancipated magazine culture. It is also reminiscent of the famous lesbian magazine *Die Freundin*, which appeared between 1924 and 1933 alongside other magazines focussing on similar themes such as *Frauenliebe* which later was named *Garçonne* (1926–1931).[16] It was rumoured that people buying *Die Freundin* at a newsstand often asked for 'Unserer kleine Zeitung' ('Our Little Newspaper').[17] The fact that not all lesbians would immediately recognise the magazine title as a reference to Weimar culture, but might associate it with its seemingly low significance was critically discussed, particularly from the 1980s onward.[18] It should not be underestimated that the pronoun 'our' in the magazine title implies a collective 'we' which ostensibly refers to an 'us' made up of the L 74 group. The title has a more profound meaning, especially for those who know the origin of the title as 'initiates' and/or for those lesbians who had lived in the Weimar Republic and were therefore able to decipher the title themselves. In this way, the title creates a community of collective memory through references to the magazine *Die Freundin* and the subculture of the Weimar Republic.

Informed by the work of Maurice Halbwachs and Aby Warburg, Aleida and Jan Assmann distinguish between a communicative, a cultural and a collective memory. According to this distinction, communicative memory is based exclusively on oral everyday conversation.[19] Essential features are its 'role reciprocity', i.e., communication that 'typically takes [place] between partners [...] who can swap roles at any time. The person sharing a joke, a memory, a gossip, an experience in this moment, will become the listener in the next'.[20] At the same time, there are certain rules governing this form of verbally transmitted knowledge: not only is the temporal horizon limited to three to four generations, representing about eighty to one hundred years, but the knowledge circulates in limited contexts, namely within a specific group; it is mostly unformed, arbitrary and not organised. This is of interest with reference to a magazine title like *Unsere kleine Zeitung*, which was rumoured to be a nickname in an anecdote. This opens up another level of meaning in the title: circulating orally and in the memory of individual contemporary witnesses, the name is preserved to a certain extent through its transformation into written form; it receives new attention in the medium of writing, thus avoiding oblivion. In other words, the name, which previously circulated in the communicative memory, becomes a knowledge base of a cultural memory of the group L 74 by being written down.

Knowledge of the colloquial name of the magazine *Die Freundin*, which was previously spread by word-of-mouth, is captured in the magazine title of the group L 74, where the reference to *Die Freundin* is not immediately recognizable. There are limits to how much one can talk about a transfer into a cultural memory, since the origins of the title are not discussed in the magazine itself. Based on Jan and Aleida Assmann's writing, however, it is possible in this context to speak of an 'identity-specific' knowledge structure. This means that organised communication, such as in the case of the magazine title *Unsere kleine Zeitung*, is structured by everyday memory and can have a 'connection to groups and group identities'.[21] By identity-specific, Aleida and Jan Assmann mean that 'a group bases an awareness of its unity and idiosyncrasies on this knowledge, and it draws the formative and normative powers to reproduce its identity from this knowledge'.[22] Likewise, L 74 and their reference to the past, which is manifested in the title as well as content published in the magazine, not only represents the possibility of continuing and further developing those lesbian feminist beginnings in the Weimar Republic in the present, but at the same time of affirmatively confirming and clarifying the self-image of the group as older lesbians.

A statement in the first edition about the magazine's aspirations and objectives also confirms that the communicative factor within the group and the magazine is given a significant role:

> UNSERE KLEINE ZEITUNG shall serve as a medium for all homosexual women and those who sympathize with us and be both ears and voices at the same time.[23]

According to this, the magazine sees itself as a medium that gives individual female actors a voice, as well as forging an audience for all topics that may be of interest to lesbian women. The magazine appears to want to take on two roles at once, i.e., that of the sender and the receiver, the voice and the ear. This is, in turn, reminiscent of the characteristics of a communicative memory, which is characterised by the role reciprocity between sender and recipient. The magazine's purpose is to contribute to networking and overcoming the isolation and loneliness of homosexual women. The aim is therefore to establish a forum or a platform for everyone who is interested, where thematic and personal plurality is just as desirable as a change in society through education.

With reference to the writing of Ann Cvetkovich, *UkZ* can also be understood as 'an archive of feelings'. Framed in this way, the traumatic loss of lesbian subculture, especially of the magazine *Die Freundin*, is remembered and commemorated in the title of *UkZ*. At the same time, the remembrance of a queer/lesbian subculture takes place in an ephemeral medium – so it is understood as an ephemeral archive.[24] For Cvetkovich, the specific role of a lesbian archive is to:

> preserve and produce not just knowledge but feeling. Lesbian and gay history demands a radical archive of emotion in order to document intimacy, sexuality, love and activism – all areas of experience that are difficult to chronicle through the materials of a traditional archive.[25]

A queer archive then, which also often is an archive of trauma, should 'enable the acknowledgment of a past that can be painful to remember, impossible to forget, and resistant to consciousness'.[26] Accordingly, the feelings of shame and grief, of fear and anger, of lust and desire – feelings which belong to a period of time to be remembered – should play a role in dealing with remembrance and with regard to the choice of location for remembrance.

The queer archive does so because 'the history of trauma often depends on the evidence of memory'.[27] In this way, the title of *UkZ* refers not only to a subculture of the past, but also to the emotions and values of this culture in the present. The title and the magazine *UkZ* therefore become an archive for the past, as well as present assessments of the past. Simultaneously, they create a connection between the emotions of these different times. Throughout this discussion, I have argued that *UkZ* committed itself at the beginning of its publication to a revival and continuation of lesbian tradition and culture of the Weimar period, even if this is not explicitly stated and addressed. For women like Hilde Radusch, Gertrude Sandmann and Kitty Kuse, this past was not something abstract, but something they experienced themselves. Dealing with Weimar's past was therefore not a nostalgic act, but rather one marked by personal experience.

LESBENPRESSE

Front cover of *Lesbenpresse*, Vol. 1, No. 1 (1975).

The radical lesbian feminist separatist newspaper *Lesbenpresse* was published irregularly between 1975 and 1982 in eleven issues. It was published by the editorial collective of the Lesbisches Aktionszentrum Westberlin (LAZ, Lesbian Action Centre West Berlin). The members in the editorial team changed several times. LAZ emerged from Homosexuellen Aktion Westberlin (HAW, Homosexual Action West Berlin) and changed its name to Lesbisches Aktionszentrum in 1975. Compared to the rather cryptic group name L 74 Berlin, which was only understandable to the initiated, the name Lesbisches Aktionszentrum is both activist and generally easy to understand. It not only refers to the central context of being a lesbian as a kind of membership, but the name also conveys a clear message: its aim is visibility and maximum awareness. 'Action centre' refers to the specific form of political grouping and makes clear that this is an active political alliance. The function of the centre that can be derived from the name should accordingly be understood as a pooled *action* of lesbian connections in a central place.[28]

The descriptive magazine title *Lesbenpresse* clearly refers to its political intentions regarding content: to create a press body by and for lesbians. The aim of *Lesbenpresse* was to promote networking among lesbians and to contribute to the development and strengthening of a decidedly lesbian identity through the exchange of conflicting experiences. The essential difference to *UkZ* is that 'lesbian' or '"lesbianism" was understood to be a political category, as a militant possibility for all women to declare war on "male domination"'.[29] Accordingly, *Lesbenpresse* was understood to be an alternative-autonomous medium of publication by and for lesbians, one that was able to and wanted to report on lesbian issues and concerns appropriately. In addition, *Lesbenpresse* was also understood as an extended representation of the LAZ and the lesbian movement. The first edition of February 1975 states in the editorial:

1) When we decided to start Lesbenpresse, we assumed that there was a big lack of communication among the lesbian groups.

2) in our group of lesbians, laz westberlin, we have already had some lousy experiences with misrepresentation in media reports[30]

Although not explicitly stated in the editorial, the 'lousy' experiences mentioned here refer to the series of articles published by *Bild* newspaper 'Die Verbrechen der lesbischen Frauen' ('The Crimes of Lesbian Women'), which was published over seventeen consecutive days in January and February 1973.[31] This series detailed in an extremely biased and clichéd way the arrest of the lesbian couple Marion Ihns and Judy Andersen, who were suspected of killing the husband of Ihns together. The reporting at the time focused largely on the two women and their scandalous relationship as well as on their supposedly deviant behaviour. The fact that Ihns' husband had mistreated and raped his wife for years was not discussed in the articles in *Bild*. The trial held in the summer of 1974, which gained notoriety as the 'Itzehoe trial', alluding to the name of the town in which the trial was held, or the 'Ihns trial', became a public media outrage. Within the women's and lesbian movement, the misogynistic and defamatory depiction of events in what was referred to as the 'Springer Press' led to a solidarity movement with Ihns and Andersen. Public protests were organised and in the courtroom a group of women announced vocally and clearly their displeasure with the prejudice and stereotypical representation of the couple in the media. In *Lesbenpresse,* the trial was discussed repeatedly in various articles, reporting on and condemning 'media misogyny', the jurisdiction, the government, and so on. Marion Ihns and Judy Andersen became prime examples of the discriminatory treatment of lesbian women in a patriarchal society. LAZ and *Lesbenpresse* were used as a place and publication medium to declare a fight against patriarchal domination and for an autonomous lesbian culture and society as well as lesbian media. Accordingly, not only was cooperation with male journalists ruled out in a 'fixed, binding media decision', but also an extensive 'list of feminist journalists' was compiled.[32] In the fourth edition, a demand was formulated to have the reproduction and printing process carried out only by women. There were no women's printing houses, but a group of women in Berlin (VIVA Women) could at least take over the reproduction of the magazine.[33] The primary aim was to no longer be dependent on men and to learn the necessary skills to produce a newspaper themselves. While the same can be claimed for *UkZ*, the editorial collective of *Lesbenpresse* placed much more emphasis on producing the magazine exclusively by women and lesbians as a political issue and an ambition to be achieved as part of a women's culture.

After internal criticism in the plenum in April 1976, the collective which had been responsible for the first three editions was ousted. The other members of LAZ criticised the fact that the editorial collective was too isolated and had not produced the journal in the interests of and in an active exchange with all LAZ women. This had the result that most of the LAZ women could only partially identify with the magazine and its contents. Eventually a new editorial team was formed for the fourth edition of *Lesbenpresse*, which addressed in its editorial statement the previous problems, and the new objectives and concerns in detail.

> It seemed particularly problematic that the conflicts in the LAZ had not been registered in the LP. These were conflicts which were reflected in the bitter disputes [within the group] and had occurred not only in our group, but also in other organized lesbian groups. This led to the accusation of unrealistic privatisation and harmonisation, which means that we are unable to identify with the LP and to view it as an instrument for discussing our issues and contradictions, our politics.[34]

To address the scope of the previous problems, the new editorial team suggested the following:

> As many LAZ women as possible (or indeed lesbian groups in the FRG [Federal Republic of Germany], too) should be involved in producing the content for the LP, as well as on its technical side, achieved through a rotating system over time – firstly so that we all acquire the important skills to make a newspaper and finally to prevent new positions of power from developing.

The layout of the front covers, as well as *Lesbenpresse*'s general design was also changed in the fourth issue. Because the previous editorial collective claimed the rights to the artistic design and the cover design used for the first three editions and did not want to pass them on to the next collective, this was a necessary measure.[35]

In comparison with the group L 74, primarily made up of older and employed lesbians, LAZ – including the editorial collective – consisted mainly of young academics and students. Group life in LAZ was therefore influenced by the academic calendar and the semester cycle. During exam periods and when there were no lectures, there was less activity than usual.[36] This could be an explanation for the greater turnover within the *Lesbenpresse* editorial departments, for the magazine's sporadic publication and for the frequent design changes, because each new editorial collective redesigned the general presentation of the magazine.[37] The fact that the LAZ experienced varying levels of popularity as a space created by lesbians could also have played a role in the frequent changes. In the opinion of Ilse Kokula and Lara Ledwa, the growth of the lesbian subculture in West Berlin as well as in West Germany and of the women's movement between 1974 and 1976 made the period 'the LAZ's most productive and effective'[38]; these years witnessed the publication of the first three issues of the magazine. In the late 1970s the movement become more diversified with numerous lesbian facilities being founded, such as book stores, publishing houses, and cafés, the 'number of LAZ members' fell, 'the activities [of the group] became increasingly infrequent and they became less outward facing'.[39] This development could have contributed to the fact that *Lesbenpresse* was not published regularly, together with the group's strong alignment to the academic calendar.

The reference to the past in *Lesbenpresse*, at least with regard to the first two editions, in my view, shows dehistoricising tendencies. Whether due to the fact that the editors of *Lesbenspresse* lacked insight into the Weimar lesbian subculture, or else didn't feel a connection to those traditions at the beginning of the publication period, they concentrated on glorious, distant times where women were imagined to have real power, for example in the myths of the Amazons or in matriarchal legends. At the beginning of the lesbian and women's movement in the Federal Republic of Germany, the search for lesbian and/or feminist traditions as well as lesbian, feminist myths and pasts was notable.[40] At the same time, alternative concepts of life and utopias were also being imagined, some of which were linked to those alternative pasts. In these imagined pasts women ruled the world or could even live without men as they were able to give birth to new generations without them. In what follows, I will illustrate the way that the past was imagined in the pages of *Lesbenpresse* through considering the sign on the cover (lesbian or vulva sign) and an article, 'The Legend of Stonehendge' [sic], that appeared in the first issue of the magazine.

The cover of the first three editions of *Lesbenpresse* feature a vulva, resembling an emblematic international lesbian sign.[41] The sign, later also used as a logo, stands out due to the bright red background and the eye-catching A3 format. It is not at all subtle. The aesthetic design of the cover is entirely committed to the moment of the late '60s. The lettering of the title *Lesbenpresse* adopts a recognised psychedelic aesthetic.[42] A similar typeface can be found in use on, for instance, the *Love* poster designed by Peter Max (1967-68), and on the cover of the Beatles' *Rubber Soul* (1965). Topics discussed in *Lesbenpresse* demonstrate a desire to follow new paths in media. This can be seen not only in the regular criticism of conventional media and its misogynistic reporting, but also at an aesthetic level. The layout and appearance are similar to or reminiscent of a DIY aesthetic. The photos and illustrations used differ in particular from mainstream women's magazines: the photos appear to have been taken privately, which not only makes their content easier to identify, but also counteracts the mostly clichéd wider representations of femininity and lesbian women. There are pictures of women laughing and embracing, women having fun in the Denmark holiday camp *Femø*, women lying in the sun or cutting their hair, all resembling holiday photos. Or just a pair of women holding hands while they walk. The photos provide an unobtrusive view of everyday lesbian relationships.

The use of the vulva sign underlines the political, combative gesture of the magazine. It was used as a hand signal in the 1970s at meetings, concerts and demonstrations of lesbians and feminists. On the inside of the front cover, in the editorial of the first edition, the editorial collective goes into detail on the meaning and the origin of the sign: 'apparently it came from France, it could have come from any other country, manhood is international'.[43] The sign was supposedly used by men:

> holding their hands shaped like this sign at penis height, in the street, in pubs, wherever they spotted a woman, when they wanted to make it clear to her that they wanted to use her for a fuck. Women have taken this sign – the sign of their own sexuality and their discrimination at the same time – and are showing it with raised arms above their heads.[44]

The use of the sign by lesbians represents a deliberate and positive reappropriation of a long-abused sign, which focuses on woman's own sexuality, a sexuality they now assert with confidence. The editorial does not go into more detail on the history or story of the sexist and misogynistic meaning of the sign and its use, which, in my opinion, suggests that its tradition should be counted as hearsay or as a form of communicative memory. Even though the feminine use of the sign does not have *one* origin or concrete source, the editorial states that it basically does not matter where the defamatory action originated from, because 'manhood' is internationally evident together with the associated defamatory and discriminatory behaviour.

What is discernible here is something I would like to describe as the appearance of the dehistoricised past in *Lesbenpresse*. To link quite different patriarchal attitudes and situations without attention to historical context leads to the impression that patriarchal behaviour has been in place forever, to the same extent. With reference to the first two editions, this has the function of creating a strong, militant, lesbian feminist 'we', which is against patriarchal oppression and men. The problem with making injustice towards lesbians and women visible is that it fails to differentiate between different forms of patriarchal structures. It also does not include the distinct experiences of women in different parts of society and the world. Through the invocation of this 'we', intersectional differences and historical differences were levelled.

The recourse, also in other places in the magazine, to signs that cannot be more specifically attributed, or historically/temporally unspecified events, figures and symbols, seems to prove this. One can argue that for the creation of a women's culture (in contrast to the patriarchal culture) it was not only necessary to research women's history, but also to create a positive, own lesbian past. The latter should enable a better self-image for women who identify with women in the present. In other words, overcoming patriarchal society and its exclusive historical narrative, its misogynistic symbols and language, should be made possible through the creation of a lesbian-feminist history and historical narrative, as well as through the re-appropriation of symbols and expressions. It was not without reason that a return to a supposedly lost feminist, matriarchal original state, a natural femininity and a matriarchal culture was postulated or suggested. Stories, myths and legends by and about women were sought and found, appropriated and rewritten, created and circulated. This narrative was centred around the sustained alienation of women through the 'shackles of patriarchal domination'. In addition, the turn toward alternative conceptualisations of living – always including the general exclusion of men – was postulated as a utopia.

In the first three issues of *Lesbenpresse*, there is not only a clear commitment to lesbian separatism, but there are also articles, such as the 'Legend of Stonehendge', which re-tell legends from a lesbian separatist perspective. This article in the first issue (1975) provides a substantial indication of a completely different way of dealing with the past in comparison to *UkZ*. The history begins as follows:

> In the dim and distant past, when women still had a history, the world was completely different. – It was the time when there were only women on earth. They lived and loved – it was a paradise that was a thousand times more beautiful than that of Eve and Adam. There was no heteronomy by humans (in this case humans = women) or by a god, every human was their own deity. And so they brought joy and pleasure to each other, without any repression or fear, possession or dependence, jealousy or being left alone. Everyone's gender was human, and each of them was a woman in body. At that time, women still had the ability to determine and control their body through intense volition. And so they gave birth to women by procreating in themselves, by resolving their bodies to do so by concentrating.[45]

'The Legend of Stonehendge' imagines a past matriarchy, characterised by not being dependent on men for its continued existence. Women are able to reproduce by themselves by sheer willpower. Temporally, the legend takes place in a 'dim and distant past', in which women are said to have had their own history. This past is set in a paradisial Garden of Eden, although it is explicitly stated that this paradise, which is only populated by women, was 'a thousand times more beautiful than that of Eve and Adam'. The conscious rewriting of a Christian state of paradise from a lesbian-separatist perspective implies an instruction for the present or for the future, which seeks to regain that state of integrity. Suggesting the genre of *legend*, this becomes possible first and foremost in writing. The textual form of a legend recalls not only the literary tradition of events, people or places shrouded in myths – their history – but also the potential of narrating to forge their own creation myths or an alternative past. In other words: writing one's own story alters the positioning in the symbolic order in the present. In this way, the text in the first edition of *Lesbenpresse* should be understood as a programme, as it tells an alternative past, alternative myths and stories, and thus at the same time writes itself into a present and describes a possible future.

At this point we can speak, following Eve Sedgwick, of a 'reparative reading', where the will to find positive characters and narratives in a story is the starting point for an orientation towards the past.[46] Elizabeth Freeman describes this turn as offering a 'different form of nourishment',[47] summarizing this kind of lustful grasping of the past under the term 'erotohistoriography'.[48] Through this Freeman marks an erotic approach to the emotions of the past, which inscribe themselves in the present. This alternative form of erotic, asynchronous and emotional historiography is characterized by a break with linear and normative temporality in history. Considering the re-written 'Legend of Stonehendge' in the lesbian press and the treatment of the past there, there seems to be – in Freeman's terminology – a lustful appropriation of depicted affects in the legend. In this way, not only is the model of an exclusively women's society interpreted with pleasure, but the model also becomes conceivable as a possible way of life for the present day.

CONCLUSION

In this essay, I have focused primarily on the earliest issues of *LP* and *UkZ* and examined their respective references to the past. *UkZ* and its editors from the group L 74 often had a personal connection to the Weimar Republic, as some of them had experienced this period themselves. For this reason, a revival and continuation of feminist discourses that had already been initiated seemed like an obvious course. The Weimar Republic as a reference point of shared memory and experience seems to have been understood within the magazine and the group as a kind of common framework or horizon. They wanted to show that some issues and discourses raised in the 1970s had already been discussed in the 1920s and '30s, and to draw attention to these traditions. However, we cannot speak of a nostalgic reference to Weimar Germany, which is evident from an article written by Gertrude Sandmann in the summer of 1976. In it, Sandmann criticizes the portrayal of the Weimar Republic in Ilse Kokula's book *Jahre des Glücks, Jahre des Leids*: in Sandmann's eyes, the portrayal of the Weimar Republic is inaccurate. Furthermore, the magazine *UkZ* and especially the title can be understood with Cvetkovich as an archive of feelings, because the title preserves not only the reference to the Weimar republic but also the lived memory and the feelings attached.

The fact that questions about memory and history in relation to gender within the new women's movement in the 1970s formed an important focus in terms of content is certainly not a new insight. In the case of *Lesbenpresse*, however, it turns out that the desire to inscribe themselves in time, which in this case meant writing themselves into a history, corresponded with the desire to write alternative pasts. Imagining alternative pasts, as exemplified by the 'Legend of Stonehendge', not only created the conditions of possibility for a lesbian-feminist present and future, but also contributed to an alternative to the patriarchal historical narrative. Elizabeth Freeman's 'erotohistoriography' is useful here, since the access to the legend of Stonehenge and the lustful emotions depicted in the legend are of particular relevance for the transformation of the present. The imagined myths and legends refer, on the one hand, to a nostalgic view of the past and on the other to the possibility of a utopian future. At the same time, these narratives also refer to the reality of life and the separatist claim of LAZ women in the present of the 1970s. The LAZ not only eschewed working with men, but also resolutely refused to. That this sometimes caused difficulties is not only made clear by the dissatisfaction with the editorial staff of the first three issues, but also by the increasingly frequent quarrels within the LAZ towards the end of the 1970s. The different dimensions of the past examined in this essay and the different ways in which the past is approached illustrate the relevance of history and historiography for the self-image of the respective groups, and further illustrate the relevance of both for the shaping of the present and the future.

ACKNOWLEDGEMENTS

I would like to thank Alastair Coates and Evelyn Barrett for their help in editing my essay on a linguistic level. I would also like to thank Naemi Eifler, Lara Ledwa, Sydney Ramirez and Lorenz Weinberg for our productive discussions and their comments in the context of our working group on queer-lesbian history. Without them I would not have been able to adequately address several questions raised in this essay.

NOTES

1 See Franka Fieseler. 2008. 'Vernetzte Netze – vielfältige Foren. Zur Geschichte lesbisch-feministischer Zeitschriften in Deutschland.' In Lea Susemichel, Saskya Rudigier and Gabi Horak. Eds. *Feministische Medien. Öffentlichkeiten jenseits des Malestreams*, Königstein/Taunus: Helmer. 134.

2 See Lara Ledwa. 2019. *Mit schwulen Lesbengrüßen. Das lesbische Aktionszentrum Westberlin (LAZ)*. Berlin: Psychosozial-Verlag. See also the unpublished Masters thesis by Lisa (now Lorenz) Weinberg, *Pleasure and Danger – Feminist Sex Wars auf Deutsch? Diskussionen über lesbisch_queere Sexualität und Butch/Femme in Wien und Westberlin in den 80er und frühen 90er Jahren*. Master's thesis at the Universität Wien 2018. (Available in the Spinnboden Lesbenarchiv Berlin.)

3 See Naemi Eifler. 2019. *Ausradierung, Verdinglichung, Identifizierung. Antisemitische Denkmuster in der deutschen Lesbenbewegung der 1970er und 1980er Jahre. Eine Analyse von Äußerungen und symbolischen Gesten in Zeitschriftenbeiträgen*. Master's thesis at the Alice Salomon Hochschule 2019. (Unpublished Masters thesis, available at the Spinnboden, Berlin).

4 *Unsere kleine Zeitung*. 1975. No. 2. 'Die Zeichnung Liebende habe ich für das Titelblatt unserer kleinen zeitung zur Verfügung gestellt, weil sie, wie ich glaube, das charakteristische gerade der lesbischen Liebe ausdrückt: Zärtlichkeit. Zärtlichkeit macht glücklich, – den, der sie gibt und den, der sie bekommt. Wo sie fehlt, kann auch die wildeste Sexualität den Menschen nicht aus seinem Alleinsein herauslösen.' 6.

5 See Claudia Schoppmann. 1985. *Der Skorpion. Frauenliebe in der Weimarer Republik*. Hamburg: Verlag Libertäre Assoziationen. 9.

6 See the detailed analysis in Weinberg, *Pleasure and Danger – Feminist Sex Wars auf Deutsch?* Op. cit.

7 Fieseler, 'Vernetzte Netze – vielfältige Foren.' Op. cit. 138.

8 To my knowledge, there is as yet no examination of the extent to which *UkZ* was distributed in East Germany after reunification.

9 See Sigrid Weigel. 1987. *Die Stimme der Medusa: Schreibweisen in der Gegenwartsliteratur von Frauen*. Hamburg: Rowohlt Taschenbuch. 16.

10 See Ludwig Levy-Lenz. Ed. 1926. *Sexual-Katastrophen: Bilder aus dem modernen Geschlechts- und Eheleben*. Leipzig: Payne.

11 'Vor 50 Jahren', *UkZ*. 1975. No. 7. 'das Thema "Homosexualität" [nicht] erst in jüngster Zeit aktuell geworden'. 4

12 Ibid. 'daß schon vor 50 Jahren Erkenntnisse veröffentlicht wurden, die heute eigentlich längst Allgemeingut sein sollten!' 4

13 Jodie Medd. 2015. 'Lesbian Literature? An Introduction'. In Medd. Ed. *The Cambridge Companion to Lesbian Literature*. Cambridge: Cambridge University Press. 3.

14 The term 'Freundinnen' (female friends) was used up until the 1970s in West Germany/FRG, and in East Germany /GDR until the '80s. The term can be understood to denote an unsuspicious connection between two females, but at the same time it was also used as a code similar to Sappho in the GDR within newspaper advertising. See: Hanna Hacker. 2015. *Frauen* und Freund_innen. Lesarten 'weiblicher Homosexualität' Österreich, 1870 –1938*, Wien: Zaglossus; Heike Schader. 2004. *Virile, Vamps und wilde Veilchen. Sexualität, Begehren und Erotik in den Zeitschriften homosexueller Frauen in Berlin der 1920er Jahre*. Königstein im Taunus: Helm; Schoppmann, *Der Skorpion*. Op. cit.

15 See Gertrude Sandmann. 1976. 'Anfang des lesbischen Zusammenschlusses: die Clubs der zwanziger Jahre'. *Unsere kleine Zeitung*. No. 7/8. 5.

16 In the late '80s and again in the '90s, the title caused resentment and a lack of understanding among new members who no longer knew about the title's origin or who were not told about it. See Fieseler, 'Vernetzte Netze – vielfältige Foren.' Op. cit. 141.

17 See Eva Bornemann and Helga Trachsel. 2007. 'Gruppe L 74 und die Zeitschrift UkZ (Unsere kleine Zeitung).' In Gabriele Dennert, Christiane Leidinger and Franziska Rauchut. Eds. *In Bewegung bleiben. 100 Jahre Politik, Kultur und Geschichte von Lesben.* Berlin: Querverlag. 78.

18 By the late 1980s, not only had the group members and the women who worked for the magazine changed, but attitudes towards sexuality had also altered. The course of these discursive transformations initiated a lot of conflict. Known as the 'Sex Wars' in the US, the topic was also hotly discussed in Germany. See Weinberg, *Pleasure and Danger – Feminist Sex Wars auf Deutsch?* Op. cit.; see also Bornemann and Trachsel, 'Gruppe L 74 und die Zeitschrift UkZ'. Op. cit. 78.

19 See Jan Assmann. 1988. 'Kollektives Gedächtnis und kulturelle Identität'. In Jan Assmann and Tonio Hölscher. Eds. *Kultur und Gedächtnis.* Frankfurt: Suhrkamp. 10; Aleida Assmann. 2009. 'Einleitung'. In Aleida Assmann. *Erinnerungsräume. Formen und Wandlungen des kulturellen Gedächtnisses.* München: C.H. Beck. 11–23.

20 Jan Assmann. 'Kollektives Gedächtnis und kulturelle Identität.' Op. cit. 10. See also Aleida Assmann, 'Einleitung'. Op. cit. 13.

21 Jan Assmann. 'Kollektives Gedächtnis und kulturelle Identität.' Op. cit. 11: 'Bindung an Gruppen und Gruppenidentitäten'.

22 Ibid. 11–12: 'daß eine Gruppe ein Bewußtsein ihrer Einheit und Eigenarten auf dieses Wissen stützt und aus diesem Wissen die formativen und normativen Kräfte bezieht, um ihre Identität zu reproduzieren.'

23 *UkZ*, No. 1, 1975, no page number, located before the table of contents: 'UNSERE KLEINE ZEITUNG

soll allen homosexuellen Frauen und den mit uns Sympathisierenden als Medium dienen und ihnen Ohr und Stimme zugleich sein.'

24 Jack Halberstam. 2005. *In a Queer Time and Place: Transgender Bodies, Subcultural Lives.* New York: New York University Press. 161.

25 Ann Cvetkovich. 2003. *An Archive of Feelings: Trauma, Sexuality and Lesbian Public Culture.* Durham, NC: Duke University Press. 241.

26 Ibid.

27 Ibid.

28 Recently, Lara Ledwa published a book about the LAZ that provides insights on the history of its origins, conflicts, and information regarding the *Lesbenpresse*. Ledwa. *Mit schwulen Lesbengrüßen.* Op. cit.

29 *Lesbenpresse*. No. 1, 1975, 2: 'Lesbianismus' als politische Kategorie verstanden [wurde], als militante Möglichkeit aller Frauen, der "Männerherrschaft" den Kampf anzusagen'.

30 '1) als wir uns entschlossen die lesbenpresse zu machen, sind wir davon ausgegangen, daß ein großer kommunikationsmangel unter den lesbengruppen besteht. 2) haben wir in unserer lesbengruppe, der laz westberlin schon etliche miese erfahrungen mit fälschlich wiedergegeben meldungen der medien gemacht. '

31 See also Clare Elizabeth Bielby. 2017. '"An jeder Straßenecke könnte praktisch ein Mannweib mit Schlagring, Lederkleidung und rauher Stimme auf ihn warten" Gewalt, Weiblichkeit und Sexualität in der Bundesrepublik der 1970er Jahre.' In Jan Feddersen et al. (eds). *Jahrbuch Sexualitäten.* 94–113.

32 *Lesbenpresse*, No. 1, 1976, 2.

33 See *Lesbenpresse*, No. 4, 1976, 4: 'sie stellen Film von den getippten Beiträgen und Fotos her und montieren diese auf eine Folie, die dann in die Druckerei geht'.

34 *Lesbenpresse*, No. 4, 1976, 3.

35 Ibid., 2–4.

36 See Ilse Kokula. 1983. *Formen lesbischer Subkultur. Vergesellschaftung und soziale Bewegung*, Hamburg: Verl. Rosa Winkel. 74.

37 Ibid. 76.

38 Ibid. 'die produktivsten und wirkungsvollsten des LAZ'.

39 Ibid. 80: 'Mitgliederinnenzahl im LAZ', 'die Aktivitäten verringerten sich zunehmend und die Außenorientierung ließ nach'.

40 For example, this can also be seen in the first edition of the magazine *Feministische Studien*, whose title 'Spuren in der Zeit' (Traces in Time) refers to the focus on women in history in various periods. But also in other non-academic magazines, in literary texts and individual articles, there is a search for what was called women's culture, which includes the search for a past, present and future, in contrast to patriarchal culture. See Susanne von Falkenhausen. 1985. 'Handelnde Phantasie – phantastisches Handeln.' In Christa Erk. Ed. *Berliner Kulturplätze 3. Frauen – Autonomie – Kreativität – Subkultur*. Berlin: NGBK. 2.

41 Evelyn Kuwertz and Ulrike Stelzl. 1976. 'Der ästhetische Anteil innerhalb der Publikationen der Neuen Frauenbewegung.' *Ästhetik und Kommunikation. Beiträge zur politischen Erziehung*. Vol 25 No 7. 116.

42 See Philippe Garner. 1996. *Sixties Design*. Köln: Taschen. 62.

43 *Lesbenpresse*. No. 1, 1975, 2.

44 Ibid. 1: 'indem sie die Hände zu diesem Zeichen geformt in Schwanzhöhe hielten, auf der Straße, in Kneipen, wo auch immer sie eine Frau entdeckten, wenn sie ihr deutlich machen wollten, daß sie sie zu einem Fick benutzen wollten. Frauen haben dieses Zeichen aufgenommen – das Zeichen ihrer Eigengeschlechtlichkeit und ihrer Diskriminierung zugleich – und zeigen es mit erhobenen Armen über ihrem Kopf.'

45 Ibid. 14: 'In dunkler Vorzeit, als die Frauen noch eine Geschichte hatten, da sah die Welt noch völlig anders aus. – Es war die Zeit, da gab es auf der Erde nur Frauen. Sie lebten und liebten – es war ein Paradies, das tausendmal schöner war als das von Eva und Adam. Da gab es keine Fremdbestimmung durch Menschen (in diesem Fall Mensch=Frau) oder durch einen Gott, [sic] Jede Mensch war ihre eigene Gottheit. Und so brachten sie sich gegenseitig Freude und Lust, ohne daß da Repression oder Angst, Besitz oder Abhängigkeit, Eifersucht oder Alleingelassensein überhaupt bekannt waren. Es war das eigentliche Geschlecht Mensch, und jede von ihnen war Frau über ihren Körper. Damals war den Frauen die Fähigkeit noch nicht verloren gegangen, durch intensives Wollen ihren Körper zu bestimmen und zu lenken. Und so gebar sie Frauen durch Zeugung in sich selbst, wenn sie ihren Körper durch Konzentration dazu bestimmten.'

46 See Eve Kosofsky Sedgwick. 2003. 'Paranoid Reading and Reparative Reading or You're So Paranoid, You Probably Think This Essay is About You.' In Sedgwick, *Touching Feeling: Affect, Pedagogy, Performativity*. Durham, NC: Duke University Press. 123–151. See also Robyn Wiegman. 2014. 'The Times We're In: Queer feminist criticism and the reparative "turn"'. *Feminist Theory*. Vol 15 No 1. 4–25.

47 Elizabeth Freeman. 2005. *Time Binds: Queer Temporalities, Queer Histories*. Durham, NC: Duke University Press. 19.

48 Ibid. 95.

12 Revisiting Lavender Menace: In Conversation With Sigrid Nielsen, Bob Orr and James Ley

FIONA ANDERSON

'And I thought, if they can do it in New York, San Francisco, Texas, New England, and Washington, there's no reason why I can't do it in Niddrie, Pilton, Marchmont, and Meadowbank.'[1]

In 1982, a year after the partial decriminalisation of sex between men in Scotland, the country's first lesbian and gay bookshop opened in a small basement space on Forth Street, on the edge of Edinburgh's New Town. Property in this stretch of the city, near the foot of Calton Hill and the top of Leith Walk, was relatively cheap. The bookshop sat close to the offices of the Scottish Campaign to Resist the Atomic Menace (SCRAM) and around the corner from the health food shop Real Foods. Lavender Menace was run by two friends, Sigrid Nielsen and Bob Orr, who shared a common belief in the value of bookshops as community resources and meeting places, drawing on their experiences working in radical leftist bookshops and with the Scottish Homosexual Rights Group (SHRG, formerly the Scottish Minorities Group, SMG) in the 1970s. Sigrid and Bob were members of the Open Gaze Collective, which ran a successful bookstall in the front room of the SHRG's Gay Centre on Edinburgh's Broughton Street until the winter of 1980. Despite only opening at evenings and weekends, Open Gaze's turnover doubled between 1977 and 1979 and, by the end of the decade, brought in enough money to cover the Centre's annual rates.[2] From the outset, its value was cultural as well as economic. 'A good bookshop', noted SHRG committee members in 1979, 'will contribute to a welcoming atmosphere, quite apart from its role as a provider of information and a source of leisure reading'.[3]

After leaving the Gay Centre in 1980 following a political disagreement about shop stock, Bob and Sigrid formed the siteless Lavender Books with former members of the Open Gaze Collective, selling paperback novels from the cloakroom at Fire Island, a popular gay nightclub on Princes Street, on Fridays and Saturdays, at book fairs in other Scottish cities such as Glasgow and Stirling, at national feminist conferences, and to Edinburgh College of Art students during their lunch breaks. When Fire Island decamped temporarily to the Playhouse Theatre during renovations in the early 1980s, Lavender Books went with them. Fiction with lesbian and gay themes, including many paperback imports from the United States, sold particularly well at Edinburgh's queer disco nights. By the summer of 1982, Sigrid and Bob had secured enough financial support to open as a bricks-and-mortar shop.

Lavender Books and Lavender Menace were, proudly, 'financially independent of the organised gay establishment in Scotland'.[4] Rather than a consequence of the legislative changes shaping gay public life in this part of the United Kingdom in this period (namely decriminalisation), the opening of Lavender Menace as an independent shop in the early 1980s signaled the growth of a more radical queer community in Edinburgh, affiliated with the political left in the city, and the desire of its constituents to distinguish themselves from established gay groups like the SHRG. As Sigrid, Bob, and James explore in this interview, gay organising in Scotland in the 1970s was shaped by the prominence of the Presbyterian Church of Scotland, the Kirk, in Scottish life in this period, which molded public discourse around same-sex desire and relationships and was a significant

Lavender Menace bookshop, 1984. Photograph courtesy of Sigrid Nielsen.

contributing factor in the country's delayed response to partial decriminalisation and the 1967 Sexual Offences Act in England and Wales.[5] Sigrid and Bob observed that a sense of disconnection from the SHRG was felt especially keenly by women, who were less likely to enter the Gay Centre in the first place, and had far fewer opportunities than gay men to attend specifically lesbian-oriented events in public venues.[6] Indeed, the bookshop opened a few months after Fire Island's women-only disco nights stopped.[7] The left-wing politics of many members of the Open Gaze and Lavender Books collectives, along with their connections to the radical political bookshop First of May, located on Candlemaker Row in Edinburgh's Old Town, signaled a divergence from the conservative political leanings of some members of the SHRG. The story of Lavender Menace, as it moved from the front room of the Gay Centre to its own premises, suggests that it is no coincidence that Open Gaze's ties with SHRG were cut in the same year as decriminalisation in Scotland was finally achieved.

Between 1982 and 1987, Lavender Menace sold novels, poetry, plays, travel guides, academic books, self-help books, political pamphlets, postcards, keyrings, badges, and posters to queer readers from across the city and the surrounding area, with customers travelling to visit the only queer bookshop in the country. A popular mail order service, supported by specialist reading lists which Sigrid and Bob developed in dialogue with friends and customers, expanded the shop's reach beyond Scotland's metropolitan central belt and, indeed, the country. At 11a Forth Street, informal conversation about books and pamphlets took place over tea and coffee. Lavender Menace hosted discussion groups and regular events with queer authors, including Jackie Kay, Jeannette Winterson, Randy Shilts, and Armistead Maupin. Conversation and dialogue were also fundamental components of the leadership of the shop and its day-to-day running. Visible collabouration between lesbians and gay men was a core aspect of the ethos of Lavender Menace, setting them apart from some of the separatist organising which had emerged in the Scottish gay scene in the 1970s, in part because of the dominance of men within the SHRG. Sigrid and Bob stocked books from a spectrum of LGBTQ communities, sometimes leading to disagreements with regular customers, as they recount in this interview. In establishing Lavender Menace, Sigrid and Bob were deeply committed to the idea that 'the power of the written word can create a gay identity and draw a gay community together'.[8] 'Reading can be one of the most important ways of learning what it is to be gay,' they observed. In a city with many bookstores, 'for those already "out" a community bookshop can offer another way of meeting other gay people', structured around a shared belief in the value of historic and contemporary lesbian and gay writing as 'a vital means of positive identity for its readers'.[9]

In 1987, Bob and his partner Raymond reopened the shop as West and Wilde, a name which, through its allusion to the writers Vita Sackville-West and Oscar Wilde, further cemented this longstanding commitment to lesbian and gay collabouration and the value of literature for sustaining queer life. In 1988, Fire Island was bought by Waterstones and became a bookshop, unintentionally memorialising the community bookselling that once went on in its cloakroom. West and Wilde's location on Dundas Street secured visibility for this queer literary hub in the early years of Section 28 of the Local Government Act (known as Clause 2a in Scotland) which outlawed the promotion of homosexuality 'as a pretended family relationship' by organisations which received local authority funding, a homophobic moral panic sparked by the availability of an English translation of Susanne Bösche's Danish-language children's book *Jenny Lives with Eric and Martin* in publicly-funded school libraries. It had been sold in Lavender Menace since its publication in 1983. Clause 2a was repealed in Scotland in 2000, three years after the closure of West and Wilde, and two years before it was repealed in England and Wales. In a conversation with *Gay News* shortly before the opening of Lavender Menace, Sigrid emphasised her and Bob's commitment to its value as a community space. Her observation that Lavender Menace could support constituents of Edinburgh's various LGBTQ communities in finding affirmation through books which reflect their lived experience underscores the powerful impact that Clause 2a had on queer people living in Scotland in the 1980s and 1990s and pre-emptively punctures its homophobic logic. An important facet of a bookshop, she noted, 'is that you're not *forced* into anything – not forced into buying or being gay in a particular way... Politics are very necessary. Without them, we'd never have this bookshop. But doing something as ordinary as selling books which are also gay is an important way of reassuring people that being gay is a perfectly all right thing to be'.[10]

In February 2016, the Traverse Theatre in Edinburgh hosted a staged reading of a new play by Scottish writer James Ley. The event marked LGBT History Month; the play recalled the fifth anniversary and imminent closure of Edinburgh's first lesbian and gay bookshop, Lavender Menace. *Love Song to Lavender Menace* follows two friends, Glen and Lewis, both volunteers in the shop, as they pack up unsold stock, share anecdotes about their friendship with Sigrid and Bob, debate the literary merits and political implications of James Baldwin's novel *Giovanni's Room* (1956), and recount nights of dancing and reading in Fire Island, also on the verge of closure. The form of the play pays tribute to the original plays and dramatic readings of queer books by Sigrid, Paul Trainer, who worked in the bookshop, and others at Lavender Menace in the 1980s. As it recalls and records independent venues closed or given over to larger corporate ownership, *Love Song to Lavender Menace* resists the gentrification of the mind that the American writer and activist Sarah Schulman has warned against.[11] This kind of gentrification, Schulman observes, impacts not only material locations for queer community, like bookshops, but the scope of queer literature itself. As bookshops with specialist stock and staff with specialist knowledge closed, as Lavender Menace and West and Wilde did, the opportunities for a nuanced understanding of the various LGBTQ communities that these spaces once catered for diminished. 'Bookshops are always full of stories', observes Lewis, but now 'Lavender Menace is disappearing for good [...] the books are checking out like fabulous people vanishing from a party without saying goodbye'.[12] The success of the play, however, which has been performed in venues across Edinburgh and in New York, has exceeded the melancholic memorial tropes that love songs sometimes deploy: in 2019, Sigrid and Bob launched Lavender Menace Returns, a pop-up iteration of the long-closed shop, selling books at fairs and conferences. They have also started work on a database and archive of LGBTQ books.[13]

The following conversation took place at the Centre for Contemporary Arts (CCA) in Glasgow in February 2017, as part of the event *Between the Sheets: Radical Print Cultures Before the Queer Bookshop*. It came after a screening of the STV documentary *Coming Out* (1983), in which Sigrid, Bob, and Lavender Menace feature prominently, and preceded a reading from *Love Song to Lavender Menace* with the playwright James Ley. For this one-off performance, Sigrid played bookshop employee Lewis performing, temporarily, as his boss, Sigrid Nielsen.

'MY SECRET BOOK COLLECTION': BEFORE LAVENDER MENACE

FA: Tell me about Open Gaze and about when you first met. How did you both end up in Edinburgh?

SN: I came to Edinburgh because I saw a BBC film [*Open Door: The Scottish Minorities Group – Glad to be Gay?*] that featured the Gay Centre, and I was coming here anyway in order to do research at the National Library of Scotland.[14] So, having seen this [film], I had to see what [the Gay Centre] was like. Open Gaze didn't exist yet at that point. That was in '76. But after that, Bob founded the bookshop that was the Open Gaze bookstore.

BO: I came through to study in '73. I was brought up in Glasgow. And before I came through [to Edinburgh] I was a member of the Scottish Minorities Group (SMG) which morphed into the Scottish Homosexual Rights Group (SHRG).[15] I already had an association, politically as it were, with being gay. Moving to Edinburgh was just part of my studies, and I stayed after I graduated. And during my time as a student, that was when I became involved in the Gay Centre and opened the bookstall which didn't have a name. It was referred to as the SMG Bookstall, just as bland as that, and the evidence for that is a [SMG] sticker inside this book [Jeffrey Weeks, *Coming Out*, Quartet Books, 1976]. The name Open Gaze came later.

FA: What kinds of things were you reading when you first came to Edinburgh?

BO: The reason I put my hand up to say 'I could do that' [run a bookstall] was that I got a job through Ian Christie [a former city councillor] in a bookshop. He was a director of Holmes McDougall in those days, an educational publisher, and they had some retail outlets. And I got a job in a bookshop, so therefore I knew all about books. And I must have done a lot of research. I can't honestly remember [what I was reading] – I wasn't a terrific reader. If I was doing any reading it was for my studies.

SN: Well, I can answer that question! I have my secret book collection with me. Some of the books are from the sixties, others are from the seventies. I think they answer some of the questions about the seventies as an in-between decade. These books [were] as much as my life was worth, if my parents had found them. The collection was lost for many years, and it turned up again in California in my partner's brother's garage.

Here's the first one: *The Problem of Homosexuality in Modern Society* [by Hendrik Marinus Ruitenbeek, E.P. Dutton, 1963]. There are a lot of gems in this, stuck between all the academic commentary. There is a story about a female transsexual warrior of a Native American tribe who insisted on learning to use spears and going to war. But that's buried in all the five syllable words and they weren't worried that anybody would find it.

Here's *Therese and Isabelle* [Dell, 1967]. This is another sixties product by a French writer [Violette Leduc]. She was well known as a rebel, and by the standard of those days it verged on porn, and it was made into a movie that was reviewed largely as verging on porn.[16]

James Ley, Bob Orr, Sigrid Nielsen and Fiona Anderson in conversation at the CCA in Glasgow, February 2017. (Photograph by Glyn Davis)

This is *I Am a Woman* by Ann Bannon [Gold Medal Books, 1959]. It's now famous as a classic of liberation, but you can see how they felt they had to sell it in the sixties. I think I plucked my courage up and bought this in a bus station bookshop in Santa Fe, New Mexico, which I was afraid to do most of the time because the attendant was always there, and he would see you. And here is another psychiatric production: *Love Between Women* [Charlotte Wolff, Duckworth, 1971], full of sordid stories which I lapped up.

And now we're in the seventies. This is what's happening. No more psychiatrists, no more pulp. This [Del Martin and Phyllis Lyon, *Lesbian/ Woman*, first published by Glide Publications, 1972] is written by two women who ran lesbian groups all through the fifties in San Francisco. They were lifelong lovers. They were heroines. And they wrote about their experience candidly, and they said many women didn't make contact with their sexuality until they were in their twenties or even later.

But here's the one that really changed things for me and many other people because this is science fiction. This [*The Left Hand of Darkness*

The Problem of Homosexuality in Modern Society. Copyright © 1969 by Hendrik M. Ruitenbeek. (Penguin Random House LLC. All rights reserved)

by Ursula K. Le Guin, Ace Books, 1969] is about a world that could be. And some of you will know it now as a classic. I bought my first copy in 1971 in the bus station in Albuquerque, New Mexico. It's a story about a planet where everyone can be both sexes and so a whole different culture comes up where there isn't one sex that's looked down on and has to lower its eyes, and the other that has to live up to its own status. Once people were writing these kinds of things, it opened minds. And this was published in '69 but it didn't get to the bus station in New Mexico until '71, and by then the books were taking off.

BO: I should have said that I bought *No End to the Way* [Neville Jackson, aka Gerald Glaskin, Corgi, 1965] in – again I can't remember because it was so long ago, but it's dated 1968. And I bought this in Central Station bookstore in Glasgow. So, this was my introduction to gay literature. And it's actually quite a positive book. Still lots of scenes I remember from it. This was really at the cusp of books that – the sort of thing that Sigrid's been talking about in the sixties where books about gay men or

Front and back covers of *Love Between Women* by Charlotte Wolff, published by Duckworth, 1971.

lesbians, usually one of the protagonists had to die at the end, usually by suicide. Just as a mark of the heterosexual culture that was around and their portrayal of us. This doesn't happen here, but they do split up. So, it's not quite as bad as it might have been five years before. And it is the beginning of a more enlightened [period] – gay authors and lesbian authors being able to express themselves in print the way they want to.

FA: Tell us about Open Gaze.

BO: Well, it was a bookstall and it was actually in what we would maybe describe as a display cabinet which was lockable so that they were safe at night – not terribly sure why! But if the Gay Centre was open then the glass doors of this display cabinet were open to the public, to anybody who came in. And you could buy books from that. We're talking about three quite short shelves, not a huge amount. But within a year,

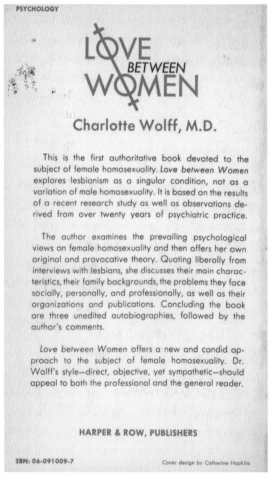

and I suspect that's when the name changed, we took over a corner of the main room in the Gay Centre and put up shelves, much bigger shelves because there was beginning to be a lot more stock available. I wasn't there all the time by any means, because the Centre was run by volunteers. But if it was open then so was the bookshop—the bookstall. It was only ever a bookstall; it was never really a fully-fledged bookshop in that sense.

SN: It was in '79, I think, that you decided to organise a collective and call on the rest of us to take part. That was when the name Open Gaze came up. I'm not sure what inspired it; it was you who thought of it. It was called the Open Gaze Books Collective. We had meetings, we all learned to do stock taking and we learned about the book trades. At that time, we had the Net Book Agreement in this country, that meant that the prices were uniform.[17] [The bookshop] Waterstones couldn't sell books at a discount – neither could [the supermarket] Tesco, if they'd ever even thought of selling books back in those days. So that meant that independent bookshops like us had a chance to compete. And because Bob worked for Holmes McDougall he could teach the rest of us how to run a bookshop. And that was what we did: we expanded the shelves, we looked over catalogues, decided what to buy, and because there were more of us we could also do our best to learn how to push the books and come up with pitches and try to make it all pay for itself.

The Left Hand of Darkness. Copyright © 1963 by Ursula K. Le Guin. (Penguin Random House LLC. All rights reserved.)

'WE WANTED TO GO A BIT FURTHER': BUILDING LAVENDER MENACE

FA: When and how did Open Gaze develop into Lavender Menace?

BO: Well, it was a reference to the anti-Christmas card. The anti-Christmas card was stocked by us [at the Gay Centre]. I can't remember what the wording of it was, but it was on that basis that the [SHRG] committee decided that we had stepped over a red line and that we should leave.

JL: It was also [because you were] stocking the *Socialist Worker*.

BO: Yes, that's right.

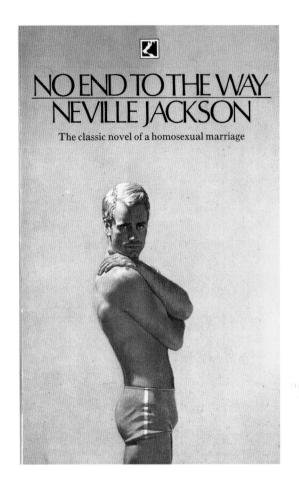

Front and back covers of *No End to the Way* by Neville Jackson, published by Corgi, 1965.

JL: There were other [left-wing] book collectives at the time—

SN: The First of May.

JL: The First of May and various others.

BO: So, we were a sort of leftist threat, I think, to this rather safe, comfortable group of people. And I think they finally felt threatened by us, really.

SN: The same thing happened with the women's group as well because we – I – felt the women might not want to buy SMG's refreshments and we had our own kettle. And the men in SMG objected deeply to that because we were depriving them of an income stream, all six of us. So, they passed a resolution forbidding us to make our own tea; it had to be bought from the café. Well that was sort of the beginning of the Christmas card [debacle]. And there are two theories about the Christmas card today. One is that it was a Christmas card which was drawn and based on a poem by a friend of mine about how poor Mary was the victim in the story and she drew the hand of God handing down Child Benefit to Mary, and that may have been part of it. The [other theory is that] there was another card that said, 'The birth of a man who thinks he's God isn't a very unusual event!'[18] Either way, it was not seen as appropriate.

BO: So, as a collective we were asked to leave, and we left. And we stayed together. This must have been late 1980.[19]

SN: That's right.

BO: And we stayed together and fought, and we went. We didn't take the stock with us, the stock stayed.

SN: It didn't belong to us.

BO: That's right. So, we must have acquired stock because we ran bookstalls at conferences around the country for about a year. And Sigrid and I… well, I guess it was really me, but you were really happy to follow, but the rest of the collective weren't.[20] We wanted to open a proper bookshop. And the rest of the collective said, 'That's fine. You get on with it. And we'll just back off, we'll just back out.' And that's basically what happened. And that would be late 1981, I think. Because early 1982, we decided – well, we needed to raise money to open the bookshop. And we started to sell books in a gay nightclub called Fire Island which was on Princes Street in Edinburgh.

SN: James' play [has] a lot more [information and detail] about [that].

BO: And that was very successful. By this time, Gay's the Word had opened [in London] so it meant that stock was much more easily attained than it had been before. And we were able to get a much wider variety of stock. One of the books I was hoping to bring which I couldn't find was called *The Lure* [Felice Picano, Delacorte, 1979], which was a sort of breakthrough, not exactly pulp, but it was very well written. It was a thriller set in the early days when AIDS was beginning taking over the New York scene. The whole nature of reading material was changing rapidly in the early eighties. And the bookstall in the cloakroom in Fire Island raised enough money that one of the banks in Edinburgh matched it as either a loan or an overdraft.

SN: It was a £2000 overdraft. That figure kept me awake at night!

BO: I get confused between the history that the play is portraying and actually what happened! Yeah, I'm pretty sure it was a £2000 overdraft. And we took over premises in the basement of rooms that the Scottish Campaign to Resist the Atomic Menace had rented.

SN: You [could] see their sticker in the window. It was the yellow one with the red sun saying, 'Nuclear Power, No Thanks!'

BO: That was at the time when Torness [Power Station] was being built. And it was known as SCRAM, that's right. So that takes us up to the beginning of Lavender Menace.

FA: You can see, James, why that anti-Christmas card story was such an appealing hook for the play as well.

JL: Yes, and I think really interesting because you've got that theme of a kind of 'necessary conservatism.' The [Scottish Homosexual Rights Group] were still pushing for legalisation of homosexuality. And then—

BO: It was 1980 when it went through.[21]

SN: Somebody said to me once that the Church of Scotland had had a great influence on the SMG. And that was the kind of organisation that I remembered it being, that they were very steady sorts of people, [but] it was very brave of them to do what they were doing. They risked a lot. But we were a bit younger, and the seventies had already happened and the kinds of thing I was thinking about with lesbian women and in *The Left Hand of Darkness* had happened to us. We wanted to go a bit further. Of course, they weren't going to like it and maybe that was a good thing.

FA: How did you keep that left-wing activism and politics alive in Lavender Menace when it opened?

SN: We had events!

FA: What kind of events were you having?

SN: Luckily the Scottish Arts Council assisted in those days. They would pay for lesbian and gay authors to come – usually from London, where most of them lived – but we got as many Scottish ones as we could. And they would pay the fare, we could have an evening. In the days of West & Wilde we could even offer wine and then people could have a discussion like this. We also had just discussions as discussions, sometimes about the books. We felt from the very beginning that we had to take it out there to people, we couldn't just sell the books. It had to be a place where people would want to come. And of course, that's totally become part of [bookshop] marketing now.

BO: Author visits were really quite new in the early eighties and we were sort of setting the trend to a certain extent. But we also put on book readings ourselves as part of the Edinburgh Fringe Festival. The Fringe catalogue wasn't huge, but it would have a huge distribution. So that's one way we got our name about. Paul Trainer would adapt some of the books that were adaptable to make into short plays.

SN: That was how it got started, just a brazen effort to push the books. And then we began to write our own plays. David Benson did a show about Kenneth Williams in the Fringe. He [would deliver readings] during the time he worked at the shop.

FA: Which is a nice connection with your own practice, James.

JL: Yeah, I think it is really interesting that there were adaptations of the books, but also some original plays. There was a really amazing energy about the shop due to some of the original plays – some by Sigrid, some by Paul Trainer.

FA: Can you remember any particular authors who came to do events at the bookshop?

SN: Well, Jackie Kay is one of them, and Ali Smith who most recently published *Autumn* [first published by Hamish Hamilton, 2016]. She wrote this book, a collection of short stories called *Free Love* [*and Other Stories*] [Virago Press, 1995]. She told me that it was because she could write [short stories] quickly and they would be made into a book more quickly. And in a damp tent on the Meadows [in Edinburgh] she did a reading from this book. At that time I was working in what later became Homebase DIY store. And I came over on my lunch hour in my brown skirt and my stripy old-time blouse and introduced her on behalf of the bookshop. Most recently she was reading *Autumn* at the Edinburgh Book Festival and the queues stretched right around the book festival [venue in Charlotte Square].

BO: Jeanette Winterson. *Oranges Are Not the Only Fruit* [Pandora Press, 1985]. We were sent plastic oranges by the publisher for display, or whatever.

SN: Edmund White.

BO: Edmund White, yes. David Leavitt, he was an early author – *The Lost Language of Cranes* [Knopf, 1986].

JL: The bookshop also predated the Book Festival.[22] And Sigrid had organised a feminist book festival prior to the Book Festival.

SN: I don't think it was a feminist book festival as such, but we had feminist readings and feminist authors during the festival.[23] And then Jenny Brown, who headed the Book Festival up, was the opening speaker when we moved and [Lavender Menace] became West & Wilde in Dundas Street. She and Iona McGregor – who was a young people's author – both gave short talks for the opening. And Iona's publisher had said: 'Now I have one thing to say to you: none of *that* stuff, you know'. So as soon as women's presses got started she was free, and she wrote a lesbian novel. She is now in her eighties, but she said, 'If I had tried to give a talk like this, even 25 years ago, the police would have been here very soon, and they would have taken Bob and Sigrid away'. So, you can see how fast things changed.

LOVE SONGS FOR A BOOKSHOP: THE AFTERLIFE OF LAVENDER MENACE

FA: James, how did you first hear about Lavender Menace?

JL: I was aware of West & Wilde. In a play that I'd written before, a character goes to West & Wilde, or mentions West & Wilde.[24] So, I'd been aware of that because it was open until the mid-nineties [1997]. But it was only when I'd arranged to meet Bob to talk more about the nightclub – as well as being involved in starting the bookstall in the nightclub, Bob had been instrumental in starting Taste nightclub in Edinburgh – so I was interested in that history as well. I met Bob and it was when we were going around Edinburgh and Bob was driving me around, showing me the locations, that we went to [the former premises of] Lavender Menace and that was the first I had heard of that. And I think I became really enamoured [with] that part of the story, the first time I heard of Sigrid and was like, 'I want to meet her as well.'

Lavender Menace
bookshop, 1984.
Photograph courtesy
of Sigrid Nielsen.

Lavender Menace
bookshop, 1984.
Photograph courtesy
of Sigrid Nielsen.

FA: How did you work together to turn [the shop's history] into a play?

BO: By this time my civil partner Raymond Rose had become my business partner, and we opened West & Wilde in '87, five years after Lavender Menace had opened. And Raymond and I met James and spent a couple of hours just talking about all sorts of things. We kept in touch, and little bits and pieces got thrown in, and you came up with this amazing play! With what seemed to be very, very little input from us, but you had interviewed lots of other people.

JL: You and Raymond and Sigrid – in fact, everyone was really generous with that. It wouldn't have been possible to get the depth that I needed – so I spent a couple of hours with you. And then [to Sigrid] we had a lunch for a couple of hours.

SN: Yes, in the French restaurant [Nom de Plume] that used to be the Gay Centre.

JL: And then I [bored Bob] to death in the LGBT Youth Centre all afternoon and interviewed him and recorded those conversations.

BO: It was about nine months of research? And it was all just interviews.

JL: Yes, interviews. And also, there is quite a lot of stuff in the National Library. Quite a lot of documents from the shop, but a lot of stuff in *Gay Scotland* magazine as well, which was really interesting to cross-reference.

SN: And you contacted David Benson and Paul Trainer by email, and Alison Dilly who worked as a volunteer in the shop in the early days.

JL: Yes, everyone was really helpful. In fact, I don't think I've ever spoken to Paul Trainer on the phone even though he's the main character in the play, but he sent wonderful emails, and I just typed them up and said that was my play.

FA: And how has [the play] been received? I am interested in your work with schools and how you work together with Sigrid and Bob to promote the play and contextualise it.

JL: We've been really lucky to have a few opportunities to work together. We were at the Book Festival in Edinburgh [in 2016]. There was a public reading in one of the marquees in the evening, which was really good to hear the play properly, like the first full reading. But we did a workshop at schools in the afternoon with about 200 kids from third – fourth year, so 15/16 [year olds]. And that was really amazing to present some scenes of the play and then talk about the books.

SN: And they asked if the bookshop still existed.

BO: Yes. It was amazing for me because they were all very curious. This is just another generation on – I could be their grandfather; they could be my grandchildren. And to me, after the hostility that I experienced when I was growing up, to have this very open-mindedness being presented to me was a really terrific experience and something I'll remember. And they went away enriched by the whole thing too, didn't they?

JL: Yes, definitely. I think it is that history. When we're describing Section 28, the piece of eighties legislation [which outlawed the promotion of homosexuality in venues which received local authority funding] to young people, it sounds so preposterous to them, and preposterous to us afresh, when you think about the fact that that came in and was upheld for such a long period of time.

FA: And to go into the early 2000s with teachers not being able to be out to their students, or talk about LGBT issues at all, to you going to speak to third- and fourth-year students about this play and about the history of Lavender Menace.

JL: Absolutely. And [it was] really driven by these school librarians who are amazing people who are really wanting to bring really diverse books in and take groups of students to these events at the Book Festival. I think it's amazing the way that's moved on, and wanting these books in the library as well, wanting to know when the play is being published so that they can get it in the library is really amazing.

'YOU HAVE TO BE DIPLOMATIC, BUT YOU ALSO HAVE TO BE BRAVE': QUESTIONS FROM THE AUDIENCE

AUD: I was wondering if you could talk about how Lavender Menace ceased to exist and, out of personal interest, what happens to all of the books in a bookstore when it closes?

SN: I left the shop because my life changed greatly. I had grown up in one of the most conservative areas of California. My uncle [reappeared] from out of the blue – he wanted to reunite me with the family. So, I was going back over to America quite a lot.

BO: The answer to 'what happened to all the books?' was they went back to the publishers. The stock that was left unsold went back to the publishers. So hopefully they were redistributed into good hands.

AUD: And there's nothing left?

BO: No. Well, funny you should say that…

AUD: Every book had a publisher you could still reach?

BO: Yes, that's right.

SN: That's what the book trades were like.

BO: This is the final booklist that we published; it's dated – brings tears to my eyes – August 1997. This is 'the Lavender List, West & Wilde's booklist for lesbian readers'. This was an element that we haven't really talked about.

SN: And it was one of the most important elements. The shop survived because of those lists.

BO: That's right. We made our own catalogues, essentially. That's what we were doing – bringing together different titles under different headings. There was a Gay Men's List, there was an AIDS List, there was a Sexual Abuse List that we did. But the Lavender List was the most popular. It was the basis of a mail-order service that we ran from day one which supplemented footfall in the shop itself.

AUD: I wanted [to go] back to the conversation you had earlier about the relationship to the [political] left more widely. Did you have a relationship to the Traverse Bookshop, based in the Edinburgh Theatre?

BO: No.

AUD: I just wondered because it was around the same kind of time they worked. They stocked things like newspapers from New York and America and stuff, so I wondered if you had any cross-overs. But there wasn't any?

SN: I hardly had even heard of them. I wish I had; I would have gone there.

JL: But the other book collective, First of May was near there, was near the Traverse.

SN: Yes, it was on Candlemaker Row.

JL: And that was before Lavender Menace wasn't it?

SN: Yes, [First of May] started in [1977]. It was a left-wing bookshop. One of the people that [James] did research with was in the First of May collective. I worked for them, but I didn't realise that it was as new as it was. Everything was coming together so fast. They had all sorts of stock of the type you're probably thinking about. People in the collective had some affiliations to the left-wing parties in Edinburgh as well.

AUD: I know it's maybe greedy to ask another two-part question but first of all I was wondering if you would consider reprinting the anti-Christmas card because I'd like to buy that. And the second question is: I was wondering if you have any advice for any members of the audience who would consider founding their own radical collective?

BO: I remember answering a long letter to a woman who wrote from Glasgow asking that very question. If you mean by 'radical collective' that you have opened a book-shop – is that what you meant?

AUD: Or maybe another means of distributing material.

BO: Well, collectives work best when there is little power struggle going on amongst the individuals. And we did work very well together, so I can advise that. We used to have collective dinners – so we all brought our own bits and pieces and had sort of a potluck evening meal before we did any business. And that was a good way of gelling the group together. Food and politics always go well – or food and anything always go well together!

But with the view of maybe starting another bookshop, what's really, really important is having enough money to sustain the business for at least a year. We were able to do it on a shoestring but very quickly within about six months we ran out of money. And we had to try and raise money privately. And we got through because the thing lasted fifteen years, but it was definitely under-capitalised, and it's really essential for any sort of business like that to get itself off the ground that there's enough money around to get you through the bad times.

SN: But if you accept that you are always going to be raising money, the other thing I would say you need is the kind of expertise that [Bob] gave the rest of us, because that impresses bank managers and funders. When we first went to the bank man-ager, we got articles from America that said that gay men had more money to spend because they didn't have any kids. And no one had ever thought of this! So never underestimate the power of being bold, but also never underestimate the power of backing that up with facts and figures, however bogus!

LG: I have a question about political affiliation and the books you stocked. I was won-dering what discussions were there around the material that you stocked and the decisions you made to stock material such as *Coming to Power* [a lesbian feminist S/M book published in the USA in 1981], at a very fraught time in terms of the queer feminist scene?

SN: This was a big, big part of our lives – and it's maybe another thing you should be prepared for – that there will be big differences in opinion in the community. It has to be that way. This is people's private world in those books. They all have secret book stashes. And they don't want to see something that doesn't stand for who they think they are, so you have to be diplomatic, but you also have to be brave. So, we were as diplomatic as we could be about *Coming to Power*. Two of the best-known [lesbian] separatists at the time were friends, and they came and had a secret discussion with me about what we could do to try and sort of keep everybody together. And one of the things they said was, "Some of these cards you've got – put them down, out of the eye line." And they were quite sincere about being separatists and they objected to *Coming to Power*, which of course for anybody who hasn't heard of it, it was published by a collective in California and is about radical lesbian S&M. But they wanted the bookshop to survive. There were others who didn't feel that way, one of whom stole some of the material and burned it ceremonially and published her exploits in [a] feminist newsletter. So, whenever we chose things like this we knew what we were going to be up against and had to think about it and prepare for it.

BO: But there was never any question that we wouldn't stock it.

SN: No. I believed in making things available.

BO: Absolutely. That was the whole point of the bookshop, wasn't it? We would be going against our own ethos.

SN: We had been through enough censorship in our lives, we weren't going to do it to others.

BO: That's right, exactly. And it caused a lot of heartache at the time, but it is very important that people make their own decisions about what's on the shelves rather than us making decisions for them.

AUD: I was wondering if you could say a little bit more about the kinds of relationships you had with presses – feminist presses and gay liberation and subsequent presses. I assume a lot of them were probably folding by the time you were dealing with West & Wilde. But I guess you were an important site of distribution for a lot of these presses.

SN: We were a lot smaller than Gay's the Word, but we were still there. And the big bookshops would pick up these titles. And the fact that we were there, I think, was important in their thinking in some ways. It has been said that when we closed, Waterstones moved their lesbian and gay section right to the back. You can say something, Bob, about the early days when you got in touch with Gay Sunshine Press and the presses in America that were virtually unknown here.

BO: The way that book distribution works is really through distributors. So, you're not dealing with an individual publisher, although we had very close relations with Gay Men's Press. There was a book distributor called Book People in California, and they published their own catalogues too, which was a very valuable resource. There was also Women's Press, which was quite young when we started [Lavender Menace] in '82, and it was publishing some really groundbreaking stuff as well.

SN: [Pandora] Books.[25] They helped set Jeanette Winterson up as a writer. She wrote them a letter that said, "Are you looking for someone who will work her ass off? I am here!" And they took her on and that's what launched her career.

BO: If we had any direct relationships it was Gay Men's Press and Women's Press. And that was part of the beauty, really, I mean it's the way book distribution works in this country – and in North America too, presumably – is that it's usually done through wholesaling. But you could negotiate discounts and what have you, more easily.

AUD: I made pilgrimages to both places – Lavender Menace and West & Wilde – when I was younger, so it's really lovely to hear this history. I wanted to ask about noticeboards, because that's something that I know very well from places in London, from doing pilgrimages to other places like Silver Moon.[26] It was all about hanging around the noticeboards. Could you talk a bit about noticeboards?

BO: Yes. There was a noticeboard. The room downstairs in Lavender Menace was—you had to walk through a sort of hallway, and it was a room in a downstairs flat as it were, the shop itself. You walked down this hallway, and all of one side was a noticeboard. And there had been boards of course in the Gay Centre, but this worked in a completely different way. This was much more open. And we had jobs and flats and all sorts of things. And it actually got us into trouble at one stage whereby… we were advertising flats – well, we weren't advertising flats, it was an open noticeboard so people who had flats to let. And it turned out that a guy who was basically pimping young lads off buses coming into town was advertising, unbeknownst to us, on our noticeboard. And it came back to us through the BBC, and we were plagued by a very tenacious journalist [from the BBC]. And she had followed up this story about this guy who had a flat with lots of rooms to let. And he basically – I don't think he was actually a pimp, he wasn't living off earnings, but he was definitely exploiting these young lads. We were interviewed on the television and all sorts of stuff and it was a complete nightmare. And we were completely innocent of the whole thing, it was just a roast. So, there was a really good side to it, and then there was this really horrible side to it as well.

AUD: I am interested in the question of collabouration between gay men and lesbians. Could you talk a little bit about the relationships within the collective and then about, possibly, conflicts?

SN: That, like the *Coming to Power* controversy, was something that became a big part of our lives. We probably had more political discussion than we ever had when we were selling left-wing newspapers, because we had to figure out different ways of working. There were conflicts. The customers were in some conflict because [lesbian] separatism was very fashionable then. Most people weren't separatists, but the separatists were the most vocal ones and they had a simple and straightforward position that anyone could understand. They did not believe in compromise. So sometimes it was hard and sometimes there were arguments. This is maybe another bit of advice and I wasn't sure how to formulate it, but it helps if you are friends to start with. It's like a good marriage, maybe. You should— if there is a time when you all worked together just as friends, then that's the best way. It always comes down to the ordinary, simple ways of getting along with people, whatever you call yourself and whatever other people call you.

JL: Sigrid, did you say as well that the women's group in Edinburgh were a bit against you working with Bob?

SN: Oh yes. There wasn't a really mixed gay scene in Edinburgh. There were just very few people. There were two other women in the original Open Gaze collective, but it wasn't an organised scene of people who had known each other forever. There had been lots of splits in the seventies between lesbians and gay men. It was something that I just had to accept that I was going to be confronted about and would have to do my best to convince people. And I imagine you went through some of the same thing, Bob?

BO: I think because we knew each other before we committed ourselves to a business that it worked, that we were able to work together. And I think that's part of your question, 'how do you get on with each other?' There were differences between us, but just like in any good relationship, you iron these things out, or make compromises.

SN: You've always got to keep talking!

NOTES

1 James Ley, *Love Song to Lavender Menace* (London: Oberon Books, 2017), 75.

2 Correspondence, publications and papers of Robert W. Orr (Bob Orr), Acc. 12766, National Library of Scotland, Folder 17.

3 Bob Orr Papers, Folder 1.

4 'The Lavender Menace' zine, Bob Orr Papers, Folder 15.

5 See Roger Davidson & Gayle Davis (2006) 'Sexuality and the State: the Campaign for Scottish Homosexual Law Reform, 1967–80', *Contemporary British History*, 20:4, 533-558.

6 'Lavender Books: A Gay And Lesbian Community Bookshop For Edinburgh', early fundraising campaign, Bob Orr Papers, Folder 11.

7 Lavender Menace Co-operative minutes book, 1981, Bob Orr Papers, Folder 5. Details of why the women-only discos stopped is not included in the archival materials.

8 'Lavender Books: A Gay And Lesbian Community Bookshop For Edinburgh', early fundraising campaign, Bob Orr Papers, Folder 11.

9 Lavender Books fundraising flyer, Bob Orr Papers, Folder 17.

10 Gay News Literary Supplement, *Gay News* 250, Bob Orr Papers, Folder 12.

11 See Sarah Schulman, *The Gentrification of the Mind: Witness to a Lost Imagination* (Berkeley, CA: University of California Press, 2012).

12 Ley, *Love Song to Lavender Menace*, 11.

13 Sigrid Nielsen, Correspondence with Fiona Anderson, 31 January 2020.

14 *Open Door: The Scottish Minorities Group – Glad to be Gay?* was made by The Scottish Minorities Group with the help of the BBC's Community Programme Unit, and broadcast on BBC2 in December 1976.

15 The Scottish Minorities Group (SMG) changed its name to the Scottish Homosexual Rights Group (SHRG) in October 1978.

16 *Therese and Isabelle* was made into a film by Radley Metzger, starring Essy Persson and Anna Gael, in 1968.

17 The Net Book Agreement was a fixed book price agreement in the United Kingdom and Ireland between The Publishers Association and booksellers which set the prices at which books were to be sold to the public. It was ruled illegal by the Restrictive Practices Court in 1997.

18 Another Christmas card stocked in Open Gaze, highlighted in a feature about the opening of Lavender Menace in *Gay News* [issue 250], featured 'pictures of a distinctly peeved Virgin saying, "So much for a woman's right to choose!"' Bob Orr Papers, Folder 12.

19 The team of volunteers who ran Open Gaze in the Gay Centre, the Open Gaze Book Collective, also tendered their resignation in a letter to the SHRG committee in February 1981, written by Sigrid Nielsen. '[A]s the bookshop has now devel[oped] to its nat. limit w/in the G.C. [Gay Centre],' Nielsen wrote, 'we doubt that our further work in finding titles, in suppliers & outlets for sales will have any further value for the branch.' Bob Orr Papers, Folder 6.

20 On rereading this interview, Sigrid recalled 'Follow? You couldn't have held me back'. Correspondence with Fiona Anderson, 31 January 2020.

21 Section 80 of the *Criminal Justice (Scotland) Act 1980*, which decriminalised sex between men over the age of twenty-one in private, according to the same terms as the 1967 *Sexual Offences Act* in England and Wales, passed in 1980 and came into effect on 1 February 1981.

22 The Edinburgh International Book Festival began in 1983. It was originally a biennial event and has been held annually since 1997. See <https://www.edbookfest.co.uk/about-us>

23 It was the 1983 Feminist Writers Conference at the Pleasance, Edinburgh.

24 In *Spain* (2011), the character Ally mentions buying a Pedro Almodóvar film on VHS from West & Wilde.

25 Pandora Books was the feminist imprint of Routledge and Kegan Paul.

26 Silver Moon Bookshop was a feminist bookshop on Charing Cross Road in London, run by Jane Cholmeley and Sue Butterworth. The bookshop opened in 1984 and closed in 2001, as a consequence of rising rents. See Maureen Paton, 'Eclipse of Silver Moon', *Guardian*, 23 October 2001 <https://www.theguardian.com/world/2001/oct/23/gender.uk2>

Index

Page references in *italics* indicate illustrations.

A

Abajo la Ley de Peligrosidad! (dir. Ahumada, J. R.), 103
academia and LGBTQ+ experiences, 6–7
activism
  British Black political activism, 11
  feminist activism, and political lesbianism, 39
  'libidinal investments,' and revolutionary movements, 33–5
  North America, HIV/AIDS related crises, 5
  people of colour, and LGBTQI activism, 9
  print culture, and role of, 3, 4–5
  race, and subversive desire, 22, 23–5, 28–30, 32
  revolutionary behaviour & the political Left, 30–1
  and social class, 27, 32
Adjusted Margin: Xerography, Art and Activism in the Late Twentieth Century (Eichorn, Kate), 8
Ahmed, Sara, 5
AIRDO (Italian Association for the Recognition of Homophile Rights), 73
Allais, Emma, 56
  FUORI! DONNA, role in, 64–6

Pezzana, Angelo, correspondence with, 64–6
Alternativa radicale, 74
Amazones d'hier, lesbiennes d'aujourd'hiu, 46
Appelqvist, Peter, 146
Arcadie Movement (France), 17, 101
Arnal, Frank, 167
Arnberg, Klara, 142
Artemide e le Furie, 67–8
Aspekt, 117–21, *119–20* , 138n2–n3
  Cviková, Jana, role in, 117
  Daučíková, Anna, role in, 119, *119–20*
  Juráňová, Jana, role in, 117
  lesbian activism, experiences of, 120
  lesbian existence, and reflections on, 120–21
  'A Letter from Bratislava' (No.1), 117–18
Assmann, Jan and Aleida, 224–5
Atribút g/l, 117, 126–30, *130*
  Fábry, Hana, role in, 126–7
  HaBiO, role in, 126
  Ištván, Milan (MP), editorial written by, 128
Axgil, Axel and Eigil, 143, 144
  International Modelfoto Service, 144
  pornography, and circulation of images by, 144
  Vennen, published by, 143

B

Babilonia, 75
  Lambda, merge with, 74
Baraghini, Marcello, 58–9
Bastille (Frank Weber), 150
  Toy, and artwork featured by, 150–152
Baudry, André, 101
Belarus
  DIK Fagazine, issue on, 193
  Forum magazine, and development of queer print culture, 188
  homosexuality, and de-criminalisation of, 178, 188
Bellezza, Dario, 74
Between the Sheets: Radical Print Cultures before the Queer Bookshop (Glasgow, 2017), 4, 9, 199, 241, 214n19
Biagini, Elena, 67
Bishopsgate Institute, 2–3
Bjurman, Lars, 145
Black Woman Talk (co-operative), 81
bookshops
  Lavender Menace (Edinburgh), 12, 237–41, *238, 250*
  Traverse Bookshop (Edinburgh), 252
  West and Wilde (Edinburgh), 12, 240, 249–50
Bourne, Bette, 205
  Life in Three Acts, A, 205

Brigate Saffo, 66–7

Brixton Black Women's Group (BWG), 81

Bühner, Maria, 9

Bulletin des Archives Recherches Cultures Lesbiennes, 46

Bulletin magazine (CHE), 1

Butt, Gavin, 7

Buying Gay (Johnson, David K.), 141

C

Campaign of Homosexual Equality (CHE), 1

CAPR (Comité d'action pédérastique révolutionnaire), 27

Carby, Hazel, 90

Castilla Homosexual Liberation Front (FLHOC)
   Aquí el FLHOC, 108
   La lada loca (newsletter), 103, 108, *108*, 109

Causse, Michèle, 49

Centre de documentation et de recherches sur le lesbianisme radical, 46

Centre of Contemporary Arts (Glasgow), 4

Chakrabarty, Dipesh, 200

Chantraine, Renaud, 161

Charting the Journey: writings by Black and Third world Women (Grewal, S., Kay, J., Landor, L., Lewis, G. & Parmar, P.), 89, *90*

Chroniques aiguës et graves, 46, 48

Clit 007, 46

Club of Lesbian Authors (KLA) (Slovakia), 125

Cobas, Lluis, 103

COC Nederland, 174n2

Col·lectiu de Lesbianes de Valencia (of MAG-PV), 109
   Dossier, 109

Come and Blow the Horn (dir. Sarno, Joseph W.), 146–7

ComeOut! 58

Coming to Power (USA, 1981), 254

Comité d'Urgence Anti-Répression Homosexuelle, 48

Communism
   Eastern Europe, and queer print in, 180–8
   and LGBTQ activism, 62
   Marxism, and homosexual 'values,' 61–2

con NOI, 10, 68, 71, 72
   Consoli, Massimo, article written for, 71–2

Consoli, Massimo, 71
   Bellezza, Dario, friendship and correspondence with, 74
   con NOI, article written by, 71–2
   Cossolo, Felix, correspondence with, 79n55
   O-MPO, role in, 73–4

conversation and language, 6

Coordinadora de Col·lectius d'Alliberament Gai (CCAG), 100, 104
   Escribano, Luis, role in, 104
   La pluma (newsletter), 104–7, *105–7*
   Manifesto (1978), 104

Coordinadora Feminista de Barcelona, 100
   Grup de Lluita per L'Alliberament de la Lesbiana (G.L.A.L.), 109–14, *111–13*

Coordinamento Donne Omosessuali (Cdo), 68

Coq International, 144

Cossolo, Felix, 74
   Consoli, Massimo, correspondence with, 79n55
   Lambda, and role in, 74–5

Cressole, Michel, 33, 35

'Cruising the Seventies: Unearthing Pre-HIV/AIDS Queer Sexual Cultures' project, 4, 6

Cuarto poder, El (dir. Lumbreras, H. & Soler, L.), 100

Cucco, Enzo, 58

Cvetkovich, Ann, 225

Cviková, Jana, 117

Cvitan, Vladimir, 182

Czechoslovakia
   decriminalization of homosexuality (1961), and response to, 128–9
   Slovakia, transition of power and impact of, 116

D

Dadzie, Stella, 86
   Heart of the Race: Black Women's Lives in Britain (Bryan, B., Dadzie, S., & Scafe, S.), 89

Organisation of Women of African and Asian Descent (OWAAD), role in, 88–9

Daučíková, Anna, 125–6
   Aspekt, work published in, 119, *119–20*
   Documentary and Information Centre (QA/DIC), role in, 131
   Iniciatíva inakosť: Spolužitie bez diskriminácie sexuálnych menšín (LGBT coalition), role in, 126
   Séparé, role in, 123, 125

de Gouges, Olympe, 42

de Keizer, Erik, 171

d'Eaubonne, Françoise, 48

Deleuze, Gilles, 32–3
   L'Anti-Œdipe, 33
   Recherches, text written by, 32–5

Délires et chuchotements, 50

Désormais, 44

Die Freundin, 224

DIK Fagazine, 12, 177, 189–91, 193–4
   Before '89 (No. 8, 2011), 182–3, *183*
   Belarus issue, 193
   Homosexualité Communiste (No. 11, 2017), 181, *182*
   Radziszewski, Karol, role in, 177, 182, 189–92

Dire nos homosexualités, 49

Doan, Laura, 199

Documentary and Information Centre (QA/DIC) (Slovakia), 131–3, 135
   Daučíková, Anna, role in, 131
   Q Archiv, production of, 133

Doms, Marielle, 121, 122

Downey, Cloud, 206

Drummer, 152

Duda, Andrzej, 180

Dullaart, Leo, 166

Duncombe, Stephen, 124

Duyves, Mattias, 159, *162*
   library and collections of, 159–61
   Mietje, role in, 162, 164, 170–1

E

Eichorn, Kate, 8

Élise ou la vraie vie (Etcherelli, Claire), 28

Emakumearen Sexual Askatasunerako Mugimendua (ESAM), 109
   Dossier on Lesbianism (1979), 109, *109*

Enke, Finn, 200

Eos, 144

Eribon, Didier, 43

Erotic Minorities, The (Ullerstam, Lars), 143

Escribano, Luis, 104

Espaces, 46, *47*

Etcherelli, Claire, 28

Euskal Herriko Gay Askapen Mugimendua (EHGAM), 100

    Gay Hosta (newsletter), 103, 108

F

Fábry, Hana, 116, 121

    Atribút g/l, role in, 126–7

    Iniciatíva inakosť: Spolužitie bez diskriminácie sexuálnych menšín (LGBT coalition), role in, 126

    LGBT activism, and related blog posts, 130

    Séparé, role in, 125

Facet (Guy), 187

Fanon, Franz, 22

    Black Skin, White Masks, 36n11

Feather, Stuart, 206, 208

feminism

    Black Feminism and Black Queer practice, 83, 84–6

    heterosexual focus of, 41

    lesbians, and Lesbian Left, 41–2, 52n1, 85

    women's movement (1970s), 53n12

feminist press

    lesbian press, and development of, 43, 50–1

    lesbians, and absence of representation in, 41–3

    and political lesbianism, 39–41

Feminist Review

    Lewis, Gail, role in, 81, 86

    Vol. 17, Issue 1: *Many Voices, One Chant: Black Feminist Perspectives*, 81–2, *82–4*

Feminist Theory, 83

Feministische Studien, 236n40

Femmes en mouvements, Des, 42–3

FHAR (Front homosexuel d'action révolutionnaire), 10, 18

    'leftist' activism, and links to, 18

    mixed-gendered alliances, and discussion of, 48

racism, and gay activism, 27

Recherches, publication of (issue 12), 18, *22–5*, 23–6, *228–9*

Tout! publication of (issue 12), 18, *20–1*, 29

Filo, 12, 177, 182–4, *184, 185*, 189–91

    Facet (Guy), renaming of, 187

    Polish Gay Guide to Socialist Countries project, 185–7, *186–7*

Fire Island (Edinburgh), 238, 239

First of May (Edinburgh), 239, 253

Flamboyant, 9

Flikkercamp (Montaigu-de-Quercy), 167

Flikkerkrant, 163, *164*

Följeslageren, 143

Forbundet af 1948, 143

Forum, 188

Foucault, Michel, 34

France

    Arcadie Movement, 17

    FHAR (Front homosexuel d'action révolutionnaire), 10, 18

    'gay liberation' publications, and treatment of race, 10, 17–18

    lesbian press (1970s and 1980s), 10, 39–41, 43

    MLF (Mouvement de Libération des Femmes), 18

    North African migrants ('Arabs'), and view of, 20–2, 27, 29–30

Free Love (Smith, Ali), 249

Freeman, Elizabeth, 232, 233

Front d'Alliberament Gai Catalunya (FAGC)

    Debat Gai (newsletter), 103–4

    Escribano, Luis, role in, 104

    Manifest (1977), 104

Front des lesbiennes radicales, 46

FUORI! 10, 56–60, *56–61*, 74

    Consoli, Massimo, role in, 71

    FUORI! DONNA, and female homosexuality, 63–6, *64–5*

    Homo, and view of, 72–3

    Mieli, Mario, article written for, 61–2

    Radical Party of Italy, and affiliation with, 63

FUORI! movement, 56–8

G

Gai Pied, 167

Ganymedes, 116–17

Ganz Junge Knaben, 150

Gay Liberation Front (GLF) (UK)

    Faraday Road women's commune, 197, 203, 206, 213n1

    Lesbians Come Together, 197–9, *198, 201*, 202, 203–4

    trans lesbians, and role of, 200

    transphobia and transmisogyny, memories and experiences of, 205–6, 208

    Transvestite, Transsexual and Drag Queen Group (GLF TS/TV Group), 197, 199

    UK movement, 85, 197

Gender and Sexuality Alliance (G&SA), 209

Germany

    feminist literature, and development of, 222–3

    Homosexuellen Aktion Westberlin network, 218

    'Itzehoe trial,' 227

    Klub Monbijou, 223

    lesbian magazines, study of, 219

    Weimar Republic, women's movement, 222–4, 232

Giansanti, Monica Galdino, 63

Gitelman, Lisa, 8

Gonnard, Catherine, 45

Gorgol, Tadeusz, 178–9

Great Vagina, The (Chordá, Mari, 1966), 110–12, *111*

Grimoire, La, 50

Groupe des Lesbiennes du Centre des Femmes de Lyon, 43

Groupe des lesbiennes féministes, 43

Groupe Lesbiennes de Paris, 43

Grupo de Lluita per L'Alliberament de la Lesbiana (GLAL), 100

Guattari, Félix, 18, 32–3

    L'Anti-Œdipe, 33

Guensberger, Ernest, 129

H

HaBiO (organization for homosexual and bisexual youth) (Slovakia), 126

Heart of the Race: Black Women's Lives in Britain (Bryan, B., Dadzie, S., & Scafe, S.), 89

Hekma, Gert, 159, *162*
    library and collections of, 159
    Mietje, role in, 162, 164–6, 170–1
Hemmings, Clare, 83
Hirschfeld, Magnus, 164
    Unsere kleine Zeitung (UkZ),
        contribution to, 223
Histoires d'Elles, 41–2
HIV/AIDS crisis, 6
    North America, HIV/AIDS related
        crises, 5
    queer print culture, as information
        source, 189
Hlas (Voice), 188
Hocquenghem, Guy, 19, 32, 37n24, 161
    'An address to those like us' (1971), 27
    Le Désir homosexuel, 31
Holm, Michael, 140, 142, 154–5
    gay publishing, role in, 143
    paedophiles, and defense of, 156n6
    Revolt: mot sexuella fördomar, role in,
        145, 147–8
    sex-liberalism, view of, 143
    Viking, role in, 143
Homo, 10, 55, 68–70, *68–9*
    FUORI! and view of, 72–3
    homophile ideal, and view represented
        in, 70–1
    Jannuzzi, Vincenzo, illustrations for, 69
    'law and against-law' article (1972),
        55–6, 70
HOMO (magazine), 143
Homophonies, 48, *49*
Homosexuellen Aktion Westberlin network,
    218, 222
    Lesbisches Aktionszentrum Westberlin
        (LAZ), renaming of, 226

I

Ifekoya, Evan, 83
Information Activism (McKinney, Cait), 2
International Lesbian Information Service
    (ILIS), 9
Ištván, Milan (MP, Slovkia), 128
Italy
    AIRDO (Italian Association for the
        Recognition of Homophile Rights),
        73
    Artemide e le Furie group (Rome), 67–8
    Brigate Saffo group (Turin), 66–7

Coordinamento Donne Omosessuali
    (Cdo) group (Milan), 68
FUORI! movement, 56–8
    homosexuality, and society's view of,
        55–56
    Political Movement of Homosexuals,
        73–4
    Radical Party of Italy, 63

J

Jannuzzi, Vincenzo, 69
Journal des lesbiennes feminists, 43, 46
Jouve, Christiane, 45
Juráňová, Jana, 117, 138n1

K

Kaczyński, Jarosław, 179
Kaveney, Roz, 199, 202
    Pollack, Rachel, friendship with, 205
    'Between the Sheets: Radical Print
        Cultures Before the Queer
        Bookshop' (conference, 2017),
        discussion at, 214n19
Kiripolská, Zuzana, 121, 122
Kisiel, Ryszard, 12, 177, *182*
    archive of, 177, 183, 192
    Polish Gay Guide to Socialist Countries
        project, 185–7, *186–7*
    Radziszewski, Karol, collabouration
        with, 182–3
Klein, Amanda, 101, 115n5
Kulick, Don, 155
Kuruc, Andrej, 136
Kuse, Käthe, 222

L

L 74 Berlin group, 219, 222, 223
    cultural and communicative memory,
        and focus on, 224–5
    Kuse, Käthe, role in, 222
    Radusch, Hilde, role in, 222
    Sandmann, Gertrude, role in, 222
    Unsere kleine Zeitung (UkZ), 219–22
LaBruce, Bruce, 7
Lambda, 66, 74, 188
    Babilonia, and merge with, 74
    'Brigate Saffo,' and contributions to,
        66–67
    Cossolo, Felix, role in, 74–75
    Pannella, Marco, fictious interview
        with, 75

Pezzana, Angelo, articles written for,
    74–75
Lambda Forum, 188
Laroche, Nadine, 50
Late Start (film collective), 81
Lavender Menace (Edinburgh), 12,
    237–40, 247, 252–53, *238, 250*
    book lists and catalogues from, 252
    Edinburgh Fringe Festival, and events
        held at, 248
    events held at, 239, 248–49
    gay men and lesbians, and relationship
        with, 255–56
    gay presses, and book distribution,
        254–55
    Lavender Books, and formation of, 238
    Lavender Menace Returns, 241
    Love Song to Lavender Menace (Ley,
        James), 12, 240–41, 250–52
    Nielsen, Sigrid, role in, 237, 245–49
    noticeboards in, 255
    Orr, Bob, role in, 237, 245–49
    political affiliations, 253–54, 256
    West and Wilde (Edinburgh), renaming
        of, 239
Left Hand of Darkness, The (Le Guin, U.),
    243, *245*
Les Gouines Rouges (Red Dykes), 27–28
Lesbenpresse, 12, 218–19, 223, 226–30,
    226
    'Itzehoe trial,' and reports on, 227
    'Legend of Stonehendge,' article (1975),
        231–32, 233
    Lesbisches Aktionszentrum Westberlin
        (LAZ), role in, 226
    vulva sign, and use of, *226,* 229–31
Lesbia, 10, 44–46, *48,* 50–51
    Lesbia Evasions, 45
    lesbian movement, and support role
        of, 45
    lesbian sadomasochism, and report
        on, 48
Lesbianaires, Les, 46
lesbianism
    activism, and radical lesbianism, 46
    feminism, and exclusion from, 41–2,
        52n1
    intimate experiences of, and literary
        expression of, 49–50
    lesbian press (France, 1970s and 1980s),
        10, 39–41, 43, 50–51

lesbianism *cont.*
 lesbian sadomasochism, 48
 mixed-gendered alliances, 48–9
 political debate, and development of,
  39, 46–8
Lesbisches Aktionszentrum Westberlin
 (LAZ), 219, 233
 Homosexuellen Aktion Westberlin
  network, renaming of, 226
 Lesbenpresse, role in, 226
Lettres à Sappho, 10, 44–5
Lewis, Abram, 200
Lewis, Gail, 82–83
 anti-imperialist view of, 85
 Black literature, and view of, 90–1
 Blackness, categorisation, and view of,
  91–5
 *Charting the Journey: writings by Black
  and Third world Women* (Grewal,
  S., Kay, J., Landor, L., Lewis, G. &
  Parmar, P.), 89
 'coming out,' and personal view of,
  84–5, 86–8
 Feminist Review, role in, 81–2, 86
 Organisation of Women of African
  and Asian Descent (OWAAD), role
  in, 88
 Trouble & Strife, interview for, 82
Ley, James, *242*
 Lavender Menace (Edinburgh), and
  links to, 249
 Love Song to Lavender Menace, 12,
  240–1, 250–2
LGBTQs, Media and Culture in Europe
 (ed. Dhoest, A., Szulc, L., Eeckhout,
 B.), 8–9
Libération, 168
Ligue communiste révolutionnaire, 39
L-Listy, 11, 117, 121–3
Lorde, Audre, 90
 'Uses of the Erotic: The Erotic as Power,'
  120
Love Between Women (Wolff, C.), 243, *244*
Lunch magazine, 1, 1–3, *2*, 13
Lure, The (Picano, F.), 247
Lutte Ouvrière, 31

M

Maasen, Thijs, 166
 Mietje, articles written by, 166–67

Magasin Gay, 155
Mammen, Jeanne, 220
Mason, Angela, 210
Masques, 39–42
Maurel, Christian, 34
McKinney, Cait, 3
 Information Activism, 2
Men, 72–3
Mieli, Mario, 58
 FUORI! article written for, 61–62
 Pezzana, Angelo, correspondence with,
  62
Mietje, 11–12, 159, 161–7, *160*, *163*,
 169–70, 169–73
 Duyves, Mattias, role in, 162, 164–6,
  170–1
 Hekma, Gert, role in, 162, 164–6,
  170–1
 Maasen, Thijs, articles written for,
  166–7
 Mietje Pietje, 171, *172*
 Rooie Flikkers (Red Faggots), link to,
  166
 van Kerkhof, Martijn, contributions
  to, 167
migrants and migration, 5
Mister SM, 148, *149*, 150
 Appelqvist, Peter, role in, 146
 'Dream in a Barn,' 146–7, *146*
Mithly (Volz, Julian), 38n57
MLF (Mouvement de Libération des
 Femmes), 18
More, Kate, 209
 Gay Liberation movement, view of, 209–10
 *Reclaiming Genders: Transsexual Grammars
  at the Fin-de-Siècle*, 209, 216n75
Morgan, Diane, 209
Morrison, Toni, 17, 18, 30, 95
Mouvement d'information et d'expression
 des lesbiennes (MIEL), 40
 mixed-gendered alliances, and discussion
  of, 48–9
Mouvement d'libéation de femmes (MLF)
 Le Torchon brûle, 41
 lesbianism, and approach to, 41–2
Movimiento Español de Liberación
 Homosexual (MELH), 100–1
 Abajo la Ley de Peligrosidad! (dir.
  Ahumada, J. R.), 103
 Aghois (newsletter), 101–103, *102–103#*

Muñoz, José Esteban, 7
Museion, 116, 121
 L-Listy, link to, 122
Musotto, Alberto, 55–6

N

Netherlands, Nijmegen, and student
 movement at, 163–4
Nielsen, Sigrid, *242*
 book collection of, 242–3
 Gay Centre bookstall (SHRG), role in,
  237–8
 Lavender Menace (Edinburgh), role in,
  237, 245–9
 Open Gaze Collective, role in, 241,
  245
 Scottish Minorities Group, and role in,
  246–7
No End to the Way (Jackson, N.), *246*
Nobili, Nella, 44
North America
 gossip, New York art world (1950s &
  1960s), 7
 HIV/AIDS related crises, 5
*Notes from Underground: Zines and
 the Politics of Alternative Culture*
 (Duncombe, S.), 124
Nouvelles Questions féministes, 39

O

O-MPO, Consoli, 73–4
Open Gaze Collective, 237
 Nielsen, Sigrid, role in, 241, 245
 Orr, Bob, role in, 241, 244
 Scottish Homosexual Rights Group
  (SHRG), and link to, 239
Ord och Bild, 152
 Revoltpornografi, concept of, 145
Organisation of Women of African and
 Asian Descent (OWAAD), 81, 86, 89
 Dadzie, Stella, role in, 88–9
 Fowaad (newsletter), 88–9, *88*
 Lewis, Gail, role in, 88
Orr, Bob, *242*
 Gay Centre bookstall (SHRG), role in,
  237–8, 241, 244–5
 gay literature, and introduction to,
  243–4
 Lavender Menace (Edinburgh), role in,
  237, 245–9

Orr, Bob *cont.*
Open Gaze Collective, role in, 241, 244
Scottish Minorities Group, and role in, 246–7
OS magazine, 72–3
Our Bodies, Ourselves, 86
Outwrite (newspaper), 81

P

Pagina frocia, La (*Lotta cointinua*), 79n50
Pannella, Marco, 75
Paper Knowledge: Toward a Media History of Documents (Gitelman, Lisa), 8
Papers Gais (Movimient d'Alliberament Gai del Pais Valencià), *110*
Parmar, Pratibha, 89
Paroles de lesbiennes féministes, 46
People's Union of Artists (UPA) (Spain), 115n2
Pezzana, Angelo, 56
Allais, Emma, correspondence with, 64–6
FUORI! magazine, and role in, 58, 63
Lambada, article written by, 74–5
Mieli, Mario, correspondence with, 62
Sanremo demonstration, role in, 58
Physique Pictorial, 144
Poland
gay activism, and development of, 192–93
homophobia, and anti-gay legislation, 180
Lambda, 179
Operation Hyacinth, 5, 6, 179, 184–5
Pink Files, 184
Pride Marches, and reactions to, 179
Queer Archives Institute, 178
queer histories and political landscape, 178, 179, 192–3
queer print culture, and development of, 182
social attitudes and gay rights, 178–9, 184
Polet, 187–8
Political Movement of Homosexuals (Italy), 73
politics
British Black political activism, 11
colonialism, and impact of, 31
feminism and political lesbianism, 39, 46–48

lesbian press, and feminist activism, 39–41
and 'libidinal investments,' 33–5
queer political movements, 5
revolutionary behaviour & the political Left, 30–1
Politics of Authenticity, The (ed. Häberlen, J.C., Keck-Szajbel, M., Mahoney, K.), 9
Pollack, Rachel, 199, 202
Beatrix Gates, The, 215n48
Kaveney, Roz, friendship with, 205
Transvestite, Transsexual and Drag Queen Group (GLF TS/TV Group), role in, 204–5
Women's and Gay Liberation movements, and impact on, 204
Pollard, Nettie, 206, 215n37
pornography
Axgil, Axel and Eigil, and circulation of images by, 144
International Modelfoto Service, 144
leather fetishism, 142–3, 146–47, 158n52
physique photography, history of, 143–4
pornographic production, 11
Sweden, and approach to, 141, 142
transnational distribution networks, 144, 146
Power, Lisa, 206
No Bath But Plenty of Bubbles, 210
Požgaj, Ivan, 116, 134
print production, 11
Problem of Homosexuality in Modern Society, The (Ruitenbeek, H.M.), 242, *243*
Psychanalyse et Politique, 42–3

Q

Q Archiv, 11, 117, 131–5, *131–2,* 139n35
Documentary and Information Centre (QA/DIC), 131–2, 135
Quand les femmes s'aiment, 43–4, *43*
lesbianism, and political debate, 46
Quashie, Agnes, 82
Queer Archives Institute, 178
Queer Between the Covers: Histories of Queer Publishing and Publishing Queer Voices (Kassir, L., Espley, R.), 9
Questions féministes, 39
Quotidiano Donna, 66–8

QYS magazine, 11, 117, *133*, 135–37, 139n43
Podpora mladých LGBTI *ludí* project, 136

R

race
Black Feminism and Black Queer practice, 83, 84–6
British Black political activism, 11
France, gay activism, and impact of, 17–18, 22, 23–5, 28–30
'gay liberation' publications, and treatment of, 10, 17–18
North African migrants ('Arabs') in France, view and treatment of, 20–2, 23–6, 29–30
'otherness' and self-definition, 30–1
people of colour, and LGBTQI activism, 9
racial-sexual prohibitions, 28–30
Radical Deviance: A Journal of Transgendered Politics, 209, 210
Radusch, Hilde, 222
Radziszewski, Karol, 6, 12, 177, 188–92
DIK Fagazine, role in, 177, 182, 189–92
Kisiel, Ryszard, collabouration with, 182–3
Queer Archives Institute, and founding of, 178
Rame, Franca, 67
Rampova, 109, 115n16
Mujer, libera tu deseo lésbico (1982), *108*
Raymond, Janice, 211–12
Transsexual Empire, The, 211–12, 215n40
Re nudo, 75
Recherches, 18–22
'The 'Arabs' and Us' article, 23–6, *23–4,* 28–9
Deleuze, Gilles, text written for, 32–5
FHAR (Front homosexuel d'action révolutionnaire), issue 12, 18, *22–3,* 23–6, *24–5*
North African migrants ('Arabs'), and expressions of race and sexuality in, 20–2, 23–6
'Three Billion Perverts' article (issue 12), 29, 31, 36n6

Reclaiming Genders: Transsexual Grammars at the Fin-de-Siècle (ed. More, K., Whittle, S.), 209

Reconstructing Womanhood (Carby, Hazel), 90

Replika, 190

Revolt: mot sexuella fördomar, 141, 144–8, *141, 153–4*
  Holm, Michael, role in, 145
  leather fetishism, articles on, 147–8
  sadomasochism, and articles on, 147–8
  Viking, former name of, 144

Revolt Press, 6, 11, 140–1, 143, 146–50, 153
  fetishism, and promotion of, 142–3, 146–7, 150–2
  Mister SM, 141
  paedophiles, and publications aimed at, 141, 150
  photoshoots arranged by, 146
  Revolt: mot sexuella fördomar, 141, *141*, 144
  Revolt Produkt, 141, 152
  Revolt Shop (Hamburg), 141
  Revoltpornografi, and promotion of, 145, 150–2
  Staal, Geurt, role in, 141
  Tom of Finland's *Kake Comics*, 146–7, 150
  Toy, 141
  Viking, 141, 143

Revoltpornografi, 145, 150–2

RFSL organization (Sweden), 140, 143
  Följeslagaren, published by, 143

RFSU organization (Sweden), 140, 152
  sex items and contraceptive devices, sales of, 152–4

Riddell, Carol, 210–12, 215n31
  Divided Sisterhood, 211–12, *211*

Rooie Flikkers (Red Faggots), 11, 161, 163
  Festival Mannen Nietwaar, and end of, 173
  Mietje, link to, 166

Rosqvist Bertilsdottir, Hanna, 142

Rosso, Enrico Colombotto, 56–58
  FUORI! illustration for (Issue 2), *60*

Rydström, Jens, 142

S

Sandmann, Gertrude, 220

L 74 group, role in, 222

Liebende illustration (UkZ), 220, *220*

Unsere kleine Zeitung (UkZ), work created for, 220

Sandström, Robert, 145

Schulman, Sarah, 240

Schwuchtel, 168

Scott, Joan W., 42

Scottish Homosexual Rights Group (SHRG), 237
  Church of Scotland, and impact on, 238–39, 248
  Gay Centre, and bookstall in, 237–8, 239, 244–5
  Nielsen, Sigrid, and role in SMG, 246–7
  Open Gaze Collective, and link to, 239
  Orr, Bob, and role in SMG, 246–7
  Scottish Minorities Group, renaming of, 241

Séparé, 11, 117, 123–6
  Club of Lesbian Authors (KLA), role in, 125
  Daučíková, Anna, role in, 123, 125
  Fábry, Hana, role in, 125
  Teocharisová, Vanda, role in, 125

Serarević, Željko, 181

Shedding (Stefan, Verena), 223

Shepard, Tom, 27

Slovakia
  anti-discrimination laws, and campaign for, 127–29
  anti-LGBTI attitudes in, 137
  Club of Lesbian Authors (KLA), 125
  Czechoslovakia, transition of power and impact of, 116
  Documentary and Information Centre (QA/DIC), 132
  Dúhový rok, 136
  gay and lesbian organizations, and emergence of, 116–17
  HaBiO (organization for homosexual and bisexual youth), 126
  Iniciatíva inakosť: Spolužitie bez diskriminácie sexuálnych menšín (LGBT coalition), 117, 126, 135
  Ištván, Milan (MP), parliamentary discussion on gay rights, 128
  LGBTI activists, social media networks and campaigning of, 135–6

Podpora mladých LGBTI ľudí project, 136

Queer Leaders Forum, and LGBTI rights advocacy, 135

queer print culture, 11, 116

samizdat and *zine* production, 124, 138n16

TransFúzia, 135

Smartt, Dorothea, 89

Smith, Ali, 248–9
  Free Love, 249

Spain
  activist media in, and emergence of (1970s), 100
  armed forces, and links to homosexuality, 115n12
  Coordinadora Feminista de Barcelona, 100, 109
  Cuarto poder, El (dir. Lumbreras, H. & Soler, L.), 100
  First National Conference of Lesbians (Madrid, 1980), 109
  Franco regime, and opposition to, 99–100
  Homosexual Liberation Fronts, 99–100, 107, 108–9, 114
  Law on Dangerousness and Social Rehabilitation (LPRS), 99
  lesbian political collectives, and emergence of, 108–9
  Pride March (Barcelona, 1977), 108
  self-published magazines, and production of, 100
  Spanish Constitution (1978), 105, 106, 114

Spartacus Gay Guide, 168

Staal, Geurt, 140, 141

Start, 181–2

Stonewall UK, 210

Stoops, Jamie, 144

Strange Fruit, 9

SUHO (Surinamese Homosexuals), 9

Suite des cris, 50

Sweden
  barn iconography, and use in pornography, 146–7, *146*
  commercial sex industry and gay consumer culture, 142, 150, 152–4
  decriminalization of homosexuality (1944), 140

Sweden *cont.*
    gay and lesbian rights, and campaigns
        for, 140
    gay economy, and market development,
        143
    leather fetishism, US culture and
        importation of, 147–8
    pornography, publishing of and impact
        on, 142
    regulation of sex and pornography, 155
    Revolt Press, 6, 11, 140
    RFSL organization, 140, 143
    RFSU organization, 140, 152
    sadomasochistic and leather fetish
        communities, development of,
        142–3
    sexual liberation, and view of, 146
Szutowicz, Margot, 180

T

Temps des Femmes, Le, 41–2
Temps des Médias, Le, 51
Teobaldelli, Ivan, 75
Teocharisová, Vanda, 125
Torchon brûle, Le, 41
Tout! 18–22, *19*
    FHAR (Front homosexuel d'action
        révolutionnaire), issue 12, 18, *20–1*,
        29
    gay activism, representations of, 30
    North African migrants ('Arabs'), and
        expressions of race and sexuality in,
        20–2
Toy, 148, 150, *151*
    Bastille (Frank Weber), and artwork
        featured in, 150–2
Trainer, Paul, 248, 251
Transvestite, Transsexual and Drag Queen
    Group (GLF TS/TV Group), 197,
    199, 202, 204–5
    gender roles, and view of, 202–3
    Lesbians Come Together (Issue 11,
        January 1972), 197–9, *198*, 202,
        203–4

Pollack, Rachel, role in, 204–5
    radical drag and transsexuality, and
        views of, 206
    trans people, experience and treatment
        of, 202–03
    transfeminist herstory, and anti-trans
        political backlash, 200–1
    transphobia and transmisogyny,
        memories and experiences of, 205–8
    Women's movement, and connection
        with, 203–4, 212
Traverse Bookshop (Edinburgh), 252
Trbuljak, Goran, 187–8
Triton, Suzette
    Masques, article written by, 42
    Vlasta, creation of, 49
Trouble & Strife, 82

U

United Kingdom
    Faraday Road women's commune, 197
    Gay Liberation Front (GLF), 85, 197
    London Pride (1996), 209
    queer memories of translife (1970s),
        200–1
    transfeminist herstory, and anti-trans
        political backlash, 200–1
    UK Gay and Women's Liberation
        movements, 199
Unsere kleine Zeitung (UkZ), 12, 218–25,
    220–1
    Hirschfeld, Magnus, contribution to,
        223
    Liebende illustration (Sandmann,
        Gertrude), 220, *220*
    queer archive, and representation of,
        225–6
    reviews and research into, 219
    Sandmann, Gertrude, work created by,
        220
    Weimar Republic, and references to,
        222–3
Usciamo Fuori! 63

V

Valcarenghi, Marina, 75
Valkovičová, Veronika, 137
van Kerkhof, Martijn, 167
Vennen, 143, 144
Vesović, Mio, 187
Viking, 144
Viks, 187
Vlasta, 49–50, *50*
Vojtek, Marián, 116
Voss, John, 146

W

Walter, Aubrey, 206
    Come Together anthology, introduction
        written by, 206–8, 214n25, 214n27
Weigel, Sigrid, 222–3
West and Wilde (Edinburgh), 12, 240,
    249–50
    Lavender Menace (Edinburgh),
        renaming of, 239
Whittle, Stephen, 201
    *Reclaiming Genders: Transsexual
        Grammars at the Fin-de-Siècle*, 209,
        216n75
Withers, D.M., 203, 215n29
Witkowski, Michał, 189–90, 191
Wittig, Monique, 39

X

Xeroxing and print culture, 8

Z

Zdravé mesto Banská Bystrica, 121
Zeffirelli, Franco, 74